I0756204

Basque Diaspora and Migration Studies
No. 14

Kaliforniakoak, 1533–1848

Basques in the Era of Exploration, Conquest, and Colonization of California

Asun Garikano

Translated by Jennifer Ottman

William A. Douglass
Center for Basque Studies
University of Nevada, Reno

This book was published with the generous financial assistance of the Basque government.

Basque Diaspora and Migration Series
No. 14
Series editor: Xabier Irujo

Cover illustration: TK
Book design by Daniel Montero

Originally published as *Kaliforniakoak (1533-1848): Euskaldunen lanak Kaliforniaren esplorazio eta kolonizazio garaian*, Pamiela 2013

Library of Congress Cataloging-in-Publication Data

To Bernardo Atxaga

Contents

Prologue

Joseba Sarrionandia

People need a place to live, and they refind that place continually, converting old countries into new ones to suit their purposes. Named and narrated, the landscape is experienced as full of memory, and if we investigate this history, we establish a strangely intimate relationship with those places in which we live or through which we pass.

During one period of my life, I accompanied an archaeologist friend in search of indigenous remains. The place was a stretch of land near the sea where a patch of woods stood among the rocks, and in front of a large cave, there was a terrace, a stratigraphic analysis of which gave surprising results. It consisted primarily of oyster shells; the people ate oysters and discarded the shells at the entrance to the cave. Interspersed darker layers of leaf litter and wood made it possible to deduce that they lived in the cave for a few years at a time and returned at intervals of around twenty years. The Indians had disappeared from that region in the sixteenth century, but their traces were still there, as if sleeping and hidden in the landscape, where we had to keep seeking them out. On one of those trips, my friend modified the object of his investigation: "They're going to lend me a metal detector," he said, "so Sunday we'll go look for the Bizkaian's treasure."

I had heard it more than once: "Oh, who could find the Bizkaian's treasure!" the old people used to say, and they sang a ballad about absolution denied, the ballad of Juan de Begoña, an early-nineteenth-century tale. According to the story, a former pirate who had abandoned his trade, thanks to a royal pardon, arrived in the city. He lived a very normal life, with neither great luxuries nor a known profession, but without pinching pennies and never without a gold coin or two to hand when the bills came due. Every so often, he saddled his horse and disappeared for an entire day, returning with a bag full of coins. There were people who followed him and tracked him from hiding on those journeys, but no one was able to find the treasure that he supposedly kept hidden. When Juan de Begoña became old and ill and was near death, the parish priest asked him where he kept the treasure, explaining that he would do a good work if before dying he left his wealth in the hands of the Church, and consequently in the hands of those most in need. The priest could think of no other way to pressure him than to deny him absolution, and that was how the old buccaneer died, without letting his arm be twisted, with his secret, and without absolution. So there we were, my archeologist friend and I, wandering from place to place in search of treasure, tired and harassed by mosquitos, lugging an unwieldy instrument that was to let us know, beep-beep-beep, if it detected gold.

Our efforts were in vain when it came to finding treasure, but I began to feel that the land was more inhabited, due to the people who had passed through. Having held in my hands the remains of the shells of the oysters eaten by those Indians who had disappeared five hundred years before, I had the impression that I glimpsed them. As for the treasure's miserly owner, from then on I had the feeling that our paths crossed in the streets of the city.

Asun Garikano has studied the written legacy left by Basque emigrants to the United States and described it in her beautiful work titled *Far Western Basque Country*, which begins on January 24, 1848, when James Marshall struck gold at Swiss immigrant Johann Sutter's sawmill. The city of San Francisco immediately emptied, and people drawn by so-called gold fever arrived in California from every corner of the globe. That book by Asun could well have been called *Kaliforniakoak, 1848–1968*, insofar as it is the chronological continuation of the one you have in your hands now.

What is California? Today, California is a state on the southwestern coast of the United States of America, and Baja California is a state on the northwestern coast of Mexico. In the sixteenth century, California was both less and more. In the beginning, it was no more than an unusual name on the maps, the name the Spaniards gave to a supposed island when they disembarked in far southern Baja California in 1533. They took the name from literature, from a bestseller of the age titled *Las sergas de Esplandián* (The Exploits of Esplandián), written by Garcí Rodríguez de Montalvo and published in Seville in 1510, which told its readers, "Know that on the right hand from the Indies exists an island called *California*." California was very close to the Earthly Paradise, according to this chivalric novel, and was an island where the women were black and "lived in the way of the Amazons," without any men. These Californians were women with robust bodies, passionate hearts, and many other good qualities. Their island was the most imposing in the world with its steep cliffs and rocky hills, and if this was not enough, it was full of gold . . .

What the Europeans who disembarked on that island found, nevertheless, were deserts and naked Indians, not gold and Amazons. It also turned out that it was not even an island, although it was a very long peninsula, as Juan de Ugarte proved in 1721 when he set out with his ship *El Triunfo de la Cruz* to measure its perimeter. From then on, the name California was extended on the maps to everything that lay to the north of that peninsula.

In this book, Asun Garikano recounts the fortunes of many individuals of Basque origin who participated in the Christianization, Hispanization, and conquest of those Californian lands. Over the course of three centuries, the Spanish monarchy tried to dominate the California coast, fighting fiercely against the native tribes. Later, other conflicts took place that had the impact of geological fault lines in the history of the Americas: with Mexico's War of Independence in 1810–1820 California became part of Mexico, and with the Mexican-American War in 1846–1848 the majority of California's territory became part of the United States. The names also changed in accordance with this succession of geological-political occurrences. Eastern Americans gave the name of "Far West" to the Western territories they considered themselves obliged to conquer and colonize, and in the process they gradually carved out and organized the states of California, Arizona, Utah, Wyoming, Nevada . . .

I think that this book will lead us to reread *Far Western Basque Country*, since this volume's endpoint demands that we continue to follow its chronological thread through that other book to our own times. Both explorations of California history show how harsh and strange human history is. Over and over, Asun surprises us with her narrative of the actions that those people were capable of, motivated, according to the beliefs of their time, by the ideals of God or gold. We should not imagine that we are less credulous, and in addition, even without believing in God or gold, we are capable of putting into practice other mad certainties. At the same time, Asun's two books demonstrate that California is another Basque province, a thesis that has to be accepted as plausible and true, all the more so if we take into account that the Basque Country has long contributed to the development of the United States.

Today, California is the most populous state in the United States and one of the strongest economic areas in the world. Sea-going ships and spaceships are built there, all branches of the construction industry and of agriculture are to be found, the arms industry continues to flourish, scrub-covered hills have given way to Hollywood, the creator of new *Sergas de Esplandián*, and on the plain, Disneyland was invented so that Silicon Valley workers could spend Sundays there with their children. In the United States, it is said that the entire country is becoming like California. In reality, not only are Americans increasingly 'California-ized', but so are Basques, and the whole world is turning into California. This is reflected in a variety of ways; for example, we view things from an aerial perspective more and more frequently.

Luis de Basabe, a Mexican writer who at a certain point in his life retired to live in Ensenada, Baja California, gave the title *Lur Berri* ('New Land' in Euskara) to a book of short stories he published in 1987. He had often flown over the old California and had contemplated from the airplane window, thousands of feet up among the clouds, the flat, blue sea below, indistinguishable from the sky at the horizon, and the interior with its desert landscape and those broken mountain ranges that were given the name of 'canyons'. It was a land that seemed from above to be a vast, ancient, wrinkled buffalo skin.

In his California stories, Luis wanted to show that the land is different down there, a maze of crevasses for the walker. Rough stones and cactus spines become embedded in the flesh of the traveler's feet. The silence is heard as a roaring noise. The warm air carries the scent of dried brambles into the lungs, and sometimes it can be suffocating. One's eyes can ache from so much sun, the rays are so strong at times, and sight hangs suspended in the burning air. The desert, the thorns, and the rattlesnakes—always lying in wait—are unpleasant. Yet at the same time, while the moon turns us to bronze, we feel that they are natural and bearable.

Asun Garikano's *Kaliforniakoak* is also like a descent to earth, a descent from the limbo of modernity, distance, and forgetfulness into the thickets of history. Conferring memory on the landscape, she provides us a strange intimacy with the lands and people of old California: Ortuño Ximenez Bertandona, a resentful cosmographer, passes before our eyes alongside Pedro de Unamuno, who holds a great oyster and its pearl in his hand; we come across Thomas Cavendish and Juan de

Ugarte in the street, chatting about globalization; and next a great herd of buffalo from Cíbola appears, in headlong flight to nowhere. We also see Olleyquotequiebe, the old Yuma chieftain who, complaining about José Joaquín Arrillaga, limps off in search of Juan Rulfo; over there is Fermín Lasuén with a small flock, but unwilling to say a word; and George Vancouver takes his place at the rail of the *HMS Discovery.* They will soon be followed by Juan Miguel Aguirre, Jean-Pierre Goytino, Mary Jeanne Goyenetche, Pete Aguereberry, and other Californians . . .

Map by Flemish cartographer Cornelis de Jode, 1593

1

First Maritime Explorations, 1533–1767

"L'America Settentrionale nuovamente corretta, et accresciuta secondo le relationi piu moderne da Guglielmo Sansone." Giacomo de Rossi, 1677.

Fortún Ximénez de Bertandona, the First European to Set Foot in California, 1533–1534

The myth of the riches of the West was an ancient one. Cities of gold and fertile lands that bore fruit for the taking, fountains of eternal youth, and other images of abundance and luxury had long slumbered in the European imagination, and with the discovery of the New World, it was as if they all suddenly awoke.

The expeditions that set out to explore Mexico's "mysterious north" in the sixteenth century were pursuing those images. Scientific expeditions were still far in the future, and these men were not inclined to embark on such adventures out of simple curiosity, only in order to get to know new seas and new lands. In reality, their goal was infinitely higher: they wanted to find the Earthly Paradise. With this aim, they ventured into unknown lands and seas, whether in search of the Seven Cities and the enigmatic kingdom of Quivira or of islands covered with pearls. Reality presented them with terrifying seas and sterile lands, but they continued their obstinate search, along the way enduring—and causing—sufferings impossible to recount.

In the third decade of the sixteenth century, Mexico City, governed by Hernán Cortés, became the point of departure for some of these expeditions. We will mention here only one of the lines of exploration: the one that ran north, toward the unknown territory that some years later would acquire the name of California. Cortés aimed to find another of those legendary places, the Strait of Anián, the passage that supposedly united the Atlantic and the Pacific. In the following centuries, both the French and the English made multiple attempts to find this strategic passage, convinced that its discoverer would have at his disposal a direct route from Europe to the riches of the Far East.

Cortés's first expedition departed in 1532, but the two ships that set sail under the command of Diego Hurtado de Mendoza found no marvels, and moreover, they came to a tragic end. One of the ships sank, and all but two or three of the men were killed by natives. The other ship, Hurtado de Mendoza's, was never heard from again.

In 1533–34, Cortés sent out another expedition, also made up of two ships: the *San Lázaro* and the *Concepción*. Hernando de Grijalva was captain of the former, and Diego de Becerra of the latter. According to the instructions they received, they were to find Hurtado de Mendoza—who had disappeared without a trace on the previous expedition—and then to search for new islands and determine whether they had pearls. The first captain, a man by the name of Fortún Ximénez, was apparently not very discreet, and before setting sail, he devoted himself to telling the whole world that he knew about lands full of riches:

> and the pilot Ortuño Ximenez, when he was conversing with other pilots about the things of the sea, before he departed on that venture, used to say and promise that he would bring them to fortunate lands, lands of riches, as they called them. And he used to say so many things about how they would all be rich that some people believed him.[1]

The conqueror and chronicler Bernal Díaz del Castillo gives additional information about this indiscreet explorer, affirming that he was a Basque and a great cosmographer. ("And a Bizkaian called Ortuño Ximenez, a great cosmographer, went as senior pilot.")

The two ships set sail from the port of Guantepeque and were already separated by the wind on the first night, never to rejoin one another. It may be that Grijalva distanced himself on purpose, in order not to have to share riches and glory with anyone or in order to free himself from serving under Becerra, who was "very proud and of a bad disposition," according to Díaz del Castillo. Becerra had some kind of disagreement with Ximénez, and the Basque seafarer decided to mutiny. He "reached agreement with other Bizkaian sailors," and they killed Becerra and some friends of his and would have killed others if two Franciscan friars travelling on the ship had not interceded on their behalf.

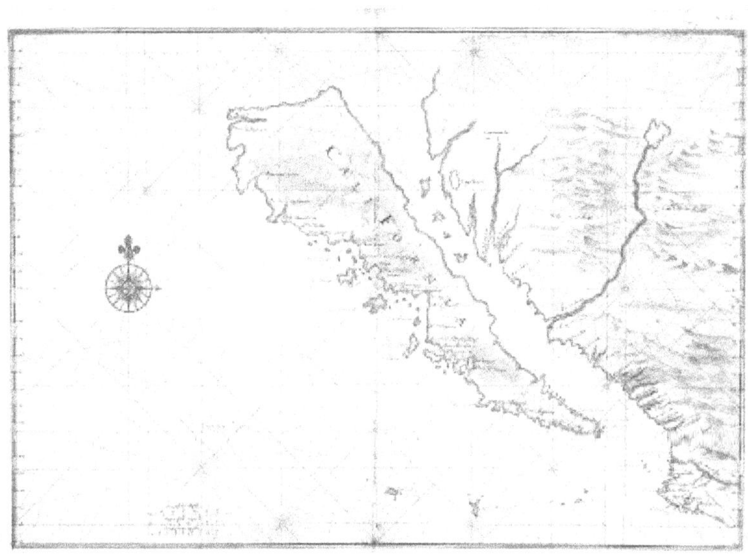

Map of California as an island, ca. 1650. Fortún Ximénez de Bertandona disembarked on the southern tip

Following these events, Ximénez himself took command of the ship. They left the two friars on land and continued northwest until they reached a handsome bay, now the port of La Paz on the Baja California peninsula. In need of water, Ximénez and a group of men disembarked, and there the Basque pilot's wanderings ended: the indigenous people killed him, along with some twenty other men, before the eyes of those who had remained on board the ship. It is impossible to say for certain whether the attack was unmotivated or whether, on the contrary, there was some kind of provocation by Ximénez and his group. Díaz del Castillo gives no explanation, only that the Indians "were set for war," but it would not be strange, if there were some kind of abuse, that the chronicler would fail to mention it. He also fails to mention that the victims of the attack included Pedro Ximénez de Bertandona, the pilot's brother.

The crew's calamities did not end there, since the ship subsequently fell into the hands of Nuño de Guzmán, a fearsome conqueror. From the perspective of future events, however, the most important thing was that on their return, the survivors declared that the coast was full of pearls. From then on, those pearls would be California's greatest attraction.

In contemporary documents, the pilot Ximénez's name appears written in various ways: Fortun or Fortin Jimenez, Ortuño Ximenez, Ortuna Ximenes . . . and also Ximenes de Bertandona. In the *Catálogo de pasajeros a Indias* (Catalog of passengers to the Indies),[2] one Fortun

Jimenez de Bertundona appears: born in Bilbao, the son of Jimeno de Bertundona and Mari Sanchez de Aregu or Araguna, and the husband of Ochanda de Hugarana. He embarked for the Indies, together with his brother Pedro, in 1527. According to historians who have studied California's early history—T. H. Hittell, F. Tuthill, W. M. Mathes, H. R. Wagner, and others—this Ximénez de Bertandona was the discoverer of Baja California. In addition, a statement by Hernán Cortés preserved in the Archivo General de Indias in Seville reports that Fortún's brother, Pedro, lost his life in the same attack.[3]

As far as the name "California" is concerned, it seems that it was Bertandona's expedition that used it for the first time, to refer to the extreme south of what is now Baja California. Later, this name would cover a much more extensive territory than today's California: everything to the north, without limits. Among the hypotheses proposed to explain the name's origin, the one most widely accepted today is that it came from a famous chivalric novel of the time, *Las sergas de Esplandián* (The exploits of Esplandián; Seville, 1510), by Garci Rodríguez de Montalvo. This novel was an enormous success and was translated into various languages. The historian Donald C. Cutter affirms that at the time California was discovered, books of this kind were easy to find in New Spain.[4] In *Las sergas de Esplandián*, the territory called "California" is described as follows:

> Know that on the right hand from the Indies exists an island called *California* very close to a side of the Earthly Paradise; and it was populated by black women, without any man existing there, because they lived in the way of the Amazons. They had beautiful and robust bodies, and were brave and very strong. Their island was the strongest of the World, with its cliffs and rocky shores. Their weapons were golden and so were the harnesses of the wild beasts that they were accustomed to tame and ride, because there was no other metal in the island than gold.[5]

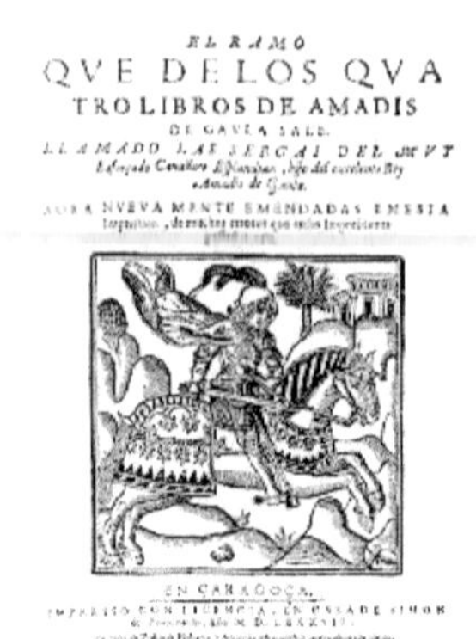

Sergas de Esplandián, where the term "California" first appeared

We do not know whether Fortún Ximénez had read the book, but what he found in California bore no resemblance to this description. Nevertheless, Cortés, with or without having read the novel, continued searching for that island that lay alongside the Earthly Paradise. After hearing the stories that the Ximénez expedition's survivors told about the quantity of pearls there, he himself took command of the following expedition.

Some years later, in 1605, Miguel de Cervantes's *Don Quixote de la Mancha* was published. At the beginning of the novel, two neighbors, the priest and the barber, attributing Don Quixote's mental disturbance to his reading of chivalric novels, decide to burn all the harmful books in his library. Strikingly, *Las sergas de Esplandián* is the first one they select to toss into the flames.

Andrés de Urdaneta, 7,644 Miles through Unknown Seas, 1565

Although the fact may appear strange today, California's destiny was long linked to the Philippine Islands, and more precisely, to the Manila galleon, which annually traversed the 7,644 miles between the Philippines and Mexico. The galleon departed for Manila at the beginning of the year, loaded with precious metals and other products of the Americas, and returned to Acapulco at the time of the summer monsoon, carrying spices, silk, Chinese porcelain, and many other exotic products. For almost two and a half centuries, this mercantile route uniting Asia and the Americas was enormously important. Logically, however, it was first necessary to work out the route, something that was not easily achieved.

Firma de Urdaneta en el testamento de Elcano. www.andresurdaneta.org

The problem was the return. Ships easily made the crossing from Mexico to the Philippines, but the return trip—the *tornaviaje*—was another story, due precisely to the winds and currents that were favorable on the trip out. The greatest seamen of the age, Magellan, García de Loaysa, Saavedra, Grijalva, and López de Villalobos, had devoted themselves to searching for a route, but crossing the Pacific from west to east seemed to be an enterprise doomed to fail.

In 1559, the king of Spain, Philip II, decided to make a new attempt. From Mexico, the viceroy, Luis de Velasco, communicated to the king the identity of the man he considered best fitted for that enterprise: Andrés de Urdaneta, "who is the person who has the most knowledge and experience of all those islands and is the best and most accurate cosmographer there is in this New Spain."[6] In making this proposal, Velasco probably took into consideration what Urdaneta had said to him some years before, seeing the failure of so many expeditions: that if he was given the opportunity, he would bring back from the Philippines

Spanish galleon

not merely a ship, but an ox cart.

Andrés de Urdaneta (Ordizia, 1508 – Mexico City, 1568), the son of Juan Ochoa de Urdaneta and Gracia de Celaya, was a seaman and cosmographer of great prestige—the two went together at the time—and he knew those islands perfectly. At the age of seventeen, he had taken part in García de Loaysa's tragic expedition to the Moluccas, along with Juan Sebastián Elcano, a Gipuzkoan. The young Urdaneta spent almost ten years in East Asia, where, in addition to learning the local languages, he had the opportunity to study the meteorology of the area and the natives' navigation methods. In reality, no one would have dared deny Urdaneta's merits, but . . . weren't his best days perhaps already behind him? When he received the royal request, Urdaneta was already, at the age of fifty-two, well on in years. In addition, he had taken vows in the Augustinian order in 1553.

In the reply he sent to the king, Urdaneta did not avoid the topics of his age and health:

> And given that in accordance with my age, which is more than fifty-two years, and the lack of health that I have at present, and the many labors I have endured since my youth, I was in need of passing the little that remains of my life in quiet.[7]

Despite all his ailments, however, he responded in the affirmative. He chose another Gipuzkoan to lead the expedition, Miguel López de Legazpi (Zumarraga, 1502 – Manila, 1572). Four Augustinians would be responsible for the work of evangelization: Martín de Rada, a cosmographer, mathematician, and astronomer, Andrés de Aguirre, Pedro Gamboa, and Diego de Herrera. The first three were fellow-countrymen of Urdaneta's, and other Basque names appear in the expedition's documents as well, including Martín de Ibarra, master of the flagship *San Pedro*; Andrés de Mirandaola, Urdaneta's nephew, senior factor; Martín de Goiti, captain of the soldiers; Guido de Labezarri, treasurer of the expedition and later the second governor of the Philippines; Juan de Lazcano, Legazpi's secretary; Francisco de Astigarribia, the *San Pedro*'s boatswain; Andrés de Ibarra, senior ensign; Asensio de Aguirre, notary; Amador de Arriarán, pilot; Pedro de Guevara, blacksmith; Juan de Aguirre, Pedro de Arana, and Alberto Orozco, soldiers; and numerous sailors and cabinboys.

After overcoming obstacles and delays, five ships and some four hundred men set sail in 1564 from the port of Navidad.[8] Four days later, three hundred miles off the coast, they opened their sealed orders and were able to read their instructions: they were to go directly to the Philippines and conquer the islands, in order to establish a permanent colony there. Afterward, they were to try to find the route back. Urdaneta and his fellow friars did not like the first part, since they thought that the Philippines belonged to Portugal according to the Treaty of Tordesillas. Nevertheless, the ships continued on their course, and in less than three months, they had arrived at their destination. There, Legazpi conquered the islands for Spain and founded Cebú, the first Spanish city in the islands. Finally, the following year,

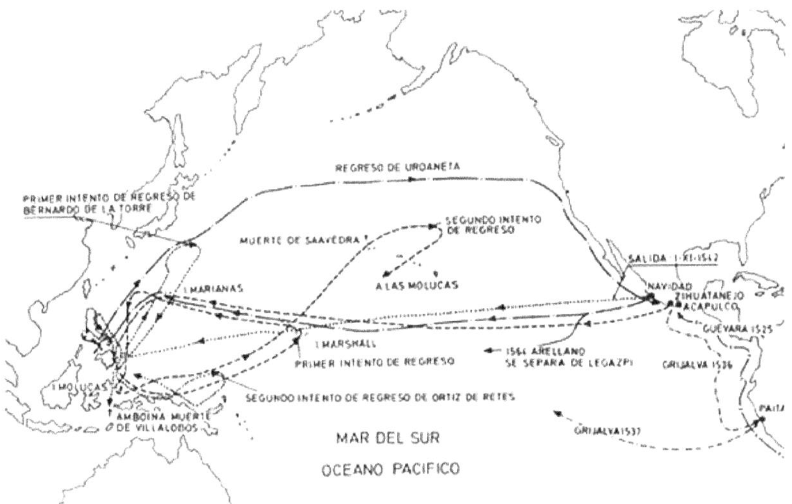

Urdaneta's routes across the Pacific. Graphic by Francisco Morales Padrón

Urdaneta undertook the *tornaviaje*.

Urdaneta's crossing holds a place of honor in the history of navigation. Never before had so long a voyage—7,644 miles—been made across an unknown ocean, and still less under the command of such an unusual pair: on the one hand, a sixteen-year-old captain, Felipe de Salcedo, Legazpi's grandson; on the other, indicating the route, the person who truly directed the ship, a friar well on in years. Urdaneta's friend Fray Andrés de Aguirre was also on board; the other three Augustinians, Rada, Gamboa, and Herrera, remained in the Philippines.

On June 1, 1565, the *San Pedro* left the port of Cebú with ten soldiers and two hundred sailors, roughly a third of whom were Gipuzkoans.

Instead of sailing south, as had been done up to that time, they headed north, with the monsoon in their favor. On July 1, they were at 39° latitude, and from there they continued to 42°. It was a detour that lengthened the crossing, but they succeeded in avoiding the trade winds that had been the downfall of previous expeditions. At that point, the ship set its course to the east, following the Kuroshio Current to what is now the United States. The men sighted land on September 26, 1565, at the latitude of Cape Mendocino, north of today's San Francisco. They then sailed south along the Mexican coast, and on October 8, the *San Pedro* entered the port of Acapulco, completing a crossing of four long months. In Urdaneta's words:

> We labored much on the return with contrary weather and illnesses. Six men died up to the time we anchored in the port, and another four after we arrived, as well as an Indian from the Ladrones Islands whom the general sent, with another three Indians whom he sent from the island of Zubu. Felipe de Salcedo, the general's grandson, who acted prudently in his post, came as captain of the ship.[9]

The pilot Rodrigo Espinosa also recorded the moment in his diary:

> we arrived in this port of Acapulco on Monday, the eighth of the present month of October, with plenty of labor endured by all the people.[10]

In the 130 long days that the voyage lasted, Urdaneta, in addition to making observations and guiding the ship, had to care for the sick and attend the dying in his capacity as a friar, along with his fellow-countryman Andrés de Aguirre. Urdaneta's crossing was different in this respect as well, however, since there were many fewer casualties than was usual. Scurvy wreaked true havoc on long maritime crossings, but not on this one: Urdaneta stocked the ship with large stores of coconuts and vegetables, which would provide the sailors with vitamins, before setting sail for the open sea.

As soon as he arrived in Acapulco, Urdaneta described and named on a map all the winds, routes, islands, and capes. In this way, one of the most important commercial routes of all time was defined, the route the Manila galleon would follow, also known as "Urdaneta's route."

The Spanish authorities' next objective was to find a port for the galleon on the California coast, so that damaged ships could be repaired and exhausted men could rest after crossing the ocean. This turned out to be no easy task.

Fray Andrés de Aguirre Gives News of the Existence of Very Rich Islands in the Middle of the Pacific, 1584–1585

On most occasions, Andrés de Aguirre's name appears united with that of Andrés de Urdaneta, unsurprisingly, since the two were together at key moments of their lives. They went to the Philippines together in 1564, and they made the memorable return voyage, the *tornaviaje*, together; they went to Madrid together to give Philip II details of their voyage, and they returned to Mexico together. There, finally, they parted ways. Aguirre returned to the Philippines in 1579, along with ten other friars. He served as prior of the Manila convent and later as provincial of his order. In 1582, we find him once again in Madrid, charged with matters relating to Philippine affairs. He succeeded in sending another nine missionaries, who arrived in Manila in 1584. In 1586, he returned to Mexico with more missionaries. In 1593, by that time a very old man, he returned to Manila, where he died the same year, having travelled more than twenty-five thousand leagues over the course of his life, an incredible distance for the time.[11]

Nevertheless, Andrés de Aguirre's presence in these pages is not due to his travels or his missionary labor, but to a remarkable text from his pen, one that, along with other, similar accounts, had a certain significance for California history. This was a letter he wrote in 1584 or 1585—the text is undated—to the archbishop of Mexico City. In this letter, Aguirre took up a common topic of conversation among the sailors of the time: that there were islands overflowing with riches in the middle of the ocean, still to be discovered. Aguirre mentioned two such islands in his letter, the so-called "Islands of the Armenian," offering details

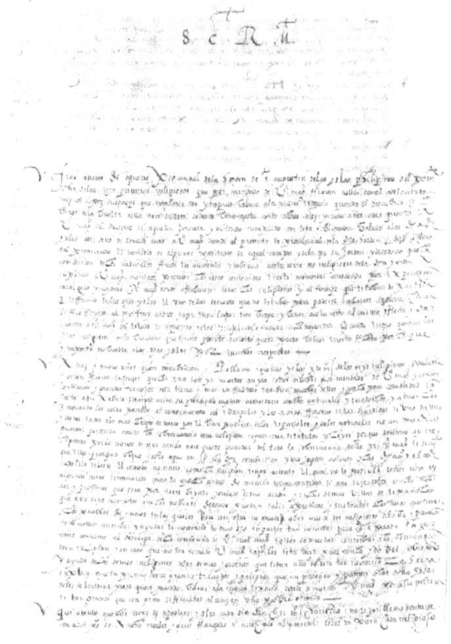

Aguirre's narrative

of all kinds that gave plausibility to his narrative.

At the beginning of the letter, Aguirre explained how he learned about those islands. Apparently, a Portuguese captain gave Andrés de Urdaneta a document that spoke about two very rich islands. Aguirre and Urdaneta were on their way to Spain to tell the king about the *tornaviaje*, so Aguirre had the opportunity to see and read the text. In Spain, Urdaneta turned the Portuguese captain's document over to the king. Aguirre had prudently kept a copy, but on his return voyage to the New World, "the ship in which I came was lost, and in it the narrative and all I was bringing with me."[12] Consequently, Aguirre was working from memory when he wrote to the archbishop of Mexico City.

Aguirre's account begins with these words: "A Portuguese ship sailed from Malacca for the islands of Japan and at the city of Canton took on board Chinese goods." After mentioning the storm that blew them off course, Aguirre described the islands the Portuguese captain found in the Pacific as follows:

> all being rich in silver and very populous. These people are white and well-formed, well cared for and clothed in silk and fine clothing of cotton; an affectionate and very affable people. The language differs from that of the Chinese as well as that of the Japanese, and is readily learned, for, in less than forty days that the Portuguese passed on the island, they were able to converse with the natives. These islands abound in the means of maintaining life well—rice, which is the bread they use; fowls like ours in great number; tame ducks and many hogs; goats; buffaloes[13] and much game with deer and wild boars in great abundance; various birds and fowls and fishes, both many and good, and a great plenty of many kinds of fruit. The climate of the land is very good and healthful.[14]

Given the name of "Isles of the Armenian," in honor of a merchant from that country who was a passenger on the ship, these islands became another entry on the list of imaginary places, on which two other Pacific islands were already found, the islands Rica de Oro ("rich in gold") and Rica de Plata ("rich in silver"). Accounts like Aguirre's, or like that found in a letter by the Navarrese Fray Martín de Rada, in which he stated that "a Bizkaian originally from San Sebastián" had told him that he had seen the Strait of Anián with his own eyes, "whaling in Newfoundland," exercised great influence.[15] In fact, when Sebastián Vizcaíno discovered the port of Monterey some years later in 1602, Viceroy Montesclaros paid no attention to its exploration and sent the age's best seamen in search of the coveted islands Rica de Oro and Rica de Plata.

Narrative of the Voyage and Navigation That Capt. Pedro de Unamuno Made, 1587

Like many other seamen of his time, Pedro de Unamuno set out to search for the islands Rica de Oro and Rica de Plata in the middle of the ocean. However, when he arrived at the latitude where, according to the maps he had, Rica de Oro was supposed to be, he could not find it, despite searching in every direction. He therefore arrived at the conclusion that it did not exist: "The said island could not be found, from which it is understood not to exist."[16] He then went in search of Rica de Plata, but despite all his efforts, he was unable to find it either, and he reached the same conclusion as before: "It must not exist, but instead, someone must have ordered it drawn on his map from hearsay." When he dedicated himself to searching for the Isles of the Armenian, the result was the same.

Nevertheless, Pedro de Unamuno is not remembered for his voyages in pursuit of legendary islands, but rather for his attempt to explore the California coast, which made the Basque captain the protagonist and narrator of one of the first documented encounters between Europeans and indigenous Californians.

The objective was, once again, to ensure the safety of the Manila galleon. The galleon easily made the trip from Acapulco to Manila, in two or three months, but in order to return from Manila to Acapulco, a minimum of four or five months was needed, across a Pacific Ocean very far from living up to the peaceful implications of its name, with a crew increasingly diminished by scurvy. For the men who had endured so hard a crossing, it was absolutely necessary to have a port available in California where they could obtain provisions, recover their health, and repair their ships, and that required exploring the entire coast, preferably as far as latitude 42° north, that is, as far as the Strait of Anián, the supposed location of the passage that united the Atlantic and Pacific.

Among the expeditions organized for this purpose, the one led by the Portuguese Juan Rodríguez Cabrillo (João Rodrigues *Cabrilho*, circa 1499–1543) deserves mention. In 1542, by order of Viceroy Antonio de Mendoza, Cabrillo made it as far as Cape Mendocino, something that no European had previously managed, but once there, he had to turn back immediately, due to the unbearable cold and the fact that a broken arm he had suffered some days earlier was turning gangrenous. Cabrillo died during the return voyage, and after so much suffering, the expedition bore scant fruit, as a consequence of the lack of descriptions and the vagueness of the maps.

For a number of years, no further expeditions were sent out, and the Manila galleon continued its voyages with no more than the usual difficulties. In 1579, however, a new enemy appeared on the scene: Francis Drake, the English corsair. The Manila galleon was undoubtedly a marvelous ship. It was laden with the most precious objects, from Indonesia, China, Japan, India, and the Middle East: Persian marbles and carpets; silks, jades, and jewels of all kinds; spices, exotic foodstuffs, and porcelain; sandalwood and women's combs. It was a true treasure, and an enormous temptation for the English corsair. In addition, with the poor weaponry it had on board, and the entire crew exhausted by the crossing, the Manila galleon could be a very easy prize. The threat was obvious, and the Spanish authorities considered it more urgent than ever to find a safe port that would allow the men to recover their strength once they reached the California coast.

The search for the desired port was entrusted to the Spanish seaman Francisco Gali. Gali left Manila in July 1584, but when he reached the California coast, with the *San Juan Bautista* fully laden with cargo, the crew was too tired to devote themselves to exploring, and scarcely anything was achieved. Gali was also going to lead a second expedition, but he died, and his second-in-command—Pedro de Unamuno, a Basque from Soraluze, Gipuzkoa—took his place.

Unamuno set sail from Manila in early summer 1586 with two ships. He had orders not to go to Macao, but for reasons that remain unclear, that was where he headed. Portugal was under the jurisdiction of Spain's King Philip II at the time, and there was a great deal of rivalry between Spaniards and Portuguese in the Far East. The Portuguese in Macao alleged that Unamuno had with him an Englishman and a Frenchman, great mariners, and "was likely to turn corsair."[17] It is possible that this was only an excuse, but Unamuno's ships were taken away from him, and he was left with no other option than to buy one, the frigate *Nuestra Señora de Buena Esperanza*, undoubtedly with money provided by Fray Martín Ignacio de Loyola, who was traveling with him and was eager to escape from the hands of the Portuguese.

The frigate left Macao on July 12, 1587, with around one hundred men, including a number of Filipinos from the island of Luzon. They would be the first Filipinos to reach California. Finally, rounding out the crew were three friars, one of them the mentioned Fray Martín

Ignacio de Loyola.

Fray Martín Ignacio de Loyola (Eibar, Gipuzkoa, circa 1550 – Buenos Aires, 1616), a nephew of St. Ignatius of Loyola whose baptismal name was Martín Ignacio Martínez de Mallea, was a great missionary and seaman as well as the author of a book much cited in its day (*Itinerario del Nuevo Mundo* [Itinerary of the New World]). When he embarked with Unamuno, he had already been around the world, sailing from Mexico to the Philippines and returning by way of the Cape of Good Hope. On the present occasion as well, a long voyage awaited him on his departure from Macao, since he was headed to Spain to report to Philip II about the problems faced by missionaries in China. When he finally reached Acapulco, he wrote to the viceroy lamenting the group's sufferings at the hands of the Portuguese and asking that the latter be punished for taking their ships, since this had delayed the voyage for almost a year. In the same letter, Loyola tried to excuse Unamuno, claiming that if he had gone to Macao, it was due to bad weather.

As far as Unamuno himself was concerned, he wrote an account of the voyage for the viceroy, ("Narrative of the voyage and navigation which Captain Pedro de Unamuno made"[18]), in which he recorded the details of his encounter with California's native inhabitants.

According to Unamuno, the *Nuestra Señora de Esperanza* sighted land on October 17, somewhere in central California. The next day, they saw smoke rising from multiple locations, and after listening to the opinions of the men on the ship, "especially Padre (Fray) Martin Ignacio de Loyola, envoy to China,"[19] Unamuno decided to disembark. It was the feast day of Saint Luke, San Lucas in Spanish, with whose name they baptized the port. From the ship, they had seen two Indians who observed them attentively from a hill, but when the landing party climbed up to the place, they found no trace of the Indians.

After choosing a route, they began to walk. "With the said Padre (Fray) Martin, his cross in hand, leading, we set out thither. Two of our Indians went ahead, as scouts."[20] They soon saw people, a group of five, including two women with children on their backs. All were naked. The Spaniards wanted to approach them, in order to speak with them, but they moved incredibly quickly, and the Spaniards were unable to get close to them. Afterward, they found something that attracted their attention:

> we found two bundles like wicker baskets wrapped up in two deerskins, and in them [the bundles] we found nothing but the two deerskins and [other] little pelts, like rabbit skins, cut and

> fashioned like a chain of skins, and a few flowers like wild marjoram . . . Of the two deerskins we took one, leaving in its place with their other bundle two handkerchiefs.[21]

Unamuno ordered one of his men, Joanes de Arraseta, to climb another hill, accompanied by the men from Luzon. They found no settlements, nor people, nor smoke, nor minerals in the soil. It was getting dark, and they decided to return to the frigate. Along the way, "we found a great quantity of very large pearl-oyster shells and other shells of many shellfish."[22] It struck them as a good place to carry out the ceremony of taking possession, so by setting up a cross, cutting branches from the trees, and performing other customary actions, they took possession of the port and the territory.[23]

The next day—Monday, October 19, 1587—Unamuno set out before dawn, together with twelve soldiers and eight Luzon Indians, accompanied on this occasion by another friar, Francisco de Noguera. Taking the greatest care to go unobserved, they found many footprints, made by people of all sizes, on the bank of a river, but they found neither settlements nor people. They continued downstream along the same bank until they reached some old *rancherías*[24] with about seventeen *ranchos* of different sizes, which reminded Unamuno of a scene from his homeland. They looked, he said, "like Biscay charcoal pits":

> a big hole in the ground, of good circumference, roofed with branches of trees—very well covered. Judging by the size of the excavations, each could hold more than a dozen persons. . . . nothing was found except some wands which seemed to be of elder, out of which they fashion their javelins, with oak points hardened by fire.[25]

In the afternoon, Unamuno sent three soldiers and three Luzon Indians to the top of another hill to look around and see whether there were settlements, people, fires, or minerals in the soil. When they came back down, not long after, they said that they had seen neither settlements nor people nor fires, and that there were no minerals in that hill.

The following day—Tuesday, October 20—they did not dare to set out early, fearing that the Indians had set a trap for them during the night. They found another ranchería, located on both sides of the river, but like the one on the previous day, it too was abandoned, so they once again set out for the shore. As they were coming down the slope, within sight of the frigate, they observed the ship's launch at the water's edge, with Joanes de Uranzu, a Basque, on board. However, before they could

Plaque for Pedro de Unamuno at Moro Bay.

reach it, they saw that the Luzon Indians, who had been sent to explore a hill, were running back down, in flight from the local Indians. They went immediately to their aid and succeeded in driving the pursuers back up the hill with harquebus fire. Juan de Aranguren, another Basque, and Joan de Mendoza arrived, "wounded with many arrow— and javelin—wounds."[26] Two other men were also wounded. One was hit by a lance that went right through his chest, "because he had taken off the coat of mail which he carried," killing him, and one of the Luzon Indians also died of "a javelin-thrust, which he failed to ward off with his target."[27]

The men were tending to the wounded when they saw many more Indians coming down the hill. Those who had remained on the frigate, realizing what was happening, came to the aid of their companions. Several Indians died in the skirmish, many more were wounded, and the rest retreated. It was starting to get dark, and Unamuno's men also retreated to their ship. There they learned the motive for the attack, and why Unamuno's group had not seen a single Indian during the entire previous day.

It was because of something that had happened the day before, Monday, October 19. Fray Martín and some men who had remained on the ship disembarked in order to obtain water and firewood, and while they were at it, to investigate something they had seen the previous night, "a great fire which lasted almost all night." Having arrived at a creek, they left a soldier, armed with a sword, standing guard over a group of Luzon Indians while the latter did laundry and collected water and firewood, and set out for the location where they had seen the fire. At that moment, while the Luzon Indians were busy with their work, twenty-three of the indigenous inhabitants came down the hill, and three of them neared the river to spy on the strangers. Seeing that they were more numerous, they seized the laundry and the containers for water and fled back up the hill. Soon afterward, when they were about to descend again, they unexpectedly saw Fray Martín and his group approaching, whereupon they "began forthwith to raise a great outcry, making many gestures and jumping from one place to another, as though they wished to attack," since they had not expected anyone else to appear.

Fray Martín's party tried to approach them peacefully, but according to Unamuno's account, the Indians

> attacked our men, making many signs that they desired to kill them. They fired many arrows without doing our men damage. Padre (Fray) Martin would not permit an arquebus to be fired until it appeared that they were arrogant, and then they fired on them with the arquebuses and wounded some and compelled them to withdraw to the top of the hill.[28]

That was how the day ended, but hostilities continued the following day. When Unamuno and his men were returning to the frigate, unaware of what had happened the previous day, they were attacked by Indians enraged by Fray Martín's group.

At nightfall, another council was held on the *Nuestra Señora de Esperanza*, and they decided to leave the following day. They were almost out of ammunition, medicine for the wounded was in equally short supply, and there were not enough men to face the enemy. They would continue on to Acapulco, trying to find a good port along the way.

So on Wednesday, October 21, the frigate continued its southward voyage, although with little luck, since for the next five days, the fog was so dense that it was impossible to fulfill the objective of finding a port for the Manila galleon on the California coast.

Unamuno's narrative of the voyage offers a quantity of details about the first contacts between Europeans and indigenous people. Obviously, however, his perspective is a partial one. As in other, similar narratives, the Indians are anonymous, condemned to the role of mere one-dimensional figures. They appear on a hilltop, rush howling down the slope, shoot off some arrows, and flee howling once again, frightened by the Spaniards' firearms.

There is also one other fact that cannot be left out. Traditionally, the spread of Old World diseases in California has been attributed to the missions, but it appears incontestable today that long before the first mission was founded at San Diego in 1769, diseases of all kinds had already spread up and down the California coast (smallpox, measles, dysentery, typhoid fever, malaria, typhus . . .). The germs sometimes traveled by land, but also by sea. During his expedition in search of the Strait of Anián (1542–43), Cabrillo had contact with the coastal inhabitants, and many of his men are known to have been weakened by illness at the end of the voyage. Several decades later, in 1579, Sir Francis Drake's men spent several weeks in close contact with the indigenous people they encountered north of San Francisco Bay. Pedro de Unamuno's men also spent a week somewhere between Monterey and Santa Barbara. Undoubtedly, all these visits were entry points for a variety of infections and are at the origin of the almost complete disappearance of California's native inhabitants.[29]

The English Corsair Thomas Cavendish Seizes the Galleon *Santa Ana* (and Hangs a Basque Canon), 1587–1588

Pedro de Unamuno's *Nuestra Señora de Esperanza* was heading toward Acapulco amid a dense fog when a launch met him off Cabo Corrientes, at 21° latitude, sent by the Acapulco authorities to warn the China ships of an English corsair's presence in the area. More than the warning, however, it was the fog that saved Unamuno's ship. The *Nuestra Señora de Esperanza* and the two ships under Thomas Cavendish's command, the flagship *Desire* and the smaller *Content, crossed paths without seeing one another, and* Cavendish continued in the direction of Cabo San Lucas, to await the arrival of the *Santa Ana*.

The *Santa Ana* had been at sea for nearly four and a half months when the California coast came into sight. Counting crew and passengers, more than one hundred fifty people were on board, including a number of women and three or four friars. The ship was carrying a true treasure: silks, embroideries, pearls, musk, and an unknown quantity of gold as well. In command was, as the sailor Antonio de Sierra testified later, "a Bizkaian named Thomas de Arzola."[30] The ship was heavily laden, but it had been carrying even more cargo when it left Manila, so much that at the beginning of the voyage, as they were approaching Mindoro, they had to throw part of the merchandise overboard.[31]

On November 14, now without fog and with a good following wind, the *Santa Ana* was drawing near to the coast, in the vicinity of Cabo San Lucas. Suddenly, the lookout at the top of the mast caught sight of some sails between the shore and the ship. At first, the crew and passengers rejoiced, thinking that it was the *Nuestra Señora de Esperanza*, since the latter ship and the *Santa Ana* had left the Philippines at roughly

Thomas Cavendish

the same time. When they came a little closer, however, the white-and-red flags and standards made clear the nationality of the two ships sailing toward them: they were English, or as Alzola put it, "the flagship of a thieving English corsair named Don Tomas Candiens of Tembley."[32]

Alzola began to give orders. The merchants who wore swords made ready to use them, the sailors armed themselves with stones, and everyone occupied his post. There were only two harquebuses on the ship, and two or three charges of powder that Alzola carried in a flask. They had neither artillery nor powder nor ammunition. Although Francis Drake had devoted himself nine years previously to attacking towns and ships in New Spain and Peru, the Spaniards felt themselves masters of the Pacific, and it did not occur to them that anyone could attack them. In addition, the Manila galleon had never faced an enemy like this Cavendish. In an instant, the *Desire* came around to the windward, and forty armed men leaped onto the galleon, engaging the men of the *Santa Ana* in hand-to-hand combat. Alzola's men held out, "doing on that occasion more than was possible,"[33] wounding several of the English and killing others or forcing them to jump overboard.

Before retreating, the English did not wish to lose their final opportunity to do damage, and with great fury one of them began to cut the ship's rigging and halyards, "which when the said Capt. Tomas de Alzola saw it, he shot him with a shotgun and killed him."[34] So ended the first English assault.

The second assault was more violent. Cannon balls tore holes in the *Santa Ana* below the waterline. On the third sally, the *Desire* boarded the *Santa Ana* at the prow. The battle lasted another five or six hours, as the situation grew increasingly desperate for the men of the *Santa Ana*. They patched the cannons' damage from the inside with leather and raw silk, but seeing that the ship was sinking, Alzola announced, "Gentlemen, see what you want us to do, because we have no remedy, for today is our day."[35] According to the sworn statement Alzola made to the Guadalajara tribunal:

> They held it better to surrender than to die by drowning,[36] and

> although for his part [Tomás de Alzola], he issued many cautions, encouraging the people above and below decks, they all, seeing the enemy's strength and that they were shooting their artillery at a great rate, sent a small boat. To authorize the negotiations, Pedro Bravo de Paredes went in it to the English flagship to treat with the general that he save their lives and that they would surrender. He returned with the message that he granted their lives to all the people of the said ship *Santa Ana*, and that in addition to this, he would put them on land.[37]

Shortly thereafter, the English captain sent six armed men in a skiff, "and he took six men as hostages."[38] Sierra, the sailor, identifies them in his testimony: the friar Francisco Ramos; Don Joan de Almendrales, canon of Manila; Antonio de Sierra himself; Don Joan Maldonado; Captain Alzola; and the pilot. From this point on, Alzola's narrative is more detailed. He also gives the Manila canon's name more exactly:

> They ordered the said Capt. Tomás de Alzola to take out and show all the treasure he was carrying in the said ship, according to the register, and he showed them three chests in which he was carrying all the gold, pearls, and other things, and His Majesty's dispatches. They took the chests out to the quarterdeck, and then in the presence of the English general and officers they broke the said chests and took out all the gold and treasure the ship was carrying and divided it there into three parts with scales. The English general took two parts, and the people of the said fleet the other part, and with this the day came to an end, although also without any occasion he then ordered the hanging of Don Juan de Almendariz, canon of the Philippines, without having an occasion for it. They hung him from an arm of the main stay, and then they threw him into the sea. He died as a good Catholic Christian.[39]

The "Joan de Almendrales" of Sierra's narrative, the canon of Manila, becomes "Juan de Almendariz" under the pen of the notary who recorded Captain Alzola's testimony. In various documents of the Archivo General de Indias, he appears as Juan de Armendáriz. As far as the motives for his hanging are concerned, the explanations could not be more varied. According to Alzola, he was executed without motive. The sailor Sierra testified that the pirates hanged him "because he did not have the temperament or endurance to bear the labors and adversities we bore there."[40] According to the researcher Héctor Santos, they hanged "Don Juan de Almendrales" for confronting the hostage-takers and cursing them.[41] There are also those who affirm that Juan de Armendáriz was one of the heroes of the battle and was killed because, when the rest had already given up, he continued making a stand and insulting the enemy . . . The only thing known for certain is that the English corsairs hung him from an arm of the main stay and then threw his lifeless body into the sea.

The *Santa Ana* was taken to the coast, near where San José del Cabo is today, and the passengers and crew were forced to disembark, together with thirty other hostages taken by Cavendish in previous assaults. After that, the pirates set a group of Indians and blacks to bailing, in order to keep the galleon afloat long enough to finish looting it.

And so the days passed. Cavendish had taken possession of the ship's register, and while his men went about the orderly transfer of the *Santa Ana*'s precious cargo to their own ship, the hostages observed from land. The English moved without haste, without fear that anyone would appear on that remote peninsula. They did not hesitate to take a break to celebrate the anniversary of Queen Elizabeth's coronation. Before departing, Cavendish took the trouble to leave arms and provisions (harquebuses, swords, candles, tools, wine, chickpeas, etc.) for those men and women who were going to be left totally isolated, and at the last moment, with no little impudence, he returned the ship's register to Alzola, signed as a receipt. After ordering the masts and rigging cut and the ship set on fire, Cavendish set out into that ocean with which he was unfamiliar, taking along Alzola's two pilots to assist him.

From this point onward, those abandoned on land thought only about how to escape from there. After twelve days, a group of men went to investigate the state in which the *Santa Ana*'s hull had been left after the fire. The lower portion, in contact with the water, was intact. At the head of the group was Sebastián Vizcaíno—"a Basque soldier of unusual talents," in the words of the historian Richard F. Pourade[42]—who would go on to play a very important role in California history. Vizcaíno had fought in Flanders before moving to Mexico and devoting himself to commerce. He had invested a large sum of money in Manila and was transporting on the *Santa Ana* the valuable products he had obtained there, and if Cavendish had not crossed his path, he would have made enormous profits.

Vizcaíno and the rest of the men spent the following days making the repairs necessary to refloat the *Santa Ana*. They constructed a mast with the pieces of wood they were able to recover and made a sail from the materials Cavendish had left them. Finally, on December 21, after

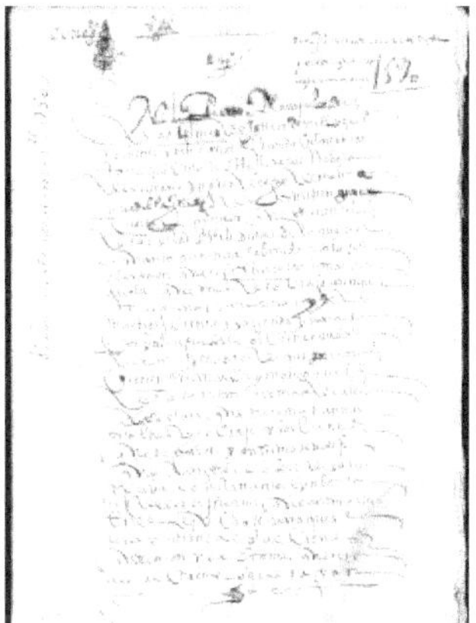

Possessions at time of death, Juan de Armendariz.

thirty-six days at San Lucas, they were able to begin their return voyage. They spent Christmas on the ship, reaching the port of Santiago on January 2, and after leaving eleven sick passengers there, they entered the port of Acapulco on January 6, 1588.

Some days later, the sailor Antonio de Sierra and Capt. Tomás de Alzola were questioned by the Guadalajara tribunal. The details given here are taken from their sworn statements. As we have seen, the names do not always agree, and the same is true of the dates and some other facts. The differences are even greater with regard to the quantity of gold the English made off with. The latter speak of a value of 22,000 pesos, the Spaniards of 600,000. In any event, it was the largest loss in the history of more than two centuries of commerce between Manila and Acapulco. The authorities of Manila and New Spain were thoroughly disconcerted. For the first time, Spanish dominion of the Pacific had been called into question. What the Portuguese and even Sir Francis Drake himself had not managed had been achieved by the young Cavendish, who at the time the *Santa Ana* was boarded was only twenty-seven years old.

Sebastián Vizcaíno Enters the History of California, 1596–1603

Sebastián Vizcaíno

Following the disaster of the *Santa Ana*, the Spanish authorities gave priority to occupying California and protecting the Manila galleon, which was so important for New Spain's economy. Thomas Cavendish's "shameless" conduct had made clear that a small number of men were enough to jeopardize the absolute dominion that Spain had enjoyed in the Pacific up to that time. There was only one way to make sure that events did not repeat themselves: having a stopover point in California where the galleon could be warned of the presence of foreign ships along the coast and, if necessary, offered an armed escort ship.

This time, the mission was entrusted to Sebastián Rodríguez Cermenho (Sebastião Rodrigues Soromenho in Portuguese). He did not lack experience, having been one of the *Santa Ana*'s pilots when Cavendish boarded Alzola's ship. Cermenho left Manila on July 5, 1595, and arrived in California on November 4. Near Drakes Bay, he decided to build a smaller ship in order to explore the coast, leaving the galleon *San Agustin*, which was heavily laden, in safer waters. It was a fortunate decision, since, for reasons that the witnesses' statements do not make clear, the *San Agustin* ran aground and sank with the treasure on board. From then on, Cermenho had to confront the sea in a miserable launch, with his men starving most of the time, and completely at the mercy of the Indians they encountered on the shore. Once he made it to Mexico, in January 1596, Cermenho provided a detailed description of the coast, including interesting information about the natives of the region, but it was all in vain, since the captain and other officers did not manage to reach agreement when the time came to report the discoveries. Consequently, after having endured so many disasters, Cermenho is remembered above all for having lost the precious galleon.

The loss of the *San Agustín*, coming on top of the disaster of the *Santa Ana*, made it very clear that it was useless to try to explore the coast with a ship crammed full of treasure and an exhausted crew. Lighter ships were needed, and they needed to set out from New Spain itself. In addition, evidently, the mission had to be entrusted to the right person.

This was when, in the words of the historian Richard F. Pourade, Sebastián Vizcaíno "entered the history of California."[43] He was that "Basque soldier of unusual talents" who helped to float the burned skeleton of the *Santa Ana* after the corsair Cavendish's assault. In effect, the viceroy of Mexico, the count of Monterrey, named Vizcaíno general of the new expedition. The choice was not without its questionable aspects. From the count's perspective, Vizcaíno was only an obscure merchant who might endanger the crown's prestige. In the end, nevertheless, he found himself forced to grant his approval. In reality, Vizcaíno was much more than a run-of-the-mill merchant. In addition to being an "ambitious and capable Basque merchant," as Iris H. W. Engstrand calls him, he had extensive experience in the Pacific: he had hunted for pearls, guarded the port of Manila, and traveled as far as China.

Vizcaíno's activities and concerns were reflected in a letter he wrote to his father in 1590, on his return from China. The text deserves special attention, since in comparison to the vast quantity of official documents preserved in the archives, very few letters addressed to family members have survived to our time:[44]

Vizcaíno wrote to his father, Antonio "Biscaino":

> this is onely to give you to understand, that foure moneths past, I came from China, and landed in Acapulco, 70 leagues from Mexico, which is the harbour where the ships that goe down to China lye; and all the marchants of Mexico bring all their Spanish commodities downe to this harbour, to ship them from that countrey. It is one of the best harbours in all Nueva Espanna; and where the ships may ride most safely without all kinde of danger. For it lyeth under a necke of land, and behind a great point.
>
> And in this harbour here are foure great ships of Mexico of 600 and 800 tunnes a piece, which onely serve to carry our commodities to China, and so to returne backe againe. The order is thus. From hence to China is above two thousand leagues, farther than from hence to Spaine. And from hence their two first ships depart at one time to China: and are 13 or 14 months returning backe againe. And when those two ships are returned, then the other twaine two moneths after depart from hence. They goe nowe from hence very strong with souldiers. I can certifie you of one thing: that 200 ducates in Spanish commodities, and some Flemish wares which I caryed with me thither, I made worth 1400 ducates there in the countrey. So I make account with those silkes, and other commodities which I brought with me from thence to Mexico, I got 2500 ducates by the voyage; and had gotten more, if one packe of fine silkes had not bene spoiled by salt water.
>
> So as I sayd, there is a great gaine to be gotten if that a man return in safetie. But the yeere 1588 I had great mischance, coming in a ship from China to Nueva Espanna: which being laden with rich commodities, was taken by an Englishman which robbed us and afterward burned our ship, wherein I lost a great deale of treasure and commodities.[45]
>
> If I should write to you of the state of this countrey of China, and of the strange things which are there, and of the wealth of the countrey, I were not able to doe it, in an whole quier of paper. Onely I may certify you, that it is the goodliest countrey, and the richest, and most plentifull in all the world.[46]

Vizcaíno ended the letter with a respectful farewell to his father: "From Mexico the 20 June, 1590. Your obedient sonne, Sebastian Biscaino." However, Vizcaíno was not only an eager merchant, as the viceroy thought and as his letter to his father seems to indicate. He had the opportunity to demonstrate as much in the two great voyages he made at the order of the Spanish authorities. The first had as its objective establishing an outpost in northern California. The second would become one of California history's turning points.

First Attempt at Establishing a Settlement in California, 1596

On April 16, 1596, the viceroy of New Spain, the count of Monterrey, wrote to the king that Vizcaíno's expedition was on the point of departure. In the same letter, the count mentioned another expedition that was completing its preparations: the one that Juan de Oñate would lead to New Mexico by land.

In the end, it was already June 15 when Vizcaíno departed the port of Acapulco with three ships (one large and two small), 230 soldiers and sailors (some of the soldiers accompanied by their wives), four Franciscans, fourteen horses, artillery, and provisions for eight months. On July 5, at the port of Salagua, they took on another 120 men, fourteen horses, and more provisions. On August 13, at the port of San Juan de Mazatlán, they had an unpleasant surprise. Fray Francisco Balda deserted, taking with him fifty men, the best soldiers.

The first Indians they encountered in California territory were "without any kind of covering or clothing, very notably large and well made."[47] They received the strangers in a friendly way, but Vizcaíno found their appearance very disagreeable, and he described them harshly:[48]

> The people are so bestial and uncivilized, that whether standing or seated, whenever they take the notion, they attend to the necessities of nature without any nicety or respect. Their language is so barbarous that it sounds more like bleating of sheep than the speech of men.[49]

At a large bay located at 24° latitude, Vizcaíno decided to go ashore to carry out the ceremony of taking possession of the territory:

> At this place there came to me a great number of Indians, who received me peacefully, and who remained at that place while I was there. What happened there is this: The clergy being

> desirous of celebrating mass, and an altar having been erected on shore, I caused the image of Our Lady to be taken out of the ship for the purpose of placing it on the altar, and it was carried in procession from the beach to the place where the altar was. At this time there appeared an Indian Chief, accompanied by more than eight hundred Indians armed with bows and arrows. I went forth to meet them and they came to me in peace. Going to where the image of Our Lady was, I fell upon my knees, kissing its feet, and also the friar who held it in his hands. Seeing this, the said Indian threw aside the bow and arrow he was grasping and humbled himself before that image, kissing its feet; looking toward the sky and the sun, he asked by gestures whether that image had come thence. Making himself understood by signs, he shouted to the other Indians, his companions, who drew near in order to do as this Indian had done—whereat all of us Spaniards who were there were content, as it was fitting we should be. And, while carrying the image in procession to place it on the altar, the Indian chief went always before it, dancing after the manner of his people.[50]

After the symbolic act of taking possession, they continued north about fifteen leagues until they reached an inlet that they named La Paz, meaning "peace," due to the good reception they were given by the inhabitants. It appeared to Vizcaíno an appropriate place for establishing a colony, and after separating out the weaker men, women, and children, he informed them of his intention to leave them there while he continued north with eighty men. However, those who had to remain rebelled. They thought that they were going to be abandoned there, and that Vizcaíno's true plan was to return to New Spain. In order to dispel these doubts, Vizcaíno told them that he would leave his seven-year-old son Juan there and proposed a bargain. If they returned from the voyage hungry and without having found prosperous lands, as many feared, they would be able to provision themselves there before returning to New Spain. If they found good lands, on the other hand, Vizcaíno would send a ship to Culiacán with the silver table service he had left and his son, in exchange for a ransom of two thousand pesos. The boy's mother would gladly pay, and with the money collected, they would be able to purchase corn, wheat, meat, and the other things they lacked.

In the end, an agreement was reached, and on October 3, Vizcaíno left the inlet of La Paz with two ships, provisions for a month and a half, and the eighty men he had chosen. From this time forward, according to his narrative, everything went against them. A large storm that blew up from the north and lasted four days was followed by a hurricane from the south that almost put an end to the expedition. Next, at 27° latitude, they found themselves amid six islands and many shoals, through which they managed to navigate safely only with great difficulty. To top it all off, the Indians who came out to meet them did not turn out to be as peaceful as they initially appeared:

> there came out to me from shore five pirogues of Indians making signs that I should go to their land, promising things to eat and water, which we were lacking, and so I arrived at the location that the Indians indicated and went on land with forty-five men. On land I was received by a large number of Indians, giving me fish and fruit and showing great happiness at having seen us, and at this location, one of my soldiers thoughtlessly hit one of the said Indians in the chest with the butt of his harquebus, without my seeing it, for which reason the said Indians became angry[51] and shot some arrows at us, although not with great effect. Having seen the Indians' boldness, I ordered four harquebuses to be fired into the air in order to startle them and not injure them. At the noise of the powder they all fell to the ground. Once the smoke of it had passed, they got up, and having seen that they had not been hurt, they began to shoot arrows again with greater force, so that I commanded my people to lower their muzzles. At the first peppering, there fell I don't know how many, for which reason the rest began to flee up into a range of mountains. Having seen that there was nothing to be done at this location, I embarked in order to continue onward, and since the shallop I had was small, we could not all embark, leaving the sergeant-major on land with half of the men, to whom I at once sent the shallop. Among the said soldiers there arose quarrels about who had done best, so that they did not embark when he ordered them. A great inquiry was made about this, and having seen the determination he had to punish some who were disobedient, they embarked. While they were on their way to the ship, already some distance from land, there arrived on the beach a large group of Indians shooting arrows into the air, one of which hit one of the sailors who was rowing in the nose. As he felt himself wounded, he stopped, and the other one in doing his job spun the shallop around, and at this disturbance the soldiers who were in the shallop began to move around in such a way that they gathered on one side. The said shallop capsized with the weight and caught them underneath, and since they were armed, they went down. Out of twenty-five, six escaped by swimming, since

> the armor they wore was of leather, and with the help of planks.[52]

From then on, they called the site of this misfortune the "port of slaughter" (Puerto de Matanzas) or the "port of death" (Puerto de la Muerte).[53]

Left without a shallop, Vizcaíno decided to return to La Paz. There, the discontent among the colonists was palpable. The provisions were running out; there was no way to fish for pearls because of the storms; and to make matters worse, a cabin caught fire, and in addition to half the encampment, all the married people's household goods burned, that is, all the household goods there were, since only the married people had brought some. In addition, the natives showed themselves increasingly rebellious and warlike, and not without reason, since the undisciplined soldiers abused their women. Finally, Vizcaíno had to give in: two of the ships would return to Mexico with those who were to have been California's first colonists.

On November 9, the third ship again sailed north, in a final attempt to explore the gulf. This time as well, eighty men accompanied Vizcaino, as well as his seven-year-old son. In his diary, Vizcaíno offers a vivid chronicle of the sufferings they endured:

> the ship began to make much water, which alarmed us considering the danger in which we were, as the winds were contrary and the sea was narrow to run before them. The islands were very close together, and full of warlike Indians, the ship was alone and very battered, and, if any disaster should occur, we could get no help from any quarter. If we accidentally struck a land so dangerous, we could not escape being drowned or eaten by the Indians. With all this, although many were discouraged, I spoke very kindly to them, exhorting them to go on with the enterprise, easing up on their work and assuring them against danger. I held up as an example my boy, a creature only seven years old who suffered as many hardships as any of them and from the same danger as all, and myself, who in seeing him suffer, suffered as much as all of them put together.[54]

It was all in vain. With the rudder broken, the water about to run out, and food scarce—the corn, the flour, and the salt meat had been ruined by water and storms—Vizcaíno had no choice but to desist in his enterprise.

So Sebastián Vizcaíno returned to Mexico without having fulfilled his mission to establish a settlement in California, but without losing his spirits as a consequence. Inclined to highlight his achievements, he provided exaggerated accounts of the wealth of pearls, the abundance of fish, and the great number of Indians they had encountered, decked with gold and silver and desirous of converting to Christianity. In his letter to the king, for example, he makes this reference to California's pearls:

> As far as pearl fishing is concerned, I believe that it is infinite, due to the extremely large number of shells of that kind that there are on the shore.[55]

Nevertheless, it should not be thought that Vizcaíno was a man who let himself be led by fantasy. In reality, this was a carefully calculated strategy: with his baseless tales and exaggerations, Sebastián Vizcaíno was trying to ensure his candidacy for the next expedition.

Sebastián Vizcaíno Reaches Cape Mendocino. During the Voyage He Sounds, Maps, and Names the California Coast, 1602–1603

After the English corsair Thomas Cavendish sacked the galleon *Santa Ana*, the Spanish authorities once again became aware of the need to explore California, and as they had done before, they entrusted the mission to Sebastián Vizcaíno. The viceroy, the count of Monterrey, gave the monarch a clear explanation of the new expedition's objective: finding out once and for all what there really was in California. According to his instructions, Vizcaíno was to head directly for Cabo San Lucas and try to enter as many bays and rivers as possible until reaching Cape Mendocino, always keeping as close to the coast as possible and avoiding clashes with the Indians. He should also mark the entrances of all ports and baptize those that were unnamed.

Following two years of preparations, the expedition that would reach Mendocino was launched in 1602. On May 5, two larger ships—the *San Diego* and the *Santo Tomás*—one frigate—the *Tres Reyes*—and a longboat sailed from the port of Acapulco, all under Vizcaíno's command. The soldiers and sailors were accompanied by three Discalced Carmelites, one of whom was Fray Antonio de la Ascensión. Vizcaíno brought along his son Juan on this occasion as well.

Prior to departure, an image of Our Lady of Mount Carmel was brought aboard in a procession of soldiers and sailors, amid artillery and musket fire.

Two chronicles of the voyage exist, in addition to other documents: the official diary, which bears Vizcaíno's name, and a summary written by the Carmelite Fray Antonio in 1620, based on his own diary.[56] We follow Vizcaíno's account here.[57]

The expedition reached Cabo San Lucas on June 8. They left the longboat there, and the three other ships continued north without losing sight of the Baja California coast, usually short on water and at a distance from one another. In addition to drawing the corresponding maps, they baptized each point on the coast with the name of the saint whose feast day it was: bays of San Bernabé (Saint Barnabas) and Magdalena (the Magdalene), port of San Bartolomé (Saint Bartholomew), bay of Santa María (Saint Mary), islands of Asunción (Ascension) and San Roque (Saint Roch) . . . Here and there, throughout the region, they encountered Indian populations of widely diverse appearance and customs, who received the strangers aggressively on some occasions, peacefully on others.[58]

On June 11, Vizcaíno and the other captains and lieutenants disembarked, armed and accompanied by fifty soldiers with harquebuses. On the beach, they found about a hundred Indians waiting for them. They embraced them and gave them food and other things, and the Indians reciprocated with "tiger" pelts and deerskins.[59]

The following day, Vizcaíno had a tent set up near the beach, in the shelter of a large hill, and after celebrating mass, they brought the image of Our Lady of Mount Carmel there—the same place where the English corsair Cavendish had abandoned the hostages from the *Santa Ana*.

The voyage continued without serious problems. The summer passed, and on October 12, having reached a very large inlet, they were approached by twenty canoes, apparently peaceful in intention, full of Indian fishermen. "They killed the fish with such ease that within two hours, they had filled their canoe full," Vizcaíno marveled in his diary.

The next day, they decided to disembark:

> He found on the shore three villages of Indians with their children and women, as calm and undisturbed as if we had been dealing with them for many days . . . Another day, the said general and friars went on land; a mass was said; some Indians came, hearing it with great attention, as if enraptured, we telling them by signs in response to their questions that this was an affair of heaven. The said Indians bowed their heads and made the sign of the cross; they said the prayers and all the words we said to them in our language.

They named the site the "Bay of the Eleven Thousand Virgins."[60]

On October 27, at barely 32° latitude, "a stiff northwest wind came up with heavy seas," for which reason they resolved to seek refuge in an inlet about nine leagues away. The following day, a group of men disembarked, "with orders to search diligently for water, and that they treat the Indians who were on the shore well." They found good and abundant water right at the shore, but on this occasion the Indians were not so hospitable.

More than a hundred Indians came out at them set for war with their bows and arrows and some throwing lances, and the said Indians very shameless, such that they bent their bows and picked up stones to throw at us.

Although the Spaniards gave them hardtack and other presents, the Indians did not let them draw water, and they tried to take away their jugs and barrels. Seeing this, Vizcaíno's men fired three harquebuses, in order to frighten them with the noise of the powder. The Indians fled, shouting, but two hours later, they were back in greater numbers, women and children among them. A lieutenant indicated to them by signs to be calm, that they should be friends. The Indians agreed, but on condition that the Spaniards not shoot the harquebuses again, since that had frightened them a great deal. Finally, the Indians returned to their rancherías, and Vizcaíno's men could continue replenishing their water supplies. They called the place the bay of Saints Simon and Jude.[61]

Continuing to hug the coast, they could see the smoke of the bonfires the Indians made on land. "There was so much smoke that the Indians made on land that at night it appeared to be a procession, and during the day it obscured the sky." In effect, the Indians were accustomed to burn large tracts of land in order to drive the game into particular areas and so be able to kill their prey more easily.

On November 10, after a voyage of almost six months, they arrived at a handsome port,

> the best there must be in all the South Sea, because in addition to being protected from all the winds and having a good bottom, it is at 33 1/2 latitude and has very good water and firewood and a lot of fish of all kinds, of which we took a great deal with the net and hooks. On land there is good hunting for rabbits, hares, and deer and very large quail, peacocks and thrushes and many other birds.

Two days later, on November 12, the feast day of Saint James (San Diego), almost all the men disembarked, and after holding a council, they agreed to take advantage of the opportunities the site offered to clean the ships and replenish their supplies of water and firewood. At that moment,

> there came into view on a hill some hundred Indians with bows and arrows and many feathers on their heads, and they called out to us with a great deal of shouting . . . The general, the admiral, and his son went toward the Indians, and when the said Indians saw this, two Indian men and two Indian women descended a hill. Upon their having reached the general, the Indian women crying, he dealt kindly with them and embraced them, giving them some things and assuring the rest of the Indians by signs. They came down in peace, for which they were well treated.

On the 15th, Vizcaíno, his son, Fray Antonio de la Ascensión, the senior pilot, and fifteen harquebusiers set out on the frigate with the aim of sounding a large inlet. After Vizcaíno had disembarked with his companions and walked more than three leagues,

> numerous Indians came out with their bows and arrows, and although he made them signs of peace, they did not dare to come close, only one very old Indian woman, who appeared to be more than a hundred and fifty years old, crying. The general dealt kindly with her, giving her some beads and something to eat. From sheer old age, this Indian woman had wrinkles on her belly that looked like a blacksmith's bellows, and her navel stuck out larger than a squash. Having seen this good treatment, the Indians came in peace and took us to their villages, where they were bringing in their harvest, having made their threshing heaps of a seed like linseed. They had clay pots in which they cooked, and the Indian women were dressed in animal skins. The general did not allow any of the soldiers to enter their villages, and it being now late in the day, he returned to the frigate, with many Indians accompanying him to the beach.

On November 20, after having taken on water, firewood, and fish, they set sail:

> I do not mention, in order not to annoy the reader, the many times that the Indians came to our camps with martin skins and other things, until the day we set sail, when they remained on the beach shouting.

Before the departure, the Indians indicated by signs to Fray Antonio de la Ascensión that they had seen other bearded men of the same appearance inland, dressed like the Spaniards.[62]

With this narrative by Vizcaíno and the details recorded by Fray Antonio de la Ascensión in his summary, San Diego entered the pages

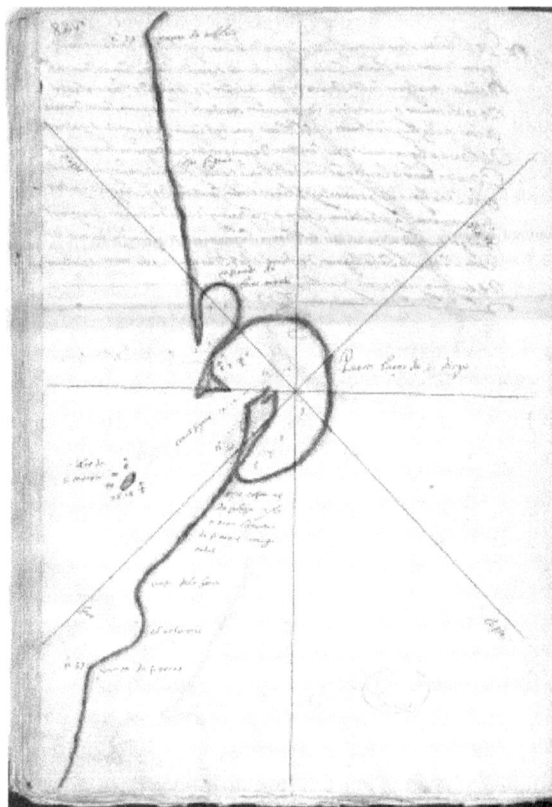

San Diego Bay. "Map a de la costa y puertos descubiertos por Sebastián Vizcayno». Archivo General de Indias. AGI,MPMEXICO, 53, fol.82v)

of California history.

A week later, the expedition discovered three large islands, the middle one of which they named Santa Catalina, since it was the eve of Saint Catherine's feast day. On November 27, before casting anchor in a cove, they were approached by a large group of Indians in handsome canoes made of cedar and pine. Each one had eight oars and fourteen or fifteen Indians, all of them very happy and inviting them by signs to come on land. The following day, a mass was said on land, in the presence of a hundred and fifty Indian men and women "not a little amazed to see the altar and the image of Our Lord Jesus Christ." When the service was over, the women, showing no sign of fear, took Vizcaíno by the hand and brought him into their huts to feed him. Without any objection from their mothers, Vizcaíno brought six girls of eight or ten years old to the ship and returned them dressed "in blouses and petticoats and bead necklaces." Seeing this, the other mothers also came with their daughters in canoes, and no one returned empty-handed. They were people used to bartering: in exchange for old clothes, they gave the soldiers skins, shells, nets, thread, cord, etc.

On the night of the 29th, Vizcaíno's men set sail, headed for another port on the same island that the Indians had recommended to them. Vizcaíno walked inland and came upon a sacred site, a very well-kept flat area where the Indians gathered to worship an idol.

> after the manner of a demon with horns, headless, and with a dog at its feet and many children painted around it. The Indians told the general that they should not go there, but he went and saw it all, and he made a cross and placed the name of Jesus over the demon's head and told the Indians that this was good and from heaven and that idol was the demon, at which the Indians were amazed, and they easily removed it and received our Holy Faith.

It was December 1 when the expedition left Santa Catalina. The cold weather and the winter were growing more severe, people were getting sick, and they lacked medicine to treat them. They needed to hurry if they wanted to complete their mission.

On the 2nd, they came in sight of two other large islands. As they approached the first,

> there came to meet us a canoe with two Indian fishermen, with a large quantity of fish, rowing so swiftly that it seemed as if they were flying. Arriving on board, without saying a word, they took two turns around with such speed that it seemed impossible, and once finished, they came to the poop deck, bowing their heads as a courtesy. The general ordered that they be given a piece of cloth with bread; they received it and gave in return the fish they brought, without any self-interest, and having giving them, they said by signs that they wanted to go. Once they were gone, another canoe came with five Indians, a canoe so well crafted and made that from Noah's Ark until now, a finer and swifter one has not been seen among barbarians, nor the planks better worked, with four of the Indians rowing and an old man in the middle singing, in the manner of a mitote[63] of the Indians of New Spain, and the others answering him.

By signs, the old man urged them to come to his land, where they would have food and water for all. In order to convince them, he also promised them another present, according to Vizcaíno: "He said that he would give each of us ten women to sleep with."

Continuing their voyage, they crossed the Santa Barbara Channel, rounded Point Conception, and having left Carmel Bay behind them, reached another handsome port on December 16, naming it Monterey in honor of the count of Monterrey, the viceroy of Mexico, who had promoted the expedition. The following day, they disembarked and set up a shelter under which to say mass, in the shadow of a live oak. There had

Plaque for Pedro de Unamuno at Moro Bay.

been a great deal of fog up to that point, and when it lifted, they could see where they were:

> we found ourselves in the best port that could be desired, because in addition to being sheltered from all winds, it has many pine forests for masts and yards and many live oaks and oaks, much water in quantity, all near the shore, fertile land, of the climate and landscape of Castile, much wild game, such as stags like young bulls, deer, buffaloes, very large bears, rabbits and hares, and many other winged animals, such as geese, partridges, quail, cranes, ducks, vultures, and many other kinds of birds that I do not mention in order not to annoy the reader.

In the following lines, Vizcaíno continues praising his discovery, making very little effort to keep close to reality. In fact, the port of Monterey was not the marvelous refuge he described, but a very open bay.

At that point in the trip, the majority of the men were suffering from scurvy, eighteen had already died, and many more were very seriously ill. A council was held to debate what should be done, and it was decided to send the *Santo Tomás* to Acapulco with the sickest men, a copy of what had been discovered to that point, and the mission of requesting reinforcements of men and supplies to finish discovering the coast. On December 29, the *Santo Tomás* left for Acapulco. Its trip turned out to be enormously difficult, and another twenty-five men lost their lives.

Meanwhile, the *San Diego* and the frigate prepared to continue their voyage to Cape Mendocino, taking on water and firewood amid terrible cold.

> The weather was extremely cold, to such a degree that on Wednesday, New Year's Day of 1603, the sun rose to reveal snow on all the mountains, so that they looked like the Mexico City volcano, and the pond where we were collecting water was covered with ice more than a palm thick, and the jugs that had been full of water overnight were all frozen, so that even when they rolled them around, not a drop came out.

The men were very sick, and the frigate was lost in a gale, but despite everything, with great labor and difficulty, they managed to continue advancing until they reached the desired location, Cape Mendocino, located at 40° latitude. It was January 12. By then, only two sailors were capable of climbing to the top of the mast, and the rain and the fog came on with such force that, in Vizcaíno's words, "it was as dark by day as by night." After holding another council, they decided to go no further.

On the 17th, they were getting ready to return to Cabo San Lucas when a terrible storm came up that "made [the ship] roll so far that it was thought to have gone bottom up and capsized, and with the great roll it knocked the sick and the healthy out of their beds, and the general out of his, knocking him against some chests, so that with the heavy blow he broke his ribs."

Fortunately—thanks be to God, according to Vizcaíno—on January 21, the wind began to blow from the northwest, easing navigation and also making it possible to map the coast. On the 25th, they reach the port of Monterey, but they did not stop, although the Indians made smoke signals to them:

> We did not enter the port, because our need for health was so great. The sick clamored without a doctor or medicine or treats we could give them, save rotten jerky and broken hardtack, beans and chickpeas full of weevils, all of them with their

> mouths damaged and their gums bigger than their teeth, so that they could scarcely get down water. The said ship appeared to be a hospital and not a naval ship, and affairs were at such a pass that someone who had never held a rudder in his life would helm the ship, climb up to the top of the mast, and do the rest of the tasks.

The sores in their mouths prevented them from eating, and the men died of hunger; the few who could get around, upright or on all fours, were incapable of handling the sails. The need for water and firewood was so pressing, however, that on February 6 they decided to stop at Cerros Island.[64] They dropped a small anchor, so that "if it could not be raised, it would be left there with the cable," and Vizcaíno went on land with half a dozen men, "the strongest of whom could not raise a jug from the ground." They were going to draw water on the beach when some Indians appeared, playing flutes and gesturing with their bows in a threatening manner. They did not want the hardtack they were offered, and Vizcaíno and his men drove them off with their harquebuses.

On the 8th, at midnight, they raised anchor and set sail. With a brisk following wind, they reached Cabo San Lucas on the 11th and retrieved the longboat they had left there on the outbound trip. They did not stop at the port of La Paz, since the people were so sick and worn down that they were afraid of not being able to bring the ship out again. Next, they crossed "the mouth of the Californias," and on the 18th, they reached the islands of Mazatlán, in a state of the greatest affliction and necessity. The following day, Vizcaíno disembarked with five soldiers; no one else on the ship was capable of walking. Uncertain of their direction, they took the wrong path, and instead of heading for Mazatlán, they walked thirteen leagues in the direction of Culiacán. They ran out of supplies and would have died of hunger "if God had not miraculously provided a remedy" in the form of a mule-driver on his way to Culiacán. He showed them the road that led to the town of Sacanta. Once they arrived there, Martín Ruiz de Aguirre, the provincial magistrate in charge, gathered as many chickens, kid goats, cows, and calves and as much bread as possible in the territory under his jurisdiction, along with something that turned out to be enormously beneficial: "A small fruit after the manner of a cypress nut, called *jucoistles*, which when the sick men who had bad mouths ate it, the strength of it healed the sores in their mouths." They spent eighteen days there, healing and recovering their strength, and finally, on March 21, they arrived in Acapulco, thereby concluding a voyage that had lasted eleven months. There they learned that only five men from the frigate *Los Tres Reyes* had reached their destination alive.

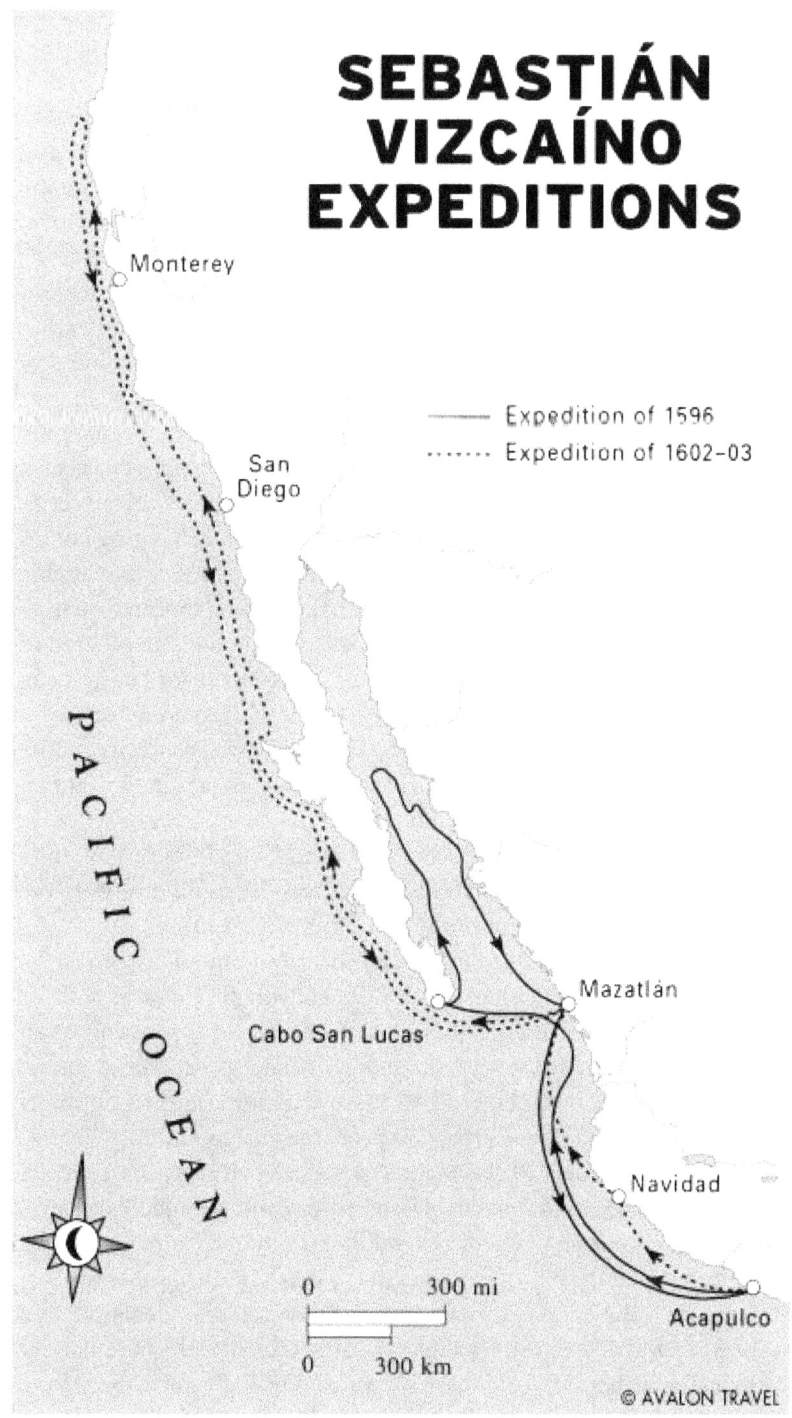
SEBASTIÁN VIZCAÍNO EXPEDITIONS
Expedition of 1596
Expedition of 1602-03
Monterey
San Diego
PACIFIC OCEAN
Mazatlán
Cabo San Lucas
Navidad
Acapulco
0
300 mi
0
300 km
© AVALON TRAVEL

Despite everything, and although more than forty men had been lost, the authorities of New Spain considered the voyage a success. Vizcaíno himself, in his letter to the king, summarized his achievements in these words: "I discovered the entire coast in great detail, without leaving a port, bay, island, or inlet that was not sounded and mapped in conformity with good cosmography and the art of seamanship."[65] A few lines further on, he recalled the expedition's objective: "Among the ports that I found of more significance there was one at 37° latitude that I named Monterey . . . that is everything that can be desired for comfort and a stopover point for the ships on the Philippines route."

It cannot be affirmed that Vizcaíno discovered new lands and new seas, since the majority of the places he visited had already been discovered by Cabrillo sixty years before, with the exception of Monterey. Vizcaíno's achievement was something else: describing the entire coast in great detail and giving names to its landmarks. Some historians criticize Vizcaíno for failing to follow his instructions and changing names that were already established, but it is possible that Vizcaíno was unable to recognize the locations that appeared on the maps elaborated on previous voyages, given their lack of exactness. It has to be remembered in this regard that there were no trustworthy instruments for taking exact measurements of longitude until well into the eighteenth century.

In any event, many locations along the California coast have maintained to the present the names Sebastián Vizcaíno assigned to them: San Diego, Monterey, La Paz, Santa Catalina Island, Santa Barbara Channel, Point Conception, Ensenada, Carmel, etc. In fact, Vizcaíno's maps were published as soon as his voyage was over, and they were the best guide to those waters until the late eighteenth century.

In recognition of his merits, the viceroy granted Vizcaíno the coveted post of commander of the next galleon that was to sail for Manila. He no longer thought of him, as he had at the beginning, as an uncouth trader. For his part, Vizcaíno continued proclaiming, orally and in writing, the advantages of Monterey Bay for establishing a port there. He convinced the viceroy, and preparations began, but a change in personnel upended all the plans. To the new viceroy, the count of Montesclaros, the recompense offered to Vizcaíno seemed excessive, and instead of commander of the galleon, he named him municipal governor (*alcalde mayor*) of Tehuantepec, a much more humble reward. Nevertheless, the court did not approve Montesclaros's decision, and in 1606, a royal decree ordered that Vizcaíno was to be the commander of the galleon that was to depart Acapulco. On his return, he was to explore the area around Monterey with the purpose of establishing a colony there. Montesclaros managed to get his way, however. When the order arrived, the galleon was already at sea, and Vizcaíno had traveled to Spain. When he returned, the viceroy had other plans.

In Montesclaros's opinion, the Manila galleon would be much better served by a stopover point somewhere in the middle of the Pacific than by the distant port of Monterey. Consequently, instead of sending Vizcaíno to occupy Monterey, he sent him in search of the legendary islands Rica de Oro and Rica de Plata. This decision put a halt to coastal exploration, and California was forgotten for the next hundred and fifty years.

There were further notable occurrences in Vizcaíno's eventful life. In 1611, he was sent to Japan as an ambassador. In 1615, back in New Spain, he took charge of the defense of the port of Salagua during an attack by the Dutch corsair Joris van Speilbergen. Nevertheless, the exploration of the California coast was his greatest achievement. For this reason, his name is borne today by Bahía Sebastián Vizcaíno on the Baja California peninsula, the Desierto del Vizcaíno Biosphere Reserve in southern Baja California, and the El Vizcaíno whale sanctuary in the same state, and for this reason, his name appears alongside those of Hernán Cortés and Juan Rodríguez Cabrillo in California children's schoolbooks.

During his lifetime, however, he received scant recognition. He was granted a small *encomienda*, an income of around two thousand pesos a year. It was not a great deal, but it did bring with it the status of a gentleman. As far as remote California was concerned, once the age of maritime explorations had been interrupted, it was left almost completely isolated, save the visits of pearl hunters and the occasional attempt at colonization.

Juan de Iturbe, a Hunter of Pearls among Dutch Corsairs, 1615–1616

> On this day there were found on the beach many large mounds of pearl-oyster shells, so beautiful and shining that, half-buried in the sand and struck by the sun's rays, they made the shore appear to be a starry heaven, so pleasing to the eye that nothing more could be desired.
>
> —Juan de Torquemada, *Monarquía indiana*, 1615

The survivors of Ximénez de Bertandona's expedition, the first Europeans to set foot on the Baja California peninsula between 1533 and 1534, returned singing the praises of its pearl fisheries. Sixty years later, Sebastián Vizcaíno's men devoted themselves to hunting pearls.

Later on as well, throughout the seventeenth century, even after the authorities had abandoned the idea of colonizing California, the hunt for pearls continued uninterrupted.

The pearl fisheries—called *placeres*—were mentioned in all the seamen's statements and in the chroniclers' writings. News of their existence even reached distant Seville, and it was there, in fact, that the Cardona company, which held a monopoly on the California pearl fisheries for ten years, was created in 1611. According to the contract signed with Philip III, the company was to explore the Gulf of California, as well as searching for pearls. The crown would receive a fifth of the proceeds, the traditional "royal fifth." Another point was also included: in the event of necessity, the ships were to be withdrawn from the search for pearls and put to other tasks.

The six ships that were to cross the ocean were built in Moguer and at the mouth of the Guadalquivir, and they finally left Cádiz in July 1613, together with the fleet commanded by Antonio de Oquendo, also headed for New Spain. Tomás de Cardona and his partners remained in Spain, and the expedition set sail under the command of Capt. Francisco Basilio. The second-in-command was Nicolás de Cardona, Tomás's nephew. Nevertheless, as we will see, the venture would soon become known as Juan de Iturbe's expedition.

The ships arrived in the Caribbean without notable misfortunes. In his account, Nicolás de Cardona described the conduct of the inhabitants of the islands with regard to the ships that arrived from Spain:

> they live . . . from piracy and doing evil to the Spaniards' ships that customarily arrive in those islands in need of taking on fresh water, and they often seize the shallops that land in search of water and capture and kill the men and eat them. If it is perhaps a ship of blacks coming from Guinea, which ships are usually poorly defended, they lie in wait for them and make sure of them, and at night they cut their cables so that they run onto the shore, killing the white people on the said ships, and they capture the blacks in order to make use of them in the fields.[66]

It was not only the Indians who "captured the blacks"; the Spaniards did so as well, but not to work the land. Capt. Francisco Basilio had purchased "twenty-eight pieces of blacks, men and women,"[67] to be used as divers. A royal decree of 1585 had prohibited the use of Indian slaves in the pearl fisheries, since it had apparently been proved that Africans did better than Indians underwater. Be that as it may, these slaves were the cause of an unpleasant surprise a few days later on Margarita:

the royal officials collected 18,093 reales in taxes from their owners. According to Nicolás de Cardona, the amount was excessive,

> the said blacks not being worth so much, because they were old, and some of them crippled and without hands as a consequence of the *niguas*[68] there are in that land, and others without noses or ears, because of the abuse they receive from the said Indians.[69]

The following year, when the men were in Veracruz and about to depart for Acapulco in order to begin the hunt for pearls, Francisco Basilio died, and Nicolás de Cardona was named captain, but on condition that he share command with a certain Rosales and with Juan de Iturbe. Nevertheless, during the investigation that took place later, in 1617,[70] all the witnesses stated that the expedition was captained by the Basque Iturbe; nobody mentioned Nicolás de Cardona as having a share in the command.

As soon as they reached Acapulco, they began to build three ships, and by early 1615, the three frigates were ready: the *San Francisco* (the flagship, two hundred tons), the *San Antonio*, and the *San Diego*. It was difficult to find material and labor in Acapulco, and according to Iturbe's testimony in the mentioned investigation, the construction and provisioning of the three ships cost the company "more than forty-five thousand ordinary gold pesos."

The ships were now about to set sail in search of pearls, but the news came that some Dutch pirates had entered the South Sea by way of the Strait of Magellan and were headed for New Spain after devastating the Peruvian coast. They were the Dutch corsair Joris van Speilbergen's men, the so-called *pichilingues*.[71] In contemporary chronicles, Admiral Speilbergen is presented as the prototypical corsair of the age: a skilled diplomat and a man of sophisticated tastes, with an elegantly furnished ship and a cellar stocked with the best wines. In view of the threat posed by the Dutchman, the Acapulco municipal governor decided to embargo the ships that were about to leave, in order to strengthen the port's defenses, as foreseen in the contract with the king. Finally, after

Joris van Speilbergen

more than two months of delay, since there was no trace of the *pichilingues*, the three ships obtained permission to leave for California.

Upon arriving at the southern tip of Baja California, the three frigates followed the coast up the gulf, disembarking often. At the same place where Vizcaíno was attacked in 1596, Iturbe's men were met with great hostility, but they had a weapon with which the natives were unfamiliar: they released two mastiffs, and the Indians fled in terror from those beasts they had never seen before.

During the months that followed, the pearl fishers were able to devote themselves to their work, until rumors of the presence of Dutch pirates arrived once again. According to Iturbe, he found out about the enemy from the Indians. Apparently, they told him that they had seen a house on the sea.[72] The *San Francisco* was immediately sent to Acapulco, captained by Nicolás de Cardona. Near Navidad, however, it encountered Speilbergen, who was waiting there for the Manila galleon. The five or six ships of the Dutch fleet easily took possession of the *San Francisco*. Some men jumped overboard and were able to reach land, but several sailors, two friars, and—the greatest loss for the company—eleven black divers fell into the corsairs' hands. According to Speilbergen's account in his diary,[73] they found nothing of value in the captured ship, only some provisions and "a few furnishings of scant importance." Not a single pearl. From then on, the *San Francisco* became part of Speilbergen's fleet, renamed the *Perel* ("Pearl" in Dutch).

Having concluded their pillaging, the corsairs headed calmly for the port of Salagua. At this moment, however, a personage of whom we have already spoken made his final appearance on the stage of California history: Sebastián Vizcaíno. Having been charged by the viceroy with the defense of the port of Salagua, Vizcaíno had immediately gathered more than four hundred men and was waiting for the Dutch. Speilbergen's fleet arrived in Salagua on November 10, 1615. Believing the port to be unprotected, the Dutch disembarked to obtain provisions and fell into the trap Vizcaíno had prepared for them. Speilbergen recounted in his diary that they killed an enemy captain in the battle and that they also killed and wounded many other men, while in his band there were only two dead and five or six wounded. Nevertheless, Vizcaíno maintained in the report sent to the king that the enemy's losses were enormous. Was he once again dressing up reality to suit his purposes? Maybe, but the king was not supposed to harbor doubts, and Vizcaíno sent along a *pichilingue*'s cut-off ears as evidence.

Meanwhile, knowing nothing of the battle of Salagua, Iturbe continued hunting for pearls. Finding the oyster beds was not difficult. The mollusks were one of the primary food sources of the indigenous people of the coast, who heated the shells over a fire until they cracked, providing easier access to the meat, and then threw the shells onto a heap. All the travelers mentioned the mountains of shells left behind, easily visible from the ships. Cardona also refers to them, affirming that all along the gulf coast, for a distance of a hundred leagues, mountains of shells could be seen everywhere. Normally, the Indians ate the shellfish near the location where they had obtained them, so a pile of shells indicated that there was an oyster bed nearby. The pearl fishers also searched the piles in hope of finding pearls among the remains, although they were often burned.

In 1616, Iturbe continued hunting for pearls in the gulf, with two ships. One of them was seized by a foreign vessel, but the other succeeded in returning to New Spain and was immediately sent to warn the Manila galleon of the enemy's presence. Having carried out this order, Iturbe returned to port without problems. In November of the same year, the Acapulco treasury officials recorded that the pearls Iturbe brought back weighed fourteen and a half ounces. The officials boxed them up, and a messenger took them to Mexico City, where their value was assessed and, as promised, the company paid the king's fifth.

That was what was registered, but it seems certain that Iturbe had gotten his hands on significantly more pearls than the ones he presented to the officials. In his *Noticia de la California* (News of California), Miguel Venegas recounts that when Iturbe arrived in Mexico, he filled the city "with the fame of the pearls that he brought."[74] The witness Esteban Carbonel, for his part, declared that Iturbe distributed the pearls among his sailors and friends; that he saw with his own eyes seven pearls in gold settings in the hands of Simon Vacilino, one of Iturbe's sailors; and that another sailor, Lorenzo Petiche, was the owner of more than twenty-four pearls, each of them the size of a harquebus ball.[75]

In his account, Tomás de Cardona refers to Iturbe with a certain disdain, alleging that he joined the company out of a thirst for adventure. Perhaps he was trying to prevent Iturbe from staining the company's name with his fraud on the royal treasury. It could also have been jealousy, however, due to the enormous profits Iturbe had amassed.

Iturbe's expeditions had other consequences that deserve mention. First, he warned of the presence of pirates, and thanks to those warnings, the Spanish authorities began to concern themselves with California once again, even if only in order to protect the Manila galleon. Second, the mistaken information Iturbe provided reinforced the belief that California was an island, not a peninsula. With this, the projects that would be concerned with the territory were decided for more than a century and a half. Every attempt to approach California would be made by sea, abandoning the idea of reaching Monterey by land. The third consequence was of a different order: the legend of Juan de Iturbe's chest of pearls, a story that has endured to our own day.[76]

According to the story, a sailing ship is buried beneath the shifting sands at the bottom of Lake Cahuilla. How did it get there? Around the year 1615, following a very successful season hunting pearls, Juan de Iturbe headed north, in search of the Strait of Anián. Having reached the furthest point of the Gulf of California, the ship continued along a channel that stretched inland; it ran aground and had to be abandoned there, since the sandbanks blocked it from moving in any direction. Almost four hundred years later, the wind sometimes uncovers the vessel's hull. The hold is still full of chests of pearls, according to the websites maintained by treasure-hunters.

Isidro de Atondo Tackles the Difficult Enterprise of Colonizing California, 1683–1685

Since the time of the Cardona company, sixty long years before, pearl hunters had been California's primary visitors. Ortega, Carboneli, Portel de Casanate, Piñadero, Lucenilla . . . they all, one after another, obtained the corresponding license and dedicated themselves to searching for oyster beds off the Baja California coasts. The contracts they signed with the crown required them to conduct reconnaissance of the territory and establish colonies, but their interests lay elsewhere, and although one expedition followed another, the crown's desires remained unfulfilled. In the end, seeing that reliance on private initiative was leading nowhere, a different contract was drawn up in 1678: an attempt would be made to colonize California with funds from the royal treasury. The next year, the person who would lead the mission was chosen: Isidro de Atondo y Antillón, a soldier of long experience and great gifts as a commander. Within a term of five years, Atondo was to establish and fortify in California a colony that would last at least one year.

Once the military commander was chosen, the clergy who would accompany him also had to be selected. It was a question of no little importance, since if the colony was to last, it was necessary for the indigenous population to gradually adopt Spanish customs and embrace the Christian faith. In the end, three Jesuits were named: the Italian Eusebio Francisco Kino (Eusebio Francesco Chini), Antonio

Suárez, and Matías Goñi.

Kino, an explorer, cartographer, geographer, and astronomer, was chosen for his reputation for learning; Suárez, because he was already an experienced missionary (ultimately he was not part of the expedition); and Matías Goñi, because Atondo wanted it that way, since they were friends. Both were Navarrese, Goñi having been born in Viana in 1647, and Atondo having been born in Valtierra and baptized in the parish church of the same locality on December 3, 1639. His parents were Luis de Atondo and Agustina de Aybar, "very well-respected members of the regional gentry."[77]

In March 1679, Atondo undertook the construction of two ships near where the town of Guasave is today, on the Sinaloa River. As H. E. Bolton comments on the basis of his familiarity with the area, unless there were more trees there in the past, they were undoubtedly cut in the mountains and then floated down the river. Everything was difficult in those remote places. To cite Bolton once again:

> In the seasoned seaport of Palos,[78] in Old Spain, Columbus´s task of equipping his vessels for his historic voyage to America was comparatively easy beside Atondo´s. Here every pound of paraphernalia had to be carried a thousand miles over tropical lowlands and rugged mountains on the back of patients animals. For the heaviest items the freight charges were almost prohibitive.[79]

Meanwhile, in central Mexico, the bureaucrats concerned themselves with provisions and selected soldiers, sailors, and colonists; messengers came and went on horseback between Sinaloa and

Guaycurak from Miguel Venegas, Noticia de California . . . , 1757

Mexico City; work went on without pause in offices in Veracruz and Guadalajara, drawing up lists, composing instructions . . . With one thing and another, more than four years went by. However, the moment for departure finally arrived. At midnight on January 17, 1683, the flagship, baptized *La Concepción*, and its fellows, the *San José* and the *San Francisco Xavier*, set sail from the port of Chacala, bound for California with more than a hundred people on board, including a number of baptized Indians, men and women, who would be employed in the cooking and other tasks.

The trip took longer than expected, due to contrary winds and other difficulties, and it was not until April 1 that they caught sight of the long line of beautiful palm trees along the La Paz coast. Many of the previous expeditions had failed due to the abuse the pearl hunters had inflicted on the Indians, but if the aim was to establish a new colony and attract the Indians to Christianity, it was absolutely necessary not to be in conflict with them. In this regard, Atondo had received very clear instructions, and he wanted to remind everyone of them before anyone set foot on land. The herald, a mulatto boy with a Basque surname named Juan de Zavala, issued the summons "to the sound of drums and with a herald's voice,"[80] and once all the people of the *Concepción* had gathered, the notary read the proclamation, "in a loud and intelligible voice." It said that the king had made great expenditures on the preparations for the voyage, in order to purchase clothing and other presents for the indigenous people, and that all this had been done in order to attract those people to the Catholic religion and His Majesty's obedience, without expecting anything in return. If, however, of their own will and as an expression of gratitude, the indigenous people wanted to offer something, whether gold, silver, pearls, amber, or anything else of value, the expedition was provided with a chest with three keys in which presents for His Majesty could be kept, in order that they might compensate at least in part the previously mentioned expenditures.

Subsequently, the proclamation announced that anyone who inflicted "the least vexation" on the natives would pay with his life. Theft was also prohibited in no uncertain terms, since serious conflicts had often arisen as a consequence of taking some trifle away from the natives:

> On account of only having a chicken taken away from them, the Indians of the Tepeguana nation rose up, and their pacification cost much blood and His Majesty much of his royal income. In this said California, when people were put on land and one of

> those who disembarked took a pearl away from an Indian, the voyage of Sevastian Viscayno obliged the said natives to fall into an uproar and obliged the men to take to their launches with great haste, at great risk to all their lives, since they killed eighteen Spaniards, and some escaped by swimming. Because there are many other examples of pagan Indians who rise up on account of only having a gourd, a bit of leather, or another item of very little value taken away from them, therefore let no one dare to enter their houses or huts without their consent, so as not to give them reason to make a complaint, in the event of which the said penalty will be imposed on those who have acted to the contrary, so that the said natives become quiet and remain content and the intention of serving both Majesties [i.e., God and the king], in an enterprise so much in their service, may be achieved.[81]

These instructions were based on the *Recopilación de Leyes de las Indias* (Recompilation of the laws of the Indies), published in 1680. Nevertheless, this statement of good intentions did not reach the Indians who were lurking on land and who continued to be on guard, without trusting the strangers in the least.

On April 5, Atondo presided over the ceremony of taking possession of the territory in the name of Spain's King Carlos II. The soldiers lined up in military formation, presenting the arms they had available. Standing out among them all was the Basque Lt. Martín de Verástegui, who "held in his hand a crimson standard, with the image of Our Lady of Los Remedios painted and embroidered on one side, and the royal arms of His Majesty, whom God preserve for many years, traced and embroidered on the other side of the said standard . . . They fired the harquebuses, and the said lieutenant waved the said standard three times."[82]

The men named the location the port of "Our Lady of Peace," Nuestra Señora de la Paz, and once the ceremony was over, they placed the standard in the shade of a palm tree.

At first, the Indians took a wait-and-see approach, but on the fifth day, they appeared armed with bows and arrows, warpaint on their faces, indicating to the strangers by signs that they were to leave their lands: *Auric! auric!* ("Out! out!"). In the following days, offering presents and tempting them with food, Atondo managed to get them to become somewhat calmer and occasionally venture down to the encampment, but only the men, since as soon as they saw the ships approaching, they had taken the women and children to the inland rancherías.

The foundations of the encampment were laid; huts, a church, and a fort were built; crops were sown; and when they considered the enclave sufficiently secured, they began to explore the region. To the east, they found the Cora Indians, who appeared weak and harmless. They lived in a very harsh and infertile landscape and had suffered a great deal at the hands of a stronger group, the Guaycuras, who lived to the west. The Cora received the colonists well, believing that they would protect them from their enemies. The Guaycuras, on the other hand, were bitter enemies of the Spaniards: they did not trust these strangers who turned up bearing gifts. It was this group who had appeared armed and with warpaint on their faces.

Meanwhile, at the encampment, the Jesuits Kino and Goñi went back and forth with pen and inkwell in hand, noting down words, since without knowledge of the native language, it would be difficult to carry out their evangelizing mission. Kino refers in his writings to the Indians' gentleness and obedience. This is the perspective of someone who desires to establish good relations with the natives, knowing that peaceful methods are the only possible ones on the road to conversion. Atondo's more suspicious pen, on the other hand, shows us proud and mocking natives. On one occasion, Atondo recounts, they saw more than fifteen hundred Indians around a "figure or idol," worshiping it. When the ceremony was over, the soldiers asked them what that "thing" was that they praised so much. "The said pagans gave them to understand that it was the one who gave them what they lived on, and the one who, when it rains, comes down from heaven to favor them and bring them the *pitahayas* and the *medese*,[83] and that he had now returned to heaven." The soldiers told them that their "thing" was not good, that it did not give them anything, and that the Holy Cross was better, because it gave them food and brought the ships. The pagans' response came immediately: "Well, tell that Cross that this here is what gives you food."[84]

Instead of decreasing with contact, the Guaycuras' hostility increased over time. They missed no opportunity to show the Spaniards their disdain and to threaten them. One day, they tried to go further. As the historian T. H. Hittell comments, however, Atondo stopped them in a quite remarkable way:

> they collected in two large armed bodies and with violent outcries advanced upon the camp. As they approached, the Spanish soldiers ran to their defenses; but the intrepid Atondo, choosing different tactics, threw himself in front of their leaders and with terrific yells and assumed fierceness challenged the entire multitude. Such gallant bravery was too much for the Indian

> warriors. Such a voice as that of Atondo they had never before heard; such a fearful spectacle as he presented they had never before seen. For the moment they were paralyzed with astonishment; and, as Atondo advanced, they precipitately turned their backs and fled in disorder to their rancheries. Thus was the battle fought and won, like some of those depicted in Homer, by mere strength of lungs.[85]

Nevertheless, the peace did not last long. A few days later, a Guaycura shot an arrow at a soldier. He did not draw blood, but it was taken as an act of rebellion; they put the rebel in the stocks and carried him off to the ship in irons. The Guaycuras were enraged. To make matters worse, a cabin boy disappeared. At first, he was thought to have run away, but then the Coras said that he had been murdered by the Guaycuras. The missing boy was the mulatto herald, Juan de Zavala, who had gathered the people "to the sound of drums and with a herald's voice."

One day, at the beginning of July, sixteen Guaycura warriors appeared at the encampment. Thinking that they came to free their imprisoned comrade or to attack, Atondo decided to take measures. He ordered that they be served *pozole*,[86] a dish they much appreciated. Suspecting nothing, the guests, who wore no clothing, sat down on the ground to eat, and as they were doing so, Atondo ordered the soldiers to fire the small cannon and the mortar. In an instant, ten Indians were dead, and the rest fled at a run, some of them seriously wounded. According to Hittell, before taking such a drastic decision, Atondo tried to raise the soldiers' spirits, but he found only cowardice and consternation among them. "With better material it is likely there would have been no necessity for firing the gun; but under the circumstances no other course seemed open."[87]

With the cannon and mortar fire, any possibility of maintaining peaceful relations with the natives disappeared. There was no more calm in the encampment. Atondo himself recounted that they were at war with the pagans of that kingdom: "They make everyone keep their weapons in hand by day and by night."[88] The Spaniards were convinced that when news of what had happened spread, all the tribes of California would rebel and kill them all. There were cases of insubordination. Soon, a request was made for permission to abandon the project of a colony, or at least transfer it to a safer location. Nor did it help that food was growing increasingly scarce. They had sent one of the ships to Sinaloa for the most necessary provisions, but two months later, there was no trace of it. Discouragement overcame them all. A council was held, and the decision was made to abandon La Paz and leave in search of a better location.

Later, it became known that one of the reasons for the attempt's failure, the supposed murder of the mulatto herald Juan de Zavala, which Atondo and his men believed without question, did not actually take place. When they fired the small cannon and the mortar, Zavala was alive. Apparently, he had committed some misdeed and, fearing punishment, fled the colony. There was a sailing vessel off the coast, engaged in fishing for pearls, and Zavala offered the captain a fine pearl in exchange for a canoe. The captain accepted the deal, and the young herald crossed the gulf with all its dangers in that cockleshell.

Many years later, the Jesuit Juan de Ugarte, serving at the time as rector of the Colegio de San Gregorio in Mexico City, had the opportunity to speak with Zavala and hear the story of what happened from his own lips. The tale came to the ears of Fr. Juan María de Salvatierra, who recounted it in a letter written on October 10, 1716, more than thirty years after the events.

A Second Failed Attempt to Establish a Colony in California

On his second attempt, Atondo dropped anchor further north, about ten leagues from Loreto. It was October 6, 1683. Everything had been prepared with great care, so that nothing would be lacking, or so the members of the expedition believed. Since the shortage of provisions had caused serious problems at La Paz, Atondo took the precaution of bringing goats, horses, and mules. Three Jesuits would once again be responsible for the spiritual work: Eusebio Francisco Kino and Matías Goñi, who had participated in the first expedition, and the Frenchman Juan Bautista Copart.

The men named the chosen site San Bruno and quickly began to set up their encampment, building huts, a church, and a fort. The Spanish authorities desired to avoid the problems they had had with the Guaycuras at La Paz, and Atondo received a letter from the royal attorney charging him to treat the Indians appropriately, so that the great expenditure the crown was making would not go to waste. Likewise, it was recommended that in his records and reports, Atondo not use the term "conquest," replacing it by "pacification."[89]

On November 30, Atondo presided over the ceremony of taking possession of the territory. As Kino wrote, "After mass, possession was taken of this California and this new province, which we call the

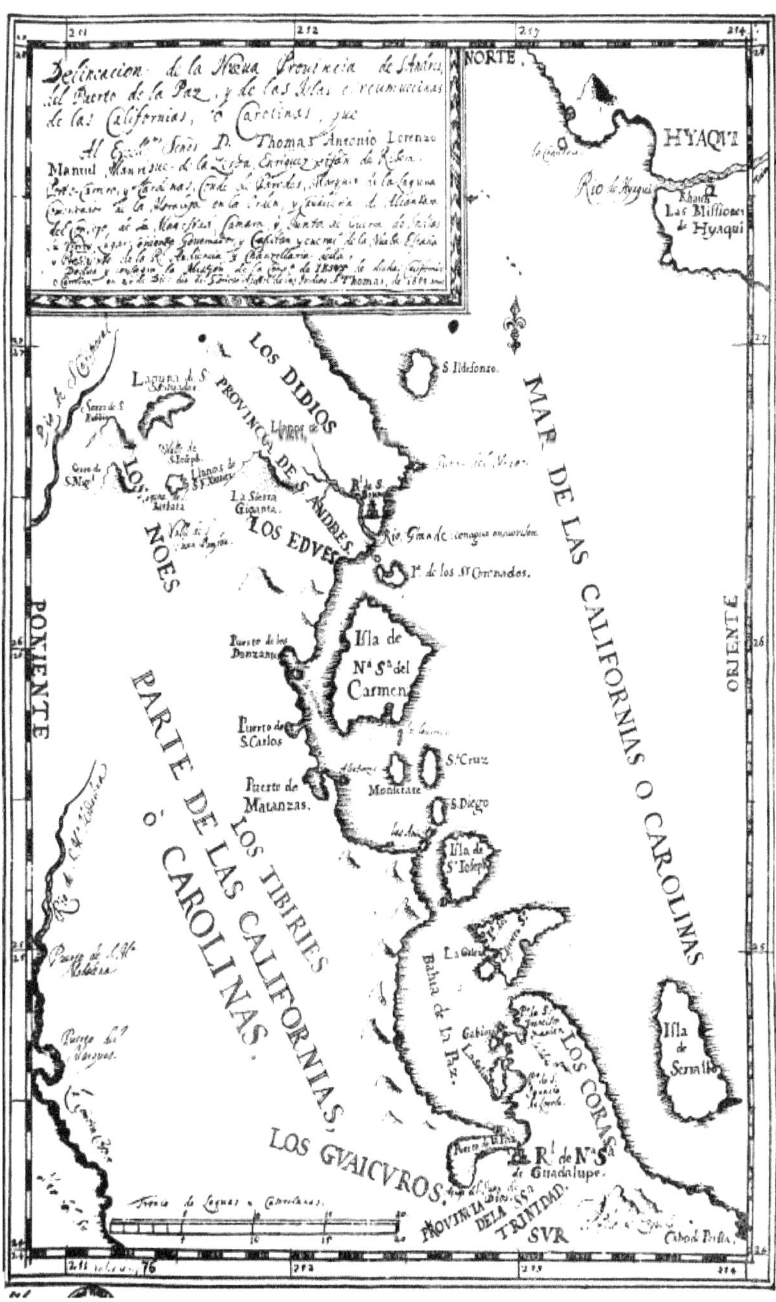

"Nueva provincia de San Andrés." W. Michael Mathes: Californiana III. Documentos para la historia de la transformación colonizadora de California (1679–1686))

province of Saint Andrew, on the part of His Majesty, Carlos II, may God preserve him, with all solemnity."[90]

The inhabitants of the region turned out to be much more receptive than the Guaycuras of La Paz. To the north lived the Didios. To the west, on the other side of the mountains, the Noys. To the south, the Edus. The chief of this last group was named Ibo, "Sun," but the Spaniards called him Dionisio, because they had met him on Saint Denis's feast day. He lived around thirty miles from San Bruno, at a location the natives called Conchó or Conunchó, but that the Spaniards rebaptized with the name of San Dionisio. Ibo or Dionisio came to be a good friend of the colonists. In that favorable atmosphere, the missionaries' work soon began to bear fruit. The children, for example, immediately learned to make the sign of the cross.

Some months later, Kino continued to express optimism:

> The boys continue to recite the prayers every day and sing the Salve, and to respond to the questions at catechism on Sunday and say which of the three divine Persons became man, died, and rose for us, and which one created the heavens and the earth.[91]

The Jesuits, intelligent men, were aware that this receptive attitude was closely connected to the *pozole* and all the other presents distributed to the Indians. In reality, presents and barter were indispensable in relations between Europeans and indigenous people, and no expedition was ever organized that did not include a good supply of gifts. At San Bruno, for example, on November 4, 1684, the following presents were distributed to the Edus:

> Mexican-style blankets [*Frezadas mestiças*], 112; children's white and blue cottons, 70; trade-quality indigenous-style blouses [*guipiles carreteros*], 36; girls' indigenous-style blouses [*guipiles de niñas*], 36; large Indian mantles [*tilmas de yndios grandes*], 6; hats, 34; Xilotepeque petticoats, 27; Crespo petticoats, 10; 50 darning needles.[92]

The following month, Atondo asked that an inventory be drawn up of the presents that remained. The list included

> Mexican-style blankets [*Frezadas mestiças*], 291; unlined Palmilla breeches, 306; children's cottons, 210; Crespo petticoats, 53; Xilotepeque petticoats, 55; trade-quality indigenous-style blouses [*quipiles carreteros*], 68; girls'

> indigenous-style blouses [*quipiles de niñas*], 34; blue indigenous-style women's ponchos [*quesquemiles azules*], 22; cheap hats [*sombreros baladies*], 104; mouth harps, 100 dozens and a half; Campeche combs, 11 dozens; a set of three flageolets; sheets of prints, 35; Michoacán paintings on wood, 6 dozens; ordinary mirrors, 8; medium mirrors, 64; flutes, 2 dozen; rattles [*sonaxas*], 5; small drums, some of them broken, 11; small vihuelas, 11; broken and coming apart, 8; large Indian dance rattles [*ayacastles de danças de indios grandes*], 22; small ones, 64; rosaries, 63 dozens; moth-eaten Mexican-style blankets [*freçadas mestiças apolilladas*], 5; Fregenal machetes, 105, plus 6 broken and 1 that was given to Fr. Eusebio Kino; small hand axes, 93.

It was at San Bruno that Fr. Kino came up with his peculiar method for explaining the concept of resurrection. No appropriate term for expressing that concept existed in the indigenous lexicon, and Kino spent a long time trying to figure out how to make the natives understand an idea they found so alien. Finally, he took some flies and submerged them in water until they appeared to be dead. He then took them out, covered them very lightly with ash, and set them in the sun. Revived by the sun's rays, the insects began to recover, and after a few moments, they shook the ash off their wings and flew away. The Indians, amazed, began to shout, "Ibimuhueite, Ibimuhueite!" The missionaries wrote the term down and subsequently, when they wanted to refer to the resurrection of Jesus and of the dead, they used that word.[93]

With such ingenious lessons—without forgetting the *pozole* and the presents—there were more than four hundred catechumens prepared for baptism before the year was out. They did not ultimately receive the sacrament, however, since the missionaries did not want to admit them to the Church until the colony's continuity was guaranteed, and San Bruno's future was increasingly uncertain. Explorations conducted in the region confirmed that it was an arid and infertile landscape. No mines were found, it did not rain in a year and a half (the Indians begged the soldiers and the missionaries over and over again to make it rain), the water was bad, the climate was damaging to the health, and the inhabitants, as the historian Charles E. Chapman described them, were peaceful but pitiable.[94]

Atondo sent a ship north in search of a better location, and meanwhile he took the other ship in search of pearls, but both endeavors failed. The harvest of the gardens was also poor, despite the fact that the vines, pomegranates, and quinces that had been sent by Fr. Diego

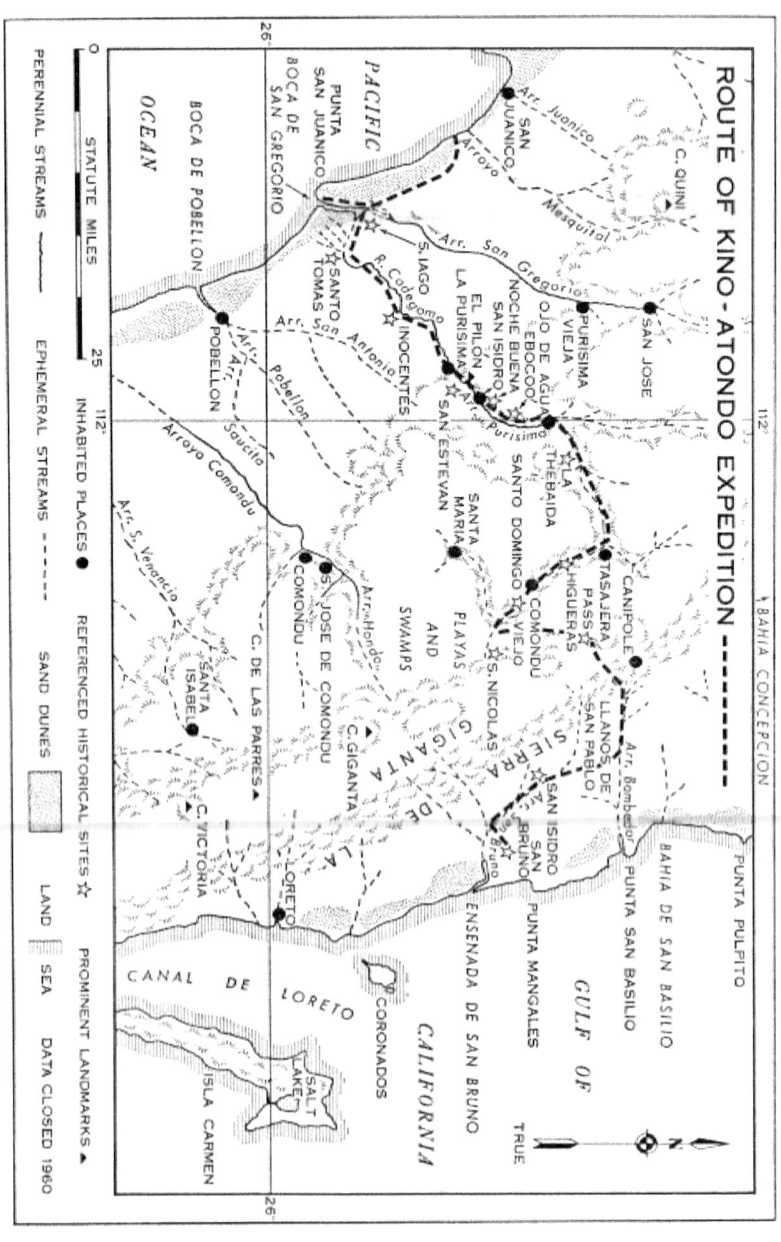
ROUTE OF KINO-ATONDO EXPEDITION
GULF OF CALIFORNIA
PACIFIC OCEAN
CANAL DE LORETO
PUNTA PULPITO
BAHIA DE SAN BASILIO
PUNTA SAN BASILIO
PUNTA MANGALES
ENSENADA DE SAN BRUNO
CORONADOS
ISLA CARMEN
SALT LAKE
LORETO
C. VICTORIA
SANTA ISABEL
C. DE LAS PARRES
C. GIGANTA
SIERRA DE LA GIGANTA
S. JOSE DE COMONDU
COMONDU
PLAYAS AND SWAMPS
SANTA MARIA
SAN ISIDRO
SAN BRUNO
LLANOS DE SAN PABLO
CANIPOLE
TASAJERA PASS
HIGUERAS
COMONDU VIEJO
S. NICOLAS
SANTO DOMINGO
LA THEBAIDA
OJO DE AGUA EBOCOO
NOCHE BUENA
SAN ISIDRO
EL PILON
LA PURISIMA
SAN ESTEVAN
PURISIMA VIEJA
SAN JOSE
INOCENTES
SANTO TOMAS
S. IAGO
SAN JUANICO
C. QUINI
PUNTA SAN JUANICO
BOCA DE SAN GREGORIO
BOCA DE POBELLON
POBELLON
Arr. Juanico
Arroyo Mesquital
Arr. San Gregorio
R. Cadegomo
Arr. San Antonio
Arr. Pobellon
Arr. Saucito
Arroyo Comondu
Arr. S. Venancio
Arr. Hondo
Arr. Purisima
Arr. Bombedor
BAHIA CONCEPCION
STATUTE MILES
0
25
26°
112°
TRUE
N
PERENNIAL STREAMS
EPHEMERAL STREAMS
INHABITED PLACES
REFERENCED HISTORICAL SITES
SAND DUNES
LAND
SEA
PROMINENT LANDMARKS
DATA CLOSED 1960

Marquina, the rector of Yaqui, had been planted with great hopes, and obtaining provisions was far from easy, as they were purchased in Sinaloa and then had to be transported to the mission.

The Jesuits were in favor of continuing, in order not to waste what had been achieved to that point, but in May 1685, seeing that hunger was at the door, Atondo decided to abandon the encampment and return to Mexico, after having dedicated three years to that enterprise. As a colophon to the unfortunate expedition, the men learned that the *pichilingues* were once again marauding in the area, and Atondo was sent to give the news to the Manila galleon.

Back in Mexico, Atondo and Kino presented reports and budgets with the objective of continuing on with the San Bruno colony, but their petitions were rejected, in light of the enormous expense the two failed attempts had meant for the royal treasury: 225,000 pesos, an enormous sum for the time, and all for nothing, according to the authorities. In addition, large sums of money had just been spent on repressing Indian uprisings in Nueva Vizcaya and New Mexico, and the crown's coffers were much diminished. Consequently, Atondo never returned to those territories. From this time forward, almost nothing is known of him, save that he served as an assistant to his uncle Isidro de Sariñana, the bishop of Oaxaca, and that when he was around fifty years old, he was admitted into the order of Santiago.

With Atondo's attempt—the most significant to date—the plan to colonize the Baja California peninsula was once again left unfulfilled. That did not mean, however, that nothing was achieved. During his explorations, in December 1684, Atondo and the group of men who accompanied him, after having crossed the La Giganta mountains, opened the route to the Pacific, thus becoming the first Europeans to cross Baja California. In addition, California's first mission was set up. A few years later, on the site of San Bruno, Fr. Juan María de Salvatierra would found the mission of Loreto, which would become the head and mother of all the missions of Baja and Alta California. The civilians had decided to abandon California, but the memory of the catechumens of San Bruno drove the Jesuits to return as soon as possible. In the words of the historian Hittell, "The cross prevailed where the sword had yielded."[95]

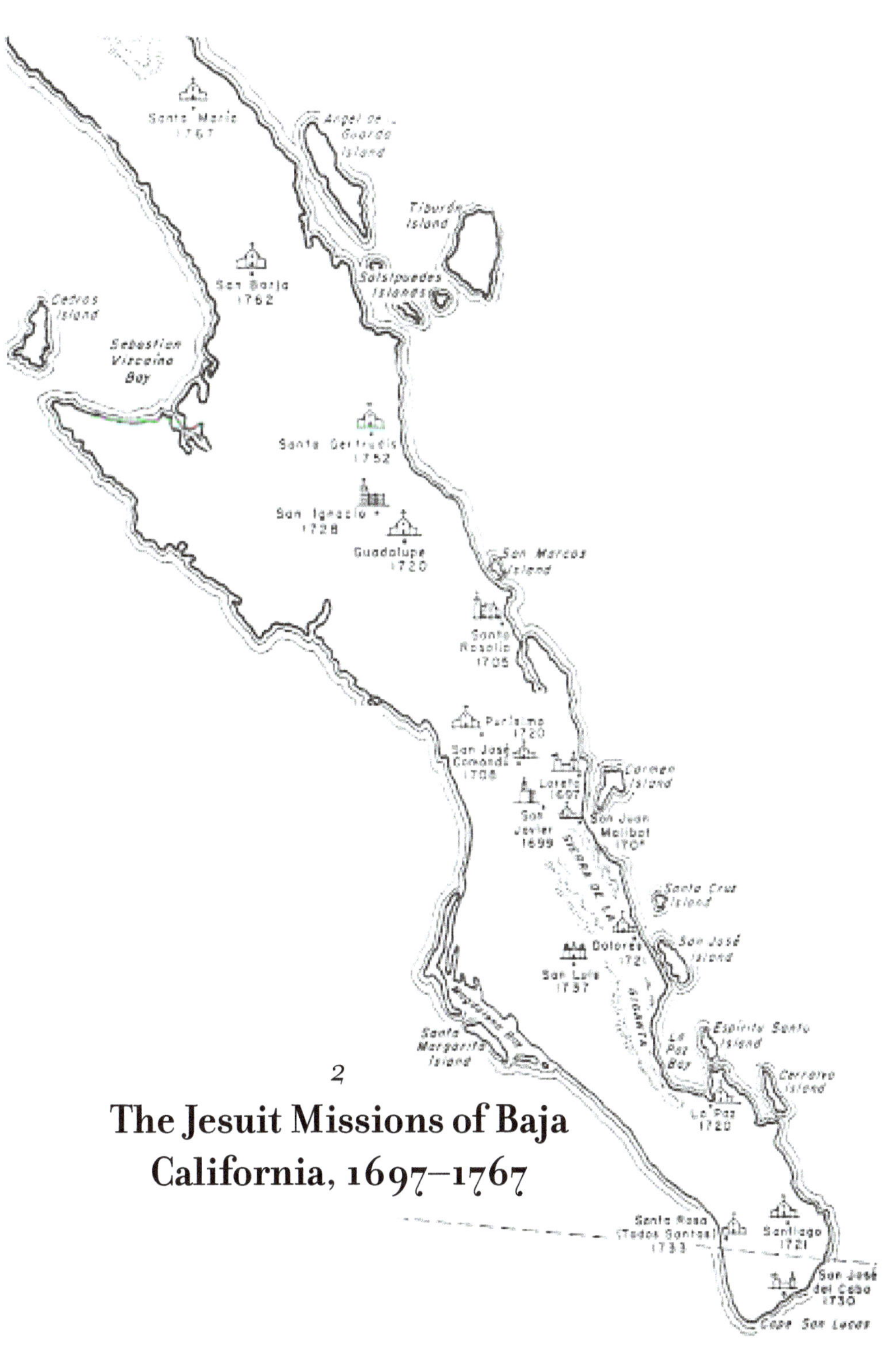

2

The Jesuit Missions of Baja California, 1697–1767

First steps

When Atondo withdrew from San Bruno, the material conquest of California was abandoned, but the same was not true of the spiritual conquest. The Jesuits who had accompanied the Navarrese admiral were fully convinced that the area's spiritual harvest would be very abundant, and they quickly moved to make arrangements to return. Fr. Eusebio Kino did not take long to find a fellow Jesuit who shared his ideas, Fr. Juan María de Salvatierra (1648–1717), originally from Milan. Salvatierra had studied theology and had taught rhetoric for a number of years, but after resigning the positions his talents had opened to him, he had spent ten years living among the Tarahumara Indians, in northern New Spain. As soon as he heard from Kino's lips about the conditions in which the inhabitants of California lived, he began to prepare to go there.

At first, Salvatierra encountered only obstacles on the part of the authorities, but finally, on February 5, 1697, he had the necessary license in his hands. The Jesuits could take possession of the lands of California in the name of the king and establish themselves there; they could take soldiers and choose their commanders; and they would have the power to appoint judges. However, they had to do all this at their own expense, without any recourse to the royal coffers.

From this time forward, Salvatierra left to Fr. Juan de Ugarte everything concerned with the preparations and with seeking donors, thereby completing the trio who were to write this important chapter in the history of California. Hittell assigns their respective merits as follows: "though Father Kino was the projector and Father Salvatierra the founder, the glory of being the preserver of the Lower Californian missions is due more to Father Juan Ugarte than to either of the others."[1]

The Basque Juan de Ugarte was born in Tegucigalpa, Honduras, around 1660 and was teaching philosophy in the Jesuit school in Mexico City when Salvatierra turned to him for help. His great intelligence was accompanied by his skill at managing worldly affairs and his perseverance in obtaining what he wanted . . . virtues that were hidden in the body of a giant.

Juan de Ugarte

Salvatierra and Kino had planned to travel to California together, but Kino had to remain on the Mexican mainland due to an Indian rebellion, and Salvatierra set out alone, without waiting for a replacement. His small ship set sail on October 10, 1697, with a crew of six soldiers, seven sailors, and three baptized Indians. Also on board was an image of Our Lady of Loreto, the patron chosen for that spiritual conquest, as well as a few other items that would turn out to be greatly useful to him: a catechism and other writings in Cochimí that Fr. Copart had prepared in Atondo's time. The crew and the baggage were decidedly scant in comparision to those of previous expeditions, and yet despite this, they succeeded in doing what no one else had managed to do before them: founding the first mission that would last. The site chosen was the bay that the natives called Conchó or Conunchó, to which the Spaniards had given the name of San Dionisio in honor of Ibo or "Sun," the chief of the Edus.

Reading Salvatierra's own texts is enough to make clear the sufferings that went into founding that mission, which took the name of Our Lady of Loreto. As soon as the ship left in search of more provisions and more soldiers, the Indians began to express their discontent to those who had remained on land. The reason was the *pozole*. The Indians demanded larger rations, and those who did not attend catechism also wanted their share, but Salvatierra did not have enough for everyone. Thefts multiplied, and faced with the threat of an attack, the soldiers and Salvatierra himself had to stand watch day and night. To top everything off, it began to rain heavily, especially at night, and since they had not brought anything with which to protect themselves from the weather, believing on the basis of Atondo's account that it did not rain in California, the group succumbed to discouragement.

Finally, on November 13, their fears came true. All the enemy Indians in the area attacked, seeking to take possession of the mission's corn and other foodstuffs. When the rivals faced off, there were around five hundred Indians on one side, and Fr. Salvatierra with five soldiers and the three mainland Indians on the other. The former group was armed with arrows, the latter with a mortar and muskets. Salvatierra, unarmed, tried to convince the Indians to stand down, but they answered by shooting arrows. Then Salvatierra decided to fire the mortar, with the aim of frightening the attackers. However, the effect was the opposite, since the weapon exploded and killed two of the soldiers. The Indians became bolder upon seeing that the Spaniards' weapons did them no harm, and they continued advancing. The musket fire caught them entirely by surprise, and as soon as the first victims began to fall, the rest all fled in terror. Shortly thereafter, peace messengers arrived, and as was customary, the women sat down around the encampment and wept, offering their small children as hostages in exchange for pardon.

The next day, as the Spaniards were preparing to give thanks for their victory, they saw the ship loaded with provisions approaching. They joyfully received the news that another, larger ship would soon arrive, with soldiers, more provisions, and Fr. Piccolo, who had been designated as Salvatierra's assistant. In the time of peace that followed, the first conversions took place. One day, Chief Ibo, "Sun," who had gotten along so well with the Spaniards in Atondo's time, made a surprise appearance. He was near death and asked for baptism for himself and his two sons, eight and four years old. His request was accepted, and he was given the name Bernardo Manuel, and his eight-year-old son that of Manuel Bernardo, since the viceroy and his wife had asked that the first two converts receive these names. The four-year-old boy was given the name of Juanico Cavallero, in honor of a gentleman who had donated money to the mission.[2]

The promised ship, the large one, arrived after ten days, carrying on board more soldiers, the provisions that Ugarte had been able to gather, and Fr. Piccolo. It was a good period for the mission. Progress was made on the construction of the church and the Jesuits' residence, more solid barracks were built for the soldiers, and the fort was expanded and strengthened. However, although this progress could be seen as a promise of better times, there were also difficult problems. On the one hand, the shamans, seeing that the Jesuits' teachings called their power into question, declared war on the new doctrine, spreading unease and discontent among their supporters. On the other hand, the problem of provisions had not been solved. Ever more *pozole* was needed for the Indians, and for the colonists as well, since their number had increased to twenty-two. The ships had returned whence they came as soon as they unloaded their cargo; days, weeks, and months passed; and no news came. At the beginning of the letter quoted previously, Salvatierra described the situation:

> I write this account without knowing whether I will finish writing it, because at the time I am writing, we are much in need here, for lack of relief, and as they press us more each day, and I am the oldest in the Camp [*Real*] of Our Lady of Loreto, I will pay the tribute first, falling as the one who is skinniest for the grave.[3]

Those primarily responsible for the situation were the Spanish authorities, due to their apathy and their refusal to grant assistance to the colonies so they could develop. On this occasion too, however, the ship carrying the provisions that Fr. Ugarte had gathered in central Mexico managed to arrive in time. As Bancroft says, it was once again Ugarte's intervention that saved the California missions from disaster. Unfortunately, the reprieve was only temporary. In the future as well, the missions would often depend on help from outside.

Juan de Ugarte Goes to California in Person to Help Consolidate the Missions, 1700

The Jesuit Juan de Ugarte had created the California Pious Fund (Fondo Piadoso de California)[4] in Mexico with the aim of collecting and managing aid for the missions. Nevertheless, after concerning himself with that institution for several years, seeing that both the authorities and the donors were increasingly reluctant to contribute, Ugarte came to think that he was not being any help there in Mexico and that it would be better to do what he needed to do for California *in situ*. He had wanted to go to the missions for a long time, and when the opportunity finally presented itself, unable to wait any longer, he set out in a poor vessel that he found abandoned on a beach.

On his arrival, the colony's situation was unsustainable, since it had received no assistance for months. Ugarte was thus able to confirm what he had been arguing for some time, that if the mission was to last, it needed to become self-sufficient.

Fr. Piccolo had created the peninsula's second mission, San Francisco Javier, about eight leagues southwest of Loreto, at a place called Viggé-Biaundó. This mission had a short life, because as soon as the first shelter and a small chapel had been built, the Indians destroyed the whole thing. Piccolo himself escaped with his life because he was elsewhere at the time of the attack. However, the location was a good one, and the surrounding lands were much better than those of Loreto, so Ugarte decided to establish himself there, after sending Piccolo to Mexico to handle other matters.

In late 1700, as soon as he was capable of stammering a few words in Cochimí, Ugarte left for Viggé-Biaundó. It was then that his courage encountered its first setback. During the years in which he was procurator for California, he had impatiently awaited the moment of joining the missions in order to devote himself supposedly to civilizing the Indians and saving their souls. Finally, he was going to see his desire fulfilled, but when he arrived at Viggé-Biaundó, there was not a soul there, only the ruins of a building. The Indians had fled, fearful of the soldiers who accompanied Ugarte. The soldiers wanted to go in search of them, but Ugarte did not allow it, since he did not want to use force. The days passed, and as no one appeared, Ugarte made a decision that is a good illustration of his character: he would send the soldiers to Loreto, remaining completely alone at the mission. The soldiers left, and Ugarte spent the entire day in his hut, "between somber and joyful thoughts of martyrdom."[5] In the afternoon, a boy approached; he had come to keep watch on him. Ugarte received him as if he were an angel from heaven and loaded him with caresses and presents. The boy then went back to his own people and reported that the soldiers had gone. Little by little, all the rest began to approach, and Ugarte could begin to work.[6]

The Jesuit had set two great objectives for himself. The first was to teach the Indians Christian doctrine, obliging them to attend mass, the rosary, and catechism every day. In this way, he hoped to wean them away little by little from "affection toward their sorcerers or fraudulent priests and attachment to their age-old superstitions."[7] The second aim was to teach them to cultivate the soil and care for livestock. That meant accustoming them to this kind of work, something new for these people who lived from fishing and from what they gathered in the mountains, with no notion of agriculture or animal husbandry. Without question, Ugarte's double plan required the Cochimís to change their way of life radically, but we must remember that in that age, not even the most farsighted minds doubted that the missionaries' plans might not be for the indigenous people's own good.

The norms that governed the operation of the missions, as well as the treatment given to the Indians, were not fixed and consequently depended on each missionary's character. The missionaries might act as kindly fathers of the natives, but also as cruel despots. In either case, they were at one and the same time civil authorities, clergy, doctors, teachers, and suppliers of provisions, who dispensed both rewards and punishments. They dictated the punishment corresponding to each offense, with a soldier to assist them in executing the sentence. The most common punishments were the whip and the stocks. The Indians were required to attend mass every day and to work, and failure to meet these obligations, apostasy, and all other offenses were judged and punished according to the mood of the missionary in charge. In summary, it was a regime very close to tyranny. For this reason, the Indians showed such a lack of enthusiasm, going to work, in the words of a Basque priest, Fr. Sebastián Sistiaga, "as if they were going to the galleys, very slowly."[8]

We are not referring specifically to the Jesuit missions, and still less to those of the pioneers Kino, Salvatierra, and Ugarte. If these three were noteworthy for anything, it was for precisely the opposite. They tried to defend the Indians, preventing the soldiers, for example, from taking them off to the pearl fisheries as slaves. However, even if they acted "obliging them gently,"[9] as Venegas says of Ugarte, it would be unjust to marvel at the achievements of California's first colonists without remembering that their actions contributed to the disappearance of many of the Indian nations they sought to save.

At the mission of San Francisco Javier, Viggé-Biaundó, Ugarte established a routine that would be repeated at California's other missions in the future. In the morning, after mass and the recitation of the corresponding prayers, *pozole* was distributed to those who were going to work, after which the Indians dedicated themselves to the construction of the church and the living quarters or were led out into the countryside to clear land for sowing, build dams and irrigation channels, or plant fruit trees and vineyards. In all these tasks, Ugarte was always carpenter, mason, and jack-of-all-trades, in addition to teacher and

Aitagurea Cochimí hizkuntzan

Pennayu nekenamba, ya ambayujup miya iro! Buhu irobojua tam mala gomenda hinnogodeño demuejua gagim. Pennayula bogodeño gagim guiki ambayujup maba, ya kaammed e decuinyi limu puegim. Ya cuhul mujua ambayujumbo dodahijua, aniel e hno guilugui ki pagagin. Tamada, ya ibo tejua guiluguigui pehiguilimo, ibo yahno puegiñ. Guihi tanna ya gambua jula kopuhui ambinyijua pennayula de daudugujua, guilugui pagagim. Guihi ya taga mugla ui, ambinyijua ki doomopuhuejua, hi doomopogounyim, tagamuajua, guihi ussi muahael kaammel e de cuiayihmu, guihi ya ui ambinyi ya gambujua pagaudugum. Amén.

Miguel del Barco: *Historia natural y crónica de la Antigua California.*

inspector, putting more effort into his work than anyone else, in order to set an example for the natives. "So he was the first to carry the stones, to tread the clay, to mix the sand, to cut, transport, and dress the lumber, to move the earth and set the materials in place."[10] Thanks to the energy that he showed in his work, many authors who have discussed this epoch of California history speak of Ugarte with admiration, since he gave up the comfortable life for which his intellectual education had prepared him in order to devote himself to much humbler tasks.

Once the day's work was over, before distributing *pozole*, Ugarte gathered the natives once again to pray the rosary and learn the catechism. To these tasks, too, like his manual labors, he devoted himself with great zeal, although his students were naked Indians, not members of the elite, as when he taught philosophy in Mexico. According to the chroniclers, Ugarte left those who went to hear him in Mexico City amazed at his rhetorical skill, but among the Indians, at least at first, he was not so successful. They were often restless during the catechism lesson, chatting among themselves, and they met the missionary's explanations with laughter and jokes, often bursting out in gales of laughter. Ugarte tolerated them patiently on some occasions and reproved them on others, but seeing that things did not improve, he had another idea. One day, he was explaining the catechism, and an Indian who liked to make himself out to be something of a tough guy started to laugh loudly and put on a show. At that moment, "the priest suddenly grabbed him by the hair, and picking him up in the air, he held him up for a certain length of time, shaking him three or four times."[11] His comrades fled in fear. When they returned, Ugarte found out the true reason for the jokes and laughter: they were laughing at "his nonsense language." From then on, Ugarte turned to the children when he needed to ask a question about the language, in order to avoid having the adults intentionally give him inappropriate answers, "so that they would have something to laugh about later at the time of the catechism."

Even with an improved knowledge of the language, the risk of misunderstanding was great. On one occasion, after having spoken at length about how terrible hell was, Ugarte was left perplexed when he realized that it was a desirable place for the Indians: at least there they would not have to look for firewood in order to keep from being cold.

Ugarte's biographers make frequent allusions to his great courage and enormous physical strength. It is said, for example, that he earned fame and respect among the Indians for what he did to a lion. Mountain lions had multiplied in the peninsula and posed a great danger to both livestock and people. Ugarte tried to convince the Indians to kill them, but in vain, since they were convinced that someone who killed a mountain lion would die himself. In order to undeceive them, Ugarte thought that there was no better method than a practical demonstration.

He was in the forest one day, riding a mule, when he saw in the distance a mountain lion heading toward him. Getting off the mule and picking up some stones, he went to meet it, and when he was within range, he threw a stone that hit the beast in the head and brought it down. This was not his greatest feat, however. He wanted to take the lion to the mission, two leagues away, so that everyone would see it, but the mule he was riding refused to carry such a load. So Ugarte, "in order to overcome this difficulty, placed the lion in a tree that stood along the path, and mounting the mule, he forced it with his spurs to pass next to the tree, and upon passing, he grabbed the lion and tossed it over the mule's rump."[12] The mule protested furiously, but it soon broke into a run and carried the priest to the mission in a few minutes. The Indians were greatly amazed when they found out what Ugarte had achieved with mere stones, and still more so when they saw that time was passing, and the missionary did not die.

The anecdote about the mountain lion and the echoes of Ugarte's other activities were collected by the chroniclers and long remembered by California's inhabitants. Among the historians, Bancroft compares him to a gladiator, and there are those who say that he was the Hercules of the Society of Jesus. Exaggerations, no doubt, but what is certain is that all speak of Ugarte with admiration.

The Jesuit's efforts soon began to bear fruit. Within a few years, in addition to constructing the mission's buildings, Ugarte succeeded in gradually converting the natives to the Christian faith. He also saw orchards, gardens, and cultivated fields multiplying around him, and in addition to corn, wheat, and other grains and vegetables, vines were planted and began to produce wine in sufficient quantity to supply all the California missions and export it to the other side of the gulf.[13] The mission also raised horses, cattle, and sheep. Little by little, San Francisco Javier became the provisioning center for the other California missions, saving them from disaster in times of hunger. Later on, Ugarte had distaffs, spinning wheels, and looms made, bringing a weaver from the other side of the gulf to teach the Indians the craft. In this way, he was soon able to see them wearing clothes. Moreover, and most important, in a very short period of time, the mission achieved self-sufficiency. In June 1707, less than seven years after the mission's foundation, Fr. Ugarte was able to write these words, at a time when the majority of New Spain was wracked by drought and hunger:

> Thanks be to God, it's now getting on for two months that we've been eating good bread from our wheat harvest here, with the seamen and landsmen, while the poor people on the other side are perishing, both in Sinaloa and in Sonora. Who would have dreamed it? Long live Jesus, and the Great Mother of Grace, and her Spouse, who obtains the impossible![14]

There were also times of poor harvest and great necessity. In 1702, the Council of the Indies decided to contribute six thousand pesos a year. In later years, the subsidies increased, and more soldiers were sent. Even so, however, there were moments when everything was very close to falling apart. In 1704, the food having entirely run out—"there remaining no more than some thin and spoiled meat, which they came to loathe"[15]—the desperation was such that they were at the point of abandoning everything and leaving. An assembly having gathered, Salvatierra addressed them and said that those who wished could return to New Spain. At that time, counting soldiers, colonists, and missionaries, the colony was made up of over sixty individuals. When it was Ugarte's turn to speak, however, he spoke with such passion, saying that it was a personal decision, but he had no thought of leaving, that following his example, they all decided to stay. At that point, Ugarte put his plan into action. The mission inhabitants went in search of pitahayas, which had been the Indians' chief sustenance for centuries, and collected them systematically, after Ugarte divided the searchers into groups.

Another problem that was never overcome was the management of the mission's military aspect. Even if the missionaries did try to attract the Indians with peaceful methods, they did not reject the use of military force to impose respect or submission. In the future, military outpost and mission would continue to be united, to such a degree that, as Fr. Sistiaga wrote in a letter, the missionaries did not take a step without the soldiers' help.[16]

According to the contract the Jesuits signed with the crown, Salvatierra, in addition to being provincial of California, was commander-in-chief of the missions of that province. Competition between the religious and military arms did not create problems with the soldiers' first commander. His successor, however, the Basque Antonio García de Mendoza—"an old soldier from Fuenterabía," in Bancroft's words[17]—turned out to be a most evil person. He aimed only to enrich himself and could not endure the authority of the missionaries, who did not permit him to take the Indians to dive in the pearl fisheries. In revenge, he dedicated himself to slandering them in letters written to the authorities of New Spain.

Very different was the case of "another Bizkaian," Juan Bautista Muguzabal.[18] Muguzabal arrived in California in 1704 as a soldier and had no conflicts with the missionaries during his time as head of the Loreto garrison. He had such good manners and was so good at his job that from the time he arrived in California, all the missionaries turned to him. Eventually, wanting to follow the missionaries' example, he decided to join the order. He did his novitiate under Ugarte's supervision, becoming the first member of a religious order to profess the vows of poverty, chastity, and obedience in California.

Conflicts between missionaries and soldiers were continuous in the history of the Alta and Baja California missions. Likewise, there were always problems between soldiers and Indians and between baptized Indians and unbaptized ones. Ugarte himself was more than once almost completely alone for weeks, after all the Indians fled with the shamans. At the same time, the problem of provisions was also a constant. The ships that sailed for New Spain were late in returning. True, when a ship finally appeared, the joy was enormous: in addition to supplies, it might bring letters, and even a new missionary. In 1705, in fact, two new missionaries arrived, making it possible to found two new missions.

Fr. Pedro de Ugarte, Juan's brother, founded the mission of San Juan Bautista de Malibar at the place called Ligüí or Liguig, about twenty leagues southeast of Loreto, and Basque-Mexican Fr. Juan Manuel Basaldúa founded the mission of Santa Rosalía de Mulegé, about forty leagues northwest of Loreto. Both attempted to imitate the procedures applied with such success by Ugarte at the mission of Viggé-Biaundó, making the natives work to increase the fertility of their lands without neglecting to teach them Christian doctrine. The inhabitants of Liguig were more reluctant to work, however, and Pedro de Ugarte had to try to get the children to do what needed to be done, making the work into a game. He challenged them to see who could clear more brush or dig the biggest hole, or he set them to dancing for a specific purpose, participating in the dance himself:

> in order to shape the adobes, making himself a child among the children, he invited them to play in the dirt and dance in the mud. The Father took his shoes off and started to tread it down, and the boys joined him. The dance started, and they jumped and danced on top of the mud, and the Father with them. The

> boys sang, and the Father sang with them. Very happy, they competed in jumping and beat and tread down the mud in different parts until the time of the afternoon refreshments.[19]

Mission Santa Rosalía de Mulegé founded by Juan Manuel Basaldúa. The rise of 10,000 pesos by Nicolás de Arteaga. The artist, Arteaga, decorated the Mexican chapel of the Hermandad de Aránzazu. When Balasaguas was beset by health problems, Juan Bautista Muguzabal took his place. Balasaguas was followed by an Italian, followed by two other Basques including Sebastián Sistiaga (1718-1726)

The years passed, the first missions consolidated their position, and new ones were founded. In 1711, Fr. Eusebio Kino died.[20] His complete legacy would occupy several pages: he demonstrated that California was a peninsula, not an island, as the majority of his contemporaries thought; he traveled hundreds of kilometers on horseback across the length and width of northern Mexico and what are now California and Arizona, drawing detailed maps of the territories explored; he founded several missions along the 240 kilometers that stretch between Sonora and Arizona . . . Juan María de Salvatierra, for his part, died in 1717. Upon his death, the position of provincial of California passed to Ugarte, as expected. Certainly, Ugarte was achieving in those remote places what no one would have imagined: self-sufficiency for the missions. Apparently, however, even that was not enough for him.

Ugarte Builds the Sloop El Triunfo de La Cruz, *the First Ship Built in California, 1719*

Ugarte had long wanted to explore the gulf's two shores, in order to demonstrate that California was a peninsula, as Kino had said, although few believed him. Also rolling around in the Jesuit's head was the idea of exploring the southern part of the so-called *contracosta* or "counter-coast," in order to finally find an appropriate port for the Manila galleon, so that the crew members who arrived from the Philippines exhausted could enjoy the necessary rest. The crossing, in truth, continued to be very difficult. The Italian Francesco Gemelli, who traveled from Manila to Acapulco in 1696, wrote in his *Giro intorno al mondo* (Trip around the world, 1699) that the tremendous storms and painful illnesses the galleon suffered, the heat and cold it had to endure, were enough to wear down a man of steel, never mind one of flesh and blood.

In order to carry out this plan, however, a good ship was indispensable, and that was where the problems began. The Baja California Jesuits had a single vessel, an old ship that had deteriorated with so many comings and goings. They had attempted to repair old ships and even ordered the construction of a new one on the other side of the gulf, but none lasted long. In that poor and infertile land, only one recourse was left:

> building a ship of entire satisfaction in that same infertile and poor California, where there was neither lumber nor nails nor cordage nor tar nor any other accouterment for that manufacture, nor a master, a builder, sawyers, or the other artisans needed for construction, nor tools for it, nor even the provisions required for so many people.[21]

The enterprise seemed impossible, but as Hittell says, for a man like Ugarte, what was necessary had to be possible. "Ugarte was not a ship-builder; but neither had he been an agriculturalist or a manufacturer. He was, however, one of those practical geniuses to whom all occupations seem subservient and to whom nothing that seems indispensable is impossible."

Ugarte learned from the natives that further north, around seventy leagues from Loreto, there were large trees, and he went there with two soldiers, some Indians, and a naval outfitter he had arranged to have come from New Spain. Fr. Sistiaga joined them along the way. Venturing into the mountain ravines, after great efforts and many difficulties, they found the trees they were looking for, but they were located in places that were difficult to reach, in hollows and ravines, and the outfitter said that it was impossible to get them out of there. Apparently discouraged, Ugarte decided to turn back, and when the group arrived back at the mission empty-handed, they were greeted with laughter and mockery, since that trip in search of timber had seemed to everyone a fool's errand, like the whole idea of building a ship. However, Ugarte had not said his final word.

As soon as he returned to the mission, he dismissed the outfitter, and as soon as he could, he returned to the mountains. He spent four months there, sleeping in a hut, and without any expert to pose obstacles, he cut down trees, opened up thirty leagues of road, and with the mission's mules and oxen, transported the roughly dressed trunks to the beach at the mouth of the Mulegé River. During all this time, Ugarte missed no opportunity to instruct the natives in Christian doctrine, and even so, he finished the ship sooner than anyone expected: "the most handsome, large, strong, and well-fitted sloop, in the judgment of Americans and Filipinos, ever seen on those coasts."[22] They nailed a cross to the bowsprit, and the *Triunfo de la Cruz* ("Triumph of the Cross"), the first ship built in California itself, cut an elegant figure on the waves. It was September 1719.

In November of the following year, the *Triunfo de la Cruz* made its first memorable voyage, from Loreto to the bay of La Paz, in order to establish another mission there. Apparently, Ugarte himself took command of the ship and showed himself as skilled a seaman as in his other activities. When they reached La Paz, Ugarte and the missionary who accompanied him, by the name of Bravo, disembarked with great caution, since they were in the territory of the Guaycuras, who had earned a reputation as a warlike people. They soon lost their fear, however. The inhabitants of La Paz had learned that the missionaries were unlike the soldiers and the pearl fishers, and instead of appearing with their weapons at the ready, they abandoned them and sat down on the ground as friends. In the following days, with the natives' help, Ugarte was able to devote himself to clearing the land, construction began on the church and the town, and to the Indians' joy, the missionaries disembarked the animals they had transported, so that by the end of 1720, the mission of Nuestra Señora del Pilar had been founded at La Paz.

At the same time, the mission of Nuestra Señora de Guadalupe was established at the place where Ugarte had found the trees for building the ship. We mentioned above that amid all his occupations, Ugarte always found time to devote himself to the conversion of the indigenous people. Apparently with good results:

> Fr. Ugarte had made all the Cochimís of the mountains where he stayed to cut the lumber for the sloop so enamored of the Christian religion that every day they sent messages for him to come back and see them.[23]

In response to these petitions, before leaving for La Paz, Ugarte had sent the German priest Everardo Helen to set up a new mission in that cold, desert, mountain location. While the foundations were being laid for these two missions, another was about to be established at the site selected by Fr. Juan Manuel Basaldúa, between Guadalupe and Comondú, so that when Ugarte returned from La Paz in 1721, there were now eight missions in California.

The *Triunfo de la Cruz* had been tested with success on the round trip to La Paz, the missions were functioning well, and the conquest of the territory seemed assured. It was the right time—so Ugarte thought—to explore the gulf. Kino had seen with his own eyes that California was a peninsula, but many continued to believe that there must be some channel between the gulf and the ocean. If so, it could become the port that the Manila galleon needed, and in consequence, perhaps the Spanish authorities would pay more attention to the region, even if only out of commercial interest.

On May 15, 1721, the *Triunfo de la Cruz* left Loreto with twenty people on board, including the English pilot William Strafford (Guillermo Estrafort in the documents written in Spanish). They disembarked first at Bahía Concepción, where they visited Fr. Sistiaga, who was at Mulegé. From there they crossed over to the Sonoran part of the gulf, and on reaching the shore, they saw a solitary Indian set up a cross on the beach and immediately withdraw. A group of men disembarked on the beach, and they all knelt in front of the cross. At that moment, the Indian gave a shout, and many more who had been hidden appeared. Making friendly gestures, many of them entered the water and swam to the ship for Fr. Ugarte to bless them. Later, the ship's party learned that Fr. Salvatierra had taught them that ships with a cross on the bowsprit usually carried missionaries, and that with them they did not need to be afraid.

Continuing north, Ugarte again crossed to the other side of the gulf, and from there he began to explore the entire coast of the peninsula. His body, now getting on in years, was beginning to show the toll of his many labors. At present, in addition, he was suffering great pain in his feet and groin. If he wanted to take a mouthful of food or rest a little, he had to do so kneeling. To make matters worse, navigation was increasingly difficult. As the ship came closer to the far end of the gulf, the sandbanks became more numerous and the water more clouded: at times it was the color of ash, other times black, but most often the reddish color of clay. The expedition had to advance with great care, one moment making use of the tides and the next hugging the coast to avoid them. In this way, they reached the mouth of the Colorado River, and they clearly saw that there was no channel there that could enable them to cross over to the Pacific.

The rainy season was about to begin, and they decided to turn back, but once more, it was not smooth sailing. Tremendous storms lashed Ugarte's ship without mercy, and they had to struggle against contrary currents, especially in the channel formed by the Salsipuedes Islands. Convinced as they were that the ship was foundering, the crew had a moment of optimism when they saw Saint Elmo's fire appear above the masts, since they considered it a good omen. A new danger arose, however. Near Bahía Concepción, they saw a giant column of water approaching the ship. It was the middle of the day, but the sky became completely dark, as if night had suddenly fallen. At the last moment, and according to Venegas, thanks to the power of prayer, the monster changed course, and the *Triunfo de la Cruz* was able to continue on its way to Loreto.

Once again, it had been demonstrated that California was not an island, and detailed information had been acquired about the coasts, ports, islands, and all the currents of the northern gulf. But Ugarte was not satisfied, since the expedition had not met all its objectives: it had not succeeded in finding a port for ships arriving from the Philippines. Consequently, as soon as he was installed at Loreto, Ugarte set about preparing the next trip. This time, the expedition would make the attempt by land, following the ocean along the coast, and due to Ugarte's ill health, Sistiaga would go in his place, but it was Ugarte who marked out the route to follow. The venture turned out to be a fruitful one: Fr. Sistiaga's group was able to make a description of the entire

San Selmo *at sea*

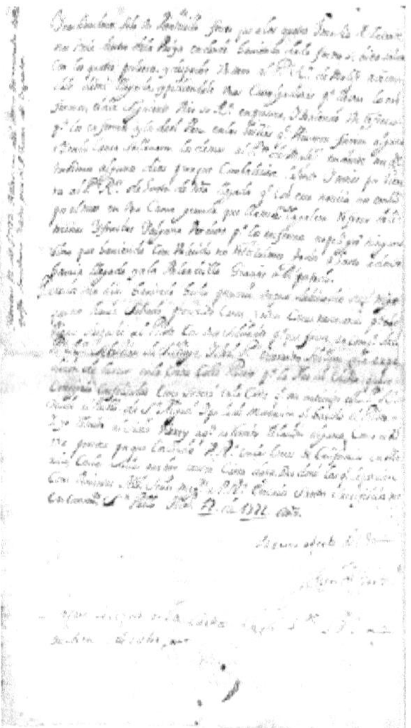

"Relación que hace el padre Juan de Ugarte al padreprocurador José de Echeverría sobre el descubrimiento del Golfo de California o Mar Lauretano a bordo de la balandra "El Triunfo de la Cruz", construida en California: San Pablo, 12 enero 1722." Mexican National Library, Special Collections, Franciscan Archive Collection.

coast, from San Francisco Javier to Cedros Island, and most important, they found three ports that offered the possibility of taking on supplies of water. All the information, maps, drawings, and the rest were sent by Ugarte to the viceroy, urging him to do something to found that long-desired port. However, the Spanish authorities were unable to bring that effort that had cost so much to a proper conclusion.

Ugarte did not plan any more expeditions, or open any more routes, or build any more ships. This man who, in Bancroft's words, "possessed in an eminent degree the qualities indispensable to a leader of pioneers,"[24] died peacefully in 1730, at the mission of San Francisco Javier, having lived seventy years, thirty of them in the California missions. By then, the Jesuits had eleven mission centers in the peninsula. The most recent had been founded a few years earlier by two Jesuits of Basque ancestry: Sebastián Sistiaga,[25] an old friend of Ugarte's, and Juan Bautista Luyando.[26]

Sebastián Sistiaga and Juan Bautista Luyando Found the Mission of San Ignacio de Kadakaamán, 1728

The mission of San Ignacio de Kadakaamán, which was for a time the largest and most prosperous in California, was founded by Sebastián Sistiaga and Juan Bautista Luyando in 1728, thanks to a ten-thousand-peso inheritance from the Luyando family, described by Clavijero as "most noble."[27] When Fr. Luyando arrived in the Cochimí territory called Kadakaamang, he found the terrain already prepared. The Indians were familiar with the basics of the catechism and had planted the fields, since Sistiaga had been there the previous year. In view of the natives' receptive attitude, Luyando sent seven of the nine soldiers who had accompanied him back to Loreto and immediately began to baptize catechumens, after arranging the burning of tablets, hats adorned with human heads, and other objects the indigenous people used in their religious ceremonies.

The natives of that region lived scattered across a very wide territory. Once, some Indians came from a great distance to seek aid for someone bitten by a snake. Accompanied by a local man who had been baptized the previous day, Luyando set out and

> arrived at the place, where he found a large ranchería of pagans who had never seen Europeans or horses; they took fright, but presents and the father's sweet manner soon took away their fear. They all surrounded him, and confident now, they held so many celebrations for him, touching him constantly, and doing the same to the horse, that they did not let him sleep all night.[28]

In order to avoid these journeys in unknown lands, Luyando had the idea of joining neighboring rancherías into towns. After that, he had roads laid out from each town to the mission.[29] However, it cost the Cochimís a great deal to settle down in their new little houses of straw and mud. Venegas explained the problem after his own fashion: "Used to being continually in the open air and under the sky, they became distressed under a roof."[30]

The Cochimís of that territory worked willingly, in shifts, since they saw that the fruits of their labor remained in their hands. They built the infrastructure needed for agriculture and prepared the ground for planting wheat, figs, grapes, dates, and pomegranates. Luyando did not escape the usual problems, however, due above all to the hostility of

Sebastián Sistiaga and Juan Bautista Luyando founded San Ignacio Kadakaamán mission in 1728. Source: Alfredo Martínez. http://www.mexicodesconocido.com.mx

the shamans and of those who did not want to abandon their traditional way of life, especially polygamy. One day, some northern Indians who could not accept the Christians' power attacked a Christian ranchería and killed a young girl and an elderly man. Luyando did not want war, and he tried to attract the attackers with presents, but it was not the best tactic. The Indians thought that he was a coward who was sending them presents because he was dying of fright, so that they became even bolder and repeated their attacks on the Christian rancherías. Luyando had only two soldiers, the mission Indians were terrified, and he decided to go to the neighboring mission, Guadalupe, where Sistiaga was at the time. The two returned together to San Ignacio, where they devoted the following days to preparations, making a great show in order to build up their own courage and frighten the enemy. When the chosen day arrived, they surrounded their adversaries while they slept and, as the missionaries desired, won the victory without firing an arrow or shedding blood.

The practice of gathering the Indians in towns facilitated their control, but it also facilitated the spread of epidemics. As the chain of missions grew in Baja California, Old World diseases spread from central Mexico toward the north. In 1729, smallpox reached San Ignacio. Luyando's efforts to provide medical and spiritual care to the sick ended up undermining his health, and in 1732 he had to abandon the mission.

It was Sistiaga who took Luyando's place at San Ignacio. There, the former teacher of literature at the Colegio de San Andrés in Mexico City found himself required to go out in search of "pagans," as Luyando had previously done. He put some corn and a little dried meat in his bag and set out for the territories of the Indians he wanted to instruct. He taught them the catechism and gave them advice until, when they were prepared, he baptized the catechumens. Sistiaga spent many seasons in the mountains without a refuge in which to take shelter and without protection against heat and cold.[31]

In a report written in 1744,[32] Sistiaga affirmed that since San Ignacio was founded in 1728, 2,746 natives had been baptized at the mission, and that the majority of deaths were due to epidemics. The population in 1744 was 1,196 inhabitants. As far as the natives were concerned, Sistiaga maintained that they were like all the pagans of the region, wild and undisciplined. They lived scattered in forests and rugged mountains. The aridity of the land and the scarcity of water forced them to move from place to place in search of roots and water, and only with great difficulty did they manage to survive thanks to the fruit of a thorny shrub, the pitahaya.

Manuscript that contains report about the San Ignacio Mission (Califorinia) that Father Miguel Venegas sent to Juan Bautista Luyando: Hacienda de San José, January 8, 1737, and reply of Father Luyando, México, January 11, 1737. Mexican National Library, Special Collections, Franciscan Archive Collection.

Sistiaga commented in his report on the progress that took place in Luyando's time, especially with regard to the task of gathering the scattered population into towns, nine of which had been formed: San Ignacio, the chief town; San Francisco de Borja; San Joaquín; San Sabas; San Atanasio; Santa Monica; Santa Marta; Santa Ninfa; and Santa Lucía. The natives did not live in the towns full-time, since they had to go into the mountains in search of food.

Sistiaga also detailed the method used for teaching Christian doctrine. Every morning, as soon as they awoke, the natives turned their thoughts to Christ and the Virgin, singing the Alabado. Following a recital of the prayers and the catechism, a catechist in each town instructed them in Christian doctrine, explaining the mysteries of the faith and encouraging them to repent of their sins. Subsequently, after the exposition of the articles of the faith, they were asked whether they believed them, to which question, Sistiaga said, they all answered in the affirmative. Finally, they prayed the rosary on their knees, after which they marchaban al monte in search of food and firewood.

On their return, before going to sleep, they said the rosary again, and they did all this, according to Sistiaga, even when they were alone and away from the missionaries. Such a routine among people who had just converted struck the Jesuit as worthy of admiration, since he knew how difficult it was among civilized nations converted centuries ago to get people to devote half an hour to prayer, not even every day, but once a week.

Sebastián Sistiaga left San Ignacio in 1747, due to old age according to some historians, due to a nervous breakdown according to others. Without doubt, he was one of the most prominent of the California missionaries. The historian Dunne considers him "a pillar of the California foundations."[33] For many years, various natives associated with the San Ignacio mission were given the name of Sistiaga in his memory. During the 1782 smallpox epidemic, for example, the first person who died at Santa Rosalía de Mulegé was the "pagan" Francisca Sistiaga.[34]

After San Ignacio, another six missions were founded, for a total of seventeen. As is well known, as the Jesuit establishments took root, the Indian population fell dramatically as a consequence of epidemics. No one was able to halt the Indians' gradual disappearance, but the Jesuits' power was done away with in a single stroke: in 1767, an order issued by Carlos III of Spain forced them to abandon his entire empire, including California and New Spain.

Following the orders of José de Gálvez, the visitor of New Spain, Gaspar de Portolà, named governor of the Californias, took charge of arranging the transfer of the California missions from Jesuit to Franciscan hands. One of the departing Jesuits, the Alsatian Johann Jakob Baegert, wrote that the soldiers continued to believe that California was paved with silver and that pearls could be gathered there with a broom.[35] They found nothing of the sort, nor any trace of the treasure that the Jesuits were said to have hidden, only the great flocks of sheep and herds of cattle raised with the sweat of the Indians and the missionaries.

A missionary carries
the word of "civilization" on earth
from coat of arms

3

First Land Explorations, 1598–1781

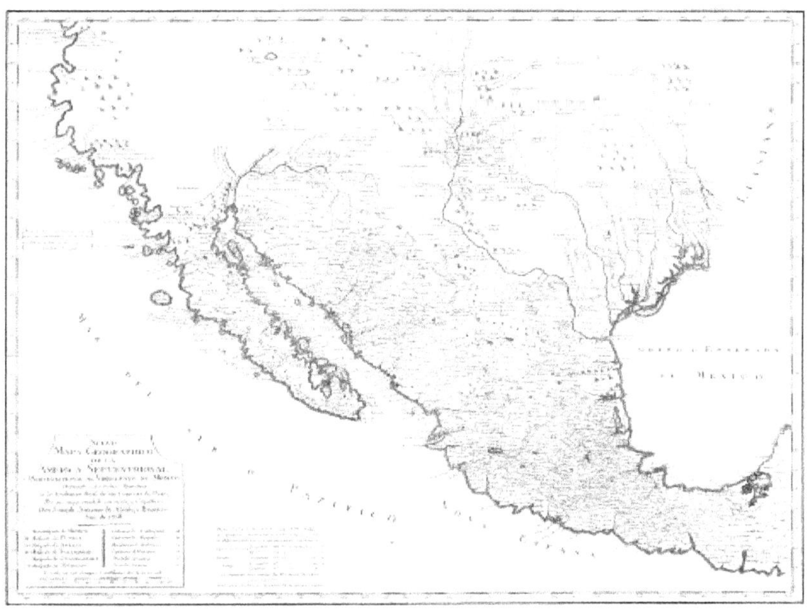

"Nuevo Mapa Geographico de la America Septentrional, Perteneciente al Virreynato de Mexico . . ." José Antonio de Alzate y Ramírez ,1768.

On How Juan de Oñate Ended Up on History's List of Villains, 1598–1605

At the same time that maritime exploration was underway, other expeditions traversed what is today Arizona, New Mexico, Colorado, and Texas by land, trying to shed light on the so-called Mystery of the North. Among the more notable such expeditions were those of the Franciscan Marcos de Niza,[1] in 1539, and Francisco Vázquez de Coronado, in 1540. All returned without having found Cíbola's seven cities of gold or La Gran Quivira, but instead of limiting themselves to describing what they had seen, they continued to foster the dream of a 'new' Mexico, adding brilliant descriptions to the real information included in their reports. It is not surprising, then, that Philip II, relying on the promising accounts brought by Antonio de Espejo in 1583, decided to promote a new attempt to colonize and conquer the territory of the Pueblo Indians. In 1595, after a long process, it was decided that Juan de Oñate would be the man responsible for the campaign.

Juan de Oñate belonged to a family that had played a major role in the conquest of New Spain. His father, Cristóbal de Oñate, one of the conquerors of Nueva Galicia and a governor of the province of the same name, was the discoverer of the giant silver mines of Zacatecas, together with three Gipuzkoan fellow-countrymen: Juan de Tolosa, Miguel de Ibarra, and the latter's nephew Diego de Ibarra. Juan de Oñate grew up in this frontier world, accompanying his father on military expeditions against the Indians from the time he was a boy. Later on, after his father's death, he managed the family's mines with great skill, thereby fulfilling the first requirement for dedicating himself to the New Mexico campaign: he was immensely wealthy.

According to the contract signed with the crown, the conquest of the new territories was to be a private enterprise; in other words, the majority of the expedition's expenses would fall to Juan de Oñate's account. Consequently, it can be affirmed that New Mexico's foundation was closely linked to the Oñate silver mines. In exchange, Juan de Oñate would obtain the title of *adelantado* and the post of governor, as well as an annual salary of six thousand ducats. In sum, Oñate risked a great deal, and the crown risked nothing. Why did Oñate accept such a contract? He could afford a comfortable life and was already forty-six years old . . . In a letter he wrote to the king before the expedition's departure, Oñate confessed his hopes that the enterprise would be one of great consequence. The thirst for recognition, the desire for immortality: this is what drove Oñate to undertake so risky a campaign.

After facing problems and obstacles of all kinds over the course of two years, during which he was occupied with provisioning the people who were to accompany him, Oñate left Santa Bárbara, Nueva Vizcaya, in early 1598. The caravan included seven thousand head of cattle and eighty-three baggage carts, along with 400 men, 120 of whom brought along their wives and children. They had decided to take part in that journey into the unknown for the privileges offered to the first colonists. Eight Franciscans were part of the group, including Cristóbal Salazar, Oñate's cousin. The brothers Vicente and Juan de Zaldívar, Oñate's young nephews, were appointed sergeant-major (*sargento mayor*) and *maese de campo* respectively. Oñate's own oldest son, eight years old and the bearer of an impressive list of surnames—Cristóbal de Naharriondo Pérez Oñate Cortés Moctezuma—was named lieutenant, and he and his horse were provided with a full set of armor. Oñate's wife, for her part, was pregnant, and the expedition had to leave without her. Isabel de Tolosa Cortés Moctezuma was the great-granddaughter of the Aztec ruler Moctezuma, the granddaughter of Hernán Cortés, the conqueror of Mexico, and the daughter of Juan de Tolosa, an extremely wealthy landowner and mine owner.[2]

The road was never easy, but the worst part came at the beginning of March, when the expedition entered the Chihuahua desert. They first suffered intense rain that lasted seven days, and then a drought that was even longer. For fifty long days, the group made its way through endless sand dunes and plains. The last five or six days, without food or water, the men, women, and children fed themselves with the desert's rare roots and plants, and both animals and people were on the brink of madness when at last they found water. Such was their thirst that two horses drank until their stomachs burst, and two others drowned in the river.

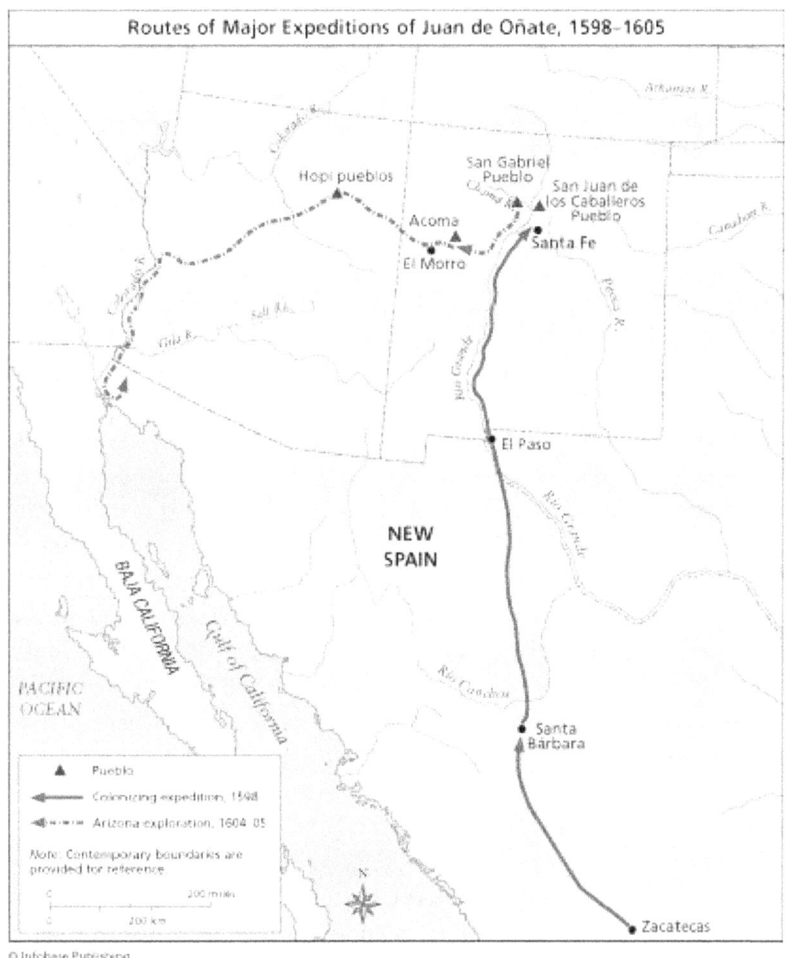

Map of the main expeditions of Juan de Oñate. http://www.fofweb.com

At the end of April, all the caravan's members gathered on the banks of the Río Grande, and Oñate decided that they would remain there for ten days, so that both people and animals could recover their strength. At the end of this period, they held a celebration to give thanks for the fact that they were still alive. There was a banquet, the Franciscans celebrated mass, the soldiers performed a brief play written by one of the expedition's captains (surely the first dramatic work staged in the United States), and Oñate led the ceremony of taking possession of the territory in the name of Philip II, following a ritual that went back to the Middle Ages. After that, they nailed a cross to a poplar tree and blew the trumpets at full blast, and the soldiers shot their harquebuses into the air.[3] It was 1598, nine years before the English founded their first North American settlement at Jamestown and twenty-two years before the first Thanksgiving. In many accounts of the foundation of the United States, Oñate's expedition goes unmentioned: the story begins with the arrival of the *Mayflower*, and the first ceremony of thanksgiving is considered to be the one celebrated by the Pilgrims at Plymouth. In reality, however, Oñate's arrival and ceremony of thanksgiving were earlier.

Subsequently, the caravan led by Oñate continued north along the river to El Paso, in what is now Texas. There, Oñate and sixty men, including the brothers Zaldívar, formed an advance party with the aim of locating a site for the colony and "pacifying" the region. In Pueblo territory, at a location they baptized Santo Domingo, they received the vassalage of the chiefs of seven provinces. Further north, having arrived at a location the natives called Ohke, they changed its name to San Juan Bautista and established their headquarters there.[4]

When the rest of the caravan joined them on August 18, they found only dust and work in recompense for all the sufferings of the journey, and a mutiny nearly broke out. According to what Oñate wrote to the viceroy,[5] the people were furious because they had not found any bars of silver lying around for the taking and because he, Oñate, had not permitted them to inflict any harm on the natives or their possessions. In view of the gravity of the situation, as several historians repeat, Oñate imposed his authority by executing two of the rebels. In Oñate's own report, nevertheless, he wrote that the sentence was handed down but not ultimately carried out, because he realized that the fault did not rise to that level and because the friars and the whole expedition pleaded with him. Either way, the threat forced Oñate to recognize the seriousness of the situation: if the colony was going to last, they needed wealth, and also food to feed so many people.

Once a church was built—the first in the United States—the eight Franciscans were sent off to their respective regions, and once the colony had been founded—the first in the United States—Oñate could devote himself to looking for riches, collecting mineral samples in the region of the Río Grande. To obtain food, he sent his nephew Vicente de Zaldívar east, to the great grasslands where the "cows of Cíbola"[6] grazed.

Vicente de Zaldívar Travels to the Lands of the Bison and the Vaquero Apaches

On April 15, 1598, the sergeant-major Vicente de Zaldívar and the administrator-general Diego de Zubía[7] left the camp accompanied by sixty soldiers. Their guide was an Indian named Jusepe, who had lived with the nomadic tribes of the region and knew how to keep his bearings in the grasslands that stretched out like an endless sea. As far as the route was concerned, they undoubtedly followed what would later be known as the Pawnee Trail, in what is now Kansas, and they may even have gone as far as Nebraska.

As was customary for expeditions of this kind, Zaldívar had to submit a report to the authorities of New Spain afterward. In his *Relación de la xornada de las bacas de Zivola* [Narrative of the enterprise of the cows of Cíbola], Zaldívar provides information about the way of life of the Vaquero Apaches[8] of the plains at the time of their first contact with Europeans. The Apaches were nomads and moved from place to place with their tipis. According to his own account, taken down by a notary, those tipis were a source of great wonder for Zaldívar:

> returning to his camp the next day he came across an encampment with fifty round tents of tanned hides, all bright red and white, with buttons and straps to close their openings as artfully made as they are in Italy, and the tents so large that the simplest among them easily held four separate beds and mattresses, and so skillfully tanned that even in a pouring rain the water cannot penetrate them, nor does the leather grow hard but, on the contrary, when it dries it is as soft and pliable as before. And since this was so astonishing he wanted to make a test; and cutting a piece of leather from a tent he soaked it in water and then set it to dry in the sun, and it came out as pliable as if it had never been wet. The said Sergeant Major obtained one tent in exchange for gifts and brought it to this camp; and though it is as large as stated above, its weight did not exceed fifty pounds.[9]

Vicente de Zaldívarren, "Relacion de la xornada de las bacas..." http://escholarship.org/

An apache dog sled.

The Apaches used dogs to transport their tipis and the rest of their possessions:[10]

> for this load and the poles with which they pitch the tent and a bag with their meat and meal or maize the said Indians use medium-sized shaggy dogs that serve as their mules, and these move in a long string, harnessed at the chest and haunches; and even carrying at least a hundred pounds they lope along as fast as their masters, and it is quite a sight, and a very amusing one, to see them trotting on their way, one after the other, the tips of the poles dragging behind them, and almost all of them with sores on their shoulders. And to load them the women hold their heads between their legs and then load them or adjust the load, which is rarely necessary, because they move along as though they had been trained with a hobble.

It is when he mentions the bison, however, that Zaldívar's account takes on more life. The expedition had set out in search of the great herds of bison of which the members of Coronado's expedition (1540–42) had spoken, with the aim of obtaining meat for the group of colonists at San Juan Bautista. Nevertheless, they did not find them easily. After riding for several days without seeing a single one, they suddenly came upon one: a single bison, separated from the rest perhaps because it was old. Zaldívar and his men broke out laughing at the clumsiness of its movements. They went a little further, however, and it became clear that they had not made the trip in vain: they found a herd of three hundred head, and a little further on, there were now four thousand . . . Finally, proceeding somewhat further, they arrived at the favorite location of the "Cíbola cows."

The favorite haunts of the abovementioned cattle are some very flat tablelands that extend for many leagues, because after climbing up to them—a very short climb, like up some hills—our men marched on for thirty leagues amid countless cattle and never found an end to them.

The next day, and the day following, they killed many animals. They now had sufficient meat. At that point, however, it occurred to them that they could make good use of some live animals. Full of optimism, they spent three days building a pen for three thousand head. Seeing the confidence with which the bison approached their horses and tents and the ridiculous way they fled, almost in little jumps, they thought that they could capture them easily, just as easily as they captured other quadrupeds with which they were familiar. They had never seen huge herds of bison charging in a full-blown stampede, and they ended up endangering their lives:

> The day after the corral was finished they rode out on a plain where the previous afternoon there had been some hundred thousand animals; and when they began to drive them the cattle headed very nicely toward the corral and in a short while turned around in a fury toward the advancing troops and broke through their ranks, though they were riding close together.

No one was hurt, but as was to be expected, they failed to catch even a single animal alive. Zaldívar blamed the animals' stubborn and wild temperament and also spoke of their craftiness:

> this is the most stubborn and fierce animal imaginable and so cunning that if you chase it, it runs, and if you stop or slow down, it stops and rolls on the ground as if it were a mule, and after this short rest it runs off again.

Bison, López de Gamararen, 1554

Nevertheless, despite all the effort expended in vain, Zaldívar does not hide in his account the sympathy he felt for the animals:

> their shape and form is so unusual and comical or astonishing that the more you see them, the more you want to see, and there is no man so melancholy that if he saw them a hundred times a day he would not laugh very heartily another hundred times and be amazed at the sight of so fierce an animal.

Nor does Zaldívar hide his admiration for the inhabitants of the plains, as can be seen in the words with which he ends his report:

> In all that land there are many Indians. They camp in the above-mentioned leather tents. They always follow the cattle and travel in their wake as cozy in their tents as they might be in any house; and since they eat their meat almost raw and a lot of fat and tallow in place of bread—a piece of meat in one hand and the hard fat in the other, taking a bite alternatively from one and the other—they grow healthy and sturdy and brave. Their weapons are flint-tipped arrows and very long Turkish bows. Our men saw some arrows with long bone tips, but just a few, because flint is better for killing the cattle than these long shafts; and they kill them at the first shot, lying in wait for them at the watering places in very skillfully made blinds, as all those who went there could see.

After a journey of fifty-four days, Zaldívar returned to the camp at San Juan Bautista on November 8, 1598, having failed to capture any bison alive, but well provided with meat and hides and having become familiar with a large stretch of territory. Nevertheless, the report we have quoted here could not be submitted until February, due to the tragic events to which we now turn.

The Massacre of the Inhabitants of Acoma

While Vicente de Zaldívar was traversing the plains where the bison flourished, the headquarters at San Juan Bautista was under the command of his brother Juan, and their uncle, Juan de Oñate, whose personality meant that he preferred devoting himself to the exploration of new lands rather than the tasks of serving as governor, continued his reconnaissance of Pueblo territory. On November 23, he left a place called Puaray, and four days later, he arrived at Acoma.

Acoma Pueblo was built on a high peak, on a mesa that offered a matchless defensive position. There, according to the eyewitness Gaspar Pérez de Villagra, who wrote an epic poem about the expedition, Oñate nearly died. One of the pueblo's chiefs, named Zutucapan,

Acoma

who had not been invited to offer his vassalage, had dedicated himself to haranguing his fellow countrymen, telling them not to submit to the pride of the "castillos,"[11] and twelve men had come together to take Oñate's life. On some pretext, they would invite him to visit a *kiva*,[12] where they would kill him.

When the *adelantado* arrived, he was very pleased with the hospitality he was given and deeply impressed by the natural strength and defensive capabilities of that pueblo built on a peak. At a certain point, one of the twelve conspirators invited him to visit one of their *kivas*, but Oñate prudently declined, thereby escaping certain death. After receiving the vassalage of Acoma's inhabitants, the small group headed west, in the direction of Zuni and Mohoqui.[13] They received the vassalage of the native chiefs there as well and continued on across what is now Arizona, with the intention of reaching the South Sea.[14]

At the beginning of his journey, Oñate had sent an order to his nephew Juan de Zaldívar, telling him that as soon as his brother Vicente returned from the plains of the bison, he should leave San Juan Bautista in Vicente's hands and come to join him. Vicente de Zaldívar returned from the tablelands on November 8, and on the 18th, Juan set out with thirty-one soldiers and eight aides to meet up with his uncle. Things did not go according to plan, however: Oñate's order could not be carried out, and the South Sea was not discovered.

Since Oñate's visit, the inhabitants of Acoma had decided to put the Spaniards' invincibility to the test the next time they arrived. They had agreed on the strategy to follow: first they would separate them, and then they would launch an attack. Hence, when they saw Juan de

Taosko kiva, "stove." Courtesy: W. H. Jackson & Co. http://commons.wikimedia.org/

Zaldívar and his men appear in the pueblo on their way to join Oñate, they came out to receive them with gifts and friendly words and showed themselves ready to assist with provisions. The following day, without suspecting anything unusual, the soldiers split up into small groups and scattered throughout the pueblo to collect the promised provisions. It was the moment the Acomas had been waiting for. They attacked and killed the foreigners. One of the victims was Juan de Zaldívar, Oñate's nephew.

What happened that day was set down in the record of a trial held in San Juan Bautista a month later. The document carries the title of *Proçeso que se hiço contra los jndios del pueblo de Acoma por aver muerto alebosamente a don Juan de Çaldivar Oñate, maese de canpo general y a dos capitanes y ocho soldados y dos moços y otros delitos* (Proceedings against the Indians of Acoma Pueblo for having treacherously killed Don Juan de Zaldívar Oñate, *maese de campo general*, and two captains and eight soldiers and two boys and other crimes). Among the witnesses who testified at the trial was one Asensio de Arechuleta,[15] "a native of the town of Ibar [Eibar] in the Kingdom of Biscay," who survived the attack. This is Arechuleta's version of events:

> this witness saw that from the time he left this said town he [the colonel] always gave orders in every place and town through which he passed that no harm was to be done to the natives, and in no ways was any done, but rather did the said colonel give the Indians hatchets and other trade goods to treat them kindly,

> and he also gave these things to the soldiers so that they might barter for whatever they might need.
>
> And when they reached the town of Acoma this witness saw that he ordered Captain Jerónimo Márquez to climb up to the said town with some soldiers for water and firewood, because there was none at their campsite; and the next day the said colonel climbed up to the said town to ask the said Indians to give him meal and corn so that they might continue their journey, which he did not bring back because, it was said, the Indians had said that they had none ready ground, that they would grind it, and that he should come back for it another day.
>
> And in view of this, and because of the lack of water, the troops moved two leagues thence to a creek that had water, whence the said colonel returned to the said town with 18 soldiers for the meal they were to give him, taking along a quantity of hatchets and other goods to trade for it; and on the said day, after nightfall, this witness saw that some of those who had gone came back very badly wounded and told how, after they had climbed up to the said town, the Indians, seeing that they had separated while seeking and bartering for the said meal, had gathered in large number and, with arrows that they had shot from the rooftops and from the ground and with stones and sticks they had likewise thrown, had killed the said colonel and Captain Felipe de Escalante and the said [sic] Diego Núñez and eight other soldiers and two servants from among those who had gone to fetch the said meal, all of which had occurred without any provocation; and this witness, because of what he has said and what he saw, believes that what the Indians did was treacherous and premeditated.
>
> And it likewise seems to this witness and is a fact that if the said town, being as strong as it is, be not destroyed so that it can never more be inhabited, it will be quite impossible to settle this country or live in it safely, because if some Indians should rebel somewhere else they could withdraw to it and fortify and defend themselves very effectively.[16]

Arechuleta affirmed that there was no provocation, but in the same trial, six inhabitants of Acoma testified to a different version. An Indian named Xunusta said that the soldiers had killed an Indian first; an Indian named Excasi said that the attack had begun because a soldier had asked for or taken a chicken; Caucachi said that it was because the interlopers had first wounded one of his people . . . What is known with certainty is that what followed was one of the largest massacres of Indians in North America, although for Oñate, his soldiers, and the friars who accompanied them, it was a "just war": the response that the trap the Acomas had set for them deserved.

In order to explain the massacre, we have to go back to the moment when Juan de Oñate received news of the ambush at Acoma and the death of his nephew Juan de Zaldívar. According to the expedition's poet, Villagra, Oñate withdrew to his tent and spent the entire night praying in front of a rough cross. Then, after assembling his men, he set out for the headquarters at San Juan Bautista, abandoning the idea of reaching the South Sea. On December 21, the group reached San Juan, where a *Te Deum* was sung to celebrate the governor's safe arrival.

Without losing time, the next day Oñate summoned the Franciscan friars to learn their opinion on the response to be made to the Acomas. After several days of hearing testimony, the friars ruled that, since the inhabitants of Acoma were subjects of the Spanish crown—they had promised obedience and vassalage a month before—their refusal to submit to Spain's authority justified war without quarter against them.

At the beginning of 1599, Vicente de Zaldívar left San Juan Bautista with seventy-two soldiers. Naturally, the official documents do not say that he intended to avenge his brother's death. According to his instructions, the inhabitants of Acoma were to hand over the murdered soldiers' weapons, abandon the heights where they lived, and settle in the plains. However, the Acomas, proud of their earlier triumph, roundly refused to comply with the terms.

Zaldívar then moved to the second point of his instructions. While the majority of the soldiers made a frontal attack, he and a dozen men went to the rear of the peak, climbed up the rocks, and before anyone realized they were there, reached the summit. For the inhabitants of Acoma, the enemy this time was not a small group of scattered men who could be taken by surprise, but a compact group trained for battle. Zaldívar's men, besides being well armed, had succeeded in bringing up two small cannons with ropes. Even so, the Acomas resisted for three days. When they surrendered, around eight hundred Acomas had lost their lives; among Zaldívar's men, there was only one casualty.

The punishment did not end there. On February 9, 1599, a trial of six hundred captives was held in Santo Domingo. On the 12th, the proceedings having come to a close, the governor issued his verdict: the Acomas were guilty. Males over twenty-five years old were to have their right feet cut off and perform twenty years of "personal service"; males between twelve and twenty-five were sentenced to twelve years of servitude, as were females over twelve. Two other Indians from the province of Mohoqui, who had fought alongside the Acomas, were to have their right hands cut off and then be set free to return to their homes and spread the news of the punishment inflicted on them. Those younger than twelve were considered innocent but were not set free: the girls were put in the care of the Franciscan superior, who was to take them to convents in New Spain, and the boys were turned over to Vicente de Zaldívar to be taught Christianity. Finally, the elderly and infirm were to be sent to "the province of the Querechos," that is, the territory of the Plains Apaches.[17]

Some historians have questioned whether Oñate carried out the sentence, arguing that there are no references to the mutilated slaves,[18] but the trial record leaves no room for doubt. According to the section titled "Execution of the sentence,"

> Which said sentence was executed and carried out as provided therein in the said town of Santo Domingo and in other neighboring towns against the Indians whose feet and hands were cut off on different days; and in regard to the servitude and commitment of the remaining Indians it was executed in the town of San Juan Bautista, which is where His Majesty's army is stationed, on the 15th day of the said month of February of the said year '99. Attest, Juan Gutiérrez Bocanegra, secretary.[19]

Juan de Oñate's signature and rubric follow.

In a report to the viceroy dated March 2, 1599, Oñate's mention of the attack on Acoma is extremely brief:

> to punish its wickedness and treason toward His Majesty, to whom it had publicly pledged allegiance, and to give an example to the others, I demolished and burned to the ground, as Your Lordship will see from the record of this trial.

The massacre and dispersion of the natives were not in reality quite that complete. The Acomas continued living atop their sandy mesa, and the "pacification" of New Mexico was only temporary (see the 1680 revolt of the Pueblo Indians discussed below). Oñate's name, nevertheless, was stained forever.

Juan de Oñate's Expedition from the Zuni Pueblos to the Colorado River, and from There to the Gulf of California

Discontent among the colonists at San Juan Bautista grew as their resources for supporting their families diminished, and Oñate had to ask the viceroy for aid, thereby making clear that the conquest of New Mexico was not turning out to be as profitable as hoped. Once the assistance arrived, Oñate set out east in search of the legendary Quivira, hoping that his luck would change, but once again, the effort was in vain. The most noteworthy episode of the journey was a battle against the inhabitants of the region. To make things worse, when Oñate returned to San Juan Bautista after five months away, he found the site almost abandoned. Most of the colonists had fled to New Spain, due to the land's harshness—eight months of winter and four months of hell—and the governor's rigor. Even the missionaries had left, since they saw that it was impossible to preach the Gospel in the face of the Indians' disdain.

The colonists' desertion was a severe blow for Oñate. Seeing that his plans were on the point of collapse, he sent Vicente de Zaldívar first to Mexico City and then to Spain in search of support. Zaldívar returned almost empty-handed in 1603.[20] After that, in late 1604, Oñate once again took up the plan that had been frozen with the Acoma Indians' attack. He would set out to explore the coast, in search of those pearl fisheries that were the subject of so much talk, or of a silver mine like the one that his family had in Zacatecas, so that the king and his counselors would continue to have confidence in his plans to colonize New Mexico. All the details of the new attempt are included in the account that Fr. Francisco Escobar wrote for Viceroy Montesclaros.

Oñate gathered a group of about thirty men and left San Gabriel on October 7, 1604. Heading west, they first encountered the inhabitants of the province of Quiñi, who welcomed the strangers into their solid stone houses with rejoicing and friendliness, offering the little they had: corn, beans, hares, and rabbits. Some twenty leagues further on, they crossed the province of Moqui, just as cold and as poor as the preceding one, and likewise inhabited by welcoming people. They were highly skilled artisans who wove the sturdiest mantles in the region and painted them better than anyone else. Continuing on in the same direction, Oñate's group then met "crossed [*cruzados*]" Indians, who wore crosses on their foreheads to please the Spaniards, in the region around the Sacramento River.[21]

On both banks of the river they baptized the Buena Esperanza ("Good Hope" in Spanish),[22] along the roughly fifty leagues that separated them from the sea, they likewise encountered numerous Indian nations, such as the Amacava and Bahacecha,[23] who left their rancherias in large groups of men, women, and children to follow Oñate's men in order to marvel at those people unlike any they had seen before. Like all the other tribes along the riverbank, they were tall and well-formed, calm in manner, and naked from head to toe, except for some grasses or cords with which the women covered their pubic area. When the Spaniards showed them a piece of coral, one of the chiefs said that it was gathered nearby, washed up on the beach at low tide. The Spaniards showed them silver, and they told them where they could find it easily. The Indians knew how to give answers that would please the strangers.

Leaving the Bahacecha nation behind, the Spaniards encountered another river, which they baptized the Nombre de Jesús ("Name of Jesus").[24] Its banks were inhabited by the Osera Indians, who were not as peaceful as those who lived along the Buena Esperanza. Oñate and his men left about twenty hungry horses in the Indian settlement's handsome meadows, intending to collect them a few days later, but when they came back, thirteen of the horses had been killed and eaten, and the Oseras, instead of admitting responsibility, claimed that it was others who had done it. From Nombre de Jesús to the sea there stretched about twenty leagues without pasture, a region of bare hills and mountains, but despite everything, it was a thickly inhabited territory, the residence of tribes as welcoming as the Amacava and Bahacecha, distinguished in bearing and affectionate in manner. We found the settlement of Alebdoma, made up of eight camps, had a total of around five thousand inhabitants, and Agalle, with five camps, and Agallecuamaya, also made up of a number of camps, had another five or six thousand inhabitants between them. Two leagues further on, Cocapa, the territory of which extended to the sea, four or five leagues away, and which appeared the largest of all to the Franciscan Escobar, also had five or six thousand inhabitants. The friars calculated that some thirty thousand souls lived along this bank of the Buena Esperanza, not counting the inhabitants of the other bank, who were enemies.

After passing through all those rancherías and nations, on October 25, 1605, Oñate's group was overjoyed to reach the sea, the Gulf of California. They saw that the coastal inhabitants wore many white and green shells and questioned them about them, to which the Indians replied that they obtained very large pearls from those shells. The governor was unable to find even a single pearl, however, despite all his efforts.

On their return trip, when they passed through Bahacecha territory again, a chief named Otata gave them information about all the Indians who lived between the Buena Esperanza and the sea and made a sketch of the region on a piece of paper. Escobar also mentions these groups in his account, apologizing to the reader for writing about what he has not seen with his own eyes, since due to the fatigue of men and horses and the scarcity of provisions, the group had no opportunity to go and confirm what Otata told them.

This is how Father Escobar reports Otata's fantastical description:

> The Indian Otata told us in the presence of many others, who corroborated his story, of a nation of people who had ears so large that they dragged on the ground, and big enough to shelter five or six persons under each one. This nation was called in its own language Esmalcatatanaaha, and in the language of this Bahacecha nation Esmalca, which means 'ear', the etymology of the word indicating the characteristic of the nation.
>
> Not far from this nation, he said, there was another whose men had virile members so long, they wrapped them four times around the waist, and that in the act of generation the man and woman were far apart. This Nation was called Medará Qualchoquata.
>
> Likewise, we learned from this Indian and the others that near the foregoing people there was another nation with only one foot, who were called Niequetata people.
>
> They told us of another nation, not far from the last, who lived on the banks of a lake in which they slept every night, entirely under the water. These people, they said, were the ones who wore handcuffs and bracelets of yellow metal, which they called *anpacha*. This nation was called Zinoes, which with more propriety we might call Hamaca Coemacha Fish. We learned from all these Indians that near this last nation there is another which always sleeps in trees. The reason we could not ascertain, whether it was for fear of wild beasts or insects, or from some natural characteristic or custom of theirs. This nation they called Ahalcos Macha.
>
> The monstrosities of another nation, which they said was near this one, did not stop here, for they sustained themselves solely on the odor of their food, prepared for this purpose, not eating it at all, since they lacked the natural means to eliminate the excrements of the body. This nation they called Xamoco Huicha.
>
> They told of another nation not far from this one which did not lie down to sleep but always slept standing up, bearing some burden on the head. This nation they called Tascaña Paycos Macha.
>
> Here we learned from all these Indians what we had learned many days before from many others, great and small, that the principal person obeyed by the people who lived on the island was a woman called Ciñaca Cohota, which signifies or means 'principal woman' or 'chieftainess'. From all these Indians we

learned that she was a giantess, and that on the island she had only a sister and no other person of her race, which must have died out with them. We learned that the men of this island were bald, and that with them the monstrosities ended.

It appears to me doubtful that there should be so many monstrosities in so short a distance, and so near us, for the Indians asserted that they were all on one river, which it was necessary to cross in order to go to the island, which was only five days' journey away (this would be twenty-five or thirty leagues). But, even though there might be still greater doubt of all these things, it seemed yet more doubtful to remain silent about things which, if discovered, would result, I believe, in glory to God and in service to the King our Lord; for although the things in themselves may be so rare and may never before have been seen, to any one who will consider the wonders which God constantly performs in the world, it will be easy to believe that since He is able to create them He may have done so.[25]

Juan de Oñate's inscription, Monument Rock. El Morro National Monument, New Mexico. From Ralph H. Anderson, 1940. Palace of the Governors Photo Archives, New Mexico History Museum, Santa Fe. http://www.palaceofthegovernors.org/. After a trip to the Gulf of California, Oñate made a roundabout return without encountering rich mines or pear trees. He may have been tired: he was 55 years old when he got to Rio de Janeiro. He carved his mark in stone: "The Adelantado Juan de Oñate made the discovery of the South Sea on 16th day of April, year 1605". In the following years, many of those who passed through the rock were from Azpilkueta, Martín de Elizacoechea, bishop of Durango (Nueva Vizcaya). Oñate's inscription is the first in Spanish; The petroglyphs were made by Indians. El Morro or Inscription Rock. Photo: Alexander Gardner, 1868. DeGolyer Library, Southern Methodist University. http://digitalcollections.smu.edu/

Oñate had fulfilled one of the expedition's objectives, reaching the sea at the northern end of the Gulf of California, but as far as the second objective was concerned, fortune had not favored him with either mines or pearl fisheries, and on April 25, 1605, he resignedly returned to San Gabriel. This was really the end of his career as an explorer and colonizer. The authorities of New Spain, after so many years of attempts, expected something more than that list of fabulous beings provided by Father Escobar, and they decided that from now on, New Mexico's governor would be appointed by the king. Consequently, when the new governor arrived in 1609, Oñate and those closest to him—his son Cristóbal, his nephew Vicente, and others—said goodbye to New Mexico and left for Mexico City.

When he arrived home, Oñate found that during his absence, the production of his family's mines had decreased. He concerned himself with the business and was quickly able to turn matters around. A more difficult problem awaited him, however. In 1601, the deserters from New Mexico had lodged accusations against him, among other

Camino Real marker.

things for the cruelty shown to the inhabitants of Acoma. In 1613, he was tried, found guilty, and sentenced to a triple punishment: he could never return to New Mexico, he was barred from Mexico City for four years, and he had to pay a specified amount of money. It was not a light penalty, but undoubtedly, for that man who had left home eleven years earlier in search of fame and honor, the worst part was the disgrace to his family name.

From then on, he devoted his time to attempting to repair his reputation. He went to Spain and settled in Madrid, thinking that being near the court would make it easier for him to clear his name. He did obtain some result: the money he had had to pay was returned to him, and he was named inspector of mines for all of Spain. In fact, he died suddenly while inspecting the Guadalcanal mines, on June 3, 1626.

Oñate's record is an extraordinary one. He founded New Mexico, and his explorations took him as far as Kansas, the Grand Canyon, and the Gulf of California. He opened the route that ran from the mines of Chihuahua to northern New Mexico, known as the Camino Real de Tierra Adentro, the "Inland Royal Road." Still today, the stretch of highway that goes from Chihuahua to El Paso is named La Ruta de Oñate, "Oñate's Route," and he was also the first to traverse the area known as the Jornada del Muerto or "Dead Man's Journey," a stretch of almost eighty miles without water. Nevertheless, despite his merits, Oñate is scarcely mentioned in most histories. The historian Marc Simmons has said that when he was writing Oñate's biography (*The Last Conquistador: Juan de Oñate and the Settling of the Far Southwest*), he was surprised by how unknown he was. More than once, when speaking at universities and schools in New Mexico, he found that the students had never heard of the man who founded that state.

If he is mentioned at all, it is on the list of history's villains, with yet another repetition of the details of the Acoma massacre and the terrible punishment of cutting off the right feet of all the men over twenty-five years old. On the occasion of the quadricentennial of New Mexico's founding, a bronze statue of Oñate was erected at the entrance of the Oñate Center in Alcalde. One morning in January 1998, it was discovered that the statue's right foot had been cut off. Around the same time, another large equestrian statue bearing Oñate's name was set up at the airport in El Paso, a city he founded. Soon after, in response to the protests of many citizens, the statue's name was changed to the generic "The Equestrian." So ended the man who left everything to set out in search of honors and immortality.

The Pueblo Revolt and the Role Played by Antonio de Otermin, the Governor of New Mexico, and Francisco de Ayeta, the Franciscan Procurator, 1680

The Acoma massacre forced the Pueblo Indians to surrender, but the "pacification" of the region was not achieved. On the contrary, indignation against and hostility toward the Spaniards increased among the natives, and revolts broke out one after another during the succeeding decades: among the Jemez in 1623, the Zuni in 1632, the Taos in 1639. In 1648 the Jemez and the Apaches rebelled, in 1650 it was the turn of the Teguas or Tewas and the Apaches, and in 1670 the Navajos attacked the Hawikuk mission . . .

The Pueblo Indians did not lack motives for desiring to free themselves from the Spanish yoke. In addition to being forced to work as captives, they had to pay taxes under the *encomienda* system; the diseases the Europeans had introduced were spreading among them with startling speed; the Spaniards took native beliefs to be idolatry or witchcraft and tried to destroy all their manifestations . . . The harshest repression took place under the administration of Gov. Juan Francisco Treviño (1675–77), who ordered the destruction of all the *kivas* the natives used for their ceremonies, as well as all paraphernalia associated with their beliefs. Forty-seven religious leaders and healers were arrested, four of them were hanged on charges of idolatry and sorcery, and the rest were publicly punished and condemned to labor as captives.

Statue of Juan de Oñate in El Paso

By then—almost a hundred years before Junípero Serra would found California's first mission in 1769, at San Diego—the Franciscans had spread throughout the extensive territory called New Mexico at the time, that is, the modern states of Arizona, Texas, and New Mexico. Since the first mission was founded at Puaray in 1581, forty-eight more had been established in New Mexico, and another sixteen in Arizona. To supply such remote locations with provisions, enormous caravans were organized every three years. The long trains made up of dozens of carts needed a year and a half to cover the distance between New Spain and Santa Fe. Along with provisions, those caravans brought missionaries, soldiers, and other officials, together with news of the world. Beginning in 1675, the man in charge of them was Francisco de Ayeta, a native of Pamplona, the Franciscan provincial custodian and general procurator. It was Ayeta, consequently, who in 1677 brought New Mexico's new governor, Antonio de Otermin, to Santa Fe to replace Treviño.

Antonio de Oterminen's signatture

Nothing is known of Antonio de Otermin's early years. A baptismal record exists in the archives of the diocese of San Sebastián for an Antonio Otermin, the son of Joanes Otermin and Catalina Recalde, baptized in the church of Santa María in Tolosa, Gipuzkoa, on December 19, 1621. Was he the same Antonio de Otermin who traveled in Ayeta's caravan?

It is also unknown to what extent he was familiar with the territory he was to govern or how much it took for him to realize the natives' discontent. In any event, his first decisions were not good ones. He retained in his position the previous governor's secretary for administration and war (*secretario de gobierno y guerra*), Francisco Javier, the man who had directed almost all the campaigns against the natives' religious practices. Under his authority, the persecutions and violence against the indigenous population continued as before.

At that time, there were around three thousand Spaniards living in the province, including thirty-three Franciscans, scattered throughout the territory and easy victims for Indian rebellions. Indians murdered at least twelve missionaries between 1540 and 1680. One of them was Fray Martín de Arbide, from Donostia, who has been called the "protomartyr of the state of Arizona."[26] The Pueblo Indian chiefs, for their part, had around six thousand warriors under their command, many of them skilled riders and owners of horses purchased from the Spaniards. They were the majority, lacking only a leader to unite them all, and that leader appeared: a healer named Poc-Pec or Popé, one of the chiefs arrested and humiliated by Governor Treviño. Popé achieved what had never been achieved before, getting the Pueblos to set aside their internal tensions and form a common front against the Spaniards, one in which they would be joined by the Apaches, who until then had been their enemies.

The Pueblo revolt of 1680 was planned and coordinated with great care. The date was set for August 11. After selecting the best runners, the organizers sent them to each pueblo with knotted ropes. These were a kind of calendar, and the knots indicated how many days remained until the revolt. They had agreed to untie the last knot on August 11. On the 9th, however, the Spaniards found out about the Pueblos' intentions from two captured messengers, and Otermin learned that the rebels wanted to kill all the missionaries and all the Spaniards, women and children included, reducing the population of the kingdom to nothing.27

Popé statue, Washington National Statuary Hall. It is one of two statues that represent New Mexico. In the wrong hand, a knot rope, a signal to start the revolution.

According to what the Santa Fe town council declared later, the rebel Indians said many times during the siege that no Spaniard was to be left alive in the entire kingdom.[28] In addition to killing them, they wanted to make every trace of them disappear: houses, fields, churches, and all Catholic religious paraphernalia. Popé ordered his followers to wash in the river, rubbing their bodies thoroughly with yucca roots, in order to make their Christian names disappear and remove the water and chrism of baptism. In the same way, it was prohibited to mention the names of Jesus, Mary, and the saints; to speak Spanish; and even to plant seeds the Spaniards had brought. From now on, they would plant only corn and beans, as their ancestors had always done.

The details of the revolt are described in a letter that Gov. Antonio de Otermin wrote to the Franciscan procurator, Francisco de Ayeta.[29] Ayeta had just arrived in El Paso, coming from Mexico City with his caravan of provisions for the Franciscans scattered throughout the province. Otermin's first words to his fellow-countryman are highly dramatic:

> My Very Reverend Father, Sir, and friend, most beloved Fray Francisco de Ayeta: The time has come when, with tears in my eyes and deep sorrow in my heart, I commence to give an account of the lamentable tragedy, such as has never before happened in the world, which has occurred in this miserable kingdom and holy custodia.

Already the day after learning of the Indians' intentions, Otermin had news of the first victim. Fray Juan Pío went to the *visita*[30] of Tesuque to say mass, accompanied by a soldier, Pedro Hidalgo. As Hidalgo would later testify, when they arrived at the town, they found it empty. They went in search of the people, since the friar wanted to celebrate mass for them. A quarter of a league away, they found many Indians, all of them prepared for war, with bows, arrows, and lances. Fray Pío spoke to them as follows, according to Hidalgo's testimony: "What is this, children? Are you crazy? Do not be disturbed, for I will help and will die a thousand deaths for you."[31]

"Nuevo Mapa Geographico de la America Septentrional . . ." in José Antonio de Alzate y Ramírez ,1768. Towns participating in the uprising of the people. http://www.texasbeyondhistory.net/

Father Ayeta included news of the murder in his annual report, giving the victim's full name—Juan Bautista Pío—and mentioning his birthplace: Vitoria, in the province of Araba. Ayeta knew him well, since Pío had arrived in the region three years earlier in the convoy that Ayeta led.

The revolt continued to spread in the following hours. As Otermin confesses in his letter to Ayeta, that kingdom, made up of small settlements at a great distance from one another, was very well suited for the rebels to carry out their plans. Making use of this advantage, the Indians began to kill all the Spaniards, men, women, and children, from Taos to Santa Fe, from La Isleta to Zuni. On the 13th, about nine o'clock in the morning, all the Indians of the Taos and Pecos nations and the Queres of San Marcos appeared, armed and yelling war cries. The governor promised them that if they returned to His Majesty's obedience, they would be pardoned, but the Indians received this offer with grimaces and mockery, demanding the release of several of their number who had been captured.

They were trying to buy time until the rebels from the Pecuris and Tigua nations arrived. All together, they would easily be able to surround the Spaniards who had taken refuge in the town. Realizing this, and seeing the Indians increasingly agitated and increasingly self-confident, appropriating whatever they could and drawing ever closer to the town, Otermin gave the order to attack. Moreover, he almost won the victory, since the Indians took refuge inside the houses, and Otermin and his men surrounded some of them and set them on fire. At that moment, however, the Tigua appeared, the Taos and Pecos succeeded in escaping, and they all gathered in the nearby mountains, where they spent that night. Otermin and the men under his command, for their part, withdrew to the church of Nuestra Señora de las Casas Reales. In this way, the following day passed, and the one after it as well, with the occasional minor skirmish. The Indians were strategically deployed on the heights of the surrounding mountains, and Otermin knew that it was useless to try to make them come out.

The next day, at night, all the Taos, Pecuris, Jemez, and Queres gathered together, and around 2,500 Indians attacked the town at dawn. They fortified themselves inside the residences and at the mouths of the streets, and they cut off the Spaniards' water supply. They were well armed, with harquebuses, powder, and plenty of ammunition. Otermin tried to barricade himself in the governor's palace, but seeing that the Indians wanted to set it on fire, he made a sally into the plaza with his men, although the majority of them were wounded. They fought all afternoon, trying to prevent the Indians from setting the palace on fire, and passed the night, like the previous one, without fighting, but half dead of thirst due to the lack of water.

According to Otermin's letter to Fr. Francisco de Ayeta, the next day, Saturday,

> they began at dawn to press us harder and more closely with gunshots, arrows, and stones, saying to us that now we should not escape them, and that, besides their own numbers, they were expecting help from the Apaches whom they had already summoned. They fatigued us greatly on this day, because all day was fighting, and above all we suffered from thirst, as we were already oppressed by it.

Things did not improve when night fell:

> Instantly all the said Indian rebels began a chant of victory and raised war whoops, burning all the houses of the villa, and they kept us in this position the entire night, which I assure your reverence was the most horrible that could be thought of or imagined, because the whole villa was a torch and everywhere were war chants and shouts. What grieved us most were the dreadful flames from the church and the scoffing and ridicule which the wretched and miserable Indian rebels made of the sacred things, intoning the alabado and the other prayers of the church with jeers.
>
> Finding myself in this state, with the church and the villa burned, and with the few horses, sheep, goats, and cattle which we had without feed or water for so long that many had already died, and the rest were about to do so, and with such a multitude of people, most of them children and women, so that our numbers in all came to about a thousand persons, perishing with thirst—for we had nothing to drink during these two days except what had been kept in some jars and pitchers that were in the casas reales—surrounded by such a wailing of women and children, with confusion everywhere, I determined to take the resolution of going out in the morning to fight with the enemy until dying or conquering.

After hearing mass at dawn, the Spaniards began the attack, those who could on horseback, others on foot with their harquebuses, and some Indian allies with bows and arrows. Amazingly—Otermin himself calls it a "miraculous event"—they succeeded in putting the Indians to flight.

The following day, a group of over 1,500 people, including 317 Indian's allies, set out for La Isleta. Provisions for so many people were scant, only a few sheep, goats, and cows. Otermin himself, like many others, was wounded, since he had been struck in the face by two arrows, and the previous day a harquebus ball had given him a considerable chest wound. When they reached La Alameda, they learned that the captain of the region and all the inhabitants had fled. This news deeply saddened the governor, since it meant that the province of New Mexico was being abandoned.

The letter mentioned above was written by Otermin on his way to El Paso to meet Ayeta's caravan, staking his hopes for his people's survival on the provisions Ayeta was transporting in his carts. The refuges arrived half dead of hunger and almost naked at the location where the convoy was, almost five weeks after the outbreak of the revolt, and just as Otermin had calculated, they were saved thanks to the Franciscan's help.

Some historians judge harshly Otermin's decisions, which had such serious consequences, in those days. The Texas State Historical Association, nevertheless, defends his legacy: "Otermín was no *conquistador* like Cortes, no explorer like Coronado, and no colonizer like Oñate, but he had laid the base for three centuries of El Paso history."[32] As far as Father Ayeta is concerned, opinions are unanimous. In the words of the mentioned Texas association, he was "one of the great men of New Mexico."

Otermin's letter narrates from the Spaniards' perspective what was, according to Bancroft, "the greatest disaster that ever befell Spain on the northern frontier, if not indeed in any part of America."[33] (It led to the deaths of hundreds, including twenty-one missionaries.) No written account from the Indians' perspective exists that we could compare with Otermin's, but we do have Indian testimony collected by the Spaniards. Those statements were often made through interpreters, obtained by force, or contaminated by the Spaniards' prejudices, but they nonetheless do not fail to offer interesting bits of information.

While Otermin was retreating south with the group of refugees, he took testimony on August 25 from a Christian Indian named Tano, who explained that he found out about the revolt from an Indian named Bartolomé.[34] This Bartolomé was the town crier of the neighboring town of Galisteo, and he apparently told Tano that the Indians wanted to kill all the friars and all the Spaniards; that whoever killed a Spaniard would obtain an Indian woman of his choice as his wife; that whoever killed four Spaniards would receive the same number of wives; and that whoever killed ten or more would be rewarded with ten or more wives.

El Paso, Texas historical marker. Reads: "First Mission and Pueblo in Texas, Corpus Christi de la Ysleta. Established by Don Antonio de Oterminek and Fray Francisco de Ayetak O.F.M. in 1682. Maintained by Franciscan Missionaries for the Civilizing and Christanizing of the T.G.T. Indians Pueblo Revolt Refuges

Asked why the Indians had rebelled, the witness repeated what Bartolomé had told him, that is, that the Pueblos were furious because of the labor they had to perform for the Spaniards and the missionaries; that doing so much work for others left them no time to plant for themselves or tend to their own affairs; and that, upset, they had decided to rebel.

On September 6, in the town of Alamillo, the governor took testimony from another Indian whom the group had encountered on the road, an elderly man named Don Pedro Gamboa, over eighty years old. Through an interpreter, Otermin asked him why the Pueblos had rebelled, and the old man answered that the Tewas, Taos, Pecuris, Pecos, and Jemez had been wanting to rebel for some time. The Spaniards prohibited them from living according to their ancestral customs, and he had been a witness of the pain this caused in the Indians' hearts since he had had the use of reason.[35]

The Indian prisoner Pedro Naranjo was asked why the rebels had burned saints' images, churches, and crosses. Naranjo answered that they wanted to go back to the old days; that they had led a better life then and wanted to go back to it; that the Spaniards' god was worthless; that their god was much more powerful, and the Spaniards' god was only rotten wood . . .[36]

Memorial for San Antonio de Senecú, founded by Otermin and Ayeto, and an uprising in the town's location.

After having linked up with Ayeta's convoy, Otermin and the refugees established themselves at El Paso and in the neighboring settlement of San Lorenzo. They spent the following months suffering hunger and fearing new Indian attacks. To deal the final blow to their spirits, Father Ayeta returned from Mexico City in late 1681 with unexpected news: according to the viceroy's orders, they were to try to reconquer New Mexico.

Against their will and poorly equipped, with few men and even fewer weapons, they set out to the north. On the way, they passed through many towns destroyed by the Indians during the previous year's uprising. Their descriptions of what they found are eloquent sources of information on the Pueblos' thoughts and intentions. When Otermin's group entered the town of Socorro, for example, they found that the mission and the church had been burned. In the sacristy, there were "two pieces of the arms of a Christ," and in the plaza, "the entire thigh, the leg, and one foot of a holy image of Christ, all in one piece, and the rest of the divine image was charred."[37] In the same plaza, they found a large cross hacked from its place in the cemetery, with the arms and almost all the rest of it charred. For Otermin and his group, all that destruction was further evidence of the Indians' savage nature, since they were incapable of attributing any kind of complexity to their actions. It did not occur to them to interpret them as symbolic acts with which the natives aimed to rehabilitate their gods and change the existing power relationships.

In another town, Sandia, Otermin saw that before setting the church on fire, they had filled it with straw and destroyed everything, desecrating the Catholic liturgical objects as obscenely as possible: the statues had been profaned with human excrement; two chalices kept in a box were found covered with dung, and the cross had also been desecrated; the location of the high altar had likewise been profaned with human excrement, and the statue of Saint Francis had been hacked to pieces.[38]

In Sandia, Alamillo, Socorro, and Zuni the clappers had been removed from the bells. The indigenous inhabitants had spent several decades subjected to those bells that marked their long days of work in the missions. By removing their clappers, they made one of the chief symbols of Spanish authority mute.

When Otermín's group entered Senecú, they found in the cemetery a bronze cannon and the cross that used to be in the plaza, together with the clapperless bell. By taking these three symbolic objects to the cemetery, the rebels had proclaimed the death of the Catholic religion and of the military force that sustained it.

In that winter of 1681, when in obedience to the viceroy's order—but with no confidence whatsoever in the forces at their disposal—they set out to reconquer the province, Otermín's men would not have drawn much encouragement from those reminders of the previous year's destruction that they found in each town. Over the course of a long month and a half, the group's indignation and frustration grew, until at a certain point they decide to ignore their orders and retreat. For the next twelve years, the province of New Mexico was in Pueblo hands.

Juan Bautista Anza I's Difficulties in the "Land of Active War," 1736–1740

Plans to open a route between Sonora and Alta California had existed for some time, but they had so far been impossible to carry out, due to the major geographical obstacles and the fact that northern New Spain was a "land of active war" (*tierra de guerra viva*) in the terminology of the time, that is, a territory inhabited by unconquered Indians. One such plan was presented to the viceroy in 1737. Its author was the Gipuzkoan Juan Bautista Anza, captain of the presidio of Fronteras.

This Anza or Anssa—he signed his name as Anssa—appears in history books as Juan Bautista Anza I, and the narrative of his actions is most often overshadowed by those of his son, Juan Bautista Anza II. As we will see in these pages, however, the father was also a witness and protagonist of exceptional events. We will begin by telling the story of two of those events, the most astonishing ones, and leave for the end Anza's destiny on the Spanish empire's frontier: unceasing war against the Apaches, in which he would find his death.

First Astonishing Event in Juan Bautista Anza's Life: The Discovery of the Arizona Silver Mine

North of Sonora, the missions founded by Father Kino formed a long chain along the continent. The Italian Jesuit had succeeded in extending the northern frontier as far as the valleys of the Gila and the Colorado, but he died in 1711 without fully achieving his goal of opening a corridor between Sonora and the port of Monterrey, the route needed in order to transport the Manila galleon's cargo to New Spain by land, avoiding a dangerous sea. With Kino's death, the opening of that much-desired route was left to await more appropriate circumstances and guides. The Spanish authorities continued to study proposals for continuing the conquest, but without making a decision to risk spending money on that remote province, the empire's most distant frontier.

The situation suddenly changed as a consequence of an extraordinary event: the 1736 discovery of a silver mine between the Guevavi mission and a ranch named Arizonac or Arizona, slightly south of the border of the modern state of Arizona. The mine was given the name "Planchas de Plata" ("Silver plaques") or "Bolas de Plata" ("Silver balls"), because the metal was found in the form of balls made up almost entirely of silver. These balls or plaques were on or very close to the surface and were enormous, some of them weighing a ton or even more. The mine had been discovered by a Yaqui Indian named Antonio Siraumea, who apparently managed to keep his discovery a secret for some days, visiting the location clandestinely with his children. It was a mining region, however, and the news spread quickly. People rushed to the site, and disputes quickly began to break out. In order to prevent further conflict, Bernardo de Urrea, deputy magistrate (*teniente alcalde*) of the province of Sonora, decided to ask for help. He went home—to the ranch named Arizona—and wrote a letter to Juan Bautista Anza, senior magistrate (*alcalde mayor*) of the province and captain of the Fronteras presidio.

Anza's company arrived at the site a few weeks later. Upon seeing the silver, the captain suspected that it might be a lost treasure and asked three Jesuits from the nearby missions for advice. If it was a mine, the king would only get a fifth, but if it was a treasure, the king would own everything. Two of the Jesuits took the view that it was a treasure. The third, Fr. Juan de Echagoyen, offered a more remarkable opinion: it could be a deception by the devil, and the balls and plaques of silver might disappear at any moment. After reading the opinions that the three Jesuits had submitted in writing, Anza took a decision that infuriated the miners: he would confiscate all the silver. A painstaking subsequent investigation concluded that the mine was a natural deposit, and the miners' shares were ordered returned to them.

Although the discovery of the mine did not mean great profits, it led the authorities to concern themselves once again with the conquest of the northwest. In reality, that palpable evidence of wealth was worth more than all the legends. There might be more mines in the vicinity. Reports and missives aimed at organizing an expedition once again began to go back and forth. On January 14, 1737, Anza wrote to Viceroy Vizarrón y Eguiarreta to try to convince him that the discovery of the region as far as the Colorado River and somewhat beyond need not cost much money. The project could be financed with donations from the devout, and he himself was prepared to contribute horses, mules, cattle, and gifts for the Indians. In addition, Anza informed the viceroy that the inhabitants of the Colorado and Gila region were industrious people and surely easy to bring into a state of submission, unlike other Indians who lived from hunting with bows and arrows and who doubtless would have condemned the enterprise to failure.[39]

The silver discovery site, about fifteen miles from the "Arizona" ranch. Source: Reba Grandrud.

Anza's plan was favorably received by the Mexican and Spanish authorities, but its implementation was paralyzed by the captain's death in 1740 in an Apache ambush.

The discovery of silver also had a consequence of another kind. All the documents about the mine were written at Bernardo de Urrea's ranch, named Arizona or Arizonac, and when the news spread, people repeated that name, speaking in wonder about "the Arizona silver" or "the Arizona treasure." In this way, "Arizona" came to be a byword for a "place of treasures" or "sudden wealth," and according to the historian Donald T. Garate, this was how the name of the modern state of Arizona spread. As far as the name's origin is concerned, Garate says that on Urrea's ranch, there were many oak trees, and the numerous Basques in the region must have called the site *(h)aritz ona* or *(h)aritz onak* (that is, 'good oak' or 'good oaks').[40]

The discovery of the Arizona silver was a noteworthy event in Anza's life and in the history of the region known as Pimería Alta,[41] but it was not the most surprising one. As captain of the Fronteras presidio, Anza was called on to intervene in other events that he himself described as the strangest ever to have taken place in that kingdom.

A Second Astonishing Event in Juan Bautista Anza's Life: The Appearance of the Prophet of the God Moctezuma

In March 1737, Anza heard the news of the appearance of a prophet of the god Moctezuma in the lands where the Guayma and Pima Bajo nations lived. They called him Arebisi in their language, and he was giving orders for the entire world to present themselves before him. Those who obeyed would receive gifts, and the rest would be punished.

Arebisi's summons received an astonishing response. "It is admirable," Anza observed in a report sent to Viceroy Vizarrón y Eguiarreta, that for a hundred leagues around, the Indians took to the road at exactly the same time.[42] The towns emptied, the mine workers stopped working, and some five thousand Indians set out for the site Arebisi indicated, carrying the sick with them in the conviction that the prophet would heal them.

Anza himself left the presidio and headed for the location set for the gathering, along with twenty-seven soldiers and twelve well-armed civilian householders, financed by Agustín de Vildósola[43] and other traders. They found Arebisi at a site near the town of Guaymas and arrested him, after which they began to question witnesses. According to their testimony, Arebisi had told them that he was a messenger of the god Moctezuma, the creator of heaven, earth, water, and all that exists. He also told them, according to Anza himself in his report to the viceroy, that he would turn those who refused to believe in him into stones, and that no one should be afraid of the soldiers, because they would also be turned into stones like all unbelievers. The world, in his words, was as thin as paper and would soon come to an end, but after this catastrophe, Moctezuma would create a new world in which the Indians would come back to life turned into Spaniards, and the Spaniards turned into Indians, so that the Indians would be the masters, and the Spaniards would be the servants. In this new world, they would not suffer food shortages, since they would eat from an inexhaustible vessel.

The people listened to these fabulous tales with so much faith that, in Anza's words, it would be difficult to believe without having seen it. Women offered him their rosaries, their religious medals, and all their valuables. Men sacrificed their cows and other animals to share them with those present and offer them to the prophet, because he had made them believe that the idol also ate. There was music of harps, guitars, and violins, creating a joyful atmosphere, as well as fireworks and dances. The celebrations lasted for several days at a time.

Subsequently, Anza took testimony from Arebisi himself. He did not want to say where he had hidden the idol, but under the pressure of blows from Anza's cane, he ended up confessing. He kept the image, Anza wrote in his report, "in a little basket, wrapped in cotton. The rosaries and crucifixes and other jewels with which they had endowed him were in a large basket." After a few further questions, Anza sentenced him to death, fearing, as many did, that the other tribes would follow Arebisi's example and might organize a general revolt. He was hanged from a tall palm tree, so that the multitude gathered there could see him. His real name was Agustín Aschuhuli, and he was around forty-five years old.

In this way, the affair of Moctezuma's prophet was brought to an end, but not the deep discontent that was at its root. For the Indians, the oppression imposed by colonial society was unendurable, and it was for this reason that the "new world" Arebisi promised them, in which they would be lords and the Spaniards would be servants, was so attractive to them. Likewise, they could not understand how it could be that there were things that the missionaries preached and imposed—monogamy especially—and the Spaniards failed to observe. In 1703, an Indian from the town of Aconchi made this complaint to his missionary:

> It is true that when we were pagans we had more than one wife, but it is also true that we only knew our legitimate wives, according to our pagan customs. Now that we are Christians, we know the wife that God gives us and no other. Those Spaniards are the ones who are not content until they know all the women in the town.[44]

Even more incomprehensible for the Indians was the rapid spread of epidemics. They knew neither their origin nor how to control them, nor why it was only they and not the Spaniards who became ill. Finding no better explanation, many thought that these illnesses had to be caused by some supernatural element, and for this reason they transported their sick dozens of leagues to the prophet Arebisi, in the hope of obtaining a similarly supernatural cure. Precisely in that year of 1737, smallpox was ravaging the Indian population. Anza mentions the fact in his report to the viceroy, although only in passing, limiting himself to saying that when he and his men were returning to the presidio—that is, on their way home—they found dead or dying Indians everywhere.

Juan Bautista Anza I's Destiny: The Unceasing War against the Apaches

The two previous events, the Arizona silver and the prophet of the god Moctezuma, were exceptional episodes in Anza's life. Juan Bautista Anza I's daily reality, the true nightmare that brought him enormous problems year after year, was the war against the Apaches.[45] When he was planning his journey to the Americas from the town where he was born, he probably never imagined anything of the sort. The Hernani apothecary's son would not have even known that the Apaches existed. Within a few years, however, he would come to know their way of life and warrior customs better than anyone else.

Juan Bautista, the son of Antonio de Anssa and Lucia de Sassoeta, was baptized on June 29, 1693, in Hernani. The priest Domingo de Sasoeta officiated at the baptism, and Theodoro de Zuaznabar and Josepha de Yrigoien served as godparents. During his childhood and adolescence, he lived a life in which he scarcely left his hometown, until at the age of nineteen he decided to go to the Americas—forever, as happened in that era, and having promised that he would go to visit his mother's two sisters, Francisca and María Josefa, who lived in Culiacán.

Juan Bautista spent little time with his aunts in Culiacán. Eager to set out in search of his fortune, he immediately went to the mines of northern Sonora, where going back to the early eighteenth century, Basques formed a large and powerful group among the communities that had grown up around the mines. According to the historian María del Valle Borrero Silva, the population was divided into two antagonistic groups: Basques and non-Basques.[46] The Basques constituted a cohesive group and were able to act jointly on occasion, as when in 1720 they expressed their disagreement with the presidio captain Gregorio Álvarez Muñoz, who was in their view not defending the province, and as when in 1741 they joined forces with the Jesuits to remove the serving provincial governor, Manuel Bernal de Huidobro, from his post and replace him with the Basque Agustín de Vildósola. The majority of them were members of the confraternity of Our Lady of Aránzazu[47] as well.

It was in those mining camps that Anza began to distinguish among the different Indian nations. He learned, for example, that the Yaquis were the best workers in the mines. At that time, the *repartimiento* still functioned in Sonora, allowing the mine owners to require the mission Indians to work for them for fifteen days, in exchange for minimal pay. There were many abuses—the periods of work grew, the pay shrank—and the Jesuits opposed the system. Anza and the other Basques were very close to the Jesuits. Did they follow their opinions on this subject?

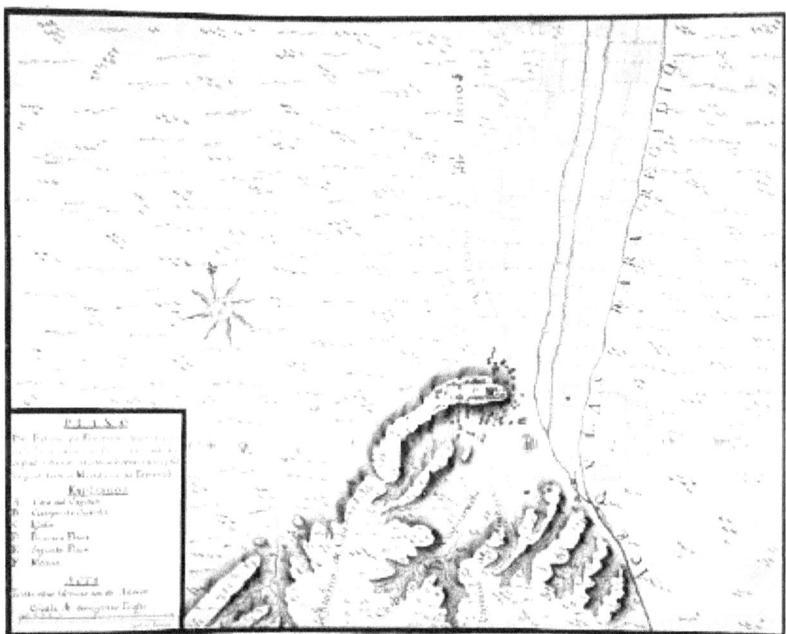

Map of frontier presidio. First Captain Juan Bautista Anza. Legend: A. Captain's House; B.Guard House; C. Church: D. First place; E. Second place; F. Mill. Note: "All of these buildings are made from fertilizers." The map shows two paths to Cuquiarach and Guchutara and Janos. It also shows "irrigation ditches, " By José de Urrutia, 1767. Courtesy British Library. http://www.nps.gov/

Likewise, Anza quickly became familiar with the group that was considered the most barbarous of all the Indian nations: the Apaches. They were a true nightmare for the inhabitants of the frontier. "The pen is horrified to indicate some of their wild customs," wrote Juan Domingo Arricivita, an eighteenth-century Franciscan chronicler.[48] The Fronteras presidio, built some years earlier at Santa Rosa de Corodeguachi, had action against them as one of its missions, and the same was true of the soldiers of Janos and El Paso.

Around 1720, Anza himself became a member of the Fronteras cavalry. Being accepted into the presidio was a way of moving up the social ladder, and Anza advanced very rapidly in his career as a soldier. Already in 1726, he was captain of the Fronteras presidio, a post of no small responsibility, from which a force of only forty men monitored a hundred thousand square miles covering a large part of Sonora and Arizona and portions of Chihuahua, Texas, and New Mexico. To the northwest, the Yuma, O'opa, Cocomaric O'opa, Papabi O'otam, and Papagos lived. To the southwest, in the region around the Gulf of California, were the

Seris. South and east of Fronteras were the Opatas and Eudeves, and the Pimas lived in the middle of them all. As far as the Yaquis were concerned, they were found everywhere in Sonora. Finally, of course, there were the indomitable Apaches, who came from the northeast.

Skilled riders, the Apaches appeared suddenly and disappeared the same way they arrived, after having robbed, killed, and destroyed everything in the camps and rancherías of other tribes and in the Spaniards' towns. They took possession of horses and cattle with such ease that, as Donald T. Garate writes, the Spaniards' enclaves and missions came to be a supermarket for them. In Anza's own words:

> From the said mountains, they spy on the horses, mules, and beef cattle that are out in the fields, and at night they gather them and drive them off, and if they see any people pass by, they come out to kill them in some narrow places.[49]

One of the presidio captain's responsibilities was escorting officials who had to cross the territory under his jurisdiction. Martín de Elizacoechea, the bishop of Durango, Nueva Vizcaya, visited the missions in Pima and Opata territory between December 13, 1737, and January 21, 1738, in the course of a journey of almost a year that had as its goal visiting all the missions of his diocese. The escort of such a high-ranking figure fell to Anza, who needed to keep Elizacoechea from becoming an easy target for the Apaches.[50] Elizacoechea was originally from Azpilkueta, Navarre. His personal secretary and his confessor, who accompanied him, Juan Ignacio de Arrasain and Pedro de Echenique, were from the same Navarrese district. When they were with Anza, traversing trails and mountains, did they speak Euskara together? Did any expression of nostalgia for their homeland escape them? The documents are mute on this subject. We know only that Elizacoechea never broke off his ties to his native region. Throughout his life, he continued writing to his family in Baztán, and he did not forget them in his will.

Once he completed his tour of Sonora, Elizacoechea headed south, escorted by soldiers from the Sinaloa presidio, and Anza and his soldiers returned to Fronteras and to their usual occupations.

In the guerrilla warfare practiced by the Apaches, their first great advantage was the immensity of their territory. Following an attack, they could hide in any mountain, canyon, or riverbank in the region. Their second advantage was the lightness of their gear, since they carried only their arrows and wore only light clothing. Anza's soldiers, in contrast, had to bear the weight of uncomfortable leather armor, as well as large and clumsy shields made from untanned hides. They offered good protection against the Apaches' arrows, but they were a great handicap in chasing after them.

The Apaches normally attacked in small groups, but it sometimes happened that a hundred, two hundred, or even three hundred warriors would gather together. On those occasions, as Anza's friend Agustín de Vildósola acknowledged, they did not lack courage, and neither were they unfamiliar with the art of war. Against their charge, Anza's fifty soldiers were of little account, even aided by the militias that existed in every town, where they were most often underfunded and very badly equipped. The ruins of horse ranches and cattle ranches destroyed by the Apaches and their allies were scattered throughout the territory. Many victims abandoned Sonora in search of more peaceful locations.

Anza knew the Apaches' warrior customs well after having fought them for fourteen long years. For this reason, the error he committed on May 9, 1740, is surprising. That morning, after having inspected the missions on the upper part of the Santa Cruz River, he was returning home with a small number of men. That is, he was headed to the presidio, located on a height that dominated the entire valley. His wife, Rosa Becerro Nieto, and his six children were awaiting him there. At a certain point, for whatever reason, the soldiers fell behind, or Anza went ahead . . . It was a matter of an instant. A group of Apaches, armed with bows and arrows, emerged from the underbrush, and before the soldiers could come to his aid, the captain lay dying on the ground.

Anza had a reputation as an upstanding and responsible man, and his death was much mourned among those who had witnessed his efforts to defend the frontier. As far as the Apaches were concerned, it seems that courage was the quality they valued most. If so, perhaps they felt a certain respect, as well as a sense of triumph, when they realized that the man they had struck down was the Fronteras captain.

As we have already said, Anza's early death meant that his most ambitious plans could not be fulfilled. He did not open a route between Sonora and Alta California, as he had discussed in his 1737 letter to the viceroy. It would be his son who would carry out his plan years later. In 1772, Juan Bautista Anza II asked Viceroy Antonio María de Bucareli y Ursúa for permission to lead an expedition, adding to his own petition the one his father had circulated to the same end, and this time, the plan prospered: Anza succeeded in opening a land route from Sonora to Monterrey and San Francisco. Thanks to this great achievement, Juan Bautista Anza II became a prominent figure in California history, and a visitor to that state today finds highways, schools, and parks that bear his name.[51] He will receive the attention he deserves in these pages as well, but for now, let us leave him in the Fronteras presidio with his widowed mother and his five siblings. He is only three years old.

The Pima Revolt of 1751 and Other News from Pimería Alta

Together with the missions, the presidios were a fundamental institution of the Spanish colonial frontier. In response to numerous Indian revolts—in 1725, the Seris rebelled; in 1737, the Pimas Bajos; in 1740, the Yaquis; in 1749, the Seris again, allied this time with the Sibubapas, Piatos, Pimas Altos, and Apaches—the number of presidios also increased: those of Fronteras, Janos, and El Paso were joined by San Pedro de la Conquista del Pitic (1741), Terrenate (1742), Altar and Tubac (1753), and San Carlos de Buenavista (1765). In 1769, Spain's empire included twenty-three frontier presidios. The long list is a clear sign of the climate of violence that existed, since all these establishments were built not to defend recently conquered areas, but to maintain those previously occupied.

In November 1751, the Pimas, who lived scattered in different territories, rebelled under the leadership of Capt. Luis Oacpicagigua or Luis de Sáric. The revolt did not take the Jesuits of the missions by surprise. In their opinion, Sonora's new governor, Diego Ortiz Parrilla, had made a mistake in naming Oacpicagigua captain-general of all the Pimas as a reward for help provided during the Seri revolt. The Jesuits thought that the governor had fostered hostility against them and also created false expectations among the Pimas, leading them to think, for example, that their territory would one day stretch as far as the Colorado River.

Abuses and exploitation by the Spanish population had generated a climate of discontent among the Pimas, and in the end, a revolt broke out, apparently in consequence of the humiliating treatment Luis de Sáric received from Father Keller. Some testimony at the trial held later indicated that Sáric was already planning a revolt before the Jesuit's action, and that the alleged humiliation was merely an excuse to justify the massacres committed. It is not easy to know the truth, but it does not seem in the witness statements that there was so much animosity between the two sides previously.

Testimony from individuals who had taken part in the repression of the rebels was also collected at the trial, including, for example, that of Gabriel Antonio Vildósola.[52] Vildósola and his young wife, Josefa Gregoria, Juan Bautista Anza I's daughter, were living on Santa Bárbara Ranch, but when the revolt broke out, they were at Sopori Ranch, owned by the Anza family. He was twenty-nine years old at the time, his wife was nineteen, and they had been married for almost five years.

Vildósola's first reaction when he learned of the attacks was to move his wife, who was pregnant. He took her to Basochuca, Sonora, and then, together with four other armed men—one of them his fifteen-year-old brother-in-law Juan Bautista Anza II—he went to San Ignacio, where the local militia was gathering.

Almost three years later, after reporting that the man responsible for the rebellion was Luis de Sáric, captain-general of all Pimería, Vildósola explained how the whole thing began:

> In his ranchería of Sáric on the afternoon of November twentieth, the actual day the uprising began because the Indians had already become restless because of what they planned to do that night. In order to conceal their scheme they set up a clamor that the Apaches were coming. Spreading the fear that the said Apaches were about to attack, they helped some ten people, all of whom were women and children, into the house that belonged to Luis, claiming that they would protect and defend them there. This is what Luis promised but did not do. Instead, upon leaving his house he locked those persons inside, even though one was his comadre (godmother of his child), the wife of one Laureano, and began his treachery by setting fire to his own house to burn inside of it (which, in effect, he did burn and incinerate) those innocent persons.[53]

The victims deceived and murdered in this way were two sisters-in-law, Inés Tisnado and Magdalena Contreras, and their nine children.

Following the massacre that began the revolt, Oacpicagigua attacked the Tubutama[54] mission and other Spanish settlements. The majority of the victims were killed in those first twenty-four hours, so that, according to Donald T. Garate, it cannot be said that the revolt was a national uprising by the Pimas. In addition, only a small number of Pimas took part in the rebellion. As we know, Indians and whites did not constitute two homogeneous blocks in these revolts. Indians often allied with Spaniards in order to oppose other Indian nations or take advantage of opportunities the Spaniards offered. In the 1751 revolt, many Pimas were already incorporated into the mission system and converted to the new religion and did not want to join the rebels. If more of them had participated in the rebellion, they would have murdered all the Spaniards, but the number of victims was around a hundred, not more. Their names are found in the mission registers. Some were Basques or of Basque heritage: José María Albizu, his wife María Candelaria, and their son Ignacio Antonio; Manuel Estevan de Amesquita ("soldier, steward") and his two children; Ignacio Amesquita ("corporal"); Juan Domingo Echeverría; Antonio Marcial Espoicucha (race/tribe: Bizkaian; Rivera's carpenter) . . .[55]

Bernardo Urrea, the owner of the Arizona Ranch that gave its name to the state of Arizona, as explained above, appears in the Mission 2000 database as a "creole Basque." Urrea was the first military officer to reach the site of the rebellion, in command of the Pimería Alta militias. Shortly thereafter, Juan Tomás de Beldarrain arrived from Sinaloa with some soldiers from his force. Captains of other presidios soon followed, all prepared for war. At the beginning, they found only abandoned settlements, since the rebels had fled to the mountains. It was already January when the two sides met face to face at Aravaca. Bernardo Urrea directed the battle and recorded the details in his diary.

According to Urrea, on January 2, 1752, the Spaniards sent three Indian messengers to speak with Don Luis Oacpicagigua. On the 4th, one of them returned with a Yaqui Indian named Joachin, who had participated in the rebellion. Asked about Don Luis's plans, Joachin replied that he was going to come to kill them with all his forces. It would be at moonrise or at dawn.

Upon learning of Joachin's confession, on the night of January 5, Urrea left twenty-three men to look after the horses, and with sixty-three others, he attacked the opposing force of over two thousand rebel warriors. Undoubtedly, Urrea exaggerated the enemy numbers in his diary. If there had really been that many Pimas, Urrea's men would not have all survived, as in fact happened. The soldiers wounded forty-three Pimas and captured one. The rest withdrew to a hill, marking the end of the first attack, at five-thirty in the morning, before the sun rose. The one prisoner pleaded with the whites not to kill him, throwing his weapons and his feather headdress to the ground.

The following day, Bernardo Urrea approached the hill with an aide and an interpreter who knew Pima. According to Urrea's own account:

> There, after Captain General Don Luis had come down the hill a short distance, we spoke with him and admonished him in the name of the Lord Governor to come down in peace, notwithstanding the fact that His Lordship had already pardoned him. To this the said Don Luis replied that he did not want to come down in peace. He was given to understand that one of the three [of us] was Don Bernardo de Urrea, godfather at the

confirmation of the said Don Luis and his wife. He responded that he did not want to come down in peace, that [Urrea] was a liar, and that he was not his godfather. [He said] that he wanted nothing more to do with the Tubutama River [Valley] that already had no Pimas to plant [its farmlands]. [He said] that we would see what there was to eat because already there are neither wheat, corn nor beans being cultivated. In anger he told us that we could do it if we were there. And, he called us mulatos, coyotes, and other indecent things, and then climbed back up to where his people were. In sight of him, we returned to our camp, where we met with all our officers and decided to move back to gain better ground and, at the same time, see if the enemy would follow us. After having marched about a half of a league we arrived at a pass that led into bad terrain with some hills that were incommodious for us but advantageous for the enemy to communicate with each other. When the rearguard, that had taken up their position at the hill where we were before, arrived at this pass, the [rebels] again fought us in a second battle. Notwithstanding the ruggedness of the aforementioned pass which caused a great impediment for managing our horses and arms, in light of which Captain General Don Luis came close to attack us on the road, we killed three of them. Among these was Cipriano, son of the referred to Captain General Don Luis and one of the chiefs of the said rebels. With these deaths they demonstrated immense sorrow, with crying and other signs of sadness, leaving behind at the said place seven horses with their blankets. These were ordered to be gathered into our caballada. Our camp attained complete victory, considering the fact that the enemy had not attained as much as the death of any one of us. Nor was there anything left in their power from our camp—not a hat, cloak, firearm, or any of the least of the things with which the enemy could derive a minimum of pleasure or comfort. In light of this we gathered the said officers together and conferred as to what was the most profitable [thing to do], considering that we had attained complete victory and broken the pride and haughtiness of the enemy. We returned to this village of San Ignacio, considering the fact that the caballada had been sorely mistreated and the said place is a long way from here. Indeed, it is more than fifty leagues distant from this village.[56]

On March 18, 1752, Oacpicagigua surrendered to the Capt. José Diaz del Carpio[57] at Tubac, offering himself as a sacrifice to keep his people from being punished for rebelling. He said that the Jesuits were the ones to blame for what had happened, because they took all the fruits of the earth for themselves, and that the majority of those who called themselves "people of reason"[58] abused the Indians. Governor Parrilla took his side and gave him permission to return home.

Other News from Pimería Alta, by Way of Capt. Juan Tomás Beldarrain and His Son

Although the Pimas had been defeated, the decision was made to build a presidio at Tubac, and the project was placed in the hands of Juan Tomás Beldarrain. Born in Durango, Bizkaia, in 1718, the son of Marcos de Beldarrain and Agustina de Zamalloa, Beldarrain was captain of the presidio of Sinaloa when the Pima rebellion took place, and as we have said, he was one of the first officers to arrive at the site of the massacre. By 1753, construction of the Tubac presidio had been completed, and it was the place of residence of Captain Beldarrain, his wife, and his two children. His wife was María Teresa Prudom Butrón y Mújica, the daughter of one of Sonora's first governors, Gabriel Prudom Butrón y Mújica.

The mission archives bear witness to the close ties Basques maintained with one another, and they also offer other interesting

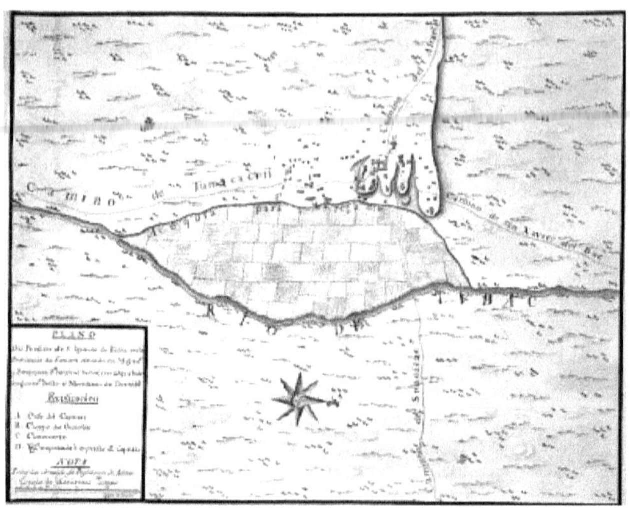

Map of the San Ignacio de Tubac. Tubac church (near Santa Cruz) and Tumacácori. Source: José de Urrutia, 1767. Courtesy British Library. http://www.nps.gov/.

Ruins of the Los Santos Ángeles de Guevavi Mission. Juan Tomás Belderrain was buried under the pillars of the altar. When Juan Bautista II's mother died, she was given a plot next to Belderrain. Photo: Steve Bass.

information, for example, the fact that Beldarrain was the owner of several Indian children. One of them, baptized as Xavier Beldarrain, was registered as follows: "Little Apache [*Apachito*] purchased by Capt. Juan Tomás de Beldarrain." In addition, Beldarrain owned three *nijoras*, a name apparently given to children of different tribes that the Yumas captured in order to sell them to the missionaries or the Spaniards. Some ended up as slaves, but there were also families that took them as paid servants or as adopted children, in order to educate them as Catholics.

From the observation post provided by the Tubac presidio, the Beldarrain-Prudom couple and their children were witnesses of the war that was part of life in those frontier territories. In 1753, a rumor spread that Oacpicagigua was preparing another rebellion. He was taken prisoner and subjected to interrogation, dying in early 1755 while a prisoner in Horcasitas. Pima and Seri attacks did not cease with their leader's death, however. In one such attack, a Seri arrow wounded Juan Tomás Beldarrain as he was fighting on Tiburón Island. It was not a very serious wound, but the Indians were in the habit of poisoning the points of their arrows, and Beldarrain died several weeks later at the Guevavi mission, where he was buried under the altar steps. After his death, command of the Tubac presidio passed to Juan Bautista Anza II, who brought his widowed mother, Doña María Rosa, to his new home. When she died a year later, she was buried alongside Beldarrain.

At the same time that the Spanish inhabitants of the frontier were growing increasingly discouraged, the Papagos, Piatos, Sobaipuris, and other tribes joined the attacks,[59] along with the Apaches. The Spaniards, for their part, stole the Indians' cattle or captured them to sell as slaves. Faced with this climate of violence, many people decided to leave.

Two or three decades later, in 1792, the viceroy, the count of Revillagigedo, asked one of the children of the Beldarrain-Prudom marriage, Luis María, to write a report summarizing the changes he had witnessed over the previous forty years. Beldarrain, who had only one hand—he had lost his left arm as the consequence of a rattlesnake bite—replied to the viceroy with a document that, according to the historian Kieran McCarty, is a unique source of information on the damage caused by the Apaches in the territory of what is now Arizona.[60]

Luis María de Beldarrain begins with the region around the source of the Santa Cruz River in Pimería Alta, specifically with the Indian town named Santa María Suamca. Together with its two satellite towns, Cocospera and Remedios, it had over two hundred families in 1759. When Beldarrain wrote his report, only Cocospera remained of the three settlements, with forty families. In 1769, the Apaches had attacked Santa María Suamca, killing the majority of the inhabitants and setting the church and all the houses on fire.

Continuing down the river, around a hundred Spanish colonists used to live on the estates and ranches of Los Divisaderos, Santa Bárbara, San Luis, El Ranchito, and Buenavista. These estates and ranches were prospering in 1750, but they were impoverished by repeated Apache attacks, and their inhabitants sought protection at the presidios of Terrenate and Tubac.

Further downstream, still following the river, was the Indian town of Guevavi and its three satellite towns, Calabazas, Tumacacori, and Sonoita, which had over three hundred families in 1750. In 1792, only two of the towns survived, with no more than fifty families between them. Sonoita was destroyed by the Apaches in 1768, and over half of its inhabitants were burned to death inside the church. This frightened the people of the area so much that, abandoning Guevavi, they clustered together in Tumacacori and Calabazas.

Luis María de Beldarrain ends his report with apologies for going on at such length, since his list does not end here, but continues on with the monotony of an inventory.

In the end, the indigenous people of the region were always divided into numerous different groups, and although they tried so many times and were fearsome warriors, they never succeeded in expelling the Spaniards from the northwest, nor the Americans later.

Fray Juan Sarobe Proposes to Dissuade the Seris, 1769

On August 5, 1767, all the members of the Santa Cruz missionary college in Querétaro, gathered in the chapel, sang the hymn *Tota pulchra es, Maria* to ask the Queen of Heaven's protection for their fourteen fellow friars who were about to leave for the Pimería Alta missions. They were to occupy the posts the Jesuits had been forced to abandon on Carlos III's orders, and there was no doubt that they would need protection in their new enterprise, since they were headed to northern New Spain, to the "land of active war." Reaching Tepic took them twenty-three days of travel. After waiting there five months, the fourteen Franciscans, accompanied by a group of missionaries headed to California, set sail from San Blas in January on the *San Carlos* and the *Lauretana*.

José de Gálvez, New Spain General Auditor. Source: Reba Grandrud

The sea voyage was far from easy, and the same was true of the two hundred leagues they had to traverse on land after that. It was the end of June when each friar reached his destination. The Franciscans had asked to assign two religious to each mission, but the request was denied, and they had to face the harsh life of that remote province of the empire alone.

One of those missions, Tecoripa, fell to a young friar, Juan Sarobe, who was a native of the village of Aduna in Gipuzkoa. According to records in the historical archive of the diocese of San Sebastián, he was the son of Peliphe Sarove and María Josepha Lizarraga and was baptized on April 11, 1742, in the Aduna parish church. An account by one of Sarobe's fellow Franciscans at Santa Cruz in Querétaro confirms his origins:

> Reverend Fr. Fray Juan de Sarobe, a native of Aduna, a small place in Bizkaia,[61] in the diocese of Pamplona, took the habit in the holy province of Cantabria, from which he came on mission to this college in the year 1763 at the blossoming age of twenty-two: a religious of great spirit, very observant, prudent, and a missionary with zeal for souls. This spirit took him to the Sonora missions in 1768, where in 1769 he gave evidence of both his courage and his apostolic zeal.[62]

First image of the Seri Tribe, by Jesuit missionary Adan Gilg at the Santa María del Pópulo mission, Sonora, 1692. Source: Julio Montané, 1996

CRONICA SERAFICA
Y APOSTOLICA
DEL COLEGIO
DE PROPAGANDA FIDE
DE LA SANTA CRUZ DE QUERETARO
EN LA NUEVA ESPAÑA,
DEDICADA
AL SANTISSIMO PATRIARCA
EL SEÑOR SAN JOSEPH
ESCRITA
SEGUNDA PARTE.
EN MEXICO:

Juan Sorobo's narrative

Juan Sarobe's Evidence of Courage When Faced with the Rebel Indians of Sonora

The same year Sarobe arrived in Tecoripa, 1768, Viceroy Teodoro de Croix, in view of the Seris' numerous attacks, gave strict orders to the visitor-general of New Spain, José de Gálvez, to go to their territory to reestablish peace and punish the rebels. Similar problems in Baja California forced Gálvez to remain there, however, and he was unable to travel to Sonora until the following year. In the meantime, he wrote to the Franciscan superior, Fr. Mariano Buena, asking him to communicate to the Indians his desire that they surrender peacefully. All those who gave up their hostile attitude would be pardoned, but those who remained obstinate in their rebelliousness would be punished.[63]

Mariano Buena attempted to convince the rebels to cease their attacks, but his efforts were in vain, and he arrived at Tecoripa in a despairing mood. At that point, when a military campaign against the Seris appeared inevitable, Juan Sarobe decided to meet with the rebels alone, to speak with them and try to "attract them to peace." All those at the mission tried to talk him out of the idea, due to the great risk it entailed, but Sarobe had made up his mind.

Not long afterward, the Franciscan Juan Domingo Arricivita recounted Sarobe's journey in his *Crónica seráfica y apostólica* (Seraphic and apostolic chronicle). The narrative shows the friar's courage and also clearly reflects the prejudices the "people of reason" held with regard to the Indians:

> Once Father Sarobe had read the proclamation, he judged that same day to be the most opportune time to go in search of the Indians and promise them that their lives would be pardoned on bond, for which he prepared himself with the greatest pleasure, but the officer who was his escort tried everything he could to convince the Father not to go, representing to him that the barbarians had no appreciation for the good, and still less for priestly rank, since they had killed a parish priest two months earlier. However, the Father replied that he was going to see whether he could liberate so many souls from hell, where they would irremediably go if they died in the hills, since in addition to being apostates, they had committed the greatest of sacrileges, homicides, and robberies, and that if they killed him, he would die for God. Even the mission Indians dissuaded the Father from his intention, because everyone expected that he could not succeed, due to the evil influences that made those who had risen up obstinate in their rebelliousness.
>
> The missionary's heart was animated by another, nobler, and more generous spirit, however, and with no more company that the crucifix he wore on his breast and an image of Our Lady of Guadalupe, with no more baggage than his breviary, with no more provisions than a little *pinole*[64] and dried meat, he took two Indians from Tecoripa and two from Suaqui as guides and interpreters, and on the 13th day of May in the year sixty-nine, he intrepidly began his journey on foot. Walking west and south, they arrived around ten in the morning on the 15th at a very steep box canyon at Cerro Verde, where the Father remained beside the stream with one Indian to pray the divine office and sent the other three to explore the land from above,

and if they found any Indians, to tell them that he was waiting for them, and if they did not want to come and see him, to tell them that he was going to discuss with them matters that were very important for their own welfare. The Father had scarcely finished praying when the three Indians came down, saying that the rebels had their ranchería on top of the hill and that although they had given them the message from a distance, they had not believed them; but that one Ignacio Tuaspa, the brother-in-law of one of the messengers, who had been a fugitive from the mission for the last year, had believed them; and that they would undoubtedly come down to where the Father was. This was news very pleasing to his heart, and more so when he saw that many were already coming down the hill with their weapons in their hands and even with arrows notched. Only Ignacio put down his weapons before reaching the Father and venerated the image of Our Lady, which he had taken out and hung from a tree.

Little by little, others arrived, without putting down their weapons, and when the Father saw that there were already thirty-two women, one of them a captive, and Ignacio's wife, he offered them the *pinole* and dried meat he had brought. As the majority of them accepted the gift, he gently persuaded them to leave that miserable life, with which they were irremediably on their way to hell, and that if they came down, they would receive many spiritual and corporal benefits, promising them that they would not be harmed or punished by the Spaniards, and although he saw that they were listening attentively, since many of them understood Spanish, he still had the interpreter repeat to them what he had said in their language, with the result that the Father came to believe that they were all convinced and resolved to come down with him. Seeing this very favorable effect, he asked them where the Seris and Piatos were, since all those who had come down were Suaquis and Pimas Bajos, and he wanted them to take him where they were, because he loved them greatly also and wanted to give them good advice. However, they replied that he should do no such thing, because they would undoubtedly tear him to pieces, but should instead write whatever he wanted on a piece of paper, as there would be someone who knew how to read among them, and he would be able to obtain what he wanted without risk. The Father accepted the advice, since he had brought the necessary supplies, but at the moment of writing, one of them suddenly grabbed his arm, and when the Father asked him in the name of the Lord whose

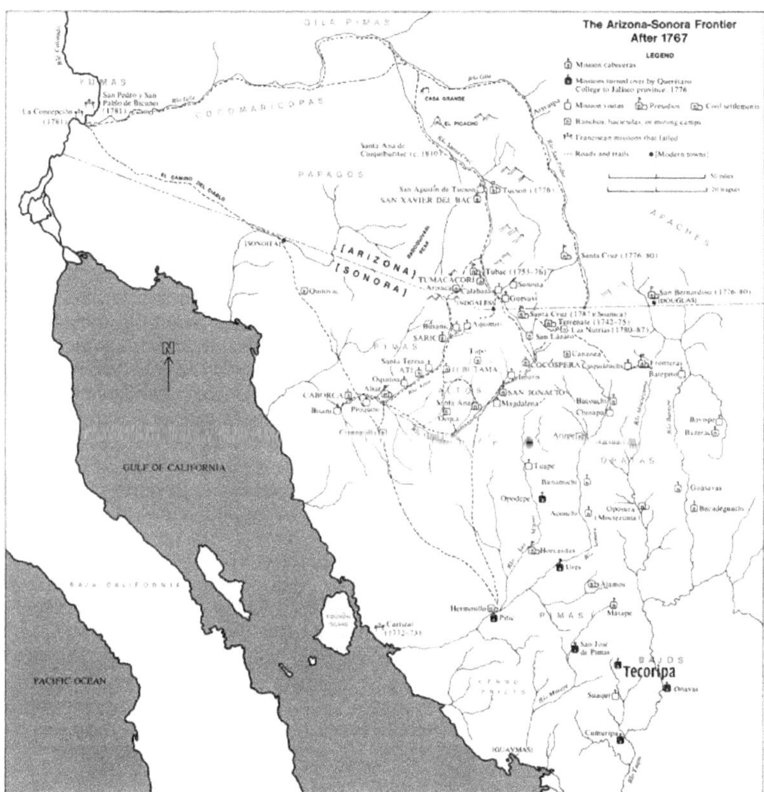

In the bottom right Juan Sarobe's mission, Tecoripa

image he wore on his breast to release him, he replied, clearly enunciating the words, "Here you are to die, you trickster." When the Father heard this, he collected himself interiorly to commend his soul to God and ask His mercy on that of the unhappy wretch who was oppressing him.

Holding on to the Father, that unfortunate asked three or four others of his party for help to hang him from a wild fig tree, in the shadow of which they were, and shoot him with arrows until he died. At that point, the Indian Ignacio picked up his weapons and, notching an arrow, asked those of his party to help him defend the Father and threaten those who wanted to take his life, placing himself at his side together with one of those who had gone with the Father, although unarmed, since the other three had already fled. The one who had grabbed hold of the Father and Ignacio argued for some time, while the Father sat on the ground without making any resistance, occupied only in sacrificing his life to God. When that bloodthirsty wolf saw that no one was helping him, he released the Father and seized his arrows, but at the same time that he bent his bow to shoot the Father, Ignacio bent his bow to shoot him. This stopped him, but he soon returned to his intent, and Ignacio repeated his, repeating as many as four times his aiming at the Father and Ignacio aiming at him. For this reason one of those of his party wrapped his arms around him, without anyone else trying to do the Father harm; only one old pagan was readying his arrows. He spoke to Ignacio, who said, "Father, let's leave." Getting up from the ground, the Father charged the mission Indian to collect his breviary and the image of Our Lady and began to leave the box canyon, accompanied only by Ignacio.

Halfway down the box canyon, they heard voices from the direction they were coming from, and although the Father did not understand them, he inferred that they were warning Ignacio that the man who wanted to take his life was coming after them. So it proved, because soon after they had left the stream, the one who had had his arms around him hurried so fast to follow them that when the Father left the box canyon, he saw him already at the side of the path and aiming at him, for which reason he broke into a run. Ignacio was unable to shoot him with an arrow, since they were within arm's length, and they were fighting hand-to-hand when the other Indian who was to bring the breviary arrived. He had already been wounded by a member of this bold and obstinate rebel's party, and he had also been unable to bring out either the breviary or the image, whether because he did not dare to collect them or because they did not permit him to do so. He did not see the Father again, however, and neither did Ignacio, because while Ignacio was struggling with the rebel, he got well away, and fearing that they would catch up with him, he headed for a low mountain where he hid until night, although with great alarms, since he heard the noise of those who were searching for him along the two paths that were on either side. He also heard from there a great deal of shouting at the stream he had come from, but he did not see anyone. There was a moon that night, and he simply walked, without a hat or any other protection than his habit, until dawn, when he could sleep a little.

The following day, he continued along what seemed to him the shortest route to his mission, among mountains and hills. Upon descending a thickly wooded hill around ten in the morning, he heard Indian cries and the sound of horses, which served only to renew his sacrifice, since he did not see anyone, and

> perceiving that the sound was heading in a different direction than the one in which he was going, he continued on his way. The next day, his journey was intolerable for him, due to the thirst that afflicted him, but in the afternoon, Providence supplied him with a stream where he could slake his mortal anguish. The day after, he walked the entire day on wide and well-trodden paths without knowing where he was going, but seeing that he was much wearied by hunger, he did not want to stop. He did the same the following day, because he said, "If the Lord gives me strength to walk, the end of the road will be some settlement; and if it is His most holy will that the violence of necessity puts an end to my life, it will be feasible for them to find my body quickly." With this conformity and resignation to the divine will, he was walking with a sense of consolation, when he suddenly encountered a horse that was dragging a halter. Although he wanted to catch it, he lacked the strength to do so, and little by little he continued on his way, not without hope of encountering someone, and so it happened that no very great distance away, he saw two men who were following the horse's tracks. Both rejoiced very much to have found him, and one of them very charitably put him on his own horse, since the Father no longer had the strength to mount on his own, and quickly brought him to Suaqui, where they gave him a little *atole de pinole*,[65] for lack of any other food, and from there to Tecoripa, which was the mission he administered, as everyone marveled at how he had survived without having taken any food from the 15th, when he ate the *pinole* and dried meat with the Indians, and having drunk water only once, until the 19th, when he arrived worn out by such a long and painful journey, with the anxiety of having the Indians searching for him, with no familiarity with the lands in which he was, and with no more guidance in finding his way out of such a furious tempest than the divine will.[66]

Juan Sarobe Lizarraga continued working with the Sonora Indians, risking his life on more than one occasion. Eventually, he returned to the Santa Cruz missionary college in Querétaro, where he served as counselor (*discreto*) and vicar. In 1787, he traveled to Spain in search of new missionaries. In 1790, after successfully recruiting twenty-two new missionaries, he embarked in Cádiz on the frigate *San Juan Nepomuceno*, alias "El Dragón," headed for Veracruz. He was forty-eight years old and ill, and the ocean voyage made his condition worse. He died while crossing the Gulf of Campeche and was buried at sea.

Col. Domingo Elizondo's Campaign against the Seris and Pimas of Cerro Prieto, 1767–1771

Sonora remained a land of active war for a long time. The situation was a frustrating one for the Spanish authorities, since with so many enemy towns, it was impossible to advance northward and conquer new lands. To the contrary, it was feared that instead of advancing toward Alta California, the frontier would recede toward Mexico.

In these circumstances, in 1764 the king asked Viceroy Teodoro de Croix to impose peace in Sonora and Sinaloa. Meetings were held in Mexico, and the decision was made to organize a military expedition. The campaign was promoted and organized by José de Gálvez with the support of Julián de Arriaga, minister of the Indies. Domingo Elizondo, the colonel of Spain's regiment of dragoons, was placed in charge of carrying it out.

The campaign's first objective was to obtain the submission of the coastal Indians, that is, the Seris, Pimas, and Sibubapas. After that, the expedition was to dedicate itself to "pacifying" all the frontier provinces in order to put an end to Apache attacks once and for all. It was an ambitious plan, and the military resources brought to bear were also ambitious, the largest force ever assembled. Elizondo had eleven hundred men under his command, including a company made up of a hundred Catalan volunteers.

From the moment that news of the expedition spread, the white population—colonists, religious, and soldiers—were in a state of anticipation. They were still waiting when one of these groups was withdrawn from the scene: the Jesuits were expelled from Spanish territory in 1767. Consequently, the conflicts between religious and laity that divided Sonora disappeared for a period of time, and there were no more revolts by Christianized Indians.

Elizondo's campaign was to have lasted a few months, but it stretched to more than three years due to the resistance mounted by the Seris and their allies. Domingo Elizondo (Pamplona, 1712–Madrid, 1783) was an experienced soldier, but he was newly arrived from Europe, and the terrain—"a labyrinth of hills, ravines, and precipices"[67]—and the Indians' way of fighting were strange to him. Knowing that the enemy was gathering at a place called Cerro Prieto, the army headed there in three divisions commanded by Elizondo, Bernardo de Urrea, and a soldier by the name of Cancio. They wanted to force the Indians to gather in a particular location in order to then massacre them all there, but they did no more than journey deeper and deeper

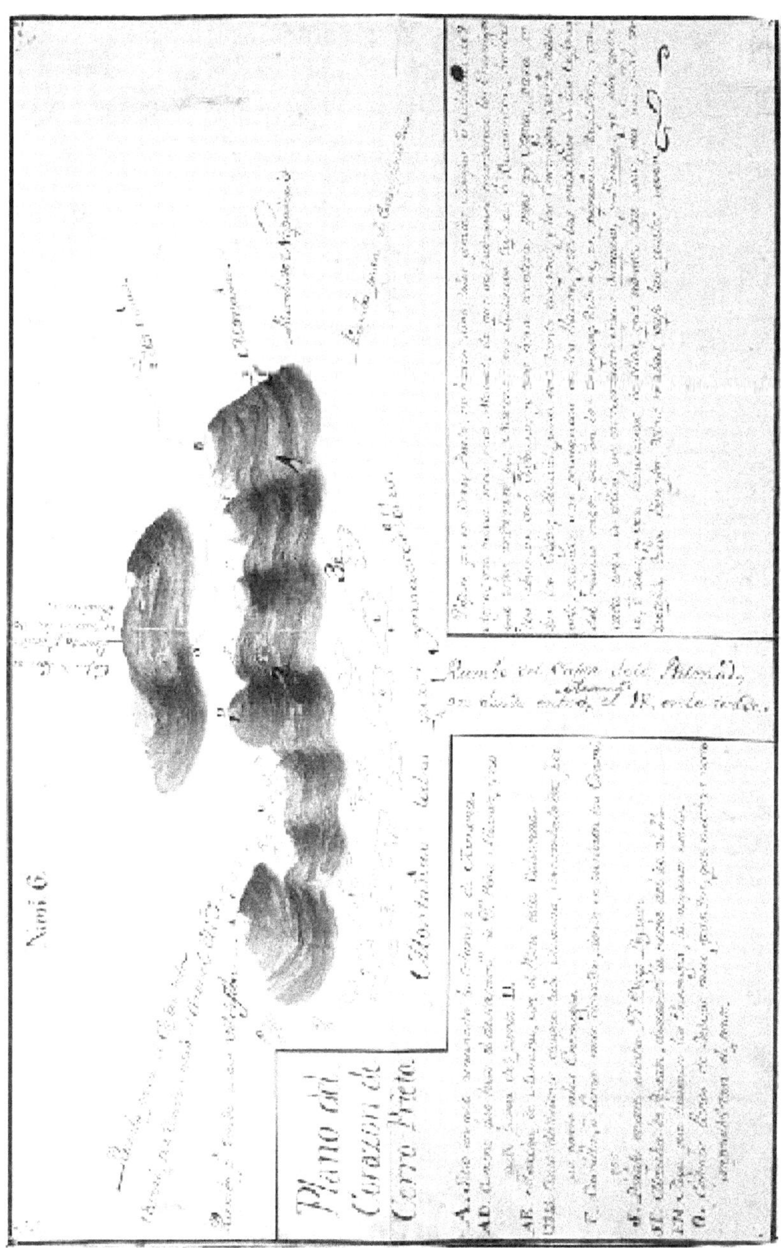

«Mapa que demuestra el ataque que se hizo al corazon del Cerro Prieto en la Sonora». (Archivo General de Indias. AGI, MP-MEXICO, 252)

into the desert, until the horses were worn out and they had to return. The Indians had learned that the best way to fight the Spaniards was to attack and then flee, and they avoided confronting large groups.

Elizondo narrated the events of those three years in a chronicle titled *Noticia de la expedición militar contra los rebeldes Seris y Pimas del Cerro Prieto, Sonora, 1767–1771 (Notice of the military expedition against the Seri and Pima rebels of Cerro Prieto, Sonora, 1767–1771)*. As the reader progresses through the text, the soldier's change in attitude, to the point of expressing his admiration for the enemy's military tactics, becomes increasingly evident:

> a little more than half a league's march on, in a narrow part of the box canyon, the enemies had taken up their position in a most warlike manner: on the right, favored by the woods; on the left, by a small hill; and in the center, where the path was, by some loose boulders, so that they could scarcely be perceived.

Otherwise, that campaign had little about it to admire. There was never a clear victory, but by dint of harassing the enemy, a surrender was finally obtained. By that point, Elizondo was familiar with the Indians' motives and had overcome many of his initial prejudices. His *Noticia* concludes with this advice:

> In order to preserve the tranquility and fidelity of those who have surrendered, no other means is understood to be necessary than that of making no innovation in the established institutions that might cause innovation in the Indians' spirits and treating them with love and sweetness, governing them with prudence and uprooting that treatment of slavery with which they have been administered, the motive on account of which many became exasperated and caused the uprisings that have just been extinguished, by dint of labor and considerable expense for the royal treasury.

At the end of the campaign, in 1771, a detachment of Elizondo's forces that was pursuing a group of Piatos in the area around Altar discovered the rich gold fields of Cieneguilla. Hundreds of people soon arrived at the site, facilitating the occupation and governance of the territory.

Elizondo's campaign had cost more energy and more money than had been foreseen, and the plan to subject the Apaches was left in abeyance. As far as Elizondo himself was concerned, he was named governor of Acapulco. From there, he asked the king for license to return to his homeland and visit his family.[68] In 1774, the king granted him two years' leave, but Elizondo was unable to make use of it until 1779. In the intervening years, specifically in 1776, the General Commandancy of the Northern Interior Provinces (*Comandancia General de las Provincias Internas del Norte*) was established in New Spain with the objective of confronting the numerous attacks by indigenous peoples of the region and halting the advance of other European powers. It included Nueva Vizcaya, Santa Fe de Nuevo México, Nuevo León, Coahuila, Sonora, Sinaloa, both Californias, and Texas, and its general headquarters was at Arizpe, Sonora.

Elizondo, once home, asked leave to stay there an additional year due to health problems. He died at the age of seventy-one as he was completing his preparations to return to the Americas. During those last two years of his life, he surely asked himself more than once how things were going in that remote part of the Spanish empire. Perhaps he learned that attacks by the majority of Indian nations were coming ever less frequently, but that the Apaches remained a threat for those who dared to head northwest, from Tubac to Gila and from there to Colorado.

Juan Bautista Anza II Opens a Route between Sonora and Alta California and Lays the Foundation for the Colonization of San Francisco, 1774–1776

In 1772, after Colonel Elizondo's campaign against the Seris and Pimas was over, Juan Bautista Anza II requested authorization to try to open a route between Sonora and Monterrey. It was a plan he had inherited from his father. As we saw earlier, Juan Bautista Anza I was struck down by Apache arrows before he was able to carry it out. His son sought permission for the first time in 1769, but Visitor-General José de Gálvez did not grant it, since the expedition would have to cross the "land of active war." At that time, in addition, another expedition was about to leave for Alta California, and Gálvez's attention was focused on that one.

The attempt with which Gálvez was concerned was to be made by both land and sea. One group, under the command of Gaspar de Portolà, set sail from the port of San Blas, and at the same time, two other groups set out by land; one of the latter included Junípero Serra, the Franciscan from Mallorca. After overcoming multiple obstacles, the three groups finally succeeded in laying the foundation for the colonization of Alta California. Serra founded the first mission, that of San

Diego de Alcalá, and Portolà, for his part, founded the San Diego presidio in 1769 and the Monterrey presidio in 1770.

In 1772, with the cities of San Diego and Monterrey now settled, Juan Bautista Anza II once again offered to open an inland route to both cities from Sonora. A reply took time to come, and in the meantime, Junípero Serra retraced his steps all the way back to Mexico with his proposals to improve California's situation. He found a receptive audience in Antonio María de Bucareli y Ursúa, one of the best and most decisive administrators New Spain ever had.[69]

Juan Bautista Anza II's signature. Courtesy of US National Park Service

Serra had turned to Bucareli in search of a resolution to the tensions between civil and religious authorities. In order to alleviate those tensions, in his opinion, it was necessary to remove California's governor, Pedro Fagés. Asked about Anza's plans, Serra showed himself in favor, arguing that if the Alta California settlements were to last, it was indispensable to open a route between Sonora and Monterrey. Baja California was too poor to provide aid to the new settlements, and the route of three hundred leagues from Loreto to San Diego was too long and difficult. As far as the sea voyage was concerned, it too was far from easy. In addition, the ships at San Blas were too small to transport entire families, so that all the Spanish settlers at San Diego and Monterrey were single men, making it more difficult to establish a stable population. If Anza succeeded in opening a route between Sonora and Alta California, this would make it easier for entire families to travel from Sonora, bringing with them grain and fruit of all kinds. Even if only in order to ensure the viability of the new settlements, supporting Anza's plan would be worth it.

There were other weighty reasons that contributed to the decision in favor of the expedition. Recent foreign aggressions in the Pacific made the need to ensure a Spanish presence more urgent. At the same time, the authorities took into account the opinion of the Franciscan Francisco Garcés (Morata de Jalón, Zaragoza, 1738 – mission of San Pedro y San Pablo del Tubutama, 1781), who had explored the area around the Gila and Colorado rivers on his own, with no more baggage than what his horse could carry. Garcés knew the paths and had lived with the Yumas of the region, and he affirmed that they were peaceful.

Bucareli continued gathering opinions and advice. He also studied the plan Anza's father had proposed years before with the same objective. Finally, the younger Anza obtained authorization to undertake the expedition that would become a true turning point in California history.

Juan Bautista Anza II's Exploratory Expedition, 1774

Juan Bautista Anza II was a three-year-old child when the Apaches put an end to his father's life; now, when he returns to our stage, he is an experienced soldier, captain of the Tubac presidio. He was born in 1735, and little is known about his first years, save that, upon his father's death, the family moved from Fronteras to Divisadero Ranch, south of Guevavi, near the location where the senior Anza was killed. We have more details, on the other hand, about the son's early adulthood, thanks to a report he himself signed in 1767, at the age of thirty-two. By that time, he already had twelve years of military service behind him, the last eight as captain. Anza says in his report that he began his military career at the Fronteras presidio and participated in five campaigns against the Apaches under the command of Capt. Gabriel de Vildósola. He was assigned the hardest and most dangerous tasks among the company, who killed forty Indians and captured more than two hundred. In the last campaign, he had to lead a detachment of soldiers and Indian allies to take a stronghold in the Chiricahua mountains defended by 180 Indians. There, he succeeded in recovering six head of cattle the Indians had previously stolen, and when the Apaches tried to prevent him from recovering the rest, Anza single-handedly captured the Indian captain. In two other campaigns, Anza killed 39 Apaches in various skirmishes and captured another 114, in addition to recovering five hundred head of cattle stolen in various parts of the province.[70]

The young Anza also participated in five campaigns against the Seris. In 1760, he crushed a revolt by more than a thousand Papagos. In the same year, he was sent to the Seri frontier five times. He killed thirty Seris in 1762 and took numerous members of their families captive, Anza reports in his curriculum vitae. Consequently, the young soldier was perfectly familiar with the trails, settlements, water sources, and pastures of the empire's northern border. Likewise, he knew the enemy's battle tactics better than anyone. He was, without doubt, the right man to lead the expedition that was to cross that region.

Once authorization had been obtained, preparations were rapidly made. When the expedition was about to set out, however, the Apaches stole 130 horses from the presidio. This delayed the departure, but it was ultimately for the best, because while new horses were being sought, an Indian who had recently arrived from Alta California was brought to Anza. His name was Sebastián Tarabal, and after deserting from the San Gabriel mission, he had succeede in reaching the Colorado River by traveling through the desert. He was the guide the expedition needed, and his arrival struck Anza as providential.

The expedition left Tubac on January 8, 1774. Anza was accompanied by twenty soldiers who had volunteered for the mission, another Mexican soldier who knew the California territory, the mentioned Sebastián Tarabal, a Pima interpreter, a carpenter who was a native of the Tubac presidio, five mule-drivers, and two servants of Anza's. Spiritual matters would be the responsibility of two Franciscan missionaries from Santa Cruz in Querétaro: the intrepid explorer Garcés and another friar named Juan Díaz. Rounding out the caravan were 140 horses and sixty-five cows. The group also brought with them "other things necessary for an unknown country," as Anza explains in his diary.[71]

In their first days of travel, they encountered abundant traces of Apache violence, what Anza called in his diary "the plague of Apaches." They were not attacked, however, but rather welcomed by Indians who offered them friendship as they crossed Papago territory. On February 7, after nearly a month on the road, they reached the banks of the Gila River, at which point over two hundred Indians were following the group:

> all of them overjoyed at our coming, which they celebrated with cheers and smiles, at the same time throwing up fistfuls of earth into the air and with other demonstrations expressing the greatest guilelessness and friendship.

When the expedition stopped at a location where there was good pasture, many natives of both sexes appeared. The closer they came to the strangers and the more they got a good look at their appearance, their clothes, and their gear, the more they marveled.

They were Indians of the Yuma nation.[72] At five in the afternoon, their chief appeared, Olleyquotequiebe, whom the Spaniards named Salvador Palma. He dismounted from his horse and asked Anza in a friendly way to embrace him, which Anza did "[w]ith every sign of affection." Subsequently, Olleyquotequiebe requested that

> I must let them look at me and touch my belongings without being offended, for they wished it, especially those who never had seen us, who were the majority, so that they might know what we were like and what things we dressed in and used were for.

Anza offered special gifts to Chief Palma, Olleyquotequiebe: a brightly-colored ribbon and a necklace made with coins that showed the king's image.

Thanks to the Indians' help, the expedition crossed the Gila and Colorado rivers fairly easily. It was Father Garcés who had the most anxious time of it: "I crossed the Colorado River in the arms of Indians, because I did not trust the horse."[73]

Anza included in his diary details about the Yumas' appearance and customs:

> The people in general are very robust and more than eight palms tall. Their temperament is the best to be found among Indians, for they are very festive, affectionate, and generous. Their color is not as dark as that of other tribes and they are less painted than some. They have naturally good features, but they make themselves ferocious by painting all the body and especially the face.
>
> The men go entirely naked, without the least sign of shame for their manhood, and to go partly covered they consider womanish, as they themselves have told us. They have good heads of hair, which they do up in many and diverse ways, with very fine mud, upon which they scatter a powder of such bright luster that it looks like silver. In order not to disturb this coiffure they sleep sitting up. It has already been said that the men paint their faces excessively with black and red colors, and this applies also to the women. The men have their ears perforated with at least three holes, five being the most common, and in all of them they wear earrings. They also perforate the nose, or its cartilage, and through it thrust a cluster of feathers, or more commonly a sprig of palm as long and thicker than the largest bird's quill, wherewith they succeed in making themselves not only ferocious but horrible.
>
> To arms and warfare they appear to be little inclined . . . At the first touch of cold in the morning or in the afternoon, those armed with bows and arrows generally lay them down wherever they happen to be, and take a firebrand which they generally put in front of their stomachs or behind their backs to warm themselves. The reason why they sleep only three hours out of the twenty-four in a day is the slender shelter they have, especially when they are outside of their rancherías, for in the rancherías they at least have their little huts in the soft earth, into which they crawl and assemble all that make up a family. Their language is easy to pronounce, and it seems to me that it would be easy to write. They pronounce Castilian as plainly as we do.
>
> The women . . . go clothed or half covered only from the waist to the thighs or knees, with little skirts which they make

> from the inner bark of the willow and the cottonwood, divided in two pieces, wearing the shortest in front. From the same kind of bark and from that of the mesquite they make some wide fabrics which, although they are more closely woven, are nearly as coarse as the cloth which in the kingdom we call guangoche bruto. These fabrics they have for clothing, and the women who wear them might be called rich, and much more so those who acquire pieces of skins of beaver, hare, and other fur-bearing animals. Both men and women go entirely barefooted.
>
> From those I have seen and from what I have heard of the rest I judge that there must be 3,500 people in the Yuma tribe, and this is the estimate given me by Father Garcés, who before now has observed these villages more at leisure. The number will not be much more or less than this estimate.

Both Anza and Father Garcés speak well of the Yumas in their respective diaries. Their way of life was fairly advanced: they had many horses, which they obtained in Sonora, and they cultivated corn, wheat, beans, squash, and melons in their fertile fields. In addition, they were so sweet in character that Anza had no doubt that the Spaniards would have no problems crossing their lands, at least while Olleyquotequiebe, Chief Palma, lived. As a show of trust, they decided to leave some cows and the most fatigued of the pack animals there until their return, as well as a few soldiers.

Nevertheless, Fr. Juan Díaz shows himself in his diary to have been less trusting. Díaz comments that, given the people's fickle character, it would not be easy to traverse their territory, since without their collaboration, it would be impossible to cross the rivers. If the Yumas refused their help or offered opposition, a large army would be needed to subdue so numerous a nation . . . Unwittingly, Díaz was announcing the revolt of 1781.

After helping Anza's group to cross the Colorado River, the Indians guided them to Santa Olaya Lake, at the edge of the great sand dunes of the Colorado desert. From that point on, the Indian Tarabal and Father Garcés, who had been there three years earlier, would be their guides. They mistook their way, however, and for fifteen days, the group wandered with no fixed direction until they reached some high mountains of sand, where the exhausted horses refused to go on. They tried to return to Santa Olaya, but windstorms had erased all the paths. Finally, they managed to reach the lake, where they rested for fifteen days, so that men and animals could recover their strength. Each day, the Yumas and their allies arrived by the hundreds to visit them, and Garcés and Diaz did all they could to convert their guests, while meanwhile, according to Bolton, "the soldiers, who had a fiddler among them, held nightly dances with the Indian girls, there on the rim of the desert, defying its menace with their jollity."[74]

Subsequently, Anza headed southwest, down the Colorado River, in search of a route that would skirt the desert's southern edge. The expedition found water and pasture north of the Cocopa mountains, and from there they turned northwest, looking for a pass that would enable them to cross the Sierra Nevada mountains. They continually encountered new Indian nations, all of them peaceful and some of them very timid and wary, including, for example, those the Spaniards called the Serrano Indians, the "mountain" Indians in Spanish, whom the people who lived along the Colorado River called the Jahueches, Caguenches, or Ajagueches. Anza described them in his diary entry for March 10:

> They say that they are as numerous as the Yumas. They live ordinarily in the mountains, subsisting on the mescal which abounds, and on seeds, supplemented by some deer hunting. They have no crops and no opportunity to plant them, for lack of water and lands. They are a naked people. They are of ordinary height, like those farther back, but less robust. With regard to the rest of their bodies they are like the people of the Colorado River. They are superior to these in the greater abundance of bows and arrows, although of the worst kind and construction, whereby they are seen to be equal. In spirit they appear to be more cowardly than the Yumas. They possess no horses, and they are so afraid of the Yumas that they are terrified even when they hear a horse whinny. They wear their hair short without adornment. In color they are petty black and their features are ugly.
>
> Their language is related somewhat to the Yuma tongue; indeed, I noticed that they understand each other to some extent, although the language of these people of whom I am speaking is very rapid and extremely explosive. Their settlements extend from the mountains which begin at the place where the Colorado River empties into the Gulf of California and run from south to north beyond the place where we are.

Anza advised these mountain Indians and all those he would encounter on his journey to live in peace, without waging war against Indians of other nations. As far as Garcés was concerned, he forgot for a moment his enthusiasm for exploration and let himself be carried away by missionary fervor: "Oh, what a vast heathendom! Oh! what lands so suitable for missions! Oh! what a heathendom so docile!"

On March 14, by which time the expedition had journeyed 221 leagues since setting out from Tubac, they arrived at "a spring or fountain of the finest water, which runs for about two leagues, having many willows most of the way," which they named Santa Catharina. The Indians of the area were unfamiliar to Anza—"What tribe this may be I cannot say with certainty"—and seemed to him much weaker in both body and character: "in stature and condition they are very timid, and are much more cowardly." They were unarmed, and out of more than a hundred who approached the Spaniards, only one had a arrow, but without a bow. In Anza's words:

> Each one carried a crooked stick something like a sickle, which serves them to hunt hares and rabbits. They throw it from a long distance, and I am informed by the soldiers who saw them hunt, that not one of these animals at which the heathen threw these sticks was missed. These poor people remained with us until they heard a horse whinny, after which they stayed until after nightfall on the hills a long distance from our camp.

San Gabriel Arcángel Mission. It is the oldest image of the California mission. By Ferdinand Deppe, 1832.

The following day's travel was historic: for the first time, white men dared to cross the great Sierra Nevada. As they journeyed upstream along the San Felipe River, they found along their path piles of huge rocks and stones of all sizes, as if they had been gathered from all around the world and placed there. Continuing upward, they were met by groups of hungry Indians who lived among the rocks and caves as if in rabbit warrens. They left the desert behind, and on the third day, they reached a pass they named Real de San Carlos. From that point on, the landscape offered ever more beautiful vistas, and Anza thought it a good location for agriculture, for planting fruit trees, and for livestock. The group encountered more than two hundred pagan natives, tremendously timid:

> It was laughable to see them when they approached us, because before doing so they delivered a very long harangue in a tone as excited as were the movements of their feet and hands. For this reason they were called the Dancers.

On March 22, the expedition finally reached the San Gabriel mission, having travelled 268 leagues since leaving Tubac. The four Franciscan friars who were there welcomed the group with surprise and joy, ringing the bells and singing a *Te Deum*. Between their tears, unable to believe that a feasible route between Sonora and Alta California existed, they could not stop asking questions of the members of the expedition.

In the end, the bells and hymns ceased resounding, and the mission's real situation became evident. Founded in 1771, San Gabriel was the fourth Franciscan mission, and like the rest, it managed to survive thanks to the provisions that arrived from the port of San Blas. A delayed ship, as was the case on that occasion, meant hunger. Father Garcés described the mission's condition in his diary:

> We found the mission in extreme poverty, as is true of all the rest. The day when we arrived our provisions for the soldiers gave out, putting us in great need because of the scarcity here, and the account would be more melancholy if the news had not come that the frigate La Galicia had put in at San Diego. The missionary fathers were delighted at our arrival, and they succored us with what little they had. We were sorry on both sides, the fathers at having so little to give, either of animals or of provisions, and we at having brought nothing to relieve them of their want.

Anza set out for Monterrey with a handful of men, and after spending three days there, returned to San Gabriel, where he had the opportunity to speak with Fray Junípero Serra. The Franciscan had just returned from Mexico, accompanied bythe Bizkaian priest Fr. Pablo José de Mugártegui. The trip had been a profitable one, since Viceroy Bucareli y Ursúa had accepted the majority of his proposals for the correct administration of California: Governor Fagés had been removed from his post, and the port of San Blas would continue supplying the Alta California missions, of which there were then five: San Diego de Alcalá, San Carlos Borromeo, San Antonio de Padua, San Gabriel Arcángel, and San Luis Obispo de Tolosa.

In Mexico, Bucareli ordered Juan José Echeveste y Arrieta,[75] treasurer of Alta California, to draw up a set of regulations specific to California. Echeveste composed what are known as the "Provisional Regulations" (*Reglamento Provisional*) or "Echeveste's Regulations" (*Reglamento de Echeveste*), California's first law code, which became an indispensable instrument for its colonization. With regard to the Indians, it established that the friars should behave toward them as fathers who love and educate their children.[76]

Without staying long at San Gabriel, Anza set out on his return trip. Six soldiers from Monterrey joined his group in order to learn the route as far as the Colorado River. When they arrived there, they discovered that the Yumas, who had shown themselves so friendly on their first visit, had tried to steal the cattle they had left there. There was also some aggression against the soldiers from Monterrey. However, all this appeared trifling in comparison to what had been achieved, and Anza headed to Mexico to give the viceroy a detailed account of the expedition's success.

Although Garcés and Anza had their ups and downs, the friar ended his diary by acknowledging the captain's merits. "The expedition has been made without molesting or vexing the Indians," he wrote on April 26, adding that this was possible thanks to "the good conduct which the commander has shown, bearing with the Indians, disciplining the soldiers gently, and respecting and sustaining the fathers."

There was, then, no molestation or vexation of the Indians, but although the expedition's members could not have suspected it, they had sowed the seeds of an evil that would have tremendous consequences. Some twenty-five years later, at that same mission of San Gabriel, the Bizkaian priest José Maria Zalvidea and his compatriot José de Miguel had more than they could do to attend to and console all who were sick. In a letter, Zalvidea gave his opinion about the origin of the illness:

> At the mission, the Indians have recently been attacked by a putrid and contagious illness. It showed itself for the first time after Don J. B. Anza's expedition stayed at San Gabriel, and with the passage of time, it has spread among the Indians to such an extent that when a child is born, it already carries the evil.[77]

The illness that Zalvidea avoids naming in his letter has been referred to in many ways: the French disease, *grosse vérole*, the Neapolitan disease, the Spanish itch, the measles of the Indies, and so on. Today, it is most commonly called syphilis, and it is known to have been one of the principal reasons for the dramatic decline in the indigenous population.

Juan Bautista Anza's Colonizing Expedition, 1775–1776

> Mass having been chanted with all the solemnity possible on the Sunday preceding for the purpose of invoking the divine aid in this expedition, all its members being present; and the Most Holy Virgin of Guadalupe, under the advocation of her Immaculate Conception, the Prince Señor San Miguel, and San Francisco de Assís having been named as its protectors, at eleven today the march was begun toward the north.[78]

With these words, Juan Bautista Anza II begins the diary that records the details of his colonizing expedition. On October 22, 1775, a solemn sung mass was celebrated. The day before, Fray Pedro de Arriquibar,[79] had arrived from Tumacácori, spending the day in Tubac with those who were about to depart. On the 23rd, at eleven o'clock in the morning, Anza shouted, "Everybody mount!"—words that would serve as the daily signal to move out—and the large group set out: the chaplain, Pedro Font, and two Franciscan missionaries, Francisco Garcés and Tomás Eixarch, who were to remain in the Colorado River region; Lt. José Joaquín Moraga,[80] the only soldier traveling without his wife, who was sick; Sgt. Juan Pablo Grijalva; ten escort soldiers; twenty-eight colonist soldiers; "[t]wenty-nine women, wives of the soldiers" (at least five of them expecting); 136 family members and civilian colonists; fifteen muleteers; three cowboys; five interpreters ("of the Pima, Yuma, Cajuenchi, and Nifora languages"); three servants of the missionaries; four servants of Anza's; and a quartermaster. Rounding out the caravan were around a thousand head of cattle, horses, cows, and mules, in addition to "baggage of all persons going, and other effects of the expedition, and presents brought in the name of his Majesty for the heathen on the way." The expedition did not have covered carts, and the muleteers had to load the mules in the morning and unload them in the evening. Guiding all those people through so many obstacles and dangers was, without doubt, one of the most difficult missions anyone had ever undertaken. Thanks to Anza's good management, however, a result was achieved that not even the most optimistic predictions had hoped for, that is, that more people arrived at the destination than had set out, since only one person died, a woman who died the first night in giving birth to her eighth child, and five babies were born.

During the preceding months, Anza himself had taken charge of all the preparations. One of the greatest difficulties was recruiting families among the settlements of the northwest and the poorest mining valleys in Mexico.[81] In effect, becoming one of California's first colonists had absolutely nothing attractive about it—the name "California" evoked only wild and unknown lands—and the pioneers had to be promised a salary for two years, rations for five years, clothes, cattle, weapons, and more in order to convince them.

For the financial aspect of the expedition, Viceroy Bucareli y Ursúa once more turned to the treasurer Juan José de Echeveste. With Anza's help, Echeveste drew up a list of provisions[82] that included cornmeal for making tortillas, beans, chocolate, white sugar, and three barrels of liquor "for necessities" (it would end up adding merriment to the expedition's more festive moments, to Father Font's annoyance). For preparing meals, there were eight griddles, ten copper kettles, twelve large chocolate pots . . . The list also details the clothes necessary to dress each man, woman, and child from head to toe: how many yards of cloth were needed to sew blouses and petticoats for the girls, how many ribbons and pairs of shoes. Curiously, the boys wore hats, but the girls did not. As far as military equipment was concerned, there was a flag with the royal coat of arms; eleven tents, ten of them for the families and the eleventh for the friars; twenty rifles; ammunition, swords, and lances; twenty-two leather jackets . . . Among the tools we find four axes from Bizkaia with steel blades.

Echeveste did not forget gifts for the Indians on his list: six boxes of glass beads ("that contain no black and abound in red"), tobacco, and above all, a very elegant military uniform, with a hat like that worn by the dragoons, to take to the Yuma captain Olleyquotequiebe (Salvador Palma), who had welcomed Anza's first expedition so warmly. Finally, Echeveste added two blank books for keeping military registers and writing the expedition's diary. Thanks to what Juan Bautista Anza and the chaplain Pedro Font noted down in them, we know what happened day by day during the long journey.

According to Echeveste's calculations, the cost of the expedition came to 21,927 pesos, a high sum that reveals the strategic value the crown placed on California at this time. It was hoped that the colonization of San Francisco would halt the expansionist tendencies of the Russians, English, and French. In addition, if all went well, the Manila galleon would finally have a good stopover point, and Spain's dominion over the California coast would be reinforced.

Hence, on October 23, 1775, following the captain's orders, everyone took their places in the caravan, and the expedition set off. From then on, the group would always organize itself for the day's march in the same way, as Father Font recounts in great detail. Every morning, while the animals were being loaded, he celebrated mass. Next,

> [a]s soon as the pack trains were ready to start the commander would say, "Everybody mount." Thereupon we all mounted our horses and at once the march began, forming a train in this fashion: Ahead went four soldiers, as scouts to show the road. Leading the vanguard went the commander, and then I came. Behind me followed the people, men, women, and children, and the soldiers who went escorting and caring for their families. The lieutenant with the rear guard concluded the train. Behind him the pack mules usually followed; after them came the loose riding animals; and finally all the cattle, so that altogether they made up a very long procession.
>
> Then we began to march, I intoning the Alabado, to which all the people responded; and this was done every day both going and coming. When the campsite was reached, after all the people had dismounted the lieutenant came to report to the commander whether everything had arrived, or if something had remained behind, in order that he might give suitable orders. At night the people said the Rosary in their tents by families, and afterward they sang the Alabado, the Salve, or something else, each one in its own way, and the result was a pleasing variety. The number of people was so large that when we halted the camp looked like a town, with the barracks which the soldiers made with their capotes, blankets, and branches, and especially with the fieldtents, which were thirteen in number, nine for the soldiers, one for the lieutenant, one for Fathers Garcés and Eixarch, one for me, and a larger one for the commander.[83]

The territory they were to cross had been severely attacked by the Apaches, but fortunately—"it is a thing to be marveled at," Font affirms in his diary—there were no problems. If this had not been the case, they would have found themselves in difficulties, since the majority of the expedition's members were poorly prepared for the journey, and there were families with two or three children to look after.

After having left the Christian settlements behind and entered pagan territory, on October 29, Anza ordered a proclamation to be read:

> At nine o'clock on the same morning, after having celebrated the holy sacrifice of the Mass, all the members of the expedition attending, I issued a proclamation making known the penalties imposed by the Ordinance on any one who should violate women, especially heathen, or steal their goods. Under the same penalties I forbade anyone to raise arms against the heathen in the country through which we pass, except in a case of necessity for the defense of life, or at my orders.

On November 1, at the town of San Juan Capistrano de Vturitue, around a thousand Indians came out to meet the expedition, and forming two lines, men in one and women in the other, they came one by one to greet and shake hands with the commander and the three friars, first the men and then the women, the elderly, the young, and the children,

> manifesting great pleasure at seeing us, putting their hands on their breasts, pronouncing the name of God, and giving other signs of good will. This handshaking took a long while, because nearly every one of them saluted us by saying, "Dios ato m'busibóy," as the Christian Pimas of Pimería Alta do, meaning "May God help us."

Anza recounts that the Pimas asked his permission to celebrate his visit with their usual dances and songs, and "with this molestation, for such in reality it is for us," they spent the rest of the day and the night.

On November 27, near the Gila River, the most memorable event of the entire journey took place. In Anza's words:

> At three o'clock in the afternoon Salvador Palma, captain of the Yumas, arrived at our camp with a following of more than thirty of his people, all unarmed. As soon as he saw me he began to embrace me and to give me the most emphatic signs of joy and satisfaction at my arrival, which he told me was shared by all his tribe and all those along the river who know me.
>
> This heathen captain had the courtesy to ask me about the

> health of his Majesty and of his Excellency the Viceroy, telling me that I was fortunate for having seen them, as they told him when he was at the presidio of San Miguel, and favored by having heard them speak; and that in order to hear them he would gladly take off his ears and put on some Spanish ears so that he might understand what they would say.

Salvador Palma asked Anza the same question he had asked the previous year; that is, he wanted to know when they would send missionaries to those lands. He said that he had scrupulously carried out everything the commantder had ordered the year before; above all, he had not fought with other nations. Anza replied that at the moment it was not possible, since he had other orders he had to fulfill, but that the time would soon come. Palma accepted the reply on a provisional basis, but he indicated to Anza that if the missionaries had not arrived by the time of Anza's return, he would go in person to Mexico to speak with Viceroy Bucareli. Once they had reached agreement, Anza presented to the Yuma captain the gift that Bucareli had sent in the king's name: the elegant blue military uniform with gold stripes. Palma appreciated the present enormously and showed it to his people, "who admired it with the same show of enthusiasm as its owner."

The expedition reached the place where the Colorado and Gila rivers came together and found that the volume of water was much greater than the previous year. They thought about building rafts, but the Indians would have had to go into the water to guide them, and this was out of the question. Inspecting the riverbank, Anza finally found a place where the river divided into three shallow arms. The caravan crossed there on November 30:

> we began to cross the first branch of the river on the largest and strongest horses, leading by the bridles those on which the women and children were riding; and as a precaution, in case any one should fall, I stationed in front ten men on the down-stream side.

Father Font, who was sick—as he was during much of the journey—crossed the river on horseback with the help of three servants who stripped for the purpose:

> I crossed over on horseback, and since I was ill and dizzy headed, three naked servants accompanied me, one in front guiding the horse, and one on each side holding me on in order that I might not fall.

It was the intrepid explorer Garcés, however, who, as in the previous year, had the most anxious crossing, due to his fear of the water. Three Yumas carried him on their shoulders, two at his head and one at his feet, while he lay face up as if he were dead.

Father Garcés and Father Eixarch were going to stay there, exploring the area, until Anza returned after completing his mission. Consequently, the expedition spent the next three days building a "shed or cabin" for the friars and the three interpreters and three servants who were to accompany them, and they left them provisions for three months. That cabin marked the first white settlement in Yuma.

It was early December when the expedition undertook the hardest part of the trip. They had to cross the *médanos*, the sand dunes "through which the Indians scarcely dare to pass because it is a land so bad that not even birds inhabit it," in Font's words.[84] Having learned a lesson from the preceding expedition, Anza divided the people into three groups at Santa Olaya Lake. Each group would set out on a specified day, allowing time for the watering holes to fill again. Anza himself guided the first group, crossing the desert by the direct route. This time, cold was their worst enemy, as thirst had been on the previous occasion. As Anza writes in his entry for December 11,

> All day and tonight the weather has been cruelly cold, and to this is added the fact that this site is lacking in firewood and it has not been possible to gather any through lack of light.

Two days later, on December 13, they camped at San Sebastián, near the pass that led across the mountains. Their joy at having arrived there vanished at the imposing sight the mountains presented, however:

> At the time when we halted the strong cold wind, which had been very hard on our people, especially the women and children, quieted down somewhat. The sky also cleared a little more, and we were able to see that the sierras through which we had to travel were more deeply covered with snow than we had ever imagined would be the case.

They stopped there to await the other groups. The next day,

> [a]t eleven o'clock at night it stopped snowing, but the mountains and plains continued to be so covered with snow that it looked like daylight.

A severe frost followed, and "this was a night of extreme hardship." On the 15th,

> several persons were frozen, one of them so badly that in order to save his life it was necessary to bundle him up for two hours between four fires.

When the three groups were reunited, the colonists were near death from cold and thirst, their two hundred head of cattle had gone four days without water, and the horses were exhausted. One of those who suffered the most was the leader of the third group, Lt. José Joaquín Moraga, who, forgetting to bundle up well himself while he was helping others and lighting bonfires to warm his people, lost his hearing in both ears. In Anza's account:

> In attending to his division, providing fire for them, and in other services for their relief, this officer so exposed himself that he contracted very severe pains in his ears, and although these have been cured, the weather is so bad that he has been left totally deaf in both ears.

Happy at being all together again, that night the expedition members "held a fandango here. It was somewhat discordant," as Father Font described it, without hiding his displeasure. Amid the celebration, "a very bold widow who came with the expedition" sang some verses that were somewhat off-color, for which "the man to whom she came attached" punished her. Anza rebuked him, but Father Font came to his defense, saying, "Leave him alone, Sir, he is doing just right." Anza replied that he would not tolerate such excesses, and the celebration ended peacefully, although not as quickly as Font would have wished: "He guarded against this excess, indeed, but not against the scandal of the fandango, which lasted until very late."

On December 19, heading northwest, they began the ascent of the formidable mountain range[85] by the same route Anza had followed on his previous journey. The sight of the snow-covered mountains before them spread discouragement among the members of the expedition. Anza describes the situation in his diary entry for the 27th:

> All the sierras . . . are so snow-covered that scarcely any trees can be seen on the summits. This sight has been terrifying to most of the people of our expedition who, since they were born in the Tierra Caliente (the Tropics), have never seen such a thing before. As a result they have become so melancholy that some of the women had to weep. Through their tears they

> managed to say, "If so many animals died of cold and the people nearly died in places where there was less snow, how will it be in the place where we see so much of it?"

More than ninety head of cattle died on the ascent. At twilight on the 26th, a great boom was heard in the distance, followed by an earthquake that lasted around four minutes. Nothing stopped the group's progress, however, and at last they reached the summit. As they descended, they left the snow and cold behind, the weather become more benign, the landscape became more agreeable, and so, without further difficulties, they arrived on January 4, 1776, at the San Gabriel mission, east of where the city of Los Angeles is today.

There, they found something they had not been expecting. They learned from Fernando Rivera y Moncada, the commander of Alta California, that on their journey they had escaped a worse danger than cold and thirst. The previous November 4, the Indians had razed the mission of San Diego, located about forty leagues from San Gabriel. It was an attack that had been planned for a long time. The natives of the region had never completely accepted the fact that the mission had been built on their land, a problem for which the soldiers were especially to blame. Fr. Luis Jayme, originally from Mallorca and assigned to the San Diego mission, had complained in a letter written two or three years earlier than many of them deserved to be hanged for devoting themselves to harassing and raping the women.[86]

Ironically, when the Indians finally revolted, the mission was their first target, and Fr. Luis Jayme himself the first victim. His body was found entirely mutilated and shot through with eighteen arrows. Two other residents of the mission also lost their lives in the attack, and none of the survivors was unwounded. Probably, Anza's caravan was not attacked on the way to San Gabriel because of the good reputation the captain had gained among the Yumas.

When Anza arrived at the mission, the situation was extremely serious. All the work of colonization carried out until then was in danger. Commander Rivera had only seventy men, split among five missions and two presidios, in a territory of more than four hundred square miles. If another attack occurred, the Spaniards would find it difficult to defend their positions. In these circumstances, Anza—the Cahuillas called him *Tomiar*, "the Great Captain"—thought it more important to capture the rebels than to continue the journey to Monterrey with the group of colonists. He pursued the rebels for four weeks, but he finally had to give up. Leaving twelve soldiers with Commander Rivera, he returned to San Gabriel to finish his mission. There, another surprise awaited him. He found out that five men had deserted, taking the best horses with them. After sending Lieutenant Moraga in pursuit of them with ten soldiers, he left for Monterrey with seventeen soldiers and the same number of families, plus six soldiers from his company.

The group set out on February 21. During the next three weeks, following the coast, they were able to advance without significant obstacles. On March 2, as they neared the mission of San Luis Obispo, Fr. José Cavaller, who was Catalan, and Fr. Pablo de Mugártegui, who was a Basque from Markina, came out to meet them. They welcomed them with pealing bells, and the whole group entered the church singing the *Te Deum*. Anza records the event in his diary as follows:

> The welcome which they gave us corresponded to their pleasure, and was such as may be imagined with people who spend all the days of their years without seeing any other faces than the twelve or thirteen to which most of these establishments are reduced, including the missionaries and the guard.

The next day, with the due solemnity, amid pealing bells and musket fire, an Indian boy was baptized. Anza was his godfather. This information and much else is recorded in the expanded version of his diary that Father Font wrote after the expedition was over. In the entry corresponding to the following day, for example, Father Font describes some birds that he found surprising:

> Along here there are some birds which they call carpenters, which make round holes in the trunks of the oaks. In each hole they insert an acorn so neatly that it can be taken out only with difficulty, and in this way they make their harvest and store, some of the oaks being all dotted with the acorns in their trunks.

Anza's diary does not mention these birds. The sensibility of a religious and that of a soldier, we might suppose, but this is not always the case. In general, the friar's prejudices and his disdain for the Indians are harsher than Anza's restrained explanations.

On March 6, the group arrived at the San Antonio mission, where they were met with a welcome similar to the previous ones and were also given a gift of bacon and two handsome pigs. The next day was one of great rejoicing, since Lieutenant Moraga arrived with the other families after having succeeded in capturing the deserters. In this way, reunited once again, the expedition made its entrance into the

Monterrey presidio on the 10th. In Anza's diary, a touch of pride is evident when he summarizes the results of the journey:

> In all these days of travel we have had no losses among the people whom I have conducted except the woman mentioned as having died of childbirth on the first night after we set forth from Tubac.

The following day also provided reason for happiness. Fray Junípero Serra came to visit them from the nearby mission of San Carlos Borromeo de Carmelo, with the friars designated for the two missions they planned to found in San Francisco: Francisco Palou, José de Murguía,[87] Pedro Cambon, and Tomás Peña.

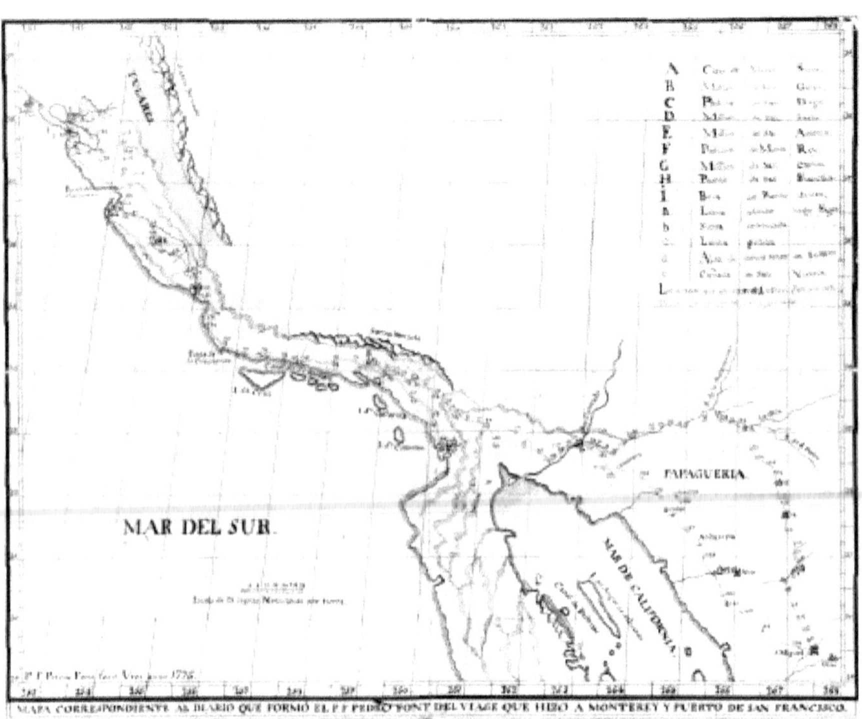

Map of the 1776 expedition of Juan Bautista Anza

The expedition had not yet reached its final destination, however, and Anza immediately began to make preparations to explore San Francisco Bay and determine a site for the colony. Nevertheless, on March 13, he writes, "I was suddenly attacked by some very severe and sharp pains in the groin, the hip, the knee, and the left thigh, which have been so violent that I could not breathe and I have thought I should be suffocated and die." The journey to San Francisco was delayed for some days, but on the 23rd, although he was not yet completely recovered, Anza was able to set out again, accompanied by Lieutenant Moraga, Father Font, and eleven soldiers.

At last, they arrived at the port of San Francisco. Even Anza, always so discreet, expressed his admiration at the sight. Font, marveling at the beauty he contemplated from atop what the Spaniards would call Punta del Cantil Blanco ("White Cliff Point," where Fort Point is today), wrote in his diary that "we saw a prodigy of nature which it is not easy to portray."

The following day, he added these words, which now appear prophetic:

> Indeed, although in my travels I saw very good sites and beautiful country, I saw none which pleased me so much as this. And I think that if it could be well settled like Europe there would not be anything more beautiful in all the world, for it has the best advantages for founding in it a most beautiful city.

After thoroughly examining the area in search of water and firewood, Anza selected the most appropriate places for building the presidio and the mission. He gave the mission the name of Dolores after Our Lady of Sorrows (*Nuestra Señora de los Dolores*), in accordance with the Catholic calendar. The building still stands and is the oldest building in San Francisco. In addition, on that day, March 28, 1776, Juan Bautista Anza II chose the site of the future city of San Francisco. He set up a cross "on the extreme point of the white cliff at the inner terminus of the mouth of the port," now Fort Point, where it was visible from the port entrance, and at the foot of the cross, he left beneath some stones a piece of paper with the record of his arrival and inspection of the port.

Nevertheless, despite so many and such great efforts, Anza began his return journey without having completed his mission, that is, without having guided the colonists to San Francisco. As it turned out, the commander of Alta California, Fernando Rivera y Moncada, surely jealous of Anza's successes, ordered that the colonists settle in Monterrey instead of San Francisco. This was a great disappointment for Anza, but nothing could be done in opposition to the governor's wishes. On April 14, the colonists bid a tearful farewell to the commander they had come to love and admire during the long journey. "This day has been the saddest one experienced by this presidio since its founding," Anza wrote in his diary; "most of them, especially the feminine sex, came to me sobbing with tears, which they declared they were shedding more because of my departure than of their exile, filling me with compassion. They showered me with embraces, best wishes, and praises which I do not merit."

A few months later, Lieutenant Moraga was able to bring Anza's enterprise to completion. He guided the group of colonists to San Francisco and founded the mission and presidio there, as well as the city of San José de Guadalupe.

On the return trip, Anza and his group again had the Yumas' help to cross the Colorado River. The river's flow was very abundant at that time of year, for which reason the travellers put all their goods "in baskets of mud and willows" to be transported by the women, "who possess greater dexterity in swimming than the men," according to Anza's account. It was even the case that "[t]here was one woman who carried a fanega of beans and asked for her labor only two strings of glass beads, although five would not have been excessive. Nevertheless they were more than satisfied, it may be said. For this pay they swam in going and returning more than fifteen hundred yards, and yet they lost no time in returning to the labor." They built rafts so that the people could cross, and several dozen men went into the water to push and guide them. They had scarcely left the bank when something fell off the raft Anza was on, and instantly, more than two hundred Indians jumped into the water to recover it.

Having crossed the river, on May 15, Anza made this reflection in his diary:

> I have said on another occasion that by keeping the tribes which dwell on this large-volumed river attached to us, we shall be able to cross it without great difficulty, but that otherwise it will be almost impossible, and I now assert this still more emphatically, since with the aid of their native experts it has cost us four days of toil. Nearly everything has been done voluntarily by these natives, and yet I am able to testify that in all this journey I have not been so overheated or so tired out anywhere else as here in effecting the crossing, and without their help it probably would have taken me twice as long.

In recognition of his labors, Juan Bautista Anza was named governor of New Mexico in 1777. In the northern part of the province, Comanche attacks on the Taos were continuous, and one of the new governor's first missions consisted in leading a punitive expedition against the Comanches. After gathering around six hundred armed men—the majority of them Pueblo Indians—and around two hundred

Orders sent May 19, 1786 by governeor Don Juan Bautista de Anza to Captain General Ecueracapa listing the captains who were to go on campaign against the Apaches, the number of men they should take, and their goals. General Archive of the Indies, AGI, MP-ESCRITURA y CIFRA, 52)

Apache and Ute allies, he headed north along an unusual route and succeeded in taking the Comanche encampment by surprise, near where the city of Pueblo, Colorado is today. Anza's forces killed eighteen of their opponents and captured many women and children. Blinded by the desire for vengeance, the Comanche chief Cuerno Verde ("Green Horn" in Spanish) attacked Anza's far more numerous group with scarcely fifty men. Cuerno Verde himself, several other Comanche chiefs, and a dozen warriors lost their lives, and Anza returned to New Mexico proudly exhibiting the headdress with green-painted buffalo horns that the Comanche chief had worn.

Juan Bautista Anza led other campaigns, sometimes victorious and sometimes not, but it is beyond doubt that his greatest achievement was uniting Sonora and Alta California. The historian Chapman dedicates these words to him:

Though he did not even suspect it himself, his work, under the guidance of the great viceroy, was to have an enduring importance beyond anything that had ever happened in the history of the Californias.[88]

For Chapman, taking the positive consequences for California into account, there has been only one event in California history more important than Anza's colonizing expedition: the 1848 gold rush.[89]

Testimony to the importance attributed to Anza in California history are the numerous places that bear his name today, the most noteworthy of which is the Juan Bautista de Anza National Historic Trail, administered by the National Park Service, which offers the opportunity to visit or travel along portions of the route Anza opened. Numerous streets, parks, schools, and other institutions in California are also named for him: De Anza Boulevard in San Mateo and Cupertino, De Anza College

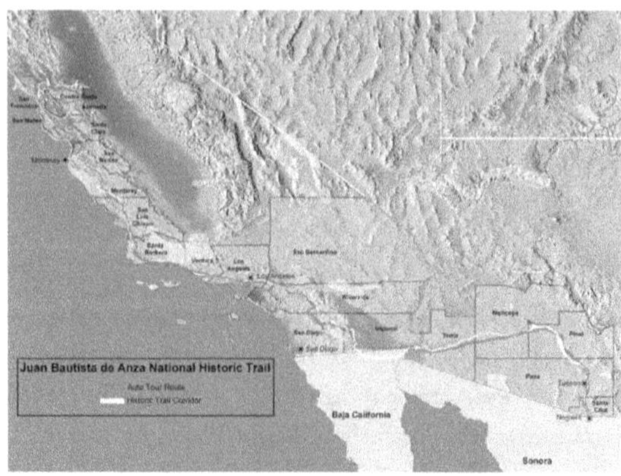

Map of the Juan Bautista de Anza National Historic Trail, a 1210-mile trail from Nogales, Arizona, to San Francisco

Remains of Juan Bautista Anza, statue on bottom left is in Riverside, California

in Cupertino, De Anza High School in Richmond, De Anza Middle School in Ontario, De Anza Middle School in Ventura, De Anza Hotel in San José, Juan Bautista De Anza Community Park in Calabasas, De Anza Elementary School in Baldwin Park in Los Angeles . . . San Francisco has an Anza Street, and there is a lake with the same name in Tilden Regional Park in the hills above Berkeley. Statues dedicated to him can be seen in Riverside and in Lake Merced Park in San Francisco. There is also a town named Anza, located in the valley of the same name, in the mountains south of Palm Springs.

In 1963, representatives from the University of California at Berkeley and the University of San Francisco gathered at the church of Nuestra Señora de la Asunción in Arizpe, Sonora to pay homage to Anza. They exhumed his body and laid him to rest again in a marble mausoleum in the same church.

During his lifetime, nonetheless, Anza did not receive great honors. This was due, above all, to the rebellion led by the Yumas in 1781.

The Yuma Rebellion, 1781

In December 1775, on his way to San Francisco with his group of colonists, Juan Bautista Anza II left the Franciscans Tomás Eixarch and Francisco

Statue of Francisco Garcés in Bakersfield, California Courtesy of Douglas Dodd

Garcés in the region of the Colorado River, having agreed to reunite on the return journey in order to go back to Sonora together. In May 1776, Anza found Eixarch at the expected location. He had established himself on the California bank of the river, dedicating himself during those five months to preparing the Indians for mission life. Garcés, on the other hand, was not there, but rather "with the tribe of the Galchedunes," some fifteen or twenty leagues away, according to what Anza was told. The tireless explorer had gone downstream along the Colorado to the river's mouth and then north to the Mohave region. From there he headed west to San Gabriel, then east to the Moqui cities. He then returned to Mohave, and continuing along the Colorado, reached San Xavier del Bac in September.

As we have said, however, Anza found Eixarch at the expected location, prepared for the return journey, and he also found there the Yuma captain Olleyquotequiebe, Salvador Palma, who, tired of waiting for missionaries to arrive in his town, joined the group in order to go to Mexico and speak to the viceroy in person. He brought three of his fellow-countrymen with him to bear witness to the welcome and treatment accorded to their chief.

In Mexico, Viceroy Bucareli y Ursúa accepted Olleyquotequiebe's petitions, and after various delays, two missions were founded on the banks of the Colorado and Gila rivers in 1780: La Purísima Concepción and San Pedro y San Pablo del Bicuñer. Four friars were also designated to take charge of them: Francisco Garcés, the navarrese Juan Antonio Barreneche, Juan Díaz, and Matías Moreno.

It seemed that Garcés's dream of founding those missions, intended to eventually become landmarks along the route to California, was finally being fulfilled. Nevertheless, it quickly became apparent that attracting the Indians to the bosom of the Church was not going to be as easy as had been thought at the time of Anza's expedition. The Yumas' desire to convert lasted as long as the presents lasted. Without presents—which did not last long—the friars lost all their enchantment. In view of the natives' evident indignation, Garcés wrote asking for the miserable sum of three hundred pesos for gifts, but his request was denied. To make things worse, Teodoro de Croix, the first commandant of the Interior Provinces, had the mad idea of building the mission, the presidio, and the town at the same place, instead of building the presidio at some distance from the mission. Croix was proud of this innovation because it saved money, but in the end, the costs were much greater than the benefits. Croix left the terrain prepared for the Yuma rebellion.

Problems between Indians and whites were there from the beginning. When troops commanded by Ensign Santiago Islas arrived at the Colorado River in December 1780, the Yumas gave them a good welcome, but the colonists chose the lands for their houses and fields with complete irresponsibility, ignoring the natives' rights. Even worse, they let their cattle damage the natives' crops. In consequence, when the colonists ran out of provisions, the Yumas refused to sell them anything. The Spaniards' reaction was not slow in coming: they imprisoned Olleyquotequiebe, the chief who had been such a loyal ally to Anza. The final insult came from an expedition headed to California under the command of Fernando Rivera y Moncada, the former governor of Alta California who had, out of jealousy, prevented Anza's group of colonists from continuing on to San Francisco and who is remembered for his incomprehensible actions and numerous mistakes. Having arrived in Yuma territory, his group let their cattle graze in the fields and mesquite[90] groves. It was Rivera's last error. On July 17, 1781, Yuma rebels destroyed the two missions and murdered the majority of the Spanish men, taking the women and children captive. Rivera, who was camped on the river's east bank, was murdered in a surprise attack, together with the sixteen men who accompanied him.

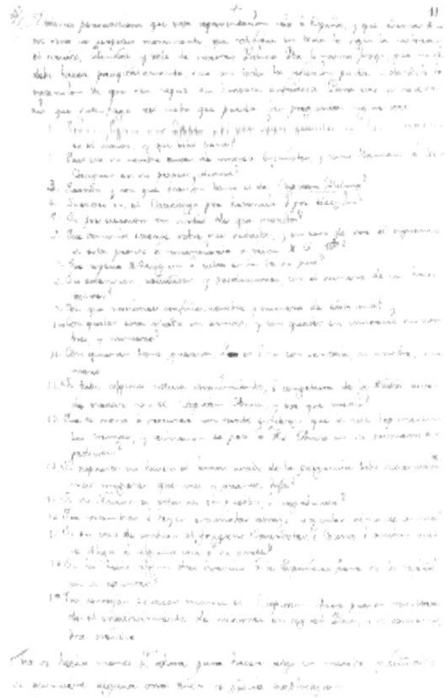

Questions by the Yuma chief Salvador Palma, after his request for baptism (1776). Palma's answers can be read here: http://lyncis.tic.unam.mx/franciscanos/ alifornia. Courtsesy of Douglas Dodd

The victims included the four friars at the two missions. The great explorer Garcés and the young Navarrese Barreneche were killed together.

Yuma Indians. Hamilton, Resources of Arizona

One of the pioneers who had settled in Yuma was a woman named María Ana Montielo. Five years after the massacre, Francisco Antonio Barbastro, the superior of the Franciscan missions of Sonora, asked her to recount what had happened. As the historian Kieran McCarty comments, this woman's handwriting is much better than that of the majority of men on the frontier, although it undoubtedly must have been difficult for her to transcribe her memories. Her own husband, Ensign Santiago Islas, the commander of the Colorado settlements, had died before her eyes during the revolt.

Ana Montielo's Letter to Fr. Francisco Antonio Barbastro

> In your much appreciated letter, Your Reverence asked me to comment on, as you phrased it, "the events surrounding the death of the missionaries on the Colorado River."
>
> Father Juan Barreneche celebrated the first mass that morning [July 17, 1781], which I myself attended. Father Francisco Garcés had the second mass. His mass-server was Ensign Santiago Islas, my deceased husband. As my husband was moving the missal from one side of the altar to the other for the gospel of the mass, the war whoops of the Indians began.
>
> Corporal Pascual Baylón was the first to fall into their hands. As they were putting him to death with their war clubs, Father Juan Barreneche rushed out just in time to force his way through the yelling Indians and witness the corporal's last act of life as he squeezed the good padre's hand. Though battered by war

clubs, Father Barreneche was able to regain the sanctuary of the church. My husband had observed a few armed Indians arriving in the village before he left for the service. As commander of the Colorado settlements, he took the precaution of placing Baylón on temporary guard, never dreaming that a full rebellion of the Yuma nation was about to break out. Though the mass was already begun, Father Garcés cut it short when the battle started.

Realizing that the whole Yuma nation had risen up against us, I gathered the women together and we fled for our lives to the church. There we found more refugee Spaniards arguing with Father Garcés about who should be blamed for the uprising. "Let's forget now whose fault it is," Father Garcés replied, "and simply consider it God's punishment for our sins." His voice was compassionate, though his face was an ashen gray.

That night the Yumas began to burn our houses and belongings and kill as many of our people as they could. That was the night my heart was broken, when my beloved husband was clubbed to death before my very eyes.

As day dawned on the 18th of July, Father Barreneche encouraged those of us who were still alive with the words: "The devil is on the side of the enemy, but God is on ours. Let us sing a hymn to Mary, most holy, that she favor us with her help, and let us praise God for sending us these trials." With great fervor of spirit, he intoned the hymn, "Arise, arise!" All during the night, he and Father Garcés had moved stealthily about the village, administering the sacraments to the wounded and dying, consoling them in their hour of death.

When the hymn was finished, Father Barreneche offered mass for all of us, as we awaited death at any moment. After mass, he occupied himself by pulling out arrows and spears from the walls of the church and the houses and climbing up onto the roofs to review the movements of the enemy.

About three o'clock in the afternoon, when the Indians had finished killing Captain Rivera and his party on the other side of the river, Father Barreneche arrived from ministering to the last of the dying and told us that each of us should try to escape as best we could. He picked up his breviary and crucifix and, together with Father Garcés, the women, and the rest of the people, started out of the settlement, leaving behind forever the new mission of La Purisima Concepcion and its property and possessions. He asked Father Garcés if they should perhaps try to reach our other settlement. Father Garcés assured him that it was completely destroyed and its inhabitants killed.

Father Barreneche was following the trail of blood of a wounded man named Pedro Burgues, who had sent for him to come and hear his confession. The trail led across a seemingly shallow lagoon. The priest waded in, armed with crucifix and breviary. Before he knew it, he was in over his head. Though he did not know how to swim, he thrashed about till he was able to grasp a log and some roots. By pulling himself along the roots, he was able to reach the other bank. Though he miraculously escaped drowning, he lost his breviary and crucifix.

From here, the two fathers went on alone. We women stayed beside the lagoon. Father Garcés warned us: "Stay together, do not resist capture, and the Yumas will not harm you." With this, he plunged into the lagoon to join Father Barreneche on the other side. This was the last we saw of the two fathers as we sat huddled together awaiting death at any moment.

Through another Spanish woman captive, who was not with my group, I later learned that Fathers Garcés and Barreneche were not killed until three days later [July 21, 1781]. After leaving the lagoon, the fathers were discovered by a friendly Yuma whose wife was a fervent Christian. He hurried the fathers to his own rancheria, where his wife was waiting.

The enemy fell upon them as they sat in the Yuma's dwelling, drinking chocolate. The rebel leader shouted: "Stop drinking that and come outside. We're going to kill you." "We'd like to finish our chocolate first," Father Garcés replied. "Just leave it!" the leader shouted. The two fathers obediently stood up and followed him.

The Indians tell the story that at the first attack of the executioners, Father Garcés disappeared from their sight, and they were left clubbing the air. Word had spread among the Yuma nation that he was more powerful than their own witch-doctors. Time and again I heard that many of the Yumas did not want to see the fathers killed. Nevertheless, their blood was spilled, and the woman who told me of this was close enough to hear their pitiful moans as they lay dying. The husband of the pious woman recovered their lifeless bodies and buried them.

The woman who told me this was Gertrudis Cantud, wife of the wounded man that Father Barreneche was following to hear his confession when the fathers crossed the lagoon.

This is all I can remember to tell Your Reverence concerning the ill-fated settlement of the Colorado River, Mission La Purisima Concepcion, and the rest of the territory we traveled until the fathers left us beside the lagoon.[91]

Juan Antonio Barreneche's biographical information is included in the Mission 2000 database, which brings together information about the California missions.

Surname:	Given Name:	Sex:
Barreneche	Juan Antonio de	M
Place of Birth:	Date of Birth:	Order:
Lecaroz, Navarra, Spain	01/01/1749	Franciscan
Place of Death:	Date of Death:	Cause of Death:
La Purisima Concepción del Rio Colorado	07/19/1781	Killed by Yuma Indians
Race or Tribe:	Residence:	Title:
Vizcaino	Lecaroz; Havana; Querétaro; Colorado River	Hijo de Juan Miguel de Barreneche y Ana Catalina de Legarreta; misionero (OFM); Martyred in the Yuma uprising on the Colorado River on Thursday, July 19, 1781.
Place of Service:	Burial Place:	
Yuma Crossing	Near La Concepción del Rio Colorado; Tubutama; Querétaro	

In a chapter of his *Crónica* (1792) titled "Virtues and happy death of Fr. Fray Juan Antonio Barreneche," Arricivita writes that as a child, Barreneche was sent by his parents to Havana with a man from a noble family to learn the profession of a trader, but he chose to become a friar. When he told his confessor about his intentions, the confessor wanted to test the strength of his vocation by making him study Latin. Barreneche dedicated himself to that task for two years, and in 1768, he was able to enter the Franciscan order in Havana, at the age of nineteen. Already as a novice, he gave evidence of his desire to live in the most absolute poverty and his propensity to mortify his body. He did not even permit himself the hot chocolate served with breakfast each day, and—another detail Arricivita found unusual—he washed his tunic himself instead of sending it to be washed.

> While he was preparing to make his religious profession, a fellow-countryman of his, Fray Enrique Echasco, stopped in Havana on his way back to his native land after twelve years in the missions. After speaking with him, Barreneche asked authorization to be admitted to the Querétaro missionary college. Echasco wrote a letter of recommendation, and the young friar's petition was accepted. On August 12, Barreneche left Havana. Once at the port of Tampico, around two hundred leagues from Querétaro, with no more baggage than his breviary, he undertook his journey alone, on foot, and relying on divine Providence for the minimum of subsistence; in

> those solitary lands, he covered up to ten leagues in a day, facing the obstacles of continuous rains and very rough paths, but it was all made tolerable for him by his longing to reach the college, which he did on September 13th of the said year.[92]

He spent six years at the Querétaro college, after which the mission superior named him Father Garcés's assistant in the Colorado River missions. Both friars shared a zeal for saving souls, and after overcoming multiple vicissitudes together, they also found death together.

Barreneche spent two years among the Indians, concerning himself especially with the children. As he wrote in a letter,

> It is a lamentable thing that so many innocent souls are lost before our eyes as are the little ones who die without baptism, and although we are not negligent in travelling throughout this nation looking out for sick little ones, even so, it cannot be helped that many die on us without the grace of baptism.[93]

The Indians lived scattered throughout the region, and the friars had no choice but to go out looking for them. Nevertheless, this was not the chief problem. The tension between the Spaniards and the natives was continually increasing. The religious did not slacken in their efforts, and each person baptized was a success. As Barreneche reported in another letter,

> Of the little ones who have been brought voluntarily by their pagan parents, more than two hundred have been baptized, some of whom have died, as well as some very old people and some young people of marriageable age, so that there will be around three hundred baptized all told.[94]

When they heard the Indians' yells on July 17, however, they immediately understood what was coming.

In all the narratives about the tragic events along the Colorado, Barreneche's courage is highlighted. There is also one other detail that is repeated, a markedly hagiographic one. When the bodies of the two friars were found some months later, in December, buried side by side in the same place where they had fallen, the searchers were surprised by the verdant grass and abundant flowers at the site. They brought the bodies to Tubutama, together with those of the other Franciscans, and buried them in front of the high altar in the church. In 1793, the remains of the four were exhumed once again and taken on muleback to the Querétaro college, the final resting place of the tireless Francisco Garcés and the young Juan Antonio Barreneche.

Consquences of the Yuma Massacre for Juan Bautista Anza II

There had never been a catastrophe to match the massacre perpetrated by the Yumas in 1781. The news roused enormous concern in Sonora and California. A large military force was gathered to suppress the rebels, but to little effect, other than recovering the captive women and children. There were no further attempts to rebuild the missions, nor to protect the route between Sonora and Alta California that Juan Bautista Anza's expedition had opened with such effort.

For Anza as well, the consequences of the Yuma rebellion were negative. The first commandant of the Interior Provinces, Teodoro de Croix, instead of acknowledging his responsibility for the mismanagement of the Colorado missions, blamed Anza for the rebellion. He accused him of having painted a too-friendly portrait of the Indians, that is, of spreading mistaken ideas, exaggerating the territory's good qualities and the Yumas' peaceful character. In the last analysis, Croix was trying to justify himself. In his diary, Anza had been absolutely clear that for the route between Sonora and Alta California to be passable, the friendship of the nations that lived along the river was indispensable. Commandant Croix did nothing to foster this friendship, and neither did the commandant who succeeded him, Felipe de Neve. Later, when the revolt broke out, both did all they could to ensure that, in the historian Chapman's words, "Thus did one of the Alta California's most intrepid heroes pass into undeserved obscurity."[95]

Commandant Neve wrote to José de Gálvez asking him to remove Anza from his post as governor of New Mexico, arguing that he did not possess the necessary qualities. The next administrator of the Interior Provinces, Jacobo de Ugarte, an old friend of Anza's, tried to straighten things out. He wrote to Gálvez that the appropriate thing to do was to reward Anza by naming him governor of Texas. Anza himself submitted a petition asking that he be appointed to a provincial governorship in order to have financial security for his last years. However, he died before anything could come to fruition, in December 1788, in Arizpe, Sonora.

Time has put each one in his place. Today, when many of his contemporaries have fallen into oblivion, Juan Bautista Anza is a respected figure in California history.

4
Exploration of the Pacific Northwest from San Blas to Alaska, 1775–1794

The Packet Boat *San Carlos*, the Frigate *Santiago*, and the Schooner *Sonora* Set Out to Explore the Pacific Northwest under the Orders of Bruno Heceta, 1775

For thirty years, from 1767 to 1797, San Blas de Nayarit[1] was the most important naval base in the North Pacific. It was from there that the Catalan Gaspar de Portolà's expedition sailed for Alta California in 1769, and it was also the point of departure for Juan Pérez's expedition in 1774. According to Viceroy Antonio María Bucareli y Ursúa's instructions, Pérez was to reach 60° latitude north, but he found himself forced to turn back upon reaching 54°. In the historian Henry R. Wagner's opinion, Pérez lacked the courage to sail the northern waters, and his effort was "a perfectly futile expedition." In fact, not only did he not reach his destination, he never disembarked, and consequently, he never took possession of the territory.[2] Nevertheless, he has the honor of being the first European to enter those seas, despite his scant scientific training and the limited resources at his disposal.

With the objective of halting the advance of the Russians, who were becoming increasingly powerful in the North Pacific, Minister of the Indies Julián de Arriaga sent six officers to San Blas in 1774. They were well-trained men, with experience in and knowledge of the art of navigation. According to the historian Michael E. Thurman, those six officers, who succeeded in shedding light on the "Mystery of the North" and bringing to the world its first news of unknown seas, lands, and peoples, have become legendary figures in the history of Old

California. These are their names: Bruno de Heceta, Juan Francisco de la Bodega y Quadra, Juan Manuel de Ayala y Aguirre, Fernando Quirós, Manuel Manrique, and Diego Choquet. The first three were Basques or of Basque origin, as was Ignacio de Arteaga, who would arrive somewhat later.

The three ships that took part in the expedition, the packet boat *San Carlos*, the frigate *Santiago*, and the schooner *Sonora*, set sail from the port of San Blas in the spring of 1775. The packet boat *San Carlos* had first of all to supply the missions of Monterrey and the north and was then to continue on to San Francisco and explore the bay that Portolà's group had seen. (Cabrillo and Vizcaíno had passed through the area but had not seen it.) The frigate *Santiago*, for its part, was to reach 65° latitude, take possession of the territory in Spain's name, and determine whether there was any sign of the Russians. In other words, it was to do what Pérez's expedition had not managed to do the previous year. The schooner *Sonora* was to assist it in its mission. Due to its small size, it was very well fitted for a detailed exploration of the coast.

The expedition's commander was to be the longest-serving officer: Bruno de Heceta y Dudagoitia[3] (Bilbao, 1744–1807). He would be the captain of the *Santiago*, and Juan Pérez would be his second-in-command. The *San Carlos*, for its part, set sail under the command of Miguel Manrique, but by the third day, Manrique was starting to show signs of serious disturbance. He cried without stopping, saying that they wanted to murder him, and did not separate himself for a moment from his six loaded pistols. The commander of the schooner *Sonora*, Lt. Juan Manuel de Ayala y Aguirre, had to take over his post, and Manrique was sent back to San Blas, accompanied by several men.

Juan Manuel de Ayala y Aguirre (Ayala y Aranza in other documents, 1745–97) was the son of Miguel Ayala Aguirre and Teresa Aranza Pleites.[4] He was not the only man of Basque origin on the *San Carlos*. The second pilot was Juan Bautista Aguirre, and the chaplain was the Navarrese Vicente Santa María. It should be noted that from this point on, Ayala made the entire voyage wounded, since one of the crazed Manrique's pistols fired by accident, wounding him in the right leg.

After Ayala moved to the *San Carlos*, command of the *Sonora* fell to Juan Francisco de la Bodega y Quadra, with the Galician Francisco Antonio Mourelle as second-in-command. Bodega y Quadra was also of Basque origin, although he was born in Lima. His father, Tomás de la Bodega y Quadra, was Bizkaian, having been born in Muskiz in 1701. Successfully established in Peru, he was a deputy of the Cuzco merchant's consulate and served as mayor *in absentia* of Somorrostro in 1761; as Donald C. Cutter describes him, he was "a minor noble (*hidalgo*) of Vizcaya."[5] Bodega y Quadra's mother, although born in Lima, was also the daughter of a Basque father, in this case from Bilbao. In 1774, Bodega had just returned from Europe with five other officers after having completed his studies at the Academia de Guardiamarinas (Coast Guard Academy) in Cádiz. He was barely thirty years old, and although he was in the same class as Ayala, he had to resign himself to occupying the second-ranking position on the schooner. Due to the prejudices of the time, the fact that he was not born in Spain was always an obstacle to his career.

The trajectory of this epic expedition can be reconstructed in great detail thanks to the six diaries that have survived to our day. The three ships left the port of San Blas with provisions for a year and with a crew of 160 men, the majority of them Mexican peasants with no experience of the sea. At the end of the first week, the other two ships lost sight of the *San Carlos*, the route and achievements of which will be described first here. Subsequently, we will follow the course of the frigate *Santiago* and the schooner *Sonora* until they separate, at which point we will travel to Alaska in the wake of the little *Sonora*.

Caption reads, "the San Carlos, pioneer of all the ships that have sailed through the Golden Gate." Source: William A Coulter, www.cable-car-guy.com/

Under the Command of Capt. Juan Manuel de Ayala y Aguirre, the Packet Boat San Carlos *Becomes the First European Ship to Pass through the Golden Gate*[6]

Because of contrary winds, it took the *San Carlos* a hundred and one long days to sail from San Blas to Monterrey. After leaving part of his supplies there, Capt. Juan Manuel de Ayala y Aguirre then received instructions to continue on to San Francisco. In effect, Viceroy Bucareli, having received news of Juan Bautista Anza's successful land expedition, was determined to colonize the port of San Francisco, as we explained in the last chapter. For this purpose, he ordered Anza to gather a group of colonists in Sonora and Sinaloa, and in the meantime, before the end of 1775, he sent Ayala to San Francisco. Ayala was to determine whether the channel or river seen by previous expeditions flowed into the bay and was also to prepare the terrain for the colonists who would come with Anza. If all went according to plan, the two expeditions would join up in San Francisco.

The *San Carlos* left Monterrey on July 27 "in search of the port of San Francisco," and it arrived at the mouth of the bay seven days later. The packet boat had a longboat the crew had made from a large sequoia tree on the banks of the Carmel River. On the morning of August 5, Ayala sent it to look for a place to anchor, with ten men and the first pilot, José Cañizares. The longboat passed through the narrow channel known today as the Golden Gate without problems, but due to the strength of the contrary currents, it was unable to return. At nightfall, concerned by the delay, Ayala decided to continue onward, and risking the ship in unknown waters, he passed through the channel by moonlight. In this way, the small sequoia longboat and the packet boat *San Carlos* became the first two European vessels to sail through the Golden Gate.

The next day, after dropping anchor at what is now North Beach, and having reunited with the longboat, the expedition proceeded to explore the bay and its surrounding area. Ayala had to limit himself to giving instructions from the ship, since the leg wound he had received from the crazed Manrique's pistol made it difficult for him to walk. He first sent the longboat with the pilot Cañizares to what is today San Pablo Bay. When this group returned, it was the turn of the second pilot, Juan Bautista Aguirre, who explored the southeastern part of the bay, determining that the bay was made up of a series of much smaller bays and that there were magnificent anchorages. He saw only three Indians, at a site now part of downtown San Francisco. They were crying, or appeared to be crying, for which reason Aguirre named the location "Ensenada de los Llorones" ("Inlet of the Crying Ones").

The group spent forty-four days in the bay, during which time they explored the entire region as far as the mouth of the San Joaquín River, took measurements of the bay's depth, and named various geographical locations. Some of these names have lasted until today, although with some alterations. Isla Nuestra Señora de los Ángeles ("Our Lady of the Angels Island") is today Angel Island. Isla de los Alcatraces ("Island of the Gannets") is today the famous Alcatraz, although the name was initially assigned to a different island. As far as the name of San Francisco is concerned, it was the one that the pilot Cañizares gave to the bay on his map, and it has been used ever since.

While the longboat came and went, the hours dragged for the *San Carlos*'s chaplain, Vicente Santa María. He was eager to disembark and meet the Indians who called out from shore, but as we have said, there was only one longboat available, and it was needed for the tasks of exploration. One day, August 18, seeing that the Indians continued calling out to them from the shore, the captain asked the second pilot, Juan Bautista Aguirre, and the surgeon whether they dared go ashore in a dilapidated dugout canoe they had on board. The two men agreed and went ashore with some beads and earrings. "I was much disappointed that I could not go along, this time," Santa María lamented in his diary,[7] but the canoe was too small for three men. The Indians on the shore, nineteen of them, offered them a gift of "pinoles, some loaves of their usual sort, and two small containers filled with mussels." One Indian approached the second pilot, Juan Bautista Aguirre, giving him to understand by gestures that he should show him his chest. Aguirre complied, and upon seeing how pale it was, the Indian shouted, "Pretty, pretty!"

Santa María also finally had the opportunity for personal encounters with the inhabitants of San Francisco Bay, although not with the frequency he would have wished, and he left a record in his diary of the close and peaceful relationships he maintained with both the Huimen and the Huchiun. The Navarrese chaplain's text is unique in the respect it shows to the Indians, although he too, with the clergy's customary paternalism, uses terms such as "infidels" and "poor unfortunates" in referring to them.

Vicente Santa María, the son of Pedro Antonio de Santa María and Ángela de Oiaga, was born in Aras, Navarre in April 1742.[8] Together with thirty-nine other Franciscans, he embarked for the Americas in Cádiz in 1769. According to the passport registers, he had a good physique, dark hair, and a "florid complexion." Before occupying the post of the *San Carlos*'s chaplain, he had been in the Baja California missions between 1771 and 1773. His contemporaries described him as a strong and impetuous man, perhaps too much so for Junípero Serra's taste, who complained that he was difficult to keep under control. The dislike must have been mutual. When Serra assigned him to San Diego in 1776, Santa María lamented that he had been left like a bird in the air. It is clear that the Navarrese friar was an unusual man. In 1793, as we will explain later, he made such an impression on the English captain George Vancouver that Vancouver named a cape situated near San Pedro for him, calling it Point Vicente.

San Francisco's Inhabitants, Huimen and Huchiun, as seen by Vicente Santa María

In his *Diario de lo acaecido en el nuevo descubrimiento del puerto de San Francisco* (Diary of what happened in the new discovery of the port of San Francisco), Vicente Santa María writes that on the morning of August 5, Captain Ayala sent the longboat to survey the rim and entrance of the bay in order to be sure that the *San Carlos* would not have problems upon entering. Around midday, they saw "a large number of smokes a short way from one another," extending over a distance of about fifteen leagues. Santa María thought that they were signals used by the natives to advise other rancherías of the strangers' arrival. The following day, the Indians came down to the shore several times and, by shouting or making gestures, leaving gifts on the beach, or dancing, tried to attract the men on the ship. On one of those occasions, seeing that some Indians were coming down a hillside, the captain gave the chaplain the opportunity to fulfill his desire, allowing him to go on land together with two pilots and the ship's surgeon. Santa María was thus finally able to see San Francisco's inhabitants up close:

> As we came near the shore, we wondered much to see Indians, lords of these coasts, quite weaponless and obedient to our least sign to them to sit down, doing just as they were bid.
>
> Their physical appearance also evoked Santa María's wonder, since "the best favoured were models of perfection; among them was a boy whose exceeding beauty stole my heart."

In his diary, Santa María recounts in great detail the visit he made to the Indians on August 9. That day, the Indians once again came to the shore with gifts, in the morning and around midday. The gesture was in vain. The *San Carlos*'s longboat was unavailable, and they could not send anyone to collect the presents. The Indians made another attempt with dances, but once more without effect. Finally, they left the shore,

72 FIRST INTO SAN FRANCISCO BAY, 1775

The last page of Vicente de Santa María's report

showing signs of irritation. Then in the afternoon the longboat, which had been exploring the surrounding area, returned to the *San Carlos*, and the captain asked Santa María whether he wanted to go on land with the surgeon. This was what the friar had been waiting for, even if it was now rather late in the day, past six o'clock.

> A VISIT THAT I MADE TO THE INDIANS
> The surgeon and I accepted the favour, and setting out in the longboat we went ashore without delay. We were mindful that the Indians might have gone away offended; so, like the hunter fearless of dangers, who leaps over the rough places and forces his way through obstacles until he meets his quarry, we went up the slopes, taking chances, hunting for our Indians until we should find them. In pursuing this venture we did not share

our intentions with the captain because, if we had, from that moment he would have had nothing to do with it in view of the risks involved in our desire to visit the ranchería at so unseasonable a time and in so remote a place. Notwithstanding all this, and even though we had no notion of how soon we might reach the Indians, we were nevertheless making our way by their very path. As night was now approaching, we were considering a return to the ship, and were of two minds about it, when we caught sight of the Indians. At the same time seeing us, they began inviting us with repeated gestures and loud cries to their ranchería, which was at the shore of a rather large round cove.

San Franciscoko natives, 1816. By Louis Choris, 1795–1828

Although we might on that occasion have succumbed to dread, we summoned our courage because we had to, lest fear make cowards of us. We thought that if we turned back and for a second time did not heed the call of the Indians, this might confirm them in their resentment or make them believe that we were very timid—not an agreeable idea, for many reasons. As none of those who came along declined to follow me, ignoring our weariness we went on toward the ranchería. As soon as the Indians saw that we were near their huts, all the men stood forward as if in defense of their women and children, whom undoubtedly they regard as their treasure and their heart's core.

They may have thought, though not expressing this openly to us, that we might do their dear ones harm; if so, their action was most praiseworthy.

We were now almost at the ranchería. As we were going to be there a while, an Indian hustled up some clean herbage for us to sit on, made with it a modest carpet, and had us sit on it. The Indians sat on the bare ground, thus giving us to understand in some degree how guests should be received. They then made quite clear to us how astonished they had been that we had not joined them at the shore; but we succeeded in giving them some reassurances. When I saw there was so large a gathering, I began to speak to them for a short time though I knew they could not understand me unless God should work a miracle. All the time that I was speaking, these Indians, silent and attentive, were as if actually comprehending, showing by their faces much satisfaction and joy. When I had finished speaking, I said to those who had come with me that we should sing the "Alabado." When we had got as far as the words "Pura Concepción," there was a great hubbub among the Indians, for some of them had come with two kinds of hot atole and some pinoles, and they gave all their attention to urging our participation in the feast. So our chorus stopped singing and we gave the Indians the pleasure they wished, which was that we should eat. After the sailors had finished with the supper that our hosts had brought, I called to the Indian who seemed to me the head man of the ranchería and, taking his hand, began to move it in the sign of the cross, and he, without resisting, began repeating my words with so great clearness that I stood amazed and so did those who were with me.

One of the sailors had brought a piece of chocolate. He gave some of it to an Indian who, finding it sweet, made signs that he would go get something of similar flavour. He did so, bringing back to him a small tamale that has a fairly sweet taste and is made from a seed resembling *polilla.* We gave the Indians, as usual, some glass beads, and received their thanks; and as they saw that the moon was rising they made signs to us to withdraw, which we then did.

Because there was not much daylight when we got to the ranchería, we couldn't take note of the appearance and the features of the Indian women, who were at some distance from us; but it was clear that they wore the pelts of otters and deer, which are plentiful in this region. There were a number of small children about. Many of the Indian men we had seen at other times,

> including some of the leaders, were not present. We headed back for the ship, and as we reached the shore we came upon the usual present, which the disquieted Indians had left in the morning.

After this visit on August 9, the crew of the *San Carlos* did not see any Indians for four days, until the 13th. On that day, Captain Ayala, the second pilot, Juan Bautista Aguirre, the surgeon, and Santa María himself again went on land. The Indians they encountered that day were much warier, however, and when Santa María took out his snuff box, because he wanted to take a pinch, they became frightened and fled, making gestures of irritation.

The next memorable encounter took place not on land, but on the *San Carlos* itself.

> THE INDIAN'S VISIT ABOARD AND THEIR WONDER ON VIEWING THE STRUCTURE OF THE SHIP
> It would be about 10 o'clock in the forenoon of the 23rd of August when, towards the point of the Isla de Santa María de los Angeles near which we stayed, two reed boats were seen approaching, in which were five Indians. As soon as the captain was informed of this, he directed that signs be made inviting them aboard, to which they promptly responded by coming, which was what they wanted to do. Leaving their boats, they climbed aboard quite fearlessly. They were in great delight, marvelling at the structure of the ship, their eyes fixed most of all on the rigging. They wondered no less at the lambs, hens, and pigeons that were providently kept to meet our needs if someone on board should fall sick. But what most captivated and pleased them was the sound of the ship's bell, which was purposely ordered to be struck so we could see what effect it had on ears that had never heard it. It pleased the Indians so much that while they were on board they went up to it from time to time to sound it themselves. They brought us, as on other occasions, gifts of pinoles, and they even remembered men's names that we had made known to them earlier. They brought among their party an Indian we had not seen before. Soon after receiving our greetings he went away alone in his boat, leaving in another direction than the one they had taken. We thought he had been sent by the others to bring us back a present; but when he did not return even after the others had gone away we dismissed this unworthy thought from our minds.

California natives, ca. 1822. By Louis Choris, 1795–1828

Throughout the time the Indians were on board we tried to attract them to Christian practices, now having them cross themselves or getting them to repeat the "Pater Noster" and "Ave María," now chanting the "Alabado," which they followed so distinctly that it was astonishing with what facility they pronounced the Spanish.

The Indian chieftain, less reserved than the others, showed how much pleased he was at our warmth of feeling; more than once he took to dancing and singing on the roundhouse. I paid close attention to their utterances that corresponded with their actions, and found that their language went like this: *pire* means, in our language, "Sit down"; *intomene,* "What is your name?"; *sumite,* "Give me"; and this last is used with respect to various things, as, a man on the ship having given an Indian a cigar, the Indian said, *sumite sot sintonau,* which means, "Give me a light to start it with." They call the sun *gismen,* the sky *carac.* And so on. Close on midday they took to their boats again, bidding farewell to us all and promising to be back on the morrow, and they made good their promise so effectually that at 7 o'clock the next morning they were already aboard. They had no sooner arrived than I went to meet and welcome these guests, although I did not stay with them as long as they wanted me to because I was about to say Matins and to prepare myself for celebrating the Holy Sacrament of the Mass. I made signs to them to wait for me until I should be through and those who occupied the cabin should get up; but they couldn't hold their expectations in suspense so long, for while I was at my prayers in the roundhouse

> the Indian chieftain, seeing that I was putting them off, began calling the surgeon by his name and saying to me, "Santa María, Vicente, Father, *ilac,*" which means "Come here"; and seeing that the surgeon did not leave his bunk, and that I did not come down, he came up to where I was reciting my prayers and, placing himself at my side on his kneecaps, began to imitate me in my manner of praying, so that I could not keep from laughing; and seeing that if the Indian should continue I would not be getting on with my duty, I made signs to him to go back down and wait for me there. He obeyed at once, but it was to set out in his boat with a chieftain, not known to us before, whom he had brought to the ship, and as if offended he left behind the daily offering of pinoles.
>
> News of the friendly treatment received spread from village to village, and soon other Indians they had not seen before came to the *San Carlos* and boarded the ship without any fear. That same afternoon, they had another visit:
>
> This visit was not a casual one, for all of them appeared to have got themselves up, each as best he could, for a festive occasion. Some had adorned their heads with a tuft of red-dyed feathers, and others with a garland of them mixed with black ones. Their chests were covered with a sort of woven jacket made with ash-coloured feathers; and the rest of their bodies, though bare, was all worked over with various designs in charcoal and red ochre, presenting a droll sight.

Following the customary exchange of gifts, they returned to the shore. Later the same afternoon, from the *San Carlos*, Santa María observed that the natives were helping the sailors who had gone on land in search of water and firewood. Once again, he did not want to lose the opportunity to be with them:

> I watched all this from the ship, and as the Indian remained seated on the shore I could not bear to lose the rest of the afternoon when I might be communicating with them; so, setting out in the dugout, I landed and remained alone with the eight Indians, so that I might communicate with them in greater peace. The dugout went back to the ship and at the same time they all crowded around me and, sitting by me, began to sing, with an accompaniment of two rattles that they had brought with them. As they finished the song all of them were shedding tears, which I wondered at for not knowing the reason. When they were through singing they handed me the rattles and by

signs asked me also to sing. I took the rattles and, to please them, began to sing to them the "Alabado" (although they would not understand it), to which they were most attentive and indicated that it pleased them. I gave them some glass beads that I had had the forethought to bring with me, and they made me with my own hands hang them in their ears, which most of them had pierced. Thus I had a very pleasant afternoon until, as nightfall neared, our captain sent the dugout for my return to the ship.

I came back well pleased, reflecting on how quick-witted the Indians were and how easy the acquisition of their language—as we all put to the test when, early next morning, the Indians came back to the ship. We designedly put before them several objects, asking what these were called in their language, to which they answered with great care; seeing that what they said was put down on paper, they came near and repeated the word as if anxious not to give occasion for any blunders in the writing. With this good opportunity we improved the occasion to acquaint ourselves with some words that tallied with what was presented to their attention; thus, their manner of counting is as follows: *imen*, one; *utin*, two; *capan*, three; *catauas*, four; *misur*, five; *saquen*, six; *quenetis*, seven; *osatis*, eight; *tulau*, nine; *iguesizu*, ten; *imeniluen*, eleven; *capanuya*, twelve; *imenaye*, thirteen; *catsuya*, fourteen; etc. We learned other words, but lest I grow tiresome I do not put them down. I shall record only some names that, like baptismal names, distinguish them one from another. Thus, the eight Indians who came to us on this occasion were named as follows: their chieftain was called *Sumu*; the second chieftain, *Jausos*; the others, *Supitacse* (1); *Tilacse* (2); *Mutuc* (3); *Logeacse* (4); *Guecpostole* (5); *Xacacse* (6). To give an example of Jausos' liveliness: on being taught to say "piloto Cañizares," he made signs that Sumu be taught to say the same thing. When Sumu mistakenly said "pinoto" instead of "piloto," Jausos corrected him, laughing so hard as to astonish all of us. They are very fond of trading. All of them hanker for our clothes, our cloaks most of all, and so as to move us to make them warm they show us with sad gestures how they suffer from the cold and even say the words *coroec cata,* "I am cold," and the like.

The Indians noticed with interest Santa María's practice of taking down their names in his diary:

> I set to inquiring their names and writing them down on paper. This gave them great amusement; for when I had finished, a number of them kept coming up and asking me how the names were spoken, and as I answered according to the paper they gave way to bursts of laughter. Thus we enjoyed ourselves that afternoon until we took our leave. The head man of this ranchería comported himself so politely that he came out with one arm around me and the other around the surgeon and went with us a part of the way until, taking leave of us, he went back to his ranchería and we returned to the ship, which was more than half a league distant. This is the manner in which these unfortunates have behaved toward us.

Governor Rivera had agreed to send a group of soldiers to San Francisco with the aim of having the site prepared by the time Anza's colonists arrived. Captain Ayala was waiting for them, but finally, since there was no sign of them, nor of Anza's colonists, he decided to return to Monterrey. Before leaving, a small group walked to the cross that Father Palou had set up the previous year on the peak of Point Lobos. Among the group was the chaplain, Vicente Santa María, who left two letters at the foot of the cross. One reported the *San Carlos*'s arrival and its successful entrance into the bay, and the other announced that they were going to return to Monterrey, but that if the group that was expected to come by land arrived, they should light a bonfire across from Angel Island, so that if Ayala and his men were still there, the two groups could find one another.

The *San Carlos* left San Francisco Bay September 18, and the group led by Bilbao native Bruno Heceta arrived three days later. They found the letters that Vicente Santa María had left at the foot of the cross and lighted a bonfire across from Angel Island, but there was no response.

It was with this expedition under Juan Manuel de Ayala y Aguirre that the fame of San Francisco's port began to spread. In Ayala's words, "the harbour of San Francisco is one of the best that I have seen in these seas, from Cape Horn northward." In his report written for Viceroy Bucareli, in addition to mentioning the beautiful harmony it offered to the eyes, he highlighted its advantages as a port, due especially to the fact that "it is free from such troublesome daily fogs as there are at Monterey," as well as the natives' docility.[234]

Having examined Ayala's report, Viceroy Bucareli y Ursúa wrote to Minister of the Indies Julián de Arriaga expressing his satisfaction with the voyage's result.

> We now know that San Francisco is a famous port, healthy, with fertile land along its coasts, and capable of everything one might want to make of it.[9]

Statue of Francisco Garcés in Bakersfield, California Courtesy of Douglas Dodd

Bruno Heceta's Frigate Santiago *Brings More News of the Pacific Northwest*

Trinidad (41° 03′ N)

On June 11, 1775, Trinity Sunday, after a maritime voyage of three months, Cmdr. Bruno Heceta disembarked and, fulfilling his instructions to the letter, led all the formalities to bring the Pacific Northwest territory under Spanish dominion. A cross was set up on top of a steep hill, and a ceremony was held, with the participation of the majority of the officers and men of the frigate *Santiago* and the schooner *Sonora*. Finally, Fray Camp celebrated mass, while the Indians observed attentively from their positions. The Spaniards named the site (41° 03′ N)—it goes without saying—Puerto de la Trinidad ("Port of the Trinity").

When the landing party returned to their ships, which were decorated for the occasion, they were welcomed with three artillery salvos. Some hours later, in the afternoon, a group of men went to the rancheria and found the Indians "dismayed with fear," in Heceta's own words,[10] but they gave them a few presents, and they became calmer.

It was the first time the Spaniards had gone on land and the first ceremony of taking possession since the expedition had left San Blas on March 16. In need of water and firewood, they decided to replenish their supplies right there. The following days were dedicated to this task and to repairing the two ships, in awareness of the misgivings they aroused among the natives, but without failing to receive their help. On the 14th, according to the Franciscan Benito de la Sierra's diary, the Indians came to ask them whether they were really men like them. Apparently, they were surprised by the scant attention they were paying to their women. Heceta was strictly enforcing the instructions he had received in this regard, in order not to have problems with the natives. Despite all these precautions, however, something happened that same night to damage their good relations. At roll call on the *Santiago*, it was discovered that the cabin boys José Antonio Rodrigues and Pedro Lorenzo were missing.

The witnesses differ notably in their accounts of these desertions. In his diary entry for the 15th, Heceta says that two suspicious native chiefs were brought on board but were quickly set free, returned to land, and given gifts, as Bodega y Quadra, the captain of the *Sonora*, and the friars had advised. The next day, one of the deserters, Pedro Lorenzo, returned and said that he had remained on land pressured by the Indians and with their help, but then thought better of it and succeeded in fleeing. After hearing this, Heceta spent the afternoon trying to extract information from the Indians on where they were keeping the second man. Around nightfall, Lorenzo confessed that he had lied and had not acted under pressure from the Indians. Heceta explains in these words the punishment he imposed on the liar:

> I punished the individual on the spot, satisfying the Indians, who throughout the length of my stay continued the same expressions of true friendship.

Juan Pérez's diary offers a different version of events. According to his account, the captain's reaction was much harsher. When he realized the desertion, "the color came and went in his face."[11] He seized two Indians, one of them elderly, and "abused them severely," trying to get them to confess where the sailors were. When Pedro Lorenzo was brought to him, he became enraged and ordered his men to tie Lorenzo up and give him a hundred lashes. All the officers on both ships disapproved of the punishment.

Pérez's criticism of Heceta did not end there. The second-in-command complains in his diary about Heceta's treatment of him and the crew and laments his tactlessness with Indians and his faults as a seaman.

Father Sierra, upon recounting the case of the two deserters, offers a third version, in which there is not even any mention of the Indians being punished. With regard to the punishment inflicted on Pedro Lorenzo, the Franciscan affirms that, when the Indians proved their innocence, "[t]he man was given a thrashing with the straps of the gun, which would have flayed him well if the compassion of the Indians had not caused them to intercede with tears in his favour."[12]

Two days later, Sierra speaks about the expedition's good relations with the Indians. According to the friar, "In the days we remained in this port the Indians behaved with the greatest friendliness and confidence, coming alongside the Frigate in our launches and taking our men ashore in their canoes."

The words of the *Sonora*'s second-in-command are similar. "We never noted in them any action contrary to the most loyal friendship," Mourelle affirms.[13]

The contradictions between the different versions are evident. It does not seem probable that relations could have been as good as Heceta, Sierra, and Mourelle affirm if Pérez's accusations were true. Was his version the fruit of jealousy and grudges? For an experienced seaman like Pérez, it could not have been easy to accept the viceroy's selection of Heceta, recently arrived from Spain, to lead the expedition. In addition, it may be that the antipathy was mutual. Heceta does not even mention in his diary Pérez's death at the end of the voyage.

Nothing more was ever learned about the second deserter. If he lived, he was the first white resident of Northern California whose name is known.

The *Santiago* and the *Sonora* left the port of Trinidad on June 19 and did not sight land again until July 11.

Rada de Bucareli (47° 24′ N)

The expedition had reached 47°, and the green, irregular coast of what is now Washington state spread out before their eyes. After trying for two days to draw near to land across dangerous sandbanks, both ships found a good bay. The *Santiago* remained at a certain distance from the rocky coast, due to the heavy seas, while the *Sonora*, for its part, maneuvered toward shore. When they reached land, several canoes approached, bringing natives who came on board the ship. The Spaniards offered them gifts, and they reciprocated with fish and whale meat and invited the schooner's men to dance with them. They seemed to Bodega y Quadra to be even more docile than those of Trinidad, although it appeared to him that night that their songs carried evil omens.

On July 14, Heceta, Fray Benito de la Sierra, the pilot, the surgeon, and twenty armed men went in the longboat to take possession of the territory. They named the site Rada de Bucareli ("Bucareli's Anchorage," 47° 24′ N) in honor of Viceroy Bucareli y Ursúa. Everything was done quickly, without even celebrating mass, due to the weather and the frigate's position: the men landed at four-thirty in the morning, the ceremony of taking possession took place at six, and by seven-thirty the group was back on the *Santiago*. In this way, Heceta and his group became the first Europeans to set foot in what would become Washington state.

After their experience with the inhabitants of the port of Trinidad, and seeing that the behavior of the inhabitants of Bucareli was equally peaceful and friendly, both Heceta and Bodega y Quadra believed that they were among friends, and they decided to stay there to take on supplies of water and firewood. The schooner, as we have said, was anchored near the coast, and the frigate further off. The same morning that the group of men from the frigate *Santiago*, with Heceta at their head, held the ceremony of taking possession, the boatswain of the schooner *Sonora* and six other men were sent to shore in a longboat. They were duly armed, but according to the viceroy's instructions, they could only use their weapons in self-defense and were to avoid molesting the Indians at all costs. While they were rowing toward shore, the waves were very high, and the longboat took on quite a bit of water. The natives were watching them from the dense pines and underbrush that came down to the water, where they remained in hiding until the longboat had come sufficiently close. At that moment, more than three hundred Indians ran toward the boat and massacred five of the men. The other two jumped into the water, attempting to flee. From the schooner, Bodega was observing what was happening through his telescope without being able to offer any help, since there was no other longboat available. A man was sent on a barrel, but in vain. The two men who had jumped into the water turned back toward land in their extremity and probably died by drowning.

Bodega and the men on the schooner saw the attackers depart after perpetrating their massacre, not all at once as they had appeared on the scene, but one by one or in twos or threes, apparently taking with them pieces of their victims' bodies and all the metal parts of the longboat. For the Quinault, there was nothing more precious than iron.

A little later, the Spaniards observed nine canoes heading toward the schooner. Only one, carrying nine Indians on board, approached the ship. They were making friendly gestures and inviting the schooner's men to a meal, but a sailor who had climbed up the mast saw that they were wearing leathers and had their bows strung. The schooner's men acted with the same dissimulation, offering the Indians glass beads. When they had drawn them close, they fired their swivel cannon and their muskets, killing seven men. The other canoes immediately fled.

All this took place without the *Santiago*'s men suspecting anything at all, since the frigate was a league away. When they found out what had happened, the officers met to decide whether or not to respond to the attack. The schooner's captain and second-in-command, Bodega y Quadra and Mourelle, declared themselves in favor of punishing the

Indians. The frigate's captain and second-in-command, on the other hand, were against a punishment. Heceta lists their reasons in his diary: their instructions were not to attack except in self-defense; many of their men were sick, and if they suffered more casualties, they would be forced to abandon the enterprise; in addition, if they decided to respond to the attack, days would be lost, and their mission would be delayed. A vote was taken, and they decided to depart as soon as possible.

Before setting sail, since the *Sonora* had lost half its men, the small schooner's crew was filled out with men from the frigate, and in memory of the dead, Bodega named the place "Punta de los Mártires" ("Martyrs' Point").[14]

Bruno Heceta Discovers the Columbia River

The two ships advanced with difficulty; each degree of latitude was gained at the cost of great suffering. On July 19, Juan Pérez informed Heceta in writing that they had to turn back, due to the difficulty of

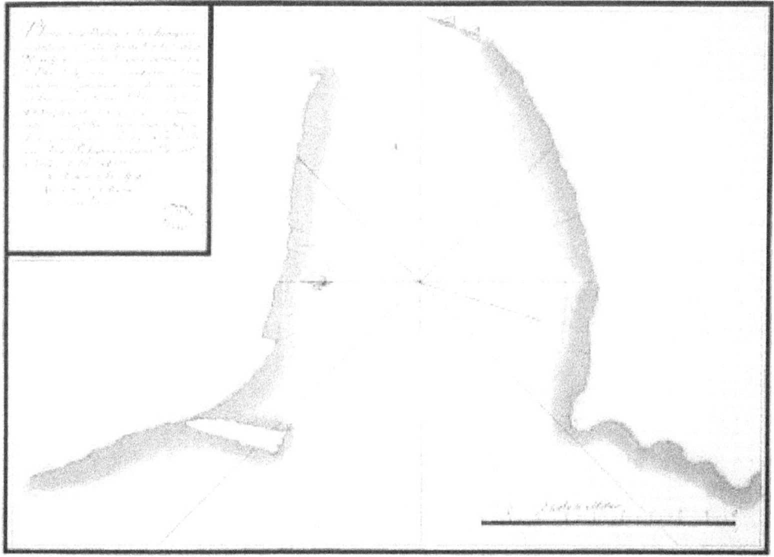

Heceta's first map of the Columbia River. it was named the Bay of the Asumption. Later, on Spanish maps, it was the entrace of Ezeta and finally it was named the Columbia River by Robert Gray. ("Plano de la Bahía de la Asumpcion ó entrada de Ezeta … descubierto y levantado por el Comandante de esta Expedicion el Teniente de Navio Don Bruno de Ezeta Dudagoitia en el viage de los descubrimientos de las costas septentrionales de California que hizo de orden del Excmo. Señor Virrei Frei Don Antonio María Bucareli y Ursua el año de 1775." Archivo General de Indias.

navigation, the terrible cold, and the general condition of the men, many of whom were ill with scurvy. Nevertheless, Heceta decided to continue, wanting to reach the 65° latitude his instructions called for.

On July 29, the skies were stormy, and the *Santiago* lost sight of the schooner *Sonora*, as had happened on many other occasions. This time, however, contact between the two ships was not reestablished, even though the *Santiago*'s crew fired rockets and mortars. Bodega states in his diary that this was a consequence of heavy cloud cover and squalls; Mourelle writes in his diary that they were at the mercy of a storm that lasted two days. Nevertheless, probably, Bodega and Mourelle had decided that they would carry out their mission better on their own.

The Santiago continued northward until it reached what is now the border between Washington state and Canada, about 49°, on August 11. There, finally, Pérez, now ill, and the rest of the officers succeeded in convincing Heceta to turn back.

On August 17, sailing for San Blas, Heceta discovered a large bay that stretched inland as far as the eye could see:

> That afternoon I discovered a large bay that I named Asuncion, the shape of which is depicted on the sketch inserted in this diary.[15]

It was what we know today as the Columbia River. Due to the strong currents and the men's feeble condition, they were unable to enter it, but the descriptions of the currents and the maps make it quite clear that Heceta was the first non-native to discover it. Seventeen years later, Robert Gray entered it and named it the Columbia River, arrogating to himself the honor of its discovery, but as the historian Donald C. Cutter writes,

> Hezeta was the initial discoverer of the mouth of the Columbia River, which was called the Entrada de Hezeta until Gray's entrance altered the name.[16]

The blame goes in large part to the Spanish authorities' obsession with secrecy. The crown's ministers and bureaucrats, instead of publicizing the voyage's diaries in Europe, kept them jealously guarded, thereby losing the opportunity to claim their rights over those territories. As a consequence, when the diary of James Cook's third voyage was published some years later, in 1784, European intellectuals were confirmed in the conviction that England had more rights than Spain over the northern American coast.

Heceta Head and Heceta Head Lighthouse

On August 29, with almost the entire crew ill with scurvy, the *Santiago* arrived in the port of Monterrey.

A few weeks later, Heceta was ordered to San Francisco, this time by land, to help Juan Manuel de Ayala y Aguirre, who had been sent there by Bucareli. Heceta was accompanied by the Franciscans Francisco Palou and Miguel de la Campa Cos, nine soldiers, three sailors, and a carpenter. They transported a small canoe on muleback. On September 22, they reached the beach south of Point Lobos, and it was then that they found, at the foot of a cross, the letters that Fr. Vicente Santa María had left. They lighted a bonfire opposite Angel Island, without response. They gave the lake alongside which they camped the name it has kept until today: Nuestra Señora de la Merced.

The following day, they continued in search of Ayala's group, but since they found no trace of them, they supposed that they must have returned to Monterrey. Heceta decided to do the same. When he arrived in Monterrey on October 1, he found Ayala's *San Carlos* anchored next to the *Santiago*, and he learned from Ayala's own lips and those of his two pilots about the explorations they had carried out in San Francisco.

Six days later, the small schooner *Sonora* entered the port of Monterrey in a pitiful state, after having succeeded in advancing farther north than any other expedition had done up to that time.

The expedition under Bruno Heceta's command explored the coast of what is now Oregon and Washington, drawing very exact maps. It was a great achievement for the time, since instruments for measuring longitude had not yet been invented, and it was necessary to rely on complex astronomical calculations. In addition, Heceta took possession of the territory in the name of the Spanish crown; discovered what is now the Columbia River; banished the fear of Russian settlements, since no trace of them was found in the entire voyage; left a diary that includes interesting information on the nations who inhabited that coast before the first Europeans arrived . . . Nevertheless, as Heceta himself wrote in a letter to the king, his achievements went unacknowledged, due to the fact that his labors were carried out so far from the scenes of honor and promotion,[17] and with time, they have fallen into oblivion. Today, no one remembers Bruno de Heceta in his native land, and in the regions he explored, historians often pass over in silence the achievements of the age when Spain was ruler and mistress of the Pacific Northwest. Even so, not everything has been erased. There is an island called Heceta in Alaska, and Heceta Head is the site of a lighthouse of the same name, the brightest on the entire Oregon coast. Apparently, however, the people who visit it are more interested in the ghost that is said to live there than in the merits of the explorer who gave his name to the location.

Bruno Heceta's expedition had a dramatic postscript. In the following decades, an epidemic of smallpox (*variola major*) struck the northwest coast, causing the region's population to fall from 37,000 inhabitants to 26,000.[18] Very likely, it was Heceta's 1775 expedition that brought the virus. On June 10, after spending the afternoon with the inhabitants of Trinidad, Heceta wrote these words in his diary: "I returned on board before it grew dark, after my crew had thoroughly mingled with them."[19] The apparently innocuous phrase acquires a sinister aspect when we consider what came after. Although the catastrophe they sowed was something that Heceta and his men could not have imagined, it casts a dark shadow over all their achievements.

The Small Schooner Sonora, *Captained by Juan Francisco de la Bodega y Quadra, Sails to Alaska Alone*

From the moment it left the port of San Blas, in the spring of 1775, it was evident that the schooner *Sonora*, which was no larger than a ship's longboat, did not handle well, and the *Santiago* had to tow it more than once in order to be able to keep the expedition moving forward. The second-in-command, the Galician Mourelle, explained in his diary that a deck and a cabin were all it offered by way of shelter and lodging. The crew had no trunks or other baggage except a cot and what would fit in a box underneath it. The size and height of their cabin allowed them only to be in a sitting position, the small deck gave them no opportunity to walk up and down, and in this state of inactivity, they spent ten months. It was painful, Mourelle commented, to see the terror that the men felt, since they had only a miserable corner for the sick, and they could not do their work without getting completely wet, except at those times when the sea was calm.[20]

For Mourelle, the ship's inadequacy could not have been more obvious. "It is not hidden from me how exposed and arduous the enterprise is, due to its smallness, poor handling, little draft, complete lack of speed," he wrote in his diary, and the crew was not much better. Of its fourteen members, only four had sailed before; the rest were cowboys recruited from the ranches around San Blas. At critical moments, when Bodega ordered all the sails set, terror mastered them. They pretended to be sick in order to transfer to the frigate. The frigate's crew, for their part, considered it a punishment to be sent to the schooner. Despite all the difficulties, the little schooner continued on its way, and thanks to its captain's good management and courage, it achieved what no one had expected from so poor a ship: reaching nearly 58°, exploring the coast in detail, and going ashore twice to take possession of the territory.

As has been said, it is likely that the *Sonora* voluntarily separated from the frigate *Santiago*. More than four months had passed since the expedition left San Blas, provisions were running low—only some rice, beans, moldy bread, and bacon were left—water was also in short supply, and they had no medicine, but the ship's captain and second-in-command, Bodega and Mourelle, were eager to cover themselves in the glory and fame of great explorers, and on July 29, under a stormy sky, they separated from the *Santiago*, beginning what would turn out to be one of the most epic voyages in the history of the exploration of the northwest American coast.

During the first two weeks of August, they sailed north without major difficulties. On the 15th, the sky grew dark, and seeing tree branches, seaweed, whales, and birds—with red beaks, breasts, and legs—Bodega and Mourelle concluded that they were near land. On the morning of the 16th, the coast came into sight at 57° 2′. It was Kruzof Island, west of what is now Sitka, Alaska. Coming closer, they saw tall mountains with snow-covered peaks, including one that they baptized with the name of San Jacinto (today Mount Edgecombe). They spent the night in a bay to which Bodega gave the name of Guadalupe. The following morning, when they were going to set sail, they were approached by two canoes, with two men and two women in each, signaling to them to come ashore. Bodega was warier after what had happened at "Martyrs' Point," however, and he did not accept the invitation.

Three days later, the *Sonora* anchored on the north side of Kruzof Island. On the coast, they saw a very well built house, surrounded by a wooden fence. Bodega went ashore and decided to take possession of the place. He did not want any more surprise attacks, so he brought along fourteen well-armed men and ordered two swivel guns and several men armed with muskets positioned where they would be able to cover a retreat, if necessary. After that, he set up a cross on a height and, with all the necessary formalities, gave the place the name of the port of Nuestra Señora de los Remedios. That port of Los Remedios, located at a latitude of 50° 20′ N, would have an important political value, since it was the northernmost Spanish possession, and Spain would use it as the basis for its claims of sovereignty.

When they returned to the ship, they observed that the Indians had left their hiding places and were carrying away the cross that the Spaniards had set up on the shore. They set it up in front of the handsome house the expedition had seen, perhaps attributing the power of a totem to it.

On August 19, the Spaniards again went ashore in search of water and firewood, taking the same precautions as on the previous day. Bodega went with six men to cut down a tree and obtain firewood. A little later, while a number of soldiers were filling their barrels with fresh water from a stream, and others were fishing, about twenty Indians[21] came out of the handsome house on the shore. Unarmed, with a small white flag on a stick, they positioned themselves on the other side of the river and harangued the foreigners for a while. They then fell silent, as if awaiting a reply. Bodega tried to give them to understand that they should not be afraid, that they would not harm them, and he indicated to them by gestures that they needed water. One of the Indians, probably the chief, then ordered that they be given water. The Indians filled a basket made from grass and, coming to the center of the river, offered it to the foreigners. In exchange for the water, Bodega gave the natives some glass beads and some handkerchiefs, and they reciprocated with dried fish.

It seemed that everything was going well, and the soldiers continued filling their water barrels. When the Indians saw that they were taking them away, however, they began to ask for compensation, giving the Spaniards to understand that the water was theirs. They rejected the trinkets they were offered, throwing them to the ground, and ran to the house, returning with very long lances with stone points. Seeing that they intended to attack, Bodega took up his musket, went to the riverbank, and told them that if they came one step farther, he would shoot, but if they put down their lances, he would also put down his musket. Apparently, the Indians understood the message, and they withdrew to their house. Without further trouble, the *Sonora*'s crew finished taking on supplies of water and firewood, and they were even able to cut a trunk for the topmast.

The *Sonora* spent three days there, enduring tremendous cold, with no trace of the sun, and permanent rain and fog. The lack of shelter was a real problem for the crew, and they decided to sail on. Consequently, on August 21, Bodega headed west in the hope of finding a breeze that would drive them north, but the winds were not in their favor. The map they had with them, by the French cartographer Jacques Nicolás Bellin, was useless to them, and they did not know where or when they might find land. Seeing that they were, in addition, entirely unfit for duty, with the crew, including the commander, suffering from scurvy and with pains in their legs, Bodega decided on the 22nd to turn back, having reached 57° 58′ N.

It is a good illustration of Bodega's personality that, instead of returning quickly, so that both he and his men could receive the care

The Sonora *discovers Bodega Bay. Source: Juan Francisco de la Bodega y Quadra, 1775. UCLA, William Andrews Clark Memorial Library.*

of which they were in so much need, he made the return voyage very slowly, keeping as close as possible to the coast at all times, in order to see whether they could find Russian settlements or the famous Strait of Anián, the supposed Northwest Passage to the Atlantic. They did not find that legendary channel, but their efforts did have another reward. On August 24, the *Sonora* arrived at a handsome bay, west of Prince of Wales Island. They took possession of it and named it Bucareli Inlet (now Bucareli Bay) in honor of the viceroy.

They continued southeast until the wind changed direction and made it impossible for them to continue on the same heading. Since the wind was now driving them north, they decided to make the effort to try to reach 60°, since the crew's health had improved somewhat with the temperate climate and fresh fish of Bucareli Bay. The temperature soon fell sharply, however. Bodega distributed among the men the only warm clothes they had: the four flannel jackets and capes that Heceta had brought to exchange with the Indians, plus some of his own and Mourelle's clothes. In addition, the wind did not maintain the expected direction: a storm blew up, and the sea became rough. It was useless to keep trying, and they turned south again. On September 6, at midnight, the wind became fierce, and the small schooner was on the point of shipwreck. From then on, seeing the crew's deplorable state, Bodega decided to give up the idea of sailing close to the coast and reconnoitering every inlet. On September 17, when they were passing opposite the Strait of Juan de Fuca, the wind shifted to the southeast and pushed them away from the coast; consequently, Bodega missed the opportunity to be the first European to see this strait.

By that point, both Bodega and Mourelle were sick with fever and scurvy, but they forced themselves to appear on deck whenever they could, so that the rest of the crew would not become discouraged.

On October 3, they reached a large bay, which they believed to be San Francisco Bay. When they dropped anchor, Indians in canoes appeared from every direction and gathered on a height, shouting at the men on the ship. When he saw them, Bodega realized that he was not in San Francisco. The Spaniards left the location without giving the bay a name, but in the future, it would come to be known as Bodega Bay.[22]

Without stopping at San Francisco, they finally saw Monterrey Bay appear from out of the fog on October 7. They did not know for sure that it was Monterrey until they saw the *Santiago* and the *San Carlos* anchored there.

The *Sonora*'s arrival was met with great rejoicing, since four long weeks had already passed since Heceta had returned with the *Santiago*, and the schooner was feared lost at sea. A cannon was fired from land in greeting, and the *Sonora* replied in kind. Heceta and Ayala, each in a longboat, went to bid the new arrivals welcome, after which they towed the schooner to the anchorage. None of the men was able to walk, and they needed help to transfer to the longboats, but surprisingly, Bodega had not lost a single man since the massacre at "Martyrs' Point." Some years later, in a 1784 letter to the king, Bodega described the sufferings undergone in epic terms:

> With the appropriate season for these voyages already well advanced, with water scarce and scurvy threatening, lacking a surgeon, without a chaplain to provide spiritual consolation, and in short, exposed to the decisions of a difficult fate, . . . placing his trust in the Almighty and devoting his efforts to honor and to leading and directing that small number of men under his command, whom he looked on as victims of bravery, without the protection of any human resource . . .[23]

Bodega spent three months in Monterrey without being able to get out of bed, and his health was permanently broken. He and Mourelle spent their convalescence in a house with a view of the port of Monterrey. The rest of the *Sonora*'s men were taken to the mission of San Carlos Borromeo de Carmelo, where they were placed under the care of the Franciscan fathers.

As soon as their health began to improve, all the officers and pilots gathered to study the expedition's maps, observations, and diaries. Heceta does not mention in his diary that Bodega and Mourelle, disobeying their orders and under cover of darkness, had decided to continue the voyage alone.

The three ships' achievements since they left San Blas on March 16 were far from insignificant. In addition to the little *Sonora*'s incredible feat, Juan Manuel de Ayala's expedition had passed through the Golden Gate and explored all of San Francisco Bay, drawing the first map that showed the bay in detail; Bruno Heceta had discovered the mouth of the Columbia River; and Juan Francisco de la Bodega y Quadra had discovered Bucareli Bay and the bay that bears his name today, as well as mapping with great accuracy the entire coastal strip north of San Francisco. Making their contribution even greater, Bodega and Mourelle recorded a great deal of information about the climate, winds, tides, and currents, providing numerous details that would be very valuable to future sailors: that the water became darker closer to shore, for example, or that birds, whales, sea otters, and other marine life became more numerous in the same locations. Certainly, their diaries are authentic treasures, in which Bodega and Mourelle, anticipating the scientific expeditions to come, collected thousands of details about the lands and, above all, the people they encountered.

Having read all the reports, Viceroy Bucareli y Ursúa wrote to Julián de Arriaga, the state secretary for the Indies, praising the expedition and the knowledge acquired "at the cost of much fatigue, continual risks, and heroic constancy,"[24] and expressing optimism about the fact that they had returned without having seen Russian settlements. This meant, in Bucareli's view, that Spain's sovereignty was not under threat. Nevertheless, the threat existed, even if the expedition had not seen it. Russian fur traders had established themselves in the Aleutian Islands and Cook Inlet, and they were about to move into Prince William Sound and the Alexander Archipelago. Soon, the Pacific Northwest would become the scene of international conflict motivated by the desire for valuable sea-otter pelts.[25]

Ignacio de Arteaga and Juan Francisco de la Bodega y Quadra Depart in Search of 70° Latitude, 1779

Rumors about an English and Russian presence in the Pacific Northwest also motivated the following expedition. Its promoter was José de Gálvez, the man who replaced Julián de Arriaga as secretary of state for the Indies after the latter's death in 1776. Once the project had been approved, the first thing to be done was to obtain ships. Since the few vessels at the port of San Blas were needed to supply the California missions and presidios, Juan Francisco Bodega y Quadra was sent to Callao, Peru, to buy a frigate. Meanwhile, Ignacio de Arteaga was to have another ship built in San Blas. By the time Bodega returned with the *Favorita* in 1778, the *Princesa*, built by the Basque outfitter Francisco de Segurola, was already finished at the port of San Blas. Both ships were more comfortable and faster than those that had participated in previous expeditions, were better prepared for long voyages, and were equipped to confront the English if necessary.

Viceroy Bucareli named Ignacio de Arteaga himself commander of the expedition. The ninety-eight men of the frigate *Princesa* would be under his orders, and Lt. Fernando Quirós would be his second-in-command. Command over the 107 men of the *Favorita*, for their part, would be in the hands of two men who had sailed those seas before: The Basque-Peruvian Juan Francisco Bodega y Quadra was to be

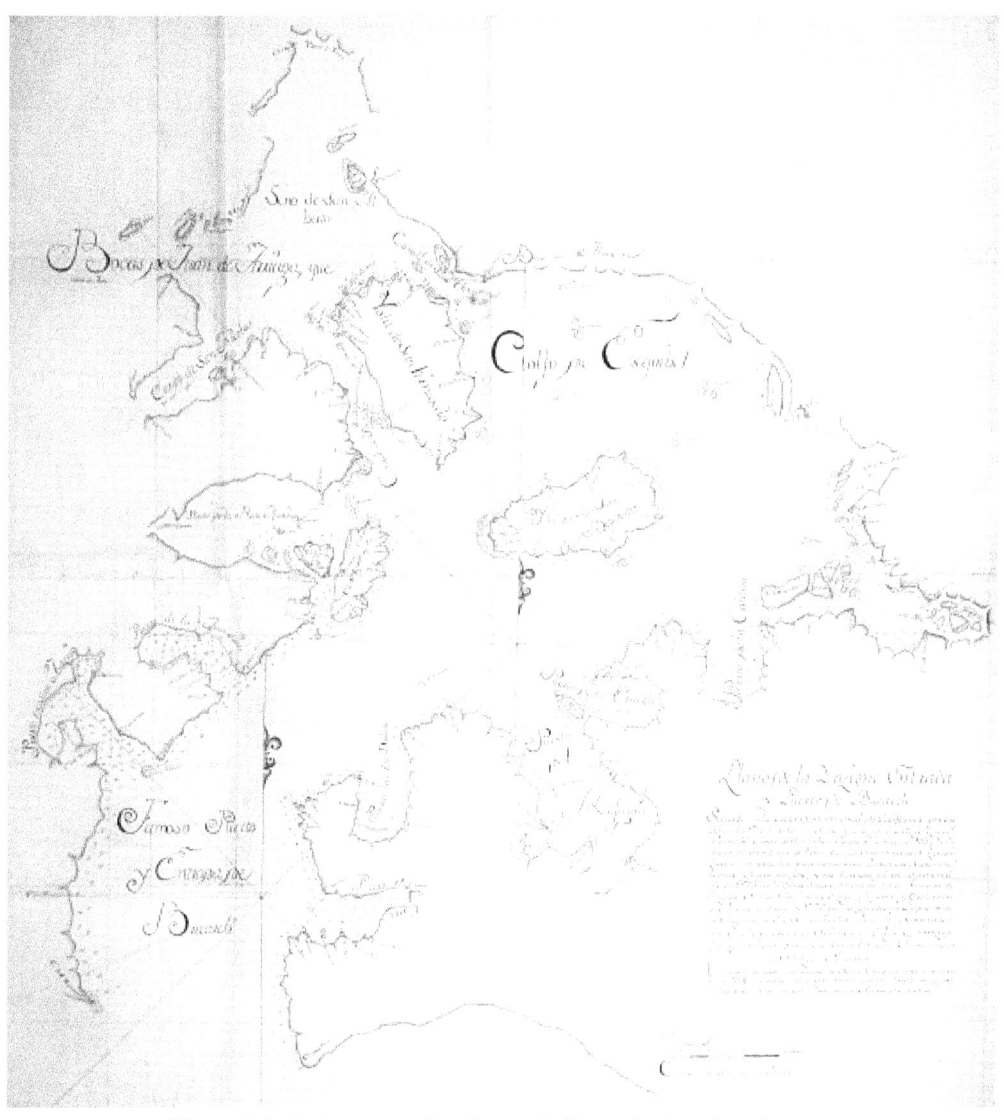

"Plano de la insigne entrada y Puerto de Bucarely situado en la costa Septentrional de California … esta entrada fué descubierta en el año de 1775 con la Goleta Sonora mandada por el teniente de Fragata Don Juan Francisco de la Bodega y Quadra y explorado este Puerto en el año de 1779 por los oficiales y pilotos de las dos fragatas de S.M.C. nombrados Princesa y Favorita mandada la primera por el Teniente de Navio Don Ignacio Arteaga y la segunda por el de la misma clase Don Juan Francisco de la Bodega y Quadra." General Archive of the Indies. AGI, MP-MEXICO,358.

captain, and Francisco Mourelle second-in-command. Juan Bautista Aguirre, another veteran explorer of the California ports, would be second pilot.

Both frigates set sail from the port of San Blas on February 11, 1779, laden with provisions for fifteen months. According to their instructions, they were to reach 70° latitude and take formal possession of the territory located between 50° and 70°. In the end, they reached 61°,[26] carried out two ceremonies taking possession of the territory, at the port of Santiago and Ensenada de Regla, and produced a detailed cartographic description of the coast of Northern California and British Colombia, as far as Alaska. On the maps they drew, there are more than a few names of Basque origin. Arteaga called a sandbar Pamplona. Among the place names on the "Carta reducida de la costa septentrional de California" (Reduced map of the northern coast of California) that he and Bodega drew between them, there appear Ureta Point, Eguía Point, Lángara Island, etc. On the "Plano de la ensenada de Nuestra Señora de la Regla" (Plan of the inlet of Our Lady of the Rule), at 59°, there is an island with the name of Arriaga.[27] All these details, along with interesting data on the flora and fauna, as well as the social organization, language, and customs of the peoples they encountered, are included in the officers' and friars' diaries. Among those that have survived from this expedition, we will follow here those signed by the Basques Ignacio Arteaga and Juan Bautista Aguirre.[28]

The *Princesa* and the *Favorita*, after a voyage of eighty-one days, came opposite the snow-covered mountains of Canada earlier than was expected, thanks to the experience and knowledge accumulated by Bodega and Mourelle on their earlier voyage. On May 3, they anchored at the port of Bucareli. Up to this point, the diaries offer only a register of latitudes, longitudes, maneuvers, and wind directions, but once the ships approach land and the natives appear in the narrative, the diaries acquire new life and become much more interesting reading:

> Immediately after we anchored, there came two canoes of Indians, who did not want to come alongside, making various gestures with their arms wide and shouting very harmoniously, as if they were singing. One of them, who was holding a dead bird in his hands, plucked the small feathers from it, crumbled them in the air, and then sprinkled them on his head and on those of the others. We realized that these demonstrations were a request for us to stop and the desire to be our friends, for which reason we reciprocated by calling out to them, manifesting many signs of kindness to them, and offering them some

> things, but they never wanted to come alongside, and when it seemed good to them, they went away.
>
> All the Indians in both canoes, who were around twelve in number, including men and women, had their faces painted, some with patches of black paint and others red, so that they were quite horrible, but in addition to the paint, the women had in their lower lips a small plaque the size of an egg, oval-shaped, that caused their lips to jut outward for a distance of around three fingers, so that they were like nuts in front of their mouths, in which conformity they were excessively ugly.[29]

The Spaniards chose a port that offered good shelter—they named it Santa Cruz ("Holy Cross")—and proceeded to reconnoiter the bay. On May 13, mass was celebrated at the port's southern end. Arteaga recounts that a group of Indians who had arrived in nine canoes, around thirty individuals in total, men, women, and children, witnessed the ceremony. They were very surprised, it seems, when they saw that the men who had arrived in the two frigates knelt to pray. Aguirre adds in his diary that before returning to the ships, they held a celebration on the beach, and once on board, they fired the cannons.

The cannon fire was part of their plans for imposing respect on the Indians. They did not want a surprise attack, as had happened on the previous expedition at "Martyrs' Point." For this reason, while they were sailing toward Bucareli, the men had practiced the use of cannons, muskets, knives, and sabers. When the two longboats left their respective ships on May 18 to reconnoiter the area and draw a map of the port, Arteaga made sure that they took along the necessary weapons, in addition to provisions for fourteen days.

Juan Bautista Aguirre, the *Favorita*'s second pilot, was part of the group of explorers. According to his diary, the Indians' boldness increased as the days passed. They thought that the Spaniards' weapons made noise but did nothing else. Aguirre complains about their continual thefts: "As they are so inclined to theft, this makes them very subtle in that damned practice."[30] He also complains about their shamelessness and their mockery. One day, things were at the point of blowing up completely. Some men had started to prepare a meal on a small point of land, while the officers proceeded to measure the terrain and organize the data gathered on the previous days. As was always the case when they went on shore, the group was made up of five armed soldiers and four sailors with rifles. The longboats were nearby, and the mortars were loaded, just in case. Suddenly,

> Canoes began to gather, and many Indians began to arrive, heading toward the inlet . . . Sometimes they manifested peace; other times they disdained our weapons, believing that they only thundered, and theirs wounded the heart and killed; other times they made threatening gestures with their lances and put on their leathers; and finally they gave a horrible cry that was able without any doubt to terrorize the sailors, seeing that number of people, incomparably more numerous than us, since the entire beach was covered. . . .
>
> Although on this occasion, shooting might have started, given the state in which we found ourselves, obliged by their daring to truly destroy the majority of them, since they were in great groups on all sides, without any precautions that would save them from our grapeshot, and we had everything excellently deployed, we judged it better despite everything to reembark without offending them in any way. This action had the result that they became more daring and insolent, fully persuaded that their threats had dismayed us, as they explained to us with the disdain they showed for our firearms. In truth, the humanity with which we looked on them, due both to obedience to the orders that had been communicated to us and to the charity with which we should behave toward our neighbors, was the fundamental cause for leaving the port to them, since we recognized the necessity of ultimately measuring the strength of each party, which would be in reality very costly for them and miserable for us.
>
> We made our retreat in the most favorable order we could, leaving behind only a barrel of water that we had landed. In truth, we were surprised at how we could have lost sight of it without noticing, since it was not a jewel that could be easily hidden, until we saw it under one of the Indians, who had it covered with the skins that he wore and was using it as a seat, and what was the greatest cause for wonder was that although he was asked for it in a friendly way, there was no persuasion that could make him give it up, with everyone mocking us because they believed that it was out of fear that we did not recover it. In order not to exacerbate matters, the commander contented himself with only making him get up from it.[31]

On another occasion, several sailors, accompanied by a number of soldiers, went on shore to do laundry, and when they were about to return to the ship, they realized that two members of the group were missing. Thinking that the Indians had kidnapped them, they took an Indian as hostage in order to arrange an exchange. In the fight that followed, the sailors overturned several canoes, the frigate fired several shots, and two Indians lost their lives. When the missing men finally returned, they confessed that they had disappeared of their own free will, just as had occurred on the previous expedition with the two deserters at the port of La Trinidad. Arteaga ordered them to be punished with one hundred lashes each for having endangered the entire expedition.

In the six weeks the expedition spent at Bucareli, Indians often came to trade. They brought fish, mats made from tree bark, deerskins, and the pelts of seals, otters, and bears. In exchange, the expeditionaries gave the Indians something that the latter desired much more than the usual trinkets, small mirrors, or glass beads: "All their esteem is given to iron," Juan Bautista de Aguirre affirms in his diary. They used the coveted metal to make a kind of knife that they wore around their necks, among other things, and they valued it so much that they stole it whenever they could. They even dared to pull down the cross that the Spaniards had set up on shore, in order to extract the nails. When they were rebuked for this, one of the Indians replied that it was the Spaniards who were behaving badly and should leave, since those seas and those lands were theirs.

There were also more unusual trades between natives and Spaniards: for example, the one that took place at the port of Santa Cruz on May 7. A father handed over his daughter in exchange for a coat and two barrel hoops. The girl was about nine years old, and one of the friars took her in charge in order to introduce her to Christian doctrine and baptize her when the time came. Another day, the Spaniards made off with "a little Indian boy, four or five years old," according to Juan Bautista Aguirre, "without anyone forcing him."[32] At the beginning, they thought that the natives sold their children driven by their passion for iron, but then they realized that none of the children offered was healthy; they were children they did not want. On another occasion, Father Noriega was given a very ill little girl as a gift. Seeing that she was going to die, the Spaniards baptized her, with Arteaga acting as godfather. For their part, the *Favorita*'s two boatswains each ended up with a little boy, one about five years old and the other about four. Bodega himself took a boy around nine or ten years old, moved by compassion, according to his own words, and with the intention of protecting and educating him. He gave him his own name, Juan Francisco. All the children died at sea or as soon as they arrived at San Blas, except for Bodega's boy. In 1783, he took him to Peru, and a friar then took charge of him when Bodega traveled to Spain in 1784.[33]

Aguirre's diary records many other details of the appearance, personality, dress, housing, language, food, and personal adornment of the Bucareli natives. He describes their swift, light canoes with admiration. All this information is of undoubted ethnographic value, but this was not the mission that had been entrusted to them. They had now spent two months at Bucareli, and they had to set sail again so as not to lose the best time of the year for exploring the cold northern regions.

Sailing North Becomes Ever More Difficult

The plan was to leave Bucareli Bay in mid-June, but due to contrary winds, the expedition had to delay its departure for twelve long days. They finally set sail on July 1, afraid of having wasted the best season of the year for sailing in the Pacific Northwest. As soon as they rounded the cape of San Bartolomé, they again encountered contrary winds. At times, the thick fog prevented them from sighting land or relying on celestial observation, and the ships lost sight of one another, even though they were very close. They managed to make progress, but much more slowly than they wished.

The crew's condition was already serious by then. The second week in July, the surgeon counted twenty-nine men sick on the *Princesa* alone. The news came at a bad time, just when they were about to enter unknown waters, since the French and Russian maps did not agree from that point on. On July 15, they began to see birds and kelp,[34] signs that they were near land. The next day, at 59° latitude, with the wind in their favor and a clear sky, the land offered them a magnificent sight. In Arteaga's words:

> At eight o'clock, four peaks that had been covered [an illegible word follows] became visible, all of them quite tall, and especially the most northern one, which might be included in the number of the most celebrated ones, due to its notable height. Both these mountains and all the land along the coast that is within sight are covered with snow, making such a beautiful view, especially if the sun communicates its rays to them, that I doubt that anything could be found more pleasing to the sight.[35]

Before their eyes was Mount Saint Elias, the second highest mountain in Canada and the United States.

On July 18, they saw a large bay, today Prince William Sound, and at the same time, they sighted Hinchinbrook Island. While they were there, two men approached them in separate canoes. Arteaga found it strange that they came so far out to sea, since they were about five miles from land. The two men first approached the flagship, singing loudly and harmoniously, without showing any fear of the strangers. In order to convey that their intentions were peaceful, they took an arrow and pulled off its point. Arteaga describes them as follows:

> Their clothes are of skins and fall from their shoulders to their knees, with sleeves. Their hair is black, long, and straight; their height is average; they are well-made and robust; and their color is white, although one of them had his face painted red; and in their language and gestures they were almost similar to those of the port of Bucareli, appearing to us to have their character, docile, peaceful, and affectionate. They carried bows, arrows, and lances, all very finely worked, with the arrow points of bone and some of copper.[36]

It was the Indians' "canoes," or rather kayaks, however, that most surprised the men of the *Princesa* and *Favorita*. As Arteaga explains, they were curved in shape and covered with a strong, tightly-sewn skin with only a single opening, like the mouth of a clay jar, into which one person could fit. Noticing the wonder that their craft aroused, one of the Indians proposed that if one of them was allowed to come on board the frigate, they would let one of the sailors come on board one of their kayaks. The Spaniards accepted the bargain, with an exchange of the usual gifts. What was most valuable, however, was the information the two men provided:

> They made signs to us that there were many to the north, and from what we understood, they meant to indicate vessels like ours and people with clothes like ours, and that there was bread like what they were given.[37]

They also indicated to them by signs that if they continued in the direction they were going, they would find a good passage. Trusting the men, and thinking that they might be referring to the passage that appeared on the Russian maps, both ships sailed in the direction proposed. They soon saw that it was a very dangerous route, however, and they managed to put about only with great effort.

Santiago, 61° 17′ N

On July 23, they anchored at a site that offered marvelous views. Arteaga convened a council, at which three important decisions were taken.

First, that they would stop there to reconnoiter the bay and make a map; second, that one pilot from each ship and a number of soldiers would go to see whether there was a passage further north; and third, that they would take formal possession of the territory.

The third item was carried out with the customary solemnity. The officers, Father Riobo, Father Noriega, the soldiers, and all the men who could be spared went ashore in procession, following a cross. Arteaga brandished his sword and cut bushes, branches, and grass. He then moved some stones around and took possession of the territory in the name of Carlos III. Next, a *Te Deum* was sung, with all the men kneeling before the cross, and the port was baptized with the name of Santiago. It was not just another ceremony: this was the northernmost point of which the Spaniards claimed possession, and it would become the new basis for their claims of sovereignty.

Those who had gone north in search of a passage did not find one, and they returned saying that the coast appeared like a great wall all along their course. This was not the only piece of bad news. The surgeon reported that ten men from Arteaga's ship were sick, five of them with scurvy. After holding another meeting, they decided to continue north despite everything, sailing west and reconnoitering the region without approaching the coast very closely, in an attempt to reach the 70° ordered by their instructions.

In addition to the testimony of the two men who had arrived at Prince William Sound in kayaks, and to the information provided by other Indians, who said they had seen ships larger than the *Favorita* and the *Princesa* in those waters, Arteaga's expedition found evidence that they were not the only Europeans in the area. The group that had gone north in search of a passage saw some natives who were carrying three small flags, one white, one blue, and one red, but they were unable to learn where they had gotten them. At the same time, when Bodega describes the natives' attire, he mentions necklaces made from large glass beads, but the Spaniards were unable to learn who had given them those beads either.

On the day after the second meeting, July 25, Arteaga gave the order to set sail, but rain and contrary winds prevented them from leaving the port of Santiago until the afternoon of the 29th.

Nuestra Señora de la Regla, 59° 08′ N

The voyage to the next anchorage was tremendously costly for both frigates. It rained harder and harder, and hurricane-force winds and storms followed one another day and night. In the rare moments when the fog lifted slightly, they could see that they were near the coast, surrounded by islands and large rocks, and they did not dare to sail onward for fear of running aground. Finally, on August 1, they sighted land to the southwest. They calculated the latitude—59° 08′ N—and decided to take possession of the territory. Since Arteaga was sick, it was Fernando Quirós who led the ceremony. They called the place Nuestra Señora de la Regla.[38]

On land, they found the natives' cabins empty, and a man who passed by in a kayak declined to approach them.

On August 3, they witnessed a strange spectacle. There was a very high mountain entirely covered with snow, and when the sun set, as Bodega explained in his diary, they saw dense smoke come down the slope, as if it were a cloud. They called the mountain Miranda Volcano.[39]

Around midnight on August 6, torrential rains and strong winds returned, and on August 8, finding himself in the middle of an archipelago, the commander gave the order to turn south. Arteaga summarized the motives for his decision in his diary:

> Attending to the weather, which is constantly severe with continual absence of visibility, in the midst of an archipelago of islands, having reconnoitered as far as the longitude of 57° 30′ west of the port of San Blas . . . without finding a passage northward for the purpose of ascending to 70° latitude, and finding ourselves at present with much of the crew sick and relapsing every day, because of the continual rain and excessive cold, I have determined to set a course for Cape Mendocino, and to decide from there what I judge appropriate.[40]

Arteaga made the decision alone, without consulting the rest of the officers, and from what can be gathered from Bodega's and Mourelle's diaries, against their wishes, since both were prepared to continue. It is possible that Arteaga acted as he did for a reason that he does not mention in his diary, but does include in the report he wrote to José de Gálvez, the minister for the Indies, after the voyage was over. In this report, he explains that he was gripped by paralysis, due to the terrible cold and the severe storms they were suffering, and that day after day, it was impossible to do anything. "Thanks be to God," however, he was capable of reaching the port of San Blas.[41]

Little Fruit for So Great a Project

The voyage to San Francisco was made without serious problems. There, the sick received the necessary care, while the pilots collated the information they had each collected separately. They were sorry to receive the news that Viceroy Antonio María de Bucareli y Ursúa, who had played such an important role in the continuity of the settlements in Alta California and the discovery of the Pacific Northwest, had died in April. They also learned that Spain and France had joined the war against Great Britain, making it necessary that they return to San Blas immediately.

The frigates arrived at the port of San Blas four days apart, on November 21 and 25. Bucareli's successor as viceroy, Martín de Mayorga, congratulated those responsible for the expedition. As was usual in such cases, a promotion was requested for all the officers who had participated, except Arteaga, who wanted a different kind of reward for his labors. He had married in violation of the applicable naval regulations, and he wanted to see to it that if he died, his two sons and two daughters would not be left without a pension.

The officers obtained their desired promotions: Bodega and Quirós were promoted from lieutenant (*teniente de navío*) to commander (*capitán de fragata*), and Mourelle and Cañizares from first pilot and ensign (*alférez de fragata*) to lieutenant junior grade (*alférez de navío*). Arteaga, for his part, was promised a pension for his family in the event of his death. The overall results of the expedition, however, were mediocre. The voyage had been prepared more carefully than any other. The ships were magnificent, the sailors were skilled, the provisions were more than sufficient, scurvy had not been the same scourge it had on other occasions, and nevertheless, the achievements had been few and the discoveries of little significance. They had spent too long exploring Bucareli, wasting the summer days they needed if they were to reach 70°. In addition, they did not pay attention to the signs that revealed the presence of other Europeans, the colored banners and glass beads. They were unaware that Capt. James Cook's ships had been there, and they returned without having seen any trace of the Russian establishments.

The supposed absence of foreigners reaffirmed the Spaniards' belief that their dominion in the Pacific was not endangered. For this reason, and because the war against England was given priority, there were no more expeditions to explore the Northwest in the following years. The *Princesa* and the *Favorita* were assigned to supplying the missions and presidios under the command of Agustín de Echeverría and his Basque compatriot Juan Bautista de Aguirre. Bodega was sent to Cádiz, and Heceta and Arteaga remained in San Blas. Meanwhile, news of the riches of northwestern North America was spreading throughout Europe. Rather than being shrouded in Spanish secrecy this time, Arteaga's and Bodega's information and maps were made public, while word of the furs Captain Cook had obtained spread throughout the European ports.

Juan Francisco de la Bodega y Quadra Gives New Impetus to the Exploration of the Northwest and Intervenes in the Nootka Crisis, 1789–1794

Juan Francisco de la Bodega y Quadra, ca. 1785. Unknown artist.

During the years in which the Basque-Peruvian Juan Francisco de la Bodega y Quadra occupied the post of commandant of the maritime department of San Blas, there was an unusual bustle in the port. Between 1789 and 1794, maritime expeditions organized by Bodega explored the Strait of Juan de Fuca, Prince William Sound, and Cook Inlet and demonstrated the falsity of the legends about the supposed transcontinental channels of Lorenzo Pérez Maldonado and Juan de Fuca. They also inspected the mouth of the Columbia River and reconnoitered the entire coastal strip between San Francisco and 56° N . . . and yet, it can be said that the chief enterprise carried out by Bodega, the culmination of his career, belonged to the diplomatic field: his participation in the Nootka crisis.

Nootka is one of the inlets or bays on the west side of Vancouver Island, today part of British Columbia, Canada. At the time of the first European expeditions, several human groups lived along these bays, each in its own territory. One of these groups was the Mowachaht. Their chief was Maquinna, and they lived in Yuquot, a settlement located on a cove at the entrance of Nootka Sound. Juan Pérez's *Santiago* was the first European ship to make landfall there, in 1774, but the formal ceremony of taking possession was carried out by Esteban Martínez in 1789. When Captain Cook visited the area in 1778, the natives showed him two silver spoons, surely obtained from the Spaniards by barter or theft. Following Cook's visit, the English became well acquainted with the route, attracted by the fur trade. As usually happened, both groups assigned new place names, in ignorance of the original ones: Martínez called the bay San Lorenzo de Nuca and gave the name of Santa Cruz de Nuca to the settlement of Yuquot. For the English, since Captain Cook's time there, it was Friendly Cove.

The Nootka crisis or Nootka incident began in July 1789, when Esteban Martínez, the Spanish commander at Nootka, seized several British merchant ships. The British asked for compensation, the Spaniards refused, and both countries prepared for war. A British squadron of twenty-nine ships sailed the length of the Spanish coast with the aim of frightening the Spaniards. Without being deterred by that show of force, the Spanish fleet set sail from Cádiz in search of the British. It all came to nothing, however, since the two groups of ships did not meet.

There was no war, but the incident was not easily resolved. At stake were, on the one hand, rights over the Pacific Northwest, and on the other, commercial interests tied to the fur trade. Spain considered herself sovereign and mistress of the Pacific on the basis of the rights derived, according to the customs of the time, from being the first country to arrive in the territory and carry out the ceremony of taking possession. For the British, in contrast, sailing in the region was a right that belonged to every nation, and without real occupation of the territory, ownership of it could not be claimed.

In 1790, the First Nootka Convention was signed. According to this agreement, British ships could not fish or sail within ten leagues of the coastal strip occupied by the Spaniards. North of Nootka, however, they would have freedom of trade wherever there were no European

Nootka's San Miguel Fort. By Sigismund Bacon, 1793.
Canadian Military History Gateway

settlements. In order to carry out the agreement and demarcate the borders of each country's territory, an expedition was organized, known as the Expedition of the Limits. The British authorities chose George Vancouver for the enterprise, and the Spanish chose the creole Basque Juan Francisco de la Bodega y Quadra.

Francisco de Eliza in Nootka, 1790–1791

When Francisco de Eliza's expedition reached its destination, the men did not find any Europeans at Nootka. They chose a sheltered cove, named Friendly Cove by the English, where Yuquot is now, and began to construct defenses. Meanwhile, seventy-six soldiers from the Catalan Free Company of Volunteers (Compañía Franca de Voluntarios de Cataluña), who formed part of the expedition under the command of Pere d'Alberni, built pens for the livestock and an oven for baking bread, prepared the ground for a large garden, built houses and a hospital, and dug wells and irrigation canals. A small fort was built on an islet located at the entrance to the cove, which they named San Miguel, and there was also time to explore. In May 1790, Salvador Fidalgo headed north to visit the Russian settlements in Alaska, and Manuel Quimper explored the Strait of Juan de Fuca.

Callicum y Maquinna, 1796. From John Meares: Voyages made in the years 1788 and 1789 from China to the Northwest Coast of America. http://www.gracegalleries.com/)

In his instructions, Bodega had underlined the necessity of making peace with the natives, since relations had deteriorated after Esteban Martínez killed one of their chiefs, Callicum, the previous summer. Eliza's efforts did not succeed in allaying their distrust, however; rather, several bloody incidents increased the Indians' hostility. One night, the Spaniards killed five natives who were trying to steal the iron hoops from their barrels. On another occasion, a large disturbance broke out when the sailors tried to steal the lumber from the Indians' cabins in order to build their houses and barracks. In order to reduce tensions, Eliza distributed copper plaques and Monterrey's valued abalone shells among the native chiefs and elders. Even so, the winter of 1790–91 was very hard for the expedition's members. Fearful of the Indians, they did not dare go hunting. The rains had ruined Alberni's garden, and without fresh food, they were completely dependent on whatever fish the natives wanted to bring them.

At the same time, the natives were anxious to recover the area where the Spaniards had established themselves. It was Chief Maquinna's summer residence and the place from which the men set out on the whale hunts that were fundamental for their subsistence. The Indians came again and again to ask the foreigners when they were going to leave. According to a letter addressed to Bodega, one day Maquinna came in person to ask, since as it was the best location in the bay, he wanted to establish himself there again with his people. The chief was very sick, because there was not sufficient food. The Spaniards told him to stay and live with them, but he replied that he could not do so, since they had raped his wives.[42]

Little by little, the tension between the two groups eased. That first winter, when the garden was ruined, Maquinna brought them venison and fresh fish. In a letter to the viceroy, Eliza spoke of the good relations he maintained with the Indians, and as evidence, he said that they were in the habit of coming to his house to eat and sleep, not just occasionally, but "too often," and not only the chiefs, but whoever came to visit the people of that bay, including members of other nations.

Commandant Juan Francisco de la Bodega y Quadra, the English Captain George Vancouver, the Artist Atanasio Echeverría, and the Frigate Aránzazu, *Protagonists of the Nootka Crisis, 1792*

Bodega had to meet the British representatives at Nootka Sound and leave the territory in their hands as recompense for the English ships that Esteban Martínez had seized, as stipulated in the First Nootka Convention. Paradoxically, nevertheless, the act of signing that accord did not mean that Spain was renouncing her interests in the Pacific, but rather the reverse. In effect, the Expedition of the Limits was planned with very ambitious goals: a settlement was to be founded at Fuca; yet another attempt was to be made to find the channel that supposedly linked the Pacific Ocean to the Atlantic; and the entire coast between San Francisco and latitude 56° N was to be explored for the purpose of demarcating the border between Spanish and English interests.

As soon as he learned the details, Bodega informed the viceroy that for an expedition on such a scale, a new ship was necessary. Having obtained the appropriate permission, he had a schooner with twelve guns built, the *Activa*. The veteran *Princesa* was also to take part in the expedition, but had to be overhauled first. The third ship chosen was the schooner *Mexicana*, but when Malaspina,[43] the commander of a contemporaneous scientific expedition, recommended taking two schooners instead of just one, the Basque Manuel Basterrechea built the *Sutil* at San Blas, a twin of the *Mexicana*. Two other ships would complete the group: the *Santa Gertrudis* and the *Aránzazu*.[44] Each ship had a function to fulfill, but it was also hoped that the ensemble would impress the English at Nootka.

While the preparations were moving forward, Bodega met at San Blas with the members of Malaspina's expedition. He thus learned about the productive work that scientists and artists could do on such voyages, and he decided to add this component to his diplomatic and exploratory expedition. The scientists selected were José Mariano Moziño and his assistant José Maldonado. The chosen artist was one of the era's most skillful drawers, Atanasio Echeverría.

Echeverría, of Basque origin, was born in Mexico and had taken part in the Royal Botanical Expedition to New Spain, led by José Mariano Mociño and Martín de Sessé, undoubtedly one of the most interesting expeditions of the time, both for its long duration and the extensive region covered and for the abundant material collected.[45] Sessé, a botanist, had highlighted the drawings Echeverría made. His plants, birds, butterflies, and fish were exceptional, as much for their beauty as for their precision. In addition, he worked very quickly. In a single day, he completed the drawings of four plants and a butterfly, and the one of the butterfly was so marvelous that it seemed that the insect was going to fly out of the paper. At the time of the expedition, Echeverría was not yet eighteen years old. Later on, the naturalist Alexander von Humboldt would write that his drawings could compete with the most perfect works of the same kind created in Europe.[46]

On February 29, 1792, the *Princesa*, the *Activa*, and the *Santa Gertrudis* were ready to set sail. The remaining ships would sail later, and the *Aránzazu* would also have to stop several times to deliver provisions and letters to the California missions and presidios.

The three ships were going to sail together, but the *Princesa* and the *Activa* had problems from the moment they put out to sea, and in the end the *Santa Gertrudis* made the voyage to Nootka alone.

Juan Francisco de la Bodega y Quadra in Nootka

The *Santa Gertrudis* arrived in Nootka without problems on April 29, 1792, after a voyage of sixty days. Francisco de Eliza's frigate *Concepción* was in the bay. Eliza and his men had been in Nootka for two years, they had been sent there with the mission of establishing a settlement. As soon as Bodega dropped anchor, Maquinna and other Indian chiefs came to welcome him. They then took him to visit the Spanish settlement, and Maquinna celebrated a potlatch[47] in his honor.

According to his *Viaje a la Costa Noroeste de la América Septentrional* (Voyage to the northwest coast of North America), the settlement made a favorable impression on Bodega. He thought the residences and gardens magnificent, and he had the impression that the crew and the soldiers enjoyed good health and were very content. Nevertheless, after speaking with Eliza, he learned that the reality was different. The site's climate was unendurable, and the two years they had spent there had been very hard, due to the cold and the unceasing rain and snow. Nine men had died of scurvy, and another thirty-two, too sick to continue there, had had to be sent to California to recover.

The other ships gradually arrived: the schooner*Activa* on May 4, the twins *Sutil* and *Mexicana* on May 11, and the frigate*Aránzazu* on May 13. In the following weeks, Bodega dedicated himself to the tasks of repair and expansion of the settlement, in order to be able to offer the English a fitting welcome. The ships also needed repair, since only the *Santa Gertrudis* had arrived in good condition. The worst storm damage had been suffered by the voluminous *Aránzazu*, which had to be careened, something that took an entire month. They also careened the *Activa*. The *Mexicana* arrived without its principal mast, and the recently built *Sutil* struck a rock upon entering the bay.

During the five months Bodega spent in Nootka, some sixteen ships, of English, French, Portuguese, and American origin, arrived in the bay for the fur trade. Seeing that activity was enough to bring home the realization that Spain was going to find it ever more difficult to maintain the hegemony she had enjoyed in the Pacific until then.

Summer came, and there was no trace of Vancouver. On July 4, the *Daedalus* arrived, loaded with provisions for him, and the Spaniards learned that he would not be there until the end of the summer. This meant the loss of precious time for exploring those latitudes. Without waiting around, Bodega acted. Since the garrison ate more than the livestock and the gardens could supply, he decided to shrink the Yuquot settlement. The *Sutil* and the *Mexicana* had previously left to explore the Strait of Juan de Fuca, and Bodega now decided to send Eliza with the *Concepción* as well. The *Santa Gertrudis*, for its part, would go to Monterrey carrying Bodega's messages. As far as the voluminous *Aránzazu* was concerned, it had sailed from Nootka on June 4, on a mission of great importance.

The Frigate Aránzazu Goes in Search of Admiral Fonte's Legendary Passage

The Northwest Passage, the legendary Strait of Anián, had been the longed-for destination of many maritime expeditions for nearly three centuries. The first recorded attempt was made in 1497 by John Cabot, who was seeking to cross from east to west. Francis Drake sought the western entrance in 1579. In 1592, the Greek Juan de Fuca, sailing from Acapulco under a Spanish flag, announced that he had succeeded in reaching the North Sea and returning by way of this passage. The Frenchman Jacques Cartier and the Englishman Henry Hudson also tried to find it. On the Russian side, the names of Vitus Bering and Aleksei Chirikov have remained forever linked to the history of this search.

In the eighteenth century, these efforts were multiplied. In 1778, Capt. James Cook's expedition sailed from Nootka Sound and reached 70° latitude, finding nothing but icebergs. On Spain's part, the passage was among the objectives of the Heceta-Bodega expedition of 1775 and the Arteaga-Bodega expedition of 1779. In 1791, Alessandro Malaspina made it as far as Yakutat Bay. In 1790 and 1791, it was Francisco de Eliza's turn, and in 1792, Dionisio Alcalá Galiano's . . . They all returned without finding what they were looking for, but this did not prevent stories about the legendary strait from continuing to circulate at the century's end.

Among those stories, that of Bartolomé de Fonte was the best known. It originated in a London publication, the *Monthly Miscellany or Memoirs for the Curious*. According to an anonymous letter published in that journal, in 1639 the Spanish authorities ordered Bartholomew de Fonte to determine whether a passage between the Atlantic and Pacific existed. In April 1640, this Fonte, "Admiral of New Spain and Peru and Prince of Chile," left Callao, the port of Lima. Having reached 53° latitude, he found a river, which he named Río de los Reyes, in an archipelago. He continued his course to the east until he reached a lake, and from there, crossing other rivers and lakes, he reached Hudson Bay. There, he met a Boston captain named Shapley, to whom Fonte gave his beautiful diamond ring in exchange for a thousand pieces-of-eight and the captain's handsome maps and diaries. Since the Boston ship came from the other direction, Fonte concluded that this was the passage that crossed the continent, and he returned to Peru without verifying that conclusion.

In the summer of 1792, in view of the presence of so many foreign ships in Nootka, all of them dedicated to the fur trade, the search for the passage became a priority for the Spanish authorities. If it really existed, and if other European nations used it, the Alta California settlements would lose the isolation in which they had existed until then. A new attempt to find the passage was urgent, and Bodega set to work. Jacinto Caamaño would be the expedition's commander, and the ship would be the old frigate *Aránzazu*.

The *Aránzazu*, the "monstrous cargo ship" of 205 tons that supplied the California missions, was to go directly to Bucareli Bay and explore all its arms. Next, it was to reconnoiter the entire coast between there and Nootka, drawing maps of all the ports, gulfs, and straits, and above all of Admiral Fonte's passage. In his diary, Captain Caamaño is pessimistic about the mission with which he was entrusted, stating clearly that the existence of such a passage, according to the latest opinions, might be doubtful and even imaginary, but notwithstanding Caamaño's lack of faith, the *Aránzazu* left Nootka on June 13, with provisions for two months.

First, the expedition explored Bucareli Bay. Next, they scrutinized all the inlets, islands, and straits in the surrounding area. They crossed Hecate Strait and entered Príncipe Strait, although it was too small for such a large ship. In sum, they examined everything . . . without finding any trace of Admiral Fonte's passage as described in the anonymous London letter. The summer was passing; it was becoming ever more difficult to navigate in those waters and continue exploring the territory, due to the rains, storms, and fogs; and believing that all his efforts were futile, Caamaño decided to return to Nootka. On the way, on August 30, he gave the name of Aristazabal[48] to an island located southwest of Princess Royal Island, British Columbia, Canada. On September 7, the *Aránzazu* was back in Nootka after a voyage of eighty-six days.

In his diary, Caamaño adds an appendix in which he again makes clear his opinion of Admiral Fonte's passage. Caamaño maintains that no such passage exists, at least not at the place mentioned by the various stories, around 53° N. In his view, Fonte's expedition of 1640 never took place; what is more, the story could have no other basis than the stupidity or ignorance of someone who knew nothing of sailing or geography.[49]

For the *Aránzazu*, this was its last great adventure. From then on, it was dedicated to more routine enterprises, fundamentally to supplying the ever-longer chain of Franciscan missions in Alta California, where for the Basque Franciscans who impatiently awaited the provisions and the news that the ship brought, it was never a monstrous cargo ship, but rather the blessed schooner of Our Lady of Aránzazu.

Bodega and Vancouver Finally Meet at Nootka

The viceroy's instructions were very clear with regard to how Bodega was to behave with the British representatives at Nootka. He was to try to maintain complete harmony and the friendliest possible relations with the commanders, officers, and crew of the British ships and to behave with the proper dignity in their presence. In sum, he was asked for diplomacy, something to which he had not previously dedicated himself, but that suited his education and temperament very well.

In order to receive the English captain as he deserved, Bodega had ordered the finest delicacies that could be obtained in Mexico:

> Barrels of brandy, table wines, cases of bottled vintage wines, wineskins of cider, and beer; Flemish [fine] lard and hams; pickled greens, vegetables in oil, jars of oil, Castilian vinegar and olives; parboiled fowl and marinated meats; flours, cookies, chocolate, coffee, sugar, and sweetmeats.[50]

He also ordered livestock, chickens, cheese, dried fruit, and other items purchased in Tepic and Ahucatlán loaded onto his ships.

In that summer of 1792, all the commanders and officers of the foreign ships that visited Nootka had the opportunity to enjoy Bodega's courtesy and the excellence of his table. It was something that they did not expect to find in that forgotten corner of the world. Exquisite dishes, served on Bodega's own silver plate! In addition, his generosity was not limited to these invitations. He supplied the visitors with fresh food. Every morning, he sent freshly baked rolls, vegetables from the garden, and fresh goat's and cow's milk to all the ships anchored in the bay. He shared his maps with those who needed them, and if a ship, even a foreign one, arrived with a problem, he had his men help to repair it.

The viceroy had ordered him to behave courteously with the aim of upholding the honor of the Spanish monarchy and its navy. And Bodega turned out to be the right man to carry out orders of this kind, due to his affability and to another trait that had characterized him since his youth: a "spendthrift spirit."[51] The viceroy's instructions were equally detailed with regard to the good relations that—if possible—he was to maintain with the natives, underlining that good treatment and harmony were necessary in order to establish friendship with them, so that the Spaniards' visits would not frighten them as much as those of other voyagers.[52]

As soon as he arrived, Bodega indicated to the captains and officers of the ships under his command and to the garrison on land that he would be greatly saddened to learn of any behavior that was not conducive to the greatest harmony with the natives.[53]

Unlike previous commanders, Bodega often visited the chiefs in their towns, taking them cloth, abalone shells, and above all, copper plaques. A special gift that he made to Chief Maquinna was a metal suit, made of tin plaques perfectly shaped in the form of fish scales, that the Indian chief kept for special ceremonies. All this—invitations, visits, gifts—was something Bodega did gladly, since as he confesses in his *Viaje*, he found it easy, as a consequence of his own personality, to maintain good relations with the natives.[54]

Summer was passing at Nootka, and Bodega and his men were growing increasingly concerned about Vancouver's failure to appear. The news of his delayed arrival had displeased Bodega. Nevertheless, when the *HMS Discovery* and the *Chatham* finally appeared in the bay in late August, they were received with the greatest courtesy. In his diary, Vancouver expressed his amazement at the meal he was offered:

> [we] were gratified with a repast we had lately been little accustomed to, or had the most distant idea of meeting with at this place. A dinner of five courses, consisting of a superfluity of the best provisions, was served with great elegance.[55]

Chief Maquinna was among the guests. He was wary of the treatment that he and his people would receive from the English when the settlement passed into their hands. Seeking to calm him, Bodega assured him that the English would treat him just as well as the Spaniards had.

Vancouver and Bodega had a very good relationship from the beginning. They both enjoyed each other's company, and they had no qualms about sharing provisions, information, and even the same doctor. When Vancouver learned of Bodega's severe headaches—he had been "in broken health" for some time—the English captain did not hesitate to send him his surgeon.

Both commanders' good will was evident, but the negotiations were a different matter. The two men did not succeed in reaching agreement when it came time to establish the borders of the territory belonging to England and Spain—Bodega proposed drawing the boundary line at Fuca, while Vancouver proposed San Francisco—or to demarcate the territory that Spain had to turn over to England.

One of the most noteworthy moments in their time together occurred during a pause in the negotiations. Taking up an invitation from Chief Maquinna, both commanders went to visit his town, at one end of Tahsis Inlet. They wanted above all to show the native chief that there was no enmity between them, and that the good relations that the indigenous people maintained with the foreigners were not going to change when the territory passed into English hands.

The visitors played music as they arrived in their boats, and they came ashore amid shouts from the natives. Maquinna welcomed them on the beach, together with his brothers and servants, and brought them to his house.

Friendly Cove (Yuquot), Nootkan. Copy of the original sketch by Atanasio Echeverría in 1792. He was La expedición de los Límites' s official artist. On the left of the image is the Bodega's two-story house. A number of other visitors from all over the world visited there. George Vancouver: A Voyage of Discovery to the North Pacific Ocean and Round the World, I. lib., plate VII. http://archive.org/

So that nothing would be lacking, Bodega had brought with him his servant, his cooks, and cooking utensils—and his silver service, of course. The artist Atanasio Echeverría was present and made a drawing in which Chief Maquinna is seen dancing before Bodega, Vancouver, and other foreign visitors in the metal garment Bodega had given him.[56] Vancouver wanted to reciprocate with a small demonstration of his own dances and had his sailors dance a reel.

When saying goodbye to his guests, Maquinna expressed his happiness at having been honored with that visit, showing himself proud that they treated him with more respect than the other chiefs.

The return to Friendly Cove or Santa Cruz de Nuca had special significance for Bodega and Vancouver. In the English captain's version:

> In our conversation whilst on this little excursion, Señor Quadra had very earnestly requested that I would name some port or island after us both, to commemorate our meeting and the very friendly intercourse that had taken place and subsisted between us. Conceiving no spot so proper for this denomination as the place where we had first met . . . I named that country the island of QUADRA and VANCOUVER; with which compliment he seemed highly pleased.[57]

Bodega mentions the matter only in passing, saying that Vancouver asked his permission to baptize an island with both their names, in order to immortalize the memory of their friendship. Which of them made the request of the other? We have no way of knowing, but the episode explains why the island appears on Spanish, French, and English maps with the compound name of Quadra and Vancouver, until in the course of the nineteenth century it lost the first element and became simply Vancouver Island.

Despite the good relations between the parties, the negotiations were at an impasse, and both representatives indicated their desire to break off the talks, leaving the final resolution of the Nootka crisis in the hands of their governments in Madrid and London. Their writings do not attempt to hide a degree of frustration about the failure of the negotiations and the waste of time. Nevertheless, they parted as friends and agreed to meet again in Monterrey in the hope of making some progress. On the eve of his departure, Vancouver invited Bodega to dine on the *HMS Discovery*. When it grew dark, they went ashore, at Bodega's request, and spent that final night in singing, dancing, and games of all kinds, enjoying themselves greatly.

The Basques Whom Captain Vancouver Met in Alta California

In his *A Voyage of Discovery*, Vancouver writes that when he left Nootka for Monterrey, he stopped in San Francisco. He was welcomed there by Fray Martín Landaeta, who invited him to his mission in the name of all the friars. Vancouver found this Bizkaian friar "very pleasing and entertaining," and the commander of the San Francisco presidio, for his part, Hermenegildo Sal, made no objection to Vancouver's moving about as he pleased, providing him with horses and an escort so that he could visit the Santa Clara mission. Consequently, when he went to the mission the next day, "we were received by the reverend fathers with every demonstration of cordiality, friendship, and the most genuine hospitality."[58]

On November 27, Vancouver met Bodega in Monterrey and showed him the results of his most recent explorations. Bodega, for his part, behaved as the best possible host, as in Nootka. The two men went to the Carmel mission, where Vancouver met Fermín Lasuén, a friar originally from Vitoria, who struck him as worthy of great esteem.

> On our arrival at the entrance of the mission the bells were rung, and the Rev. Fermin Francisco de Lasuen, father president of the missionaries of the order of St. Francisco in New Albion, together with the fathers of this mission, came out to meet us, and conduct us to the principal residence of the father president.[59]

Vancouver spent fifty days at the port of Monterrey while he made observations on land and his ships were repaired. The Spaniards accepted no payment of any kind in exchange, and on January 15, 1793, the English and Spanish ships sailed out of the bay together.

In May of the same year, Vancouver was back on the California coast. In San Francisco, Commander Sal received him with courtesy, but not as generously as the previous year. In November, in Monterrey, he had a meeting with the interim governor, the Basque José Joaquín Arrillaga. Trying to prevent the English from realizing the weakness of the Spanish defenses, Arrillaga set limits on the English captain's movements. The latter took offense and sailed south as soon as he could, without replenishing his supplies of water and without loading the provisions that had been prepared for him. Arrillaga sent a message to the presidios not to provision the English ships, but they reached Santa Bárbara before the messenger did. Felipe Goicoechea,[60] the presidio commander, welcomed the foreigners with open arms, giving them all facilities for supplying themselves with everything they needed, although he also put some limits on their movements.

Felipe Goicoechea appeared to Vancouver to be a man of "noble and generous mind."[61] It was someone else who made the greatest impression on the Englishman during his stay in Santa Bárbara, however: the Navarrese friar Vicente Santa María, the chaplain of the first European ship to pass through the Golden Gate almost twenty years before.

According to Vancouver, on the day before his planned departure from Santa Bárbara, a friar appeared with a small flock and twenty mules laden with foodstuffs. It was Vicente Santa María, and he was coming from the mission of San Buenaventura. He had made more than one ocean voyage, and he was very well aware of how necessary fresh food was for seamen. For this reason, in addition to making Vancouver a gift of everything he had brought with him, he invited him to visit the mission, where he might find more things that would be useful to him on his voyage. The captain did not accept the invitation, so as not to delay his departure, but pleasantly surprised by friar's generosity, he invited Santa María—"this excellently-good man," as he called him—to a meal on the *HMS Discovery*. The commander Felipe Goicoechea and Fray José de Miguel, a native of Treviño, from the Santa Bárbara mission, were also invited. In their agreeable table conversation, Santa María's character seemed even more admirable to Vancouver:

> I had only reason to regret the short time I was to be indulged with the society of a gentleman, whose observations through life, and general knowledge of mankind, rendered him a most pleasing and instructive companion.[62]

When night fell, before the guests returned to shore, Vancouver, who wanted to continue enjoying the friendly friar's company, offered to take him to the mission the following day on the *Discovery*, so that he would not have to walk all the way. Santa María happily accepted the offer.

The *Discovery* left for San Buenaventura the following morning. Along the way, Vancouver gave a cape the name of Point Felipe, in a gesture of thanks to Cmdr. Felipe Goicoechea. They made the trip slowly, and it was already eight o'clock in the evening when they came within a league of the mission. Santa María was pleased; he hoped that this friendly relationship with the English captain would set a good example for the Indians, who were convinced that all strangers were enemies. That same morning, Vancouver had seen evidence of this. When Santa María told the four or five Indians who had accompanied him to return

Point Vicente, in Palos Verdes, north of the port of Los Angeles. Source: josefrancisco.org

to the mission on their own, while he went by ship, they begged the friar for the love of God to do nothing of the sort, because if he went off with strangers, they would never see him again. Santa María tried to reassure them, but in vain. They remained on the beach until the last moment, unceasingly begging the friar not to go on the ship.

The following day, after an early breakfast, Vancouver and Santa María set out for shore together in a longboat, but the sea was rough, and they had to return to the *HMS Discovery*. While they were waiting to be able to land, the Indians brought four canoes loaded with lambs, birds, and all kinds of vegetables for the English, on Santa María's orders.[63]

The next morning, the natives returned to the *HMS Discovery* to report that the sea was calm. On shore, a new supply of provisions awaited Vancouver, including a young bull that was brought on board alive, with the intention of taking it to "Owhyhe" (Hawaii). The most surprising thing, however, was what happened when Vancouver and Santa María began their walk. Although it was very early, an enormous number of Indians, men and women, old and young, came out to meet them. Vancouver thought at first that they were coming to see him and his men, the foreigners, but he quickly realized that they only wanted to welcome Santa María and ask for his blessing. They wanted to know whether the English had treated him well and asked him many questions in their language, since, as Vancouver was able to verify, the friar spoke the natives' language "very fluently."

Vancouver left the mission very grateful for the warm welcome he had been given. Back on the *Discovery*, he set sail southeast, and on reaching a bay, he gave its most prominent cape the name of Point Vicente, in homage to his friend.[64]

In this way, on December 9, Vancouver began his return voyage, after having baptized various locations along the California coast with the names of his Basque friends: Point Fermín, Point Lasuén, Point Felipe, Point Vicente . . . The cautious Arrillaga, who wanted to restrict the Englishman's movements, did not receive any similar honor.

Bodega's End

The final agreement resolving the Nootka crisis was signed on January 11, 1794. The two governments agreed to leave Nootka Sound by way of a ceremony in which Santa Cruz de Nuca or Friendly Cove would be transferred to the British. The count of Floridablanca sent Bodega y Quadra detailed instructions from Spain, with the aim that he take care of everything. By the time the instructions arrived, however, Bodega was dead. He had never completely recovered after he returned from his 1775 voyage sick with scurvy, and in the last few years, his "broken health" had been accompanied by worry over the debts he had contracted.

Bodega's father, the Bizkaian Tomás de la Bodega y Quadra, had become a prosperous businessman in Peru and left a considerable inheritance to each of his children, but Bodega, following the inclinations of his "spendthrift spirit," had committed his own wealth to the missions with which he was entrusted. In 1779, he used part of his inheritance to buy the *Favorita* in Peru; later on, in his eagerness to show himself to be generous to the foreigners in Nootka, he contracted numerous debts. Back from Nootka and knowing that he was ill, he wanted to improve his financial situation so that his wife and children would not find themselves in difficulties in the event of his death. He wrote to the king, recalling that he had sacrificed his life for his country and requesting the post of governor of Lima's port of Callao, or a similar position, appropriate for his "poor talents," and with a healthy climate, something that he needed after having served the crown for thirty years in unhealthy climates.[65] It was all in vain, however. Bodega got nothing back from the royal treasury and ended up ruined, without receiving any recompense after so much effort.

His health worsened, and on March 24, 1793, he wrote to the viceroy in these terms:

Stained glass showing the moment Bodega y Quadra and Vancouver met.

Quadra Park, Victoria, British Columbia, Canada

> For many days, I have lived mortified by a pain that it is no longer possible for me to resist, and as the physicians assure me that I will be able to heal if I withdraw for a while from the department's affairs, I must deserve from Your Excellency permission to turn them over to the appropriate officer until I obtain some relief.[66]

The viceroy granted him license, and Bodega departed for Mexico City, accompanied by two or three servants, in search of medical care. Along the way, between Irapuato and Querétaro, they were robbed of everything they had with them, along with about a thousand pesos. When they reached Mexico City, Bodega was very ill. It seems that he was taken to the Colegio de San Fernando, the Franciscan missionary seminary, where he died on March 26, 1794.

After Bodega's death, the Vitorian José Manuel de Álava took on the task of putting the accord reached with the British into effect in Nootka, presiding over the formal ceremony. From then on, both nations would be able to pursue commerce in the area around Nootka Sound, but neither one would be permitted to construct permanent buildings there. The agreement had another, broader consequence: the Pacific Coast from Chile to Alaska could not be considered Spanish property.

For Nootka as well, the accord had significant consequences. It ceased to be a center of international diplomacy, and at the same time, due to a fall in the sea-otter population, it ceased to interest fur traders. In these new circumstances, it went back to being what it had always been: a remote location.

Legacy

In the mid-sixteenth century, the Pacific Northwest coast was an empty space on the maps. Those who explored and named the region include some of the most important figures in the history of maritime navigation: Bering and Chirikov, Cook and Vancouver, La Pérouse and Malaspina. More than a few Basque surnames appear on the roll of honor: Heceta, Ayala y Aguirre, Arteaga . . . and standing out among them all, the Basque-Peruvian Bodega y Quadra.

Juan Francisco Bodega y Quadra is considered one of the greatest explorers of the Pacific Northwest, and his name has received the recognition it deserves. In 1903, the Washington University State Historical Society set up a granite monument at the site in Canada where the battery that defended the entrance to Nootka Sound was located. In Victoria, the capital of British Colombia, one of the major streets that crosses the city is named Quadra Street. There is also an elementary school named for Quadra in this city, and there is a statue of the explorer, dedicated by Spain's King Juan Carlos I in 1984, in a park that bears his name.

A number of geographical locations in British Colombia are also named for him. Between Vancouver Island and the mainland, in Discovery Passage, there is a large island named Quadra Island; on Galiano Island, in the Strait of Georgia, there is a Quadra Hill; in Houston Stewart Channel, in the Queen Charlotte Islands, there are the Quadra Rocks . . . Even so, as we have already mentioned, his name has been erased from one geographical location, the most important of all, since it is the largest island on the entire Pacific Coast.[67] What the two captains named Quadra and Vancouver Island is today Vancouver Island, just as what was "Ezeta's Inlet" on late-eighteenth-century maps is today the Columbia River.

5
The Franciscan Missions in Alta California

Two Franciscan missionaries. By Alexander Harmer

The Mission, a Basic Frontier Institution

Missions played a fundamental role in Spanish colonial policy. As H. E. Bolton explains in his synthesis of the subject,[1] each of the nations that participated in the colonization of the Americas brought specific types of institutions and people to frontier lands. In the French colonies, the pioneers were trappers, fur traders, and missionaries. In the English colonies, the first to arrive, and the ones who opened new paths, were again trappers, but they were immediately followed by colonists who cut down the forests and, step by step, displaced the Indians without ever mixing with them. In the Spanish colonies, there were three categories of people who were responsible for expanding and maintaining the frontiers: the conqueror, the presidio soldier, and the missionary. Of the three, it was undoubtedly the missionary, the first European inhabitant of those lands, who was the most influential, serving both the Church and the state.

The missionaries' primary objective was to spread the Christian faith among the pagans. So Bolton affirms, and anyone who reads the numerous texts the missionaries wrote will come to the same conclusion: they were drawn to those lands by religious fervor. Once they established themselves, however, they were called on to act at the same time as scientists, geographers, ethnographers, schoolteachers, masons, and farmers, becoming, voluntarily or involuntarily, the state's best allies in its effort to expand its borders and subject the native inhabitants to the yoke of civilization.

At first, the missions were founded as provisional institutions. After ten years, they were to pass into the hands of the secular clergy, and their lands were to be returned to their original owners, that is, the Indians. However, this plan, which had been designed on the basis of experience with the inhabitants of Mexico, Central America, and Peru, turned out to be inappropriate for Alta California's inhabitants, as a consequence, in the friars' opinion, of their lower level of civilization,[2] and because the Indians of Alta California clung to their way of life much more fiercely than those of Baja California. According to Fr. Fermín Lasuén, it was impossible for someone who had not seen it to have an idea of the attachment that "these poor creatures" had to the forest. There, they had neither shelter nor protection, nor food, nor medicine, nor help of any kind. In the mission, they could cheer their hearts with all these things; the dead were far fewer there than in the forest. They saw all this, and despite everything, they continued yearning for the forest.[3]

Another obstacle that the missionaries faced was the hostility that existed between the different Indian nations. In effect, the inhabitants whom the Europeans found in those lands bore no resemblance to Rousseau's "noble savage." Lasuén himself described them in a letter he wrote to the viceroy in 1797 in this way:

> Among the nations that have been discovered here, I do not know even one that would keep the peace with its neighbor. Those living adjacent to one another are accustomed at times to be in communication and to preserve some sort of harmony. But when one of them enters the territory of another, they invariably take up arms, because among them to speak a different dialect and to be an enemy are one and the same thing.[4]

The friars immediately understood that in order to attract the Indians to Christian doctrine, they first needed to get them to accept the basics of what they understood as civilization. The Indians needed to wear clothes, practice monogamy, and live in houses of adobe or stone; as far as social organization was concerned, they had to submit to the Spanish authorities and Spanish laws. The missionaries' interests and those of the civil authorities coincided in this regard, and as a consequence, the missions were designed as institutions intended to civilize and control the frontier, as well as to Christianize it.

The first step was to gather the Indians into populated centers. The Pueblos of New Mexico and the Pimas of Arizona could be given instruction in their rancherías, since they were sedentary, but the nomadic and scattered nations of California had to be brought together in towns and kept there, by force if necessary. For this purpose, each mission customarily had the assistance of a few soldiers, and the friars sought reinforcements in the event that a group of Indians escaped and had to be searched for. Over time, both in order to defend the missionaries and in order to protect the mission Indians, as well as in order to defend the frontier, a long line of presidios was established all along the route from San Agustín to San Francisco. In general, the missionaries' opinion was that the presidios were necessary, but there were many tensions on account of the men stationed in them. The friars often complained it was the lowest sort of people who were sent from Mexico, wretches often fresh out of prison and setting a bad example for the Indians.

In the documents of the time and in the literature that has grown up around the missions, references to the abuses and punishments inflicted on the Indians are abundant. The harshness of the punishments was decided in accordance with each friar's personality, but in all cases, punishment was considered something necessary. Indians who disobeyed orders were shackled, put in the stocks, or whipped. Nevertheless, the dramatic decline in the native population is explained not by these punishments, but by the Indians' living conditions and the spread of disease.[5] The Indians were at the center of Spain's entire colonial policy, since the aim was to populate the new colonies with native inhabitants, not with individuals of Spanish origin, and that meant that the friars and the civil authorities had to act with prudence. It would only be possible to Christianize and instruct the Indians if they were treated well and trained in agriculture, livestock raising, and various trades. According to Bolton, the English colonists did not go to so much trouble:

> The missions were a force which made for the preservation of the Indians, as opposed to their destruction, so characteristic of the Anglo-American frontier. In the English colonies the only good Indians were dead Indians. In the Spanish colonies it was thought worthwhile to improve the natives for this life as well as for the next.[6]

Bolton's words are illuminating. The missions were not the oases depicted in California tourist brochures, and in order to become familiar with their reality, it is necessary to puncture the veil of romanticism with which they have been covered. It is also necessary, however, if the aim is to arrive at a minimally accurate view, to get rid of the layer of grime with which the Black Legend of Anglo-American historiography has covered them.

The Long List of Basque Missionaries in Alta California

Among the 142 Franciscan missionaries sent to Alta California between 1769 and 1848, the most numerous group is made up of those from the Basque Country, with the following members: Marcos Amestoy (Treviño), Gregorio Amurrio (Bastida, Araba), Francisco José de Arroita (Abadiño?), Juan Antonio Barreneche (Lekaroz, Navarre), Domingo Carranza (Loza, Navarre), Tomás Eleuterio Esténaga (Antzuola, Gipuzkoa), Román Fernández de Ulíbarri (Ali, Araba), Francisco González de Ibarra (Viana, Navarre), Domingo Santiago Martínez de Iturrate (Lukiano, Araba), Martín de Landaeta (Kortezubi, Bizkaia), Fermín Francisco Lasuén (Vitoria), Marcelino Marquínez (Treviño), Manuel José Martiarena (Errenteria, Gipuzkoa), Pascual Martínez de Arenaza (Araba), José Miguel y Bermeo (Zurbitu-Treviño), Pablo José de Mugártegui (Markina, Bizkaia), José de Murguía (Domaikia, Araba), Juan Prestamero (Bastida, Araba), Andrés Quintana (Antoñana, Araba), Marcos Antonio Saizar de Vitoria y Odriozola (Vitoria), Isidro Alonso y Salazar (Araba), Vicente Santa María (Aras, Navarre), Juan Norberto Santiago (Treviño), Vicente Francisco de Sarriá (Etxebarri, Bizkaia), Faustino Solá (Arrasate, Gipuzkoa), Francisco Xavier de la Concepción Uría (Aizarna, Gipuzkoa), Jose Antonio Uría (Azkoitia, Gipuzkoa), José Antonio Urresti (Mañaria, Bizkaia), Marcos Antonio Vitoria (Vitoria), and José María Zalvidea (Bilbao). The second most numerous group was made up of the twenty-two friars who came from Catalonia. Next were the groups from Mallorca and Aragon, with sixteen and fourteen friars respectively, and the remainder came from other Spanish provinces.[7]

The friars destined for Alta California, who were missionaries from the colleges of San Fernando, Zacatecas, and Querétaro, had to complete at least ten years of service. Some had difficulty lasting that long, due to the harshness of the land and the way of life. José Manuel de Martiarena, for example, suffered a deep depression accompanied by severe headaches, and Fermín Lasuén, in his role as father president of the missions, found it difficult to assign him to an appropriate post. Martiarena left for the Colegio de San Fernando as soon as his term of ten years was over. Francisco José Arroita also served out his ten years, but when he left in 1796, Lasuén described him as worn out by his efforts. Domingo Carranza had been in California eight years when he wrote to Fr. Tomás de la Peña Sarabia on February 26, 1806, announcing his desire to leave two years later. He did not hide his discontent in his letter: "I no longer even take pleasure in anything, and in Californias even less."[8] His stay turned out to be longer than he wished, since Governor Arrillaga did not grant him permission to return to the Colegio de San Fernando until 1810.

Lasuén gave Martín de Landaeta permission to leave Alta California before his ten years were up, since he found it entirely impossible to continue in his ministry, due to the emotional disturbances he suffered. In one letter, Lasuén gave Landaeta's illness a name: hypochondria.[9] Lasuén often mentions Landaeta in his correspondence, although not on the subject of health, but rather in relation to a problem that had arisen at the San Francisco mission. In effect, José María Fernández and Diego García, Landaeta's companions at that mission, accused him of making the Indians work too much. Lasuén investigated the facts and came to the conclusion that it was a plot hatched by the other two friars to expel the Bizkaian from the mission.

Landaeta left California in 1798, but not for long. In 1800, now recovered, he was back in San Francisco. "The neophytes received me with joy and applause, however long it will last," he wrote to Fray Tomás de la Peña, procurator of the missions, once he was back in his post.[10]

Landaeta's letters to Tomás de la Peña at the Colegio de San Fernando were collected in a small book (*Noticias acerca del puerto de San Francisco* [News of the port of San Francisco]). In one such letter, dated August 30, 1803, the friar speaks of his health problems:

> with last winter's sickness, I'm sick in my feet, and I'm in better shape to get kicked, as they say, than to govern the mission's material affairs.[11]

The chief topic of the letters is the mission's temporal administration. Everything else is mentioned only in passing. For example, a brief reference to the fact that around seventy Indians have died in San Francisco in an epidemic is immediately followed by this request for the procurator:

> It's been three or four days since I sat down to write this, so it's inevitable that there are a lot of loose ends. What I was forgetting is for you to please advise the chocolate maker not to make the chocolate so sweet, since everyone is complaining, and what has arrived here is even cloying. Amid so many troubles, we should at least have good chocolate.[12]

As we have previously mentioned, Vancouver met Landaeta in San Francisco in 1792 and considered him "very pleasing and entertaining." Georg Heinrich Langsdorff also found him very agreeable in 1806.[13] As far as his complaints of ill health are concerned, it is possible that they were not the result of hypochondria but had a real basis, since he died before the age of forty. His fellow-countryman Marcos Antonio Saizar buried him.

José Antonio Uría y Larrañaga also had health problems starting with his arrival, and when he was sent to San Fernando in 1806, it seemed to him the culmination of all his miseries and sufferings. "At San Fernando he succumbed to melancholy," Maynard Geiger writes in a study that collects the biographies of all these friars.[14] Uría was a musician, and in 1808 he requested a piano and an instructional treatise on the clavichord for his mission. Nevertheless, it did not take San Fernando long to reply that they would not be sending the piano, since Father José Antonio was leaving and there was no one else there who could play it.

The Russian naturalist Georg Heinrich Langsdorff, who met Jose Antonio Uría in San Francisco in 1806, found him a very intelligent man, but perhaps overly serious. Langsdorff recounts an anecdote that illustrates the friar's character very well:

> Our cicerone, Padre Uría, who, generally speaking, seemed to be a man of sound and accurate judgement upon most matters, understanding that I was a naturalist, took me by the hand when we were in the chapel and forced upon my attention a painting representing the Agave Americana, Linn., from the middle of which, instead of a flower-stalk, rose a holy virgin, by whom, as he assured me, many extraordinary miracles were wrought. His story was related with such an air of belief and certainty that, through an assumed appearance of courtesy and admiration of this phenomenon, I thus expressed my envy of the painter who had witnessed it with his own eyes.[15]

As Langsdorff himself reports, an expedition to cross the Sierra Nevada was being prepared in San Francisco at the time of his visit. Uría was going to participate in it with the aim of finding an appropriate location for founding a new mission.[16]

Five years later, in 1811, Uría requested license and a passport to return "to Cantabria," once again because of his poor health:

> experiencing in these last two years such a decadence in my health that I believe that I am declining toward a complete collapse and probably the end of my existence, I find myself in need of seeking a climate more adaptable to my constitution, which is that of the kingdoms of Spain.[17]

He was granted license the following year, in 1812, but it was not a good time to return to the "kingdoms of Spain," and he died in Mexico in 1815, without having benefited from the air of his native region.

There is also another Uría on the long list of Basque Franciscan missionaries in Alta California: Francisco Xavier de la Concepción Uría, born in 1770 in Aizarna, Gipuzkoa, the son of Antonio Uría Iraola and Polonia Arruti Astiasarán. Starting in 1808, Uría was a capable manager of the mission of Santa Inés. He was there when the revolt of the Chumash Indians broke out in 1824, as we will mention later. Nevertheless, what his contemporaries and future historians highlighted about him, more than anything else, was his good humor and love of jokes. In Bancroft's words,

> Padre Uría was stout in physique, jolly in manner, addicted to pleasantries and jokes, indulging sometimes in coarse language, kind-hearted and well liked though at times very quick-tempered. He was an excellent manager of temporal affairs, and was noted for his generosity, especially to the Indians.[18]

Angustias de la Guerra, who knew Uría from the time she was very young, described him as a Bizkaian and a magnificent farmer.[19] Alfred Robinson, a businessman and writer, had the opportunity to enjoy Uría's hospitality and his sense of humor:

> At dinner the fare was sumptuous, and I was much amused at the eccentricity of the old padre, who kept constantly annoying four large cats, his daily companions; or with a long stick thumped upon the heads of his Indian boys, who seemed delighted thus to gratify his singular propensities.[20]

The information available to us portrays Martiarena, Arroita, Carranza, Landaeta, and the two Urías as normal men of flesh and blood. The same is surely true of many others about whom we know almost nothing: all that has remained of them are their signatures in the registers. In Geiger's words, "[t]he preponderance might be classed as men of ordinary ability, zeal, learning, and virtue."[21] There were also extraordinary individuals, however.

José Manuel de Martiarena

Francisco Xavier Uría

Martín de Landaeta

José de Arroíta

Thomás Esténaga

José Antonio de Uría

Marcos Amestoy

José María de Zalvidea

The Araban José de Murguía, for example. After serving twenty years in the Sierra Gorda, Mexico, and another five years in Baja California, Murguía arrived in Alta California in 1773 as part of the group of eight Franciscans who were to undertake the region's spiritual conquest. On January 12, 1777, he participated in founding the mission of Santa Clara, and over time, he became its leading missionary. During his years in the Sierra Gorda, he had built a handsome stone church, the first of its kind in those mountains. Upon reaching his post at Santa Clara, he proposed to construct a similar building there, using adobe instead of stone. The work dragged on, since Murguía had to combine an architect's labors with those of a builder. The church was finished in 1784, however, and it remained only to consecrate it. May 16 was the date chosen, but Murguía became suddenly ill and died on the 11th. He was buried in the church that he himself had just finished building. As planned, the consecration took place on the 16th, with great admiration among those present: the church was the largest and most beautiful in California. Junípero Serra, Gov. Pedro Fages, all the inhabitants of the mission and the neighboring settlement of San José, and all the Indians of the surrounding area attended the ceremony.[22] Serra judged that, of the nine churches that had been built at the missions up to that point, Murguía's was the "prettiest."

The Bizkaian Pablo José de Mugártegui also deserves special mention among these pioneers in religious habits. Born in Markina, in the palace that continues to carry his family's name in the Mugartegi palace, he was Junípero Serra's assistant—they made the historic journey from San Blas to San Diego together in 1774—the highest-ranking supervisor of the southern missions during the period when Fermín Lasuén was father president, and the latter's possible replacement in the event that something happened to him. Both Mugártegui's own writings and others' opinions about him clearly show that he had one of the best minds among the missionaries. Nevertheless, the passage of time has blotted out all of this, and his name only lives on in historic texts related to the origins of Californian viticulture.

We know that the first vineyards in California were planted by missionaries in the last years of the eighteenth century. What were called "mission grapes" were the primary kind of grapes in California throughout almost the entire nineteenth century. It is unknown who planted the first vines, but opinions agree on the name of the first winemaker and the place where that wine was made: Pablo de Mugártegui at the mission of San Juan Capistrano. In 1779, on Mugártegui's orders, six farmers from Baja California began to plant vines brought by ship from Mexico or Baja California. By 1781, working side by side with the friar, those six farmers had planted more than two thousand vines. The historian Richard Steven Street, who has researched the subject, affirms that the first California wine was produced in 1783 or 1784.[23] The Franciscan historian *Zephyrin* Engelhardt, nevertheless, dates the event slightly earlier, on the basis of some casual remarks by Fr. Fermín Lasuén in a letter. In effect, Lasuén wrote to the viceroy in 1781 that they had began to press the grapes at San Juan Capistrano.[24] For Engelhardt, who spent his life collecting and analyzing the California Franciscans' writings, the wine Mugártegui made at San Juan Capistrano was the origin of viticulture in California.

That first wine made by the friars was part of a much broader effort. Mugártegui and his companions, convinced that the cross and the plow had to advance together, proposed to spread agriculture and livestock raising among the natives. In their view, without material progress, it was impossible to think of spiritual progress, and they applied themselves to this end, putting into practice among the California Indians the Illustration ideas that the members of the Real Sociedad Bascongada de Amigos del País were spreading in the Basque Country at this same time.[25] This progressive impulse is especially evident in Mugártegui's case, his older brother, Pedro Valentín, was one of the founders of the

Bascongada. The two brothers maintained a correspondence even after the friar established himself in California.

The tone of Mugártegui's letters to his brother Pedro Valentín is a good reflection of the friar's character and his well-honed sense of irony. In one letter, speaking about the Indians he has come to know in California, and after dispatching their clothing in two words—complete nakedness—he describes their dwellings in this way:

Building mission. By Alexander Harmer. http://www.missionscalifornia.com/

> The houses they live in correspond to their clothing, since they are no more than huts, or better, a cage made from four sticks covered with straw, over which, in order to better protect themselves from inclement weather, they spread some mats, if they have them. The amusing thing is that some of them burn their houses when summer arrives, only so that the fleas that bother them will die, and build new ones when winter comes; and this is every year, due to the ease of construction of palaces of this sort.[26]

He goes on to mention their beds—the bare ground—and their food: "they eat grass, especially when it is fresh, in the way you might eat a Bizkaian stew with all the trimmings [*una olla vizcaína con todos sus sainetes*]."

It was, then, a Bizkaian, Pablo José de Mugártegui, who was the first to make wine in California, and it was also a Bizkaian, José María Zalvidea, a native of Bilbao, who was the first to make it on a large scale. This took place at the mission of San Gabriel between 1806 and 1826.

Under Zalvidea's direction, San Gabriel, located a few miles from the present city of Los Angeles, became the largest and most prosperous mission of its time. It was where the largest vineyards were planted and where the most wine was obtained. An irrigation system was set up, and olive trees, fruit trees, and citrus trees were planted, including California's first orange trees, more than two thousand of them. In 1811, San Gabriel brought in the largest wheat harvest ever recorded in the missions: 18,710 celemines.[27] The following year, the volume rose to 32,618 celemines. Cotton also prospered: it seemed that nothing was impossible for Zalvidea. The orchards and fields stretched for hundreds of acres, and in order to protect them all from the horses and wild animals that roamed the area, the friar planted an enormous hedge of cactus, parts of which still remain.

Zalvidea is one of the most interesting individuals among the group of Basque Franciscans, and we will have more to say about him later. For the moment, to end this general introduction, it is enough to note that the continual appearance of Basque Franciscans in accounts of this period of California history is surprising. When the border between Alta and Baja California was established in 1773, four Basque missionaries took part in the ceremony: José de Murguía, Juan Prestamero, Gregorio Amurrio, and Fermín Lasuén. Vicente Santa María was the chaplain of the *San Carlos* when in 1775 this packet boat captained by Juan Bautista de Ayala y Aguirre became the first European ship to pass through the

Part of the cactus fence planted in San Gabriel, with a horseman in front. Source: George Wharton James; Hervey Friend, ca. 1886. University of Southern California.

Golden Gate. José de Murguía was in Monterrey when in 1776 Anza arrived with the group of colonists who were to found the first settlement at San Francisco. When Vancouver visited San Francisco in 1792, he was welcomed by Martín Landaeta. Later on, when the Chumash Indians rebelled, it was Vicente de Sarría, then father president of the California missions, who succeeded in convincing them to return to the mission . . . Standing out from the long list is the figure of Fermín Lasuén. He was one of the chief protagonists of the historical era we are discussing, and deserves a separate chapter.

Fermín Lasuén, Father President of the Alta California Missions

Fermín Lasuén is present in history textbooks used in California schools; Stanford University has a Lasuen Mall; we find a Lasuen Drive in Sacramento, Carmel, San Juan Bautista, Ashland, Millbrae, Sonoma, and other California cities; a monument has been erected in his honor at the San Fernando mission; a bust of him can be seen at the San Juan Bautista mission . . . What do we know about this man, who became the highest religious authority of Alta California.

Fermín Francisco Lasuén was born on July 7, 1736, in Vitoria, Araba. His father was Lorenzo de Lasuén, and his mother was María Francisca de Arizqueta; both were resident in Vitoria but originally from Bizkaia. He took the Franciscan habit at the age of fifteen, on March 19, 1751, in the convent of San Francisco of his native city, and he professed as a Franciscan on July 7, 1752. During the following years, until 1759, he studied philosophy and theology in Arantzazu.[28]

Father Fermín Lasuén

It was precisely in Arantzazu that Lasuén learned that the "collector" of the Colegio de San Fernando had come to Spain to "collect" volunteer friars and novices. The colleges and provinces under the jurisdiction of the Congregation for the Propagation of the Faith (Propaganda Fide) sent collectors to Spain to recruit friars for teaching positions and to serve as preachers and in the missions. Pedro Pérez de Mezquía (1688–1764), from Vitoria, like Lasuén, took the first "boatload," made up of twelve friars, in 1742. In 1749, he acted as guide to another group of thirty-three friars, including Junípero Serra and Francisco Palou. Lasuén went in the "boatload" of 1759, along with seventeen other friars. The patent that the collector that year, Fray Gaspar Gómez, sent to Arantzazu explained what Lasuén's obligations would be in the New World:

> the holy exercise of the missions and propagation of our Holy Catholic Faith among the pagan Indians called Apaches and other innumerable barbarian nations, who, blinded by their pagan errors, live without the Gospel's clear light in the vast mountains and regions of that wide kingdom.[29]

Lasuén left Arantzazu on March 6, 1759, prepared for the journey of 153 leagues to Cádiz. He probably passed through Vitoria in order to say goodbye to his relatives, since his letters of later years testify that he maintained close ties to his family, but there is no way to be certain of this. What we do know is that his group of eighteen friars included several fellow-countrymen of his who would work in the California missions in subsequent years: Dionisio de Basterra, Fermín Juanena, Juan de Medinaveitia, Francisco Pangua, Esteban Pérez de Arenaza, and Juan de Prestamero. We also know that Lasuén was "of proportionate height, with a flushed face and smallpox scars, enough of a beard, and

Fermín Lasuén's baptismal certificate, San Juan Bautista Mission

black, curly hair."[30] He was twenty-three years old when he embarked for Veracruz on the *Jasón*.

Lasuén's first home in the New World was the Colegio de San Fernando. He was ordained a priest there, and in 1762 he was assigned to his first post as a missionary, among the Pame Indians of the Sierra Gorda, in northeastern Mexico. No documents exist to inform us about what he did during the five years he spent there. In 1767, when the Colegio de San Fernando took charge of the Baja California missions, Lasuén was one of the five missionaries sent there. The five friars left Loreto together, headed north. Each time they arrived at a mission, the one who was to stay there celebrated a sung mass, assisted by the others. Then they took their leave, and the group continued on its way with one member fewer. Finally, only two remained: Lasuén and his fellow countryman Juan de Medinaveitia. Medinaveitia had been assigned to the northernmost mission. When they reached San Francisco de Borja, the two said goodbye, promising to help one another in case of need, and Medinaveitia continued his journey.

The Years at San Francisco de Borja: Similitudo est causa amoris

There is no doubt that Serra chose Lasuén to take charge of San Francisco de Borja because he had full confidence in Lasuén's great abilities. It was a difficult posting, remote and isolated, but of great strategic value. To the south, the nearest mission was Santa Gertrudis, about 150 kilometers away; to the north, Santa María, about 160 kilometers. The mission was located around fifty kilometers from the Pacific and around forty kilometers from the Gulf of Mexico. Including the inhabitants of the region's rancherías, San Borja had around 1,500 Indians and was the most populous of the thirteen Baja California missions.

When Lasuén arrived, the mission was abandoned, as a consequence of the irresponsibility of the soldiers who replaced the Jesuits when the latter were expelled. The following year, 1769, the situation deteriorated further, since the mission found itself obligated to supply the expeditions headed for Alta California. San Borja was far to the north—only Santa María de los Angeles, Medinaveitia's mission, lay beyond—and provisions very rarely made it that far. On occasion, the situation became so serious that Lasuén, "with great sorrow of heart," found himself forced to cut the Indians' ration, "serving it to them with a ladle that is much smaller than usual."[31]

During the first months he spent at San Borja, from May to October 1768, the mission received no aid. Lasuén sent a letter to José de Gálvez, the visitor-general of New Spain, informing him that his "children" were very numerous and that they were hungry and naked.[32] Gálvez then had a remarkable idea. He proposed that Lasuén take some of those neophytes to the better-supplied southern missions. Two ships would provide transportation, and Lasuén was to decide who would leave and who would stay at San Borja.

Lasuén thought the plan was nonsense, since it took into account neither the Indians' attachment to their land nor their mistrust of the recently arrived friar, but he did not express this opinion in his reply. Demonstrating his good sense and diplomatic skill, he indicated to Gálvez that, "[a]lthough I recognize that the order is very just and necessary," it was not advisable at that time. The Indians of his mission had not yet been instructed and had just begun to learn Christian doctrine; consequently, it would be difficult to make them understand "the benefits" and all the advantages that the change would mean for them.[33]

The first ship that was to transport the Indians arrived before Gálvez's reply. Lasuén informed the captain that no one would embark before receiving the visitor's latest orders. In the end, Gálvez agreed with Lasuén, and no Indians left San Borja.

At San Francisco de Borja, in addition to running the mission, Lasuén had to attend to the six rancherías in the surrounding area. Their inhabitants, Cochimí Indians, had neither houses nor huts in which to live. In Lasuén's words,

> one sees in [these regions] scarcely more evidence of life than would mark the place where a chance wanderer rested or slept.[34]

Lasuén himself also had no shelter at the mission, and he immediately began to build in adobe. Soon, the results of his dedication could be seen. In his report for 1771, he affirmed that there was not a single pagan left in the entire region. The Cochimí Indians had demonstrated

San Borja

their agreeable and receptive character since the Jesuits' times. As far as temporal affairs were concerned, despite the lack of water and the scarcity of arable land, Lasuén had planted vines, figs, pomegranates, and cotton. The cotton was used to make shawls for the Indians, along with wool cloaks. When the Baja California missions passed into the Dominicans' hands in 1773, there were a thousand people at San Borja, 648 head of cattle, 387 horses and mules, 2,343 sheep, and 1,003 goats. At the fourteen Baja California missions, there were a total of 4,268 people and 14,716 domestic animals, leading to the conclusion that San Borja in Lasuén's time had almost a quarter of the mission Indians and more than a quarter of the domestic animals.

The figures are even more surprising if we take into account that Lasuén was alone for the five years he spent at San Borja. He had a soldier as an escort, and occasionally two, but he was the only friar. It is necessary to make an enormous effort in order to understand what it meant for the friars, on a personal level, to live in what Lasuén himself called "this place of seclusion and exile from the civilized world."[35] In Bancroft's words,

> We can in some degree imagine the desolate loneliness of a padre's life at a frontier mission; but the reality must have been far worse that anything our fancy can picture. [36]

The friars also suffered the lack of the most everyday objects. How to acquire a nail, a cooking pot, or a pair of shoes? Or a new habit? In 1774, a year after leaving San Borja, Lasuén wrote in a letter from San Gabriel that he was very short of clothing, to the point that, without exaggerating, it could be said that he had fallen into an embarrassing state. He had not had a new habit in five years, and although he tried to keep his clothing in good condition, he could not do so, since in addition to not having anything to keep in good condition, he had nothing to keep it in good condition with.[37]

Again, in another letter to the Colegio de San Fernando, he wrote:

> I am also asking the Reverend Father Guardian to do me the kindness of furnishing me a complete outfit of clothes, because in the five years during which I was in charge of the Mission of San Borja I did not receive as much as a single stipend. I left that unfortunate province entirely devoid even of under-clothing and sandals . . . Perhaps it was because of my very necessities that the Indians became so devoted to me, for if "*Similitudo est causa amoris*" I resemble them closely in scantiness of attire.[38]

Lasuén's words clearly express how difficult it was for those friars to meet their most basic needs. They also show that he did not lose his good humor even in the most difficult situations.

Unwanted Years in Alta California

After his time in Baja California ended, Lasuén would have preferred to return to the Colegio de San Fernando in Mexico. As he himself explained,

> I had already left my few belongings in Loreto, and only awaited the handing over of my Mission of San Borja before going down to the presidio so as to embark and return to the college.[39]

He now had a new reason to want to leave that exile behind. News had reached him that his parents were in poverty and asking for his help. Lasuén thought that it would be easier to arrange matters in Mexico, but when he spoke with Father Palou, the latter convinced him to join the group that was preparing to undertake the spiritual conquest of Alta California, promising that the Colegio would see to helping his parents. Lasuén agreed, thinking that this would be a provisional arrangement, with no suspicion that there would be no turning back from this decision and that he would spend the next thirty years of his life in California.

The other missionaries who made up that first group were Francisco Palou himself, José de Murguía, Juan Prestamero, Gregorio Amurrio, Vicente Fuster, Miguel de la Campa Cos, and Pedro Benito. Palou left Loreto alone. On the journey, as he passed through the missions of Muleguė, Guadalupe, San Ignacio, Santa Gertrudis, and San Borja, he was joined by Murguía, Prestamero, Amurrio, and Lasuén. At the mission of San Fernando de Velicatá, Father Fuster was added to the group. The six—there were two others who travelled later—headed north, very slowly, carrying their few possessions on mules. They were accompanied by fourteen soldiers, six Indian families, and a train of mules loaded with corn for the missions.

They left Velicatá on July 21, 1773. It was the height of summer, and the sun beat down by day; at night, they had only the hard ground to rest on. On August 19, they reached the border between the two Californias, where they set up a cross made the previous day from alder wood, with this inscription: "The year 1773. Division between the missions of Our Father Saint Dominic and Our Father Saint Francis." Glad to have arrived, they sang a *Te Deum*. It was a memorable moment: for the first time, they crossed what would from then on be the border between Baja California and Alta California. The line was drawn about fifteen leagues south of San Diego, thirty miles south of today's border between Mexico and the United States. Once the ceremony was over, they set out again, reaching San Diego on August 30.

It is useful to remember what California was at that time before colonization, in order to understand the reality that the missionaries faced and properly appreciate the magnitude of the transformation that would soon result. When the friars arrived in Alta California, they found no white towns or settlements there. There were only five missions in the entire territory, mere shelters of branches covered with mud, roofed with *tule*.[40] Each mission had a few soldiers, and for the defense of the entire region, there were only two presidios, one at each end of the province, separated by a distance of some five hundred miles. There were no highways, only a route that linked the presidios and missions from north to south. It was called the Camino Real, the "Royal Road" in Spanish, an undoubtedly pompous name for what was scarcely a cart track.

The Indians were more numerous there than in Baja California, but also more reserved in their relations with the missionaries. In San Diego, a whole year passed before the first Indian was baptized; in San Gabriel, the number of baptisms in three years did not reach eighty. It was precisely San Gabriel that was Lasuén's first posting in Alta California.

Lasuén arrived in San Gabriel in September 1773. "The land is very beautiful," he wrote in a letter.[41] Times were bad, however. The famine that had endangered the survival of the settlements in the province was at its height. When Juan Bautista Anza's exploratory expedition arrived at San Gabriel on March 22 of the following year, having used up all their provisions on the long journey from Sonora, they found the mission in a deplorable state. During the nineteen days that Anza spent at San Gabriel, the captain and the friar had the opportunity to get to know one another. Lasuén wrote to the Colegio de San Fernando that Anza was "a distinguished benefactor, and a source of great encouragement to the missionaries of the Pimería."[42]

The group's arrival turned out to be beneficial for Lasuén. Upon seeing him with a habit that was so ragged and full of patches and almost barefoot, the two friars who arrived with Anza, Francisco Garcés and Juan Diaz, took pity on him. One gave him "a light habit and cowl," and the other a tunic and sandals.[43]

His two years at San Gabriel were unhappy ones for Lasuén. He had agreed to go to California due to the scarcity of missionaries, but once there, he found himself relegated to the position of a supernumerary.

Each of the Alta California missions had its corresponding minister, and although the authorities had promised to create new establishments, the promise was not carried out. In his letters from San Gabriel, Lasuén speaks ironically about his situation—"Just a supernumerary with nothing in particular to do"[44]—openly confessing his dislike of the place and his desire to go back to the college.

His discontent was aggravated when he learned that the promise to send help to his impoverished parents remained unfulfilled:

> I am much perturbed these days, for I find myself obliged to solicit help for my poor, aged, beloved, and venerated parents. They are in need of help, and they have asked me for help. My efforts failed, for no one would answer the pleas which I made for that purpose.[45]

In order to solve that problem, which was so urgent for him, he proposed to send his parents the salary he had not received during his five years at San Borja. In the end, Lasuén's parents received the promised assistance by way of another native of Vitoria, Francisco Pangua, who was the guardian of the Colegio de San Fernando at the time.

Many years later, in the last part of his life, Lasuén faced a similar problem, to which he responded with the same diligence, In 1797, the sister of Gov. Diego de Borica, a fellow-countryman of Lasuén's, sent a letter from Vitoria requesting help for Clara, the friar's sister, who was in straitened circumstances. Lasuén was at that time the highest-ranking friar in charge of the California missions, but although the friars received a payment of four hundred pesos, the father president made no profit from it, and Lasuén did not have a cent. "I venture to say that if I had large resources I would gladly spend them for the purpose of helping her, even to the point of reducing myself to the state of a mendicant, the state in which I am,"[46] Lasuén wrote to Governor Borica. In the end, the college again took charge of the matter, sending the elderly Clara Lasuén two hundred pesos.

The "great perturbation" Lasuén felt at not being able to help his parents and his quick response to his sister's request are evidence of the close ties that continued to unite him to his family. Elsewhere, Lasuén mentions letters sent to Spain.[47] No personal letters of his or of any other friar have survived, however, except for an occasional one sent by Pablo de Mugártegui to his brother. Among the hundreds of pages written by the friars that are preserved in California's archives, these by the "mendicant" Lasuén are the only ones we have found that speak of family affairs.

Lasuén did not succeed in becoming comfortable at the San Gabriel mission, and year after year, he continued asking permission to go back to the college. Instead, however, Junípero Serra charged him with founding the mission of San Juan Capistrano, halfway between San Diego and San Gabriel. According to Lasuén himself, there was no place that attracted him less, and for this reason, he happily accepted his fate.[48] He had an additional motive for rejoicing: he would have his fellow-countryman and friend Gregorio Amurrio as a companion.

On October 30, 1775, at the chosen location—the natives called it Quanis-savit—Lasuén set up a large cross and a set of bells and celebrated his first mass in a shelter made of branches. The ceremony was attended by numerous Indians, who showed their goodwill by helping to cut and transport wood for building the church and the residential quarters. Less than a week had passed, and everything was moving forward at a good pace. Amurrio was to arrive from San Gabriel on the 6th, with more men, animals, and provisions, enabling them to progress even more rapidly. On the same day that Amurrio was expected, however, everything came to a standstill, as a consequence of the terrible news a messenger brought. The previous morning, the Indians had rebelled and set fire to the San Diego mission, murdering Fr. Luis Jayme. According to Lasuén's own account, the San Juan Capistrano contingent buried the bells and two *metates*,[49] since they did not have enough mules to carry everything, and set out for San Diego.[50]

The two friars and the soldiers began their journey full of apprehension, fearing that the Indians would attack again. It would not have been the first attack Lasuén suffered. In May of the same year, travelling with a friar who was leading a pack train, he nearly lost his life in a ranchería in the region of the Santa Barbara Channel.

> It happened in the ranchería that a soldier struck a pagan a sharp blow with the flat side of his sword, for the latter had cut off the tail of the soldier's mule and had tried to disarm him. In a rage the Indian ran to fetch his arms, raised the alarm, and excited his neighbors to follow his example. They all rushed out armed and caught us in their midst, the soldier and myself. I was on foot, for I had just dismounted from the mule in order to give glass beads to the children whom the Indian mothers were bringing to me in their arms.[51]

The Indians began to shoot arrows, and Lasuén wanted to get away on his mule, but he was unable to do so, "for the animal had become very restive because of the vociferous yelling." He had to "make my escape on foot." When the fight was over, six Indians were dead:

> six of these unfortunate Indians met death at the hands of our soldiers; and the greatest wonder is that the losses were not on our side instead, and that I was not one of them.[52]

The clash had occurred several months before. Now, as he made his way to San Diego with Gregorio Amurrio, those images surely returned to Lasuén's mind. Nevertheless, there was no attack this time. The two friars reached the mission without problems, and as the messenger had said, they found it burned down.

Fernando Rivera y Moncada ravaged the church asylum in the San Diego mission, March 26, 1776. Engelhardt, 1920: 75

Following the revolt, the friars set the pacification of San Diego as their first goal. Gov. Fernando Rivera y Moncada preferred the method of punishment and repression, however. An incident occurred that brought the disagreement into the open. A neophyte who had participated in the rebellion returned, having repented of his actions, and the friars—Fuster, Lasuén, and Amurrio—gave him permission to take refuge in the storehouse that was serving as a church. For believers, a church was a place of sanctuary, and no one could be forced to leave it. Nevertheless, Rivera informed the friars that if they did not turn the man over, he would bring him out by force. The friars replied that if he did such a thing, they would excommunicate him. Rivera carried out his threat, the missionaries considered that he had committed a sacrilege, and they decreed the excommunication of the governor and his helpers.

When the governor appeared at mass a few days later, Lasuén, far from quailing before the region's highest authority, asked him to leave, despite the fact that he and Rivera had maintained a close relationship, since excommunicates could not participate in the celebration. Rivera and his men left the church.[53]

A year after the San Diego rebellion, Junípero Serra went to the site chosen for the San Juan Capistrano mission and found the large cross that Lasuén had set up still standing. They dug up the bells and performed the usual ceremonies, and on November 10, 1776, San Juan Capistrano was founded for the second time. Gregorio Amurrio and Pablo de Mugártegui were to be responsible for the new mission, while Lasuén, for his part, was appointed minister at San Diego.

San Diego was the worst posting a missionary could be offered, due to the aridity of the land and the character of the inhabitants. Lasuén took up his post in the summer of 1777, and during the next eight years, he commented often that he remained there out of obedience alone. In Maynard Geiger's words, "the crude and dangerous surroundings were hard on his refined character."[54] Lasuén himself summarized the obstacles he encountered in San Diego in this way:

> I am much perturbed that I am having difficulty with the inflections of this dialect, for I cannot grasp its syllables, although I have been here a long time. This is an experience I did not have at the other missions. It may be that there are circumstances peculiar to this mission which are responsible for this difference which is so notable and so obvious. I am not pleased with the interpreters, and I have but little time to devote to study, for I have to devote a great deal of attention to the Christian converts. These latter are quite numerous and are widely scattered. Then, on the part of the Indians, there is no love whatever for anything resembling civilization or rational culture. And worst of all, the duties at the presidio are burdensome and almost insupportable, overcrowded as it is with so many families.[55]

It is not surprising that, required to remain there, Lasuén asked Junípero Serra for permission to spend a few weeks at San Juan Capistrano, a request that shows us that even in those difficult times, the friars were able to permit themselves a vacation. We also see that Lasuén sought the company of his fellow-countrymen, since the ministers at San Juan Capistrano were Mugártegui and Amurrio, as we have already mentioned. On another occasion, when San Diego's new church was consecrated in August 1781, Lasuén had Mugártegui come to preach.[56] It surely must have been a joyful day: the new church was replacing the one that the Indians had burned down. Nevertheless, threats persisted. Not long before, the previous month, another terrible Indian attack had taken place. The Yumas who lived along the banks of the Colorado had rebelled, murdering all the whites who fell into their hands, including the veteran explorer Francisco Garcés, the same one who, when he passed through San Gabriel with Anza in 1774 and saw Lasuén's tattered habit, gave him "a light habit and cowl." The young Navarrese friar Juan Antonio Barreneche and Governor Rivera were also among the victims.

Lasuén never got used to the harshness of the San Diego mission. When he finished his fifth year there, he wrote these words to a fellow Franciscan at the Colegio de San Fernando:

> I am already an old man and completely grey; and although it is the toll of years, the pace has been accelerated by the heavy burden of this office which I hold, and especially by the five years which I am completing as superior at San Diego. This land is for apostles only, and its people should be cared for by those more mission-minded than I; but, thanks be to God, I enjoy good health, and I shall try to use it for some good purpose, even though my strength be waning.[57]

The words seem to be those of someone who has reached the last stage of life, but when he wrote this letter in 1782, Lasuén was only forty-six years old. Three years later, when his time at San Diego came to an end, baptisms had increased from 431 to 1,075, and the number of cattle had risen from 245 head to 2,462. The person who had achieved such results in so difficult a place could not be an ordinary man. That was the opinion, apparently, of the Franciscans at the Colegio de San Fernando, since when the president of the California missions, Junípero Serra, died in 1784, the college decided that it would be the friar from Vitoria who would succeed him.

It was around this same time that Lasuén learned that his father had died, but nothing is said about the matter in the letters that have survived.

Fermín Lasuén and Diego de Borica, California's Highest Religious and Civil Authorities

On February 6, 1785, Fermín Lasuén was named president of all the California missions. If anything happened to him, he would be replaced by Pablo de Mugártegui. Lasuén was also to be licensed to administer the sacrament of confirmation, a faculty that only Serra had been granted up to that time. In ten years, Serra had confirmed 5,309 individuals. Lasuén was also given a term of ten years, but the document did not arrive until 1790; despite this, in the following five years, he confirmed around nine thousand people. In 1795, he was named commissioner of the Mexican Inquisition (as such, he is merely credited with the publication of the occasional edict sent from Mexico). Finally, the bishop of Sonora named him vicar forane and vicar for military services in 1796, and he was appointed an ecclesiastical judge around the same time.

While serving as father president, Lasuén maintained good relations with California's successive governors: Fages, Romeu, Arrillaga, Borica, and Alberni. The usual clashes between the military and the religious authorities were not lacking, but Lasuén always sought harmony. As Bancroft described him, he was a prudent man who, lacking Serra's intolerance, was superior to his environment and ahead of his time.[58]

One of the most difficult episodes that Lasuén would face came immediately after he was appointed president, as a consequence of the Neve regulations of 1779. According to these regulations, the missionaries' only responsibilities from then on would be spiritual ones. The missions would consist solely of the churches and the friars' residences. The natives would receive the missionaries' instruction and then return to their customary way of life. Each friar was to receive four hundred pesos for his maintenance, but there would be no presents for attracting the Indians, there would be no agriculture or livestock raising, and the neophytes would not be taught trades. These new regulations proposed a true revolution in the mission system, with a logical consequence that no missionary wanted: since they were to concern themselves only with spiritual matters, there would be a single friar at each mission, not two, as there had been until then.

After having lived five years in the complete solitude of San Francisco de Borja, and knowing perfectly well what that meant, Lasuén roundly opposed the Neve regulations, declaring that, if they were approved without an appeal to the Council of the Indies, he would take advantage of whatever means were available to withdraw to the Colegio de San Fernando.[59] In Lasuén's opinion, the new regulations aimed only at saving the royal treasury money. "[T]his is to condemn a religious to a life that is more than a burden, to sickness without attendance, and to death without the sacraments,"[60] he maintained in a letter, adding a little further on, "For me the solitude of this occupation is a cruel and terrible enemy which has struck me heavily, like a blow. I escaped from it, thank God, after evident risk of dying on account of it, and now that I see its shadow again, even from afar, I am full of trembling at the mere prospect of having to return to the struggle."

Going back to the college was not a mere threat. Lasuén had completed his required ten-year term in the missions some time previously, and he had the right to leave. When he had to deal with the problem in his capacity as president of the missions, however, his thirteen-page response was energetic ("I oppose and resist . . . the project of being alone at a mission")[61] but carefully considered. Bancroft praises Lasuén's literary abilities: "His writings, of which I have many, both original and copied, prepossess the reader in favor of the author by their comparative conciseness of style."[62] In the end, Governor Fages also decided in Lasuén's favor. The issue was resolved without conflict, and new missions were founded on the same terms as the previous ones, as Lasuén and the other friars wanted.

Following Pedro Fages's administration (1782–91), José Antonio Romeu briefly served as governor of the Californias (1791–92), and when he died, José Joaquín Arrillaga became interim governor (1792–94). If Lasuén knew how to get along with the previous authorities, his understanding with Arrillaga, a native of Aia, Gipuzkoa, was complete. Lasuén wanted him definitively named to the position, and in late 1794, he wrote to the guardian of the Colegio de San Fernando, Fray Francisco Pangua, urging him to support Arrillaga's appointment wherever he could: "He is a very gifted person and, in short, knows a great deal, or all that is to be known, about this country," Lasuén said.[63] Nevertheless, less than two months later, another Basque became the seventh governor of the Californias: Diego de Borica y Retegui.

Diego de Borica[64] was from Vitoria, so that, surprisingly, two men from Vitoria, Lasuén and Borica, became California's highest-ranking religious and civil authorities. Historians emphasize that, in addition to fellow-countrymen, they were good friends—"devoted friends," Chapman says—and that during their joint time in office, the two institutions worked together better and more progress was made than at any other time during the colonial period. The two men's shared origin must have helped to some degree, but so did their agreeable personalities and the intelligence with which they worked out how to solve their many disagreements. Their contemporaries agreed that Borica was one of the best governors of the colonial period. "I remember Gov. Don Diego de Borica well," José María Romero says in his memoirs. "He was a very happy and good-humored man, agreeable to the whole world."[65] Among the historians, Bancroft says that "he was a prudent, sensible man, honest and zealous in the discharge of his public duties."[66] For Hittell, he was the best educated of all the governors of the colonial period, and also the most sensible and the most industrious.

Diego de Borica y Retegui was a lieutenant colonel with a long military career in New Spain. When he received news of his appointment, he was around fifty years old and was living in Arizpe, where he enjoyed the company of a circle of cultivated friends. In the letters they exchanged, a much more refined atmosphere is evident, according to the historian Hittell, than would be expected from the inhabitants of such a remote location. Borica himself was a member of the Real Sociedad Bascongada de Amigos del País, and other members of the Arizpe circle probably were as well.

Borica left Arizpe in the spring of 1794, together with his wife and daughter. His wife, who owned large tracts of land in Nueva Vizcaya, was María Magdalena de Urquidi, also of Basque origin. The journey to Loreto did not turn out to be a very pleasant one. "On Tuesday at three in the afternoon, we reached the peninsula. María Magdalena and my daughter were quite seasick. They spewed, among other things, rage,"[67] Borica wrote to his friends on May 15. By the time they arrived at the governor's residence in Monterrey, on November 9, the provisional governor, José Joaquín Arrillaga, had returned to his post in Loreto. They were in Monterrey at the same time as Capt. George Vancouver, and Borica and his wife had the opportunity to converse with and enjoy the company of the English explorer.

Unlike the majority of previous governors, Borica liked California from the first. He wrote that it was the most peaceful and tranquil region on earth, and that one could live there better than at the most cultivated European court. It was:

> a grand country, with a healthy climate intermediate between cold and temperate, especially rich in beef, fish, table delicacies and, best of all, in "bonne humeur."[68]

One of the first goals the new governor set for himself was to complete the chain of missions, in collaboration with Lasuén. Their larger objectives were different: one was thinking about evangelization, the other about subjecting the territory by putting it in the missionaries' hands. Nevertheless, in order to obtain either objective, more missions were needed. On this point, they were in agreement, and they set to work. The period between June 11 and September 8, 1797, saw the foundation of the missions of San José, San Juan Bautista, San Miguel, and San Fernando, with one more, San Luis Rey, coming on June 13 of the following year. Never had so much been done in so short a time. Lasuén went to each site in person and personally led the consecration ceremonies. In other words, at the age of sixty-one, he travelled over five hundred miles, at a time when today's travel facilities were unimaginable. When he finally returned to San Carlos, he received a letter from Borica in which the governor congratulated his friend and jokingly asked him whether he had dunked himself in the sacred waters of another Jordan in order to renew his youth.

This increase in the number of missions was the most obvious achievement of Lasuén's time in office, since the total grew from nine to eighteen during his administration. The chain of California missions along the Camino Real stretched almost a thousand kilometers from south to north. There were large gaps between them, and it was apparently Lasuén's idea to fill in those gaps with new missions. The

Alta California mission map. It shows "El Camino Real" in 1821, when it was Just a trail. Source: California from the Conquistadores to the Legends of Laguna

sites were chosen so as to leave an interval of around fifty kilometers, so that the missionaries could cover the distance from one mission to the next in a single day on horseback. Before Borica became governor, Lasuén had already founded four missions, and Santa Bárbara was the first in that long chain.[69]

The mission of Santa Bárbara was founded on a site selected by Lasuén, and he himself formally consecrated it on December 4, 1786. The first entries in the mission's baptismal register are for three young Indian men: the first was Catuya, around twenty-two years old, from the ranchería of Guainonase, whom Lasuén baptized with the name of Antonio María; the second was Sioctu, around fifteen years old, from the ranchería of Sisabanonase, baptized with the name of Vicente María; and the third was Mumiyaut, around twelve years old, from the ranchería of Janaya, given the name of Vicente de Paul. The commander of the Santa Bárbara presidio, Felipe de Goicoechea, served as godfather for all three.

The remaining missions were consecrated in the following order: La Purísima Concepción, December 8, 1787; Santa Cruz, August 28, 1791; and Soledad, October 9, 1791. Then came a pause of several years, after which all the rest were consecrated within a short period.

Just as important as founding new missions was maintaining those that were already functioning, and noteworthy progress was made in this area as well during Lasuén's and Borica's administrations. Between 1785 and 1803, at the same time that the number of missions grew from nine to eighteen, the number of missionaries increased from eighteen to forty. Baptisms also notably increased, from 6,736 to 37,976. The number of Indians who lived in the missions was 4,646 in 1784 and 18,185 in 1803. Over the same period of time, the number of cattle increased from 5,384 to 77,578 head, and the number of sheep from 5,384 to 117,736. The harvest was 15,796 fanegas[70] at the end of 1784 and 48,003 fanegas at the end of 1803.[71]

At the same time, between 1792 and 1795, Lasuén and Borica decided to contract carpenters, blacksmiths, masons, and other artisans from New Spain to teach the Indians their various trades. It was an important step toward enabling the missions to be self-sufficient in the future, without depending on the ships laden with provisions sent from New Spain. Around twenty "masters" arrived on four- or five-year contracts. Some settled permanently, but the majority returned to New Spain when their time was up. It was these artisans, in large part, who were responsible for the transformation the missions underwent in this period. Up to this point, the mission buildings had been of very poor quality, and it was under Lasuén and Borica that what is today considered "mission style" came into being. It was at this time that the Carmel church was built of stone, and the San Gabriel church of stone and brick.

So Lasuén and Borica worked side by side in the effort to found new missions, but as we have noted, these two "devoted friends" also had their differences. One of the latter had to do with the friars' escorts. In 1795, Borica ordered that the friars do without an escort when they had to spend the night away from the mission in order to baptize a pagan or hear a Christian's confession. Lasuén could not agree with this measure:

> Your Lordship must not conclude that when we say the missionary is away overnight we mean that he retires to rest in the place to which he goes, or even on the road. We simply mean that he utilizes the night to complete the task he was not able to complete during the day. Or it may be a case of waiting for daylight, for only with the aid of that would it be possible to negotiate some dangerous pass where, in the darkness, there is risk of falling over a precipice. Or it may be a case of taking some rest so as to be able to continue the task.[72]

Lasuén had situations from his own experience in mind. In the same letter, he tells Borica about the following episode:

> I myself have set out to do something that seemed to require but a half a day, and not even in a day and a half, and taking in the night, too, has it been possible to conclude the task. I have gone on a journey with the intention of returning the next day, in order to baptize a pagan woman who had sent for me. I began that night to instruct her in the Christian doctrine, and before I could finish I had to hasten to another who was dying. I instructed and baptized her; then returned to the first and did the same for her. I retired a distance of two or three musket shots to the ranchería to rest for what little remained of the night, and there I learned that the ranchería was suffering from the plague. This I saw for myself the following morning. The sick wanted my help, and those who were well pressed for it, too. In the end I had to stay for nine nights and days with these pagans, a dozen leagues from the mission, and I baptized and buried many.[73]

On that occasion, Lasuén had the help of two escorts. In his letter to Borica, he asks himself whether the natives would have been so peaceful without their presence. In addition, Lasuén's fears did not concern the natives only:

> Furthermore, Sir, it is worthy of consideration that the rugged sierras, the valleys, and the beaches where the Indians live abound in bears, and other wild animals. And I am inclined to say that above all others I fear the very animal on which I ride, for I am quite unskilled in managing it—a failing in which we, the Franciscans, all share alike in these parts.[74]

Lasuén ends with a question:

> What heart, then, (and least of all that of Your Lordship), will bear to see a poor Friar on a dark night . . . surrounded by so much danger, so many things that cause anguish and anxiety, all of which can be remedied with two or three soldiers?[75]

On this subject, it was the viceroy who had the last word, and he decided to rescind Governor Borica's order.

Another of the moments of tension between Lasuén and Borica arose when the governor, motivated by the war between Spain and France, wrote to Lasuén asking the missions to contribute with donations. The friar replied with his usual courtesy, offering spiritual assistance in place of material aid, since the missions were in no position to contribute in any other way. Lasuén and Borica also maintained opposing views on the foundation of towns alongside the missions. In 1797, when Branciforte was founded alongside the Santa Cruz mission and the first group of colonists arrived—outlaws and delinquents sent from Mexico, who arrived almost naked, some of them ill with the "French disease"—Lasuén expressed to Borica his displeasure at setting such a bad example for the Indians whom the friars were trying to "educate." The same year, Borica wanted to give new momentum to the project of uniting California and New Mexico by organizing an expedition in which the Indians were to play a significant part. As the reader will remember, the route that was to unite Sonora and California, opened by Juan Bautista Anza, had been abandoned after the rebellion of the Yuma Indians along the Colorado. On this matter also, Lasuén and Borica did not agree. All these disagreements did not affect their relationship, however. At the same time that they were trying to sort out their differences, Lasuén, prostrated by what he called a "a troublesome cold or influenza," wrote to Borica in a familiar tone:

> I am troubled a great deal night and day by a dry hard cough. I cannot recall ever having suffered from such a thing in all my life. Perhaps I did once in the old country when I was a small boy, for I can recall that I was told "That's the drum of death." It was like a warning then; who knows but the same will be true now? God's will be done. This at least is certain, that if I were at the college I would now be receiving treatments and good care in the infirmary, for that is the way Divine Providence disposes things down there. Up here things are different.[76]

During the time that this double administration lasted, the competition between the two powers was continuous, but the way of proceeding changed radically between Serra's time and Lasuén's. Serra went to Mexico and accused Governor Fages publicly. Lasuén, in contrast, was always in favor of solving problems discreetly. It was for this reason that the scandal that broke out at the San Francisco mission was so painful for him, since he found himself obliged to publicly defend the honor of the friars accused of abusing the Indians and the prestige of the missions.

The Accusations against the Mission as an Institution; Borica's Death

One of Gov. Diego de Borica's greatest concerns was the situation of the mission neophytes. He had no sooner arrived in California than he expressed his indignation at the Indians' high rate of mortality, and during his administration, he was always ready to collaborate on anything that entailed an improvement in their conditions of life. For this reason, when in 1796 he read a letter by Father Fernández of the San Francisco mission in which the friar denounced the abuses of which the Indians of his mission were allegedly the victims, he immediately wrote to Lasuén. It was a scandal, the governor said, that in a single year, 1795, 203 Indians had died, and 200 others had fled. "It is a matter that keeps me from sleeping and makes me talk to myself," Borica confessed.[77]

"It would have been impossible for the poor creatures to have found a more firm and steadfast advocate, friend and protector than Borica at once showed himself to be,"[78] Hittell writes in his *History of California*. Borica's letter has a threatening tone, but at the same time, it expresses a hope of being able to solve the problem: "Won't it be a shame for two fellow-countrymen to have to sue one another, with the scandal of the province? And it's necessary for things to happen this way, because the fulfillment of my obligation does not permit me further dissimulation in so serious a matter."[79] In his reply, Lasuén also made reference to their shared origin—"No, my lord and my countryman, there will be no lawsuits"[80]—but without forgetting each one's place in the social scale: "What chance has a poor father Lasuén against a señor like Don Borica?"

When a problem arose, Lasuén preferred to make a personal appearance at the location and examine the matter *in situ*, and this is what he did on this occasion as well. When the storm had blown over, he confessed to the guardian of the Colegio de San Fernando that it had been the most serious problem he had confronted in his entire life.[81] In the same letter, he explained that the accusations had been the consequence of a conspiracy against the friars responsible for the San Francisco mission and had no other objective than getting Father Dantí and Father Landaeta removed from there. The natives' high rate of mortality, according to Lasuén, had been due to a contagious illness. The epidemic, and not abuse, was the reason that so many had fled the mission.

The matter fell into abeyance for a time, but a year later, when Fernández repeated his accusations in another letter to Borica, Lasuén considered that enough was enough, and in response to Fernández's request, granted him permission to leave the missions.

Two years later, Lasuén faced a similar accusation. In a letter dated July 12, 1798, fray Antonio de la Concepción Horra, who had been sent back to Mexico with signs of mental illness, wrote a long letter to the Viceroy Miguel José de Azanza (Aoitz, Navarre, 1746 – Bordeaux, 1826), harsly criticizing the California missions. Borica sent a questionnaire to which the commanders of the four presidios were to respond. Lasuén, for his part, began to prepare the missionaries'defense. Meanwhile, Borica's health deteriorated alarmingly in Monterrey. He began to lose his sight, and an old illness reappeared, the consequence of his long journeys on horseback. His letters grew shorter; it took great effort for him either to write them himself or to dictate them to others. Seeing that he could not carry out his obligations, he wrote to the viceroy on April 1, 1799, that after thirty-five years of service, and after having covered more than ten thousand leagues on horseback during this time, his body was destroyed, and he wished to return to Mexico, in case the doctors there could help him.

The viceroy granted him license, and José Joaquín Arrillaga again occupied the post of governor *ad interim*. Before embarking for Mexico, Borica passed through San Luis Obispo to take his leave of Lasuén, and on January 16, 1800, from the ship *Concepción*, together with his wife and children—there were three of them by this time—he bid farewell forever to San Diego and to Alta California. After disembarking at the port of San Blas, he made it as far as Durango, Nueva Vizcaya, where he died on July 19, 1800.

In general, California historians write about Borica admiringly. Bancroft describes him in this way:

> Going beyond the routine duties of his position, the governor devoted himself faithfully and intelligently to the general advancement of his province. . . . Missionaries, neophytes, pagans, soldiers, and settlers, each received sympathy, encouragement, and aid from the government. No industry or institution was neglected.[82]

Hittell, for his part, says that it is impossible to mention a topic with which Borica did not concern himself:

> Entirely apart from what may be called his political and military duties, . . . he found other matters to busy himself with more than sufficient in themselves to engage the time of an ordinary governor. Few other men would have done, or could have done, what he did. He was a remarkable man. His intelligence and ability, his benevolence, integrity and energy were uncommon. In view of his time and surroundings, he was an extraordinary governor.[83]

Among the "other matters" to which Borica devoted himself, it should not be forgotten that he was the one who established the official border between Baja and Alta California, nor that he was the sponsor of California's first secular school, a fitting enterprise for a committed member of the Real Sociedad Bascongada de Amigos del País.

Lasuén received the news of Borica's death as he was reflecting on how to defend the missions against Horra's serious accusations. It is logical to suppose that, while he was preparing the forty pages of his reply to Horra's charges, he must have had more than one occasion to remember the governor with whom he had worked in close collaboration so many times—a devoted friend who, alas, was too quick to believe accusations against the friars.

Lasuén's Reply to the Accusations against the Missions: "The Refutation"

The document Lasuén wrote between November 12, 1800, and June 19, 1801, known as "The Refutation," is "the most eloquent and complete defence and presentment of the mission system in many of its phases which is extant,"[84] in Bancroft's opinion. This is how Lasuén formulates the missions' greatest challenge:

> How to transform a savage race such as these into a society that is human, Christian, civil and industrious . . . it is being done successfully by means of patience, and by an unrelenting effort to make them realize that they are men. They are treated with tolerance, or dealt with more or less firmly, depending on the longer or shorter time that has elapsed since their conversion, while awaiting the time when they will gently submit themselves to rational restraint, something they had not known before.[85]

The conviction with which Lasuén refers to the goodness of their effort is, from our point of view, distasteful, but at that time, no one posed the topic of the Indians in other terms, neither the soldiers nor the friars nor the "people of reason." If there were disagreements, they were about means, not ends.

According to Lasuén, the Indians did not flee the missions because of abuse, but because they were forbidden their previous way of life. That was the key: the Indians loved freedom and had "an affinity for the mountains."[86] As the friar explained:

> On an occasion like that, when someone asked permission for some of this group who get "hungry" to go to the mountains for a week, I said to them with some annoyance: "Why, you make me think that if one were to give you a young bull, a sheep, and a fanega of grain every day you would still be yearning for your mountains and your beaches." Then the brightest of the Indians who were listening to me said, smiling and half ashamed of himself, "What you say is true, Father. It's the truth."[87]

This "addiction" of the Indians to the mountains made the missionaries' work enormously more difficult, but it was something that Lasuén could understand:

> The effort entailed in procuring a sustenance from the open spaces is incomparably greater than what is now enjoined on them so that they can sustain themselves; but the former is free and according to their liking, and the latter prescribed, and not according to their liking.[88]

This was, in Lasuén's opinion, the reason for the Indians' discontent, and it was a complete injustice to bring these complaints to the authorities as if they were serious accusations, without first being aware of the friars' perspective.

In his refutation, Lasuén also mentions the problem of language. Horra had accused the friars of speaking to the Indians in the Indians' language and not in Spanish. On this point, Lasuén vigorously defends the use of the native language:

> How can you teach when the other does not understand? The pagans have not even heard Spanish—how can they understand it? And there are persons of fifty or sixty or more years to be baptized—how are they to understand it?[89]

After reading Lasuén's report and examining the replies of the presidio commanders, it was clear to the viceroy that there were major contradictions between them, and he requested further investigation. Governor Arrillaga completed a report that he sent to the new viceroy, José de Iturrigaray y Aróstegui (Baztan, Navarre, 1742 – Madrid, 1815), on November 3, 1804. Finally, after reading all the documentation, Iturrigaray ruled that Horra's accusations lacked foundation.

The historian Bancroft, after having read and examined all the papers, including Lasuén's report, reached the same conclusion:

> The venerable friar's words and manner impress the reader most forcibly, and a close study of the subject has convinced me that he was right; that down to 1800 and considerably later the natives were as a rule most kindly treated; . . . in the matter of neophyte labor at presidio, pueblo, and rancho the friars here as elsewhere were usually right and the military wrong.[90]
> No one today would maintain that "the natives were as a rule most kindly treated," but in the long struggle between the missionaries and the military men, it is easier to side with the missionaries. The soldiers exploited the Indians for their own benefit; the missionaries, on the other hand, tried to strengthen the mission as an institution, in expectation of the day when all the lands and property would pass into the natives' hands. Rumors circulated that the missionaries were accumulating great wealth at the Indians' expense, but no trace of the Jesuits' and Franciscans' alleged gold and silver was ever found. The poverty in which Lasuén spent his last years is good evidence of this lack of interest in personal benefit. When news arrived from Vitoria in 1797 of the indigent state of his sister Clara, Lasuén did not have a cent to

> send her. When they entered the Franciscan order, the friars renounced the right to possess anything in their own names. If they occasionally sought to make a profit, as when Lasuén himself and his fellow missionary from Markina, Pablo de Mugártegui, agreed to trade in sea-otter pelts, for example—the plan was not ultimately put into practice—it was in order to enable the missions to subsist.

Lasuén's Writings and References to Him in the Works of Other Writers

Of the many tasks of all kinds that occupied Lasuén over the course of his life, one of the most wearying, according to his own confession, was having to write so much, especially during the eighteen years he served as president of the missions. Including only the papers that have survived to our day, the Franciscan historian Finbar Kenneally put together two thick volumes of more than four hundred pages each.

In the course of editing all the texts and translating them into English, Kenneally came to know Lasuén's writings better than anyone; yet even so, it seems to us, he let himself be carried away by his admiration for the Basque people when he affirmed that Lasuén's Spanish shows signs of the friar's *euskaldun* origin. On one occasion, Lasuén spoke of "my limited knowledge of Spanish,"[91] and Kenneally sees in these words a confession of the friar's difficulties with the Spanish language. In context, however, the phrase has a different meaning. If there is anything noteworthy about Lasuén's writings, it is the complete absence of Basque.

Euskara is also absent in the written legacy left behind by other friars, and the same is true, evidently, of the writings of explorers, soldiers, and governors. The documents that have survived are almost entirely official letters and reports. Were things different in private correspondence? It seems that Father Uría, a native of Aizarna, Gipuzkoa, interspersed phrases in Euskara in the letters he wrote to Gov. Pablo Vicente Solá,[92] but we have not been able to locate any examples of this. In all the documentation consulted, we have found only one case in which a few words appear in Euskara: "Agur, frailea, agindu,"[93] Gov. José Joaquín Arrillaga told Fray Martín Landaeta at the end of a letter.

If they did not use Euskara to write, did they use it to speak? As far as Lasuén is concerned, Kenneally believes that the answer is yes:

> No letter of his is written in Basque, but there can be little doubt that he used his native language often, for many of the

missionaries, and some of the governors, were Basques.[94]

Nonetheless, Kenneally does not believe that Lasuén showed favoritism toward his fellow-countrymen in his role as a superior.[95]

In Kenneally's collection, Lasuén's letters break off in April 1803. There are no letters written in May, and in June there is only a brief note on the 3rd. Was Lasuén sick? Had that "drum of death" he heard as a child begun to sound again, keeping him from his occupations? We know nothing about Lasuén's illness, only where he died, at San Carlos de Carmelo, and when, on June 26, 1803, at the age of sixty-seven. He was buried the next day in the mission church, beside the high altar. Visitors who go up to the altar can see his tomb there, alongside that of Junípero Serra, with a stone on which his name is engraved.

During the years in which he was president of the missions, Lasuén had the opportunity to meet great travellers and explorers, as well as dealing with the authorities of the time. Some of them recorded details about him in writing. In reality, it is rare to find so much unanimity about a historical figure: we have not found a single negative or lukewarm opinion about Lasuén.

When the great French explorer Jean-François de Galaup, the count of La Pérouse, was in Monterrey in 1786, he went to visit the mission of San Carlos. Although in his description of the province he shows himself opposed to the missions, he has only words of praise for Lasuén:

> Father Fermín de Lasuén, president of the missions of New California, is one of the most worthy of esteem and respect of all the men I have ever met. His sweetness of temper, his benevolence, and his love for the Indians are beyond expression.[96]

As a demonstration of goodwill, and knowing that the French explorer was interested in unique objects from the places he visited, Lasuén gave him three items made from reeds and a stone carved by the Indians of the Santa Barbara Channel.

Carmel San Carlos mission in 1792, when visited by the captain George Vancouver it was the official headquarters of San Carlos Fermín Lasuén. Vancouver: A Voyage of Discovery to the North Pacific Ocean and Round the World, 2. lib.

The explorer Alessandro Malaspina,[97] who visited Monterrey and the San Carlos mission, where he met Lasuén, in 1791, was also impressed by the friar's personality:

> He was a man who in Christian lore, mien, and conduct was truly apostolic, and his good manners and learning were unusual. This religious had with good reason merited the esteem and friendship of both French commanders [of La Pérouse's expedition] and the majority of their subordinates.[98]

More surprising is the praise he received from the English captain George Vancouver at a moment when the dominant opinion in England was opposed to anything that came from Spain. After enjoying a warm welcome from the friars of San Carlos during his visit in December 1792, Vancouver described Lasuén in these terms:

> [his] gentle manners, united to a most venerable and placid countenance, indicated that tranquilized state of mind that fitted him in an eminent degree for presiding over so benevolent an institution.[99]

The friar made such a good impression on Vancouver that, as we have already mentioned, the Englishman named two promontories

Fermin lighthouse, at the Cape Fermin designated by Fermin Lasguenas in Vancouver. It is currently one of the attractions of the Los Angeles port. In 1972 it was designated to the National Register of Historic Places. http://www.uscg.mil/

for him in San Pedro Bay, near Los Angeles, the following year, in November 1793: Point Fermín and Point Lasuén.

On his second visit, Vancouver showed his esteem for the friar by giving him an organ. Lasuén had seen the instrument in the captain's cabin during his previous visit, but it never occurred to him that it might one day be his. "By merely turning a small handle you get the most beautiful sound. It plays thirty-four brief melodies [*tocadas*], and none is far removed from what is sacred. It is an instrument of beauty and a truly precious piece," Lasuén explained in a letter to Fray Tomás Pangua,[100] adding a little further on, "It is now here in San Juan, and on Christmas Night and Christmas Day it was played to the indescribable delight and amazement of the Indians."[101] The instrument was not the most appropriate one for the purposes to which the friars put it. Among those thirty-four melodies were pieces such as "Go to the Devil" and "Lady Campbell's Reel," which would have disturbed the friars if they had understood the titles.

Among the historians who have studied Lasuén, Hittell attributes to him a much broader perspective than would be expected from a man in his position. Chapman, for his part, wishes to rescue him from the second rank:

> Lasuén worthily filled the post of the great Junípero. As a mission-founder he achieved as much; indeed, it might be argued that he did more . . . He travelled fully as much as Father Serra from mission to mission and perhaps more. He baptized a far greater number of Indians. He built up the missions economically and architecturally. He was far more successful than Serra in maintaining harmonious relations with the military. In zeal as a Christian and missionary he equaled, though he could not surpass, Father Junípero.[102]

Nevertheless, the highest praise comes from Bancroft's pen:

> Though Lasuen's name stands second and not first chronologically in the list of Franciscan prelates, though no pen of brother friar or friend has recorded his life and virtues, I cannot but regard Lasuen as first thus far in California, both as a man and a missionary. In him were united the qualities that make up the model or ideal padre, without taint of hypocrisy or cant.[103]

The recipient of such eulogies is practically forgotten in his native country. May these pages contribute to making him and his work better known.

Fermín Lasuén statue at the San Fernando mission.

6
Other Protagonists of Alta California History

Port of Monterrey, ca. 1840. (Eugène Duflot de Mofras: Exploration du territoire de l'Orégon, des Californies et de la Mer Vermeille).

The period between 1792 and 1822 was the age of Basque governors of California. José Joaquín Arrillaga, a native of Aia, Gipuzkoa, was governor *ad interim* from 1792 to 1794; he was succeeded by Diego de Borica, a native of Vitoria, who occupied the post from 1794 to 1800; Arrillaga then returned from 1800 to 1814; it was the turn of the Mexican José Darío Argüello during the brief period from 1814 to 1815; and finally, the post was occupied by Pablo Vicente de Solá from Arrasate, Gipuzkoa from 1815 to 1822.

Moreover, it was not only the governors. In the last decade of the eighteenth century, the principal administrative posts, both civil and religious, were in Basque hands. We've already referred to Diego de Borica and to Fermín Lasuén . Andrés de Mendívil y Amirola was postmaster and handled all the mission correspondence. Jacobo Ugarte y Loyola was the highest-ranking authority in the Interior Provinces, and the strategic port of San Blas was led, como se ha dicho, by Juan Francisco de la Bodega y Quadra. Esteban Lazcano was the Colegio de San Fernando's syndic in Tepic, responsible for obtaining the items that the missionaries requested in their annual reports. The list would be unending. Thus, we will focus on the most representative figures.

José Joaquín Arrillaga: From the Manterola Ironworks in Aia to the Post of Governor of California

In the National Park Service's Mission 2000 database, we find the following information about the first of the Basque governors, José Joaquín Arrillaga:

Race or Tribe: Vizcaíno [Bizkaian].
Place of Service: Sonora; Tejas; California.
Residence: Aya; Horcasitas; San Saba; La Bahía; Loreto.
Title: Alférez; Teniente; Capitán; Teniente Coronel; Gobernador de las Californias [Ensign; Lieutenant; Captain; Lieutenant Colonel; Governor of the Californias].

The database also includes the details recorded by the Aia parish priest in his baptismal register:

Event ID: 9487 Book: Aya B2 Page Number: 74
Event: Baptism Event Date: 03/18/1750 Event Place: Aya, Gipuzkoa
Notes:
Joseph Joachin de Arrillaga
On the 18th of March [1750], I, the Rector, baptized Joseph Joachin, legitimate son of Domingo de Arrillaga and Ana Joachina de Embil, paternal grandson of Ignacio de Arrillaga and Catalina de Iruretagoena, and maternal grandson of Don Manuel de Embil and María Lorenza de Lizardi. Godparents were Joseph Joachin de Embil and María Joachina de Embil. He was born the said day at the Manterola Ironworks. In certification of this, and having explained the spiritual relationship and obligation as instructed in Christian doctrine, I signed.
Don Juan de Zulaica (rubric)

The Manterola Ironworks and the residential cluster of the same name were in Aia's Laurgain neighborhood. It seems that the ironworks were built in the first half of the sixteenth century. According to archival records, there were five ironworks in Aia in 1752. Manterola produced six hundred quintales[1] and was operated by Ignacio de Arrillaga.[2]

Manterola iron works remains, 1988 in Aia, Gipuzkoa. Province of Gipuzkoa archives, http://www.guregipuzkoa.net

Nuestra Señora de Loreto Misson, Baja California, ca. 1700.

The name of Ignacio was common among the Arrillagas. It was the name of José Joaquín's grandfather, and he also had an uncle named Francisco Ignacio and three siblings named Miguel Ygnacio, Ignacio, and Francisca Ygnacia. There were nine siblings in total, whose names were, in order of birth and in the spelling of the time, Miguel Ygnacio, Julia Antonia, José Joaquín, Lorenza Antonia, Micaela Juachina Jazinta, María Agustina, Ignacio, Francisa Ygnacia, and María Xaviera Josepha.[3]As far as their ancestry is concerned, Bancroft says, and American historians repeat, that José Joaquín Arrillaga was "of noble parentage."

Having established himself in Mexico, he enlisted in the company of the presidio of San Miguel de Horcasitas, Sonora, as a volunteer in 1777; on March 30, 1778, he was named ensign; starting in 1780, he served as a lieutenant in the San Sabas and La Bahía companies in Texas; and in 1783, he was named captain of the Loreto presidio and vice governor of the Californias.[4] By that time, he had already received commendation from his superiors for his participation in three campaigns under Col. Juan Bautista Anza and two battles against the Seris and the Pimas. In 1792, when Gov. José Antonio Romeu died, Arrillaga became provisional governor of the Californias. During the brief period he occupied the post, from 1792 to 1794, he showed himself to be a competent and diligent man. According to the historian Chapman, the good reputation he earned at that time and his good character were the reason that he was named governor later.

Among the enterprises with which he concerned himself during this brief administration, two are worth mentioning. The first is the decree he issued in 1793 to prevent fires. While brief, it is a document of great historical value, since it was the first attempt to prevent fires in California. Appropriately for the diligent character of which Chapman speaks, Arrillaga did not limit himself to just issuing the order, but traveled from mission to mission explaining the instructions to the Indians.

The second enterprise—the governor's chief occupation—consisted in reinforcing the territory's defenses. California's military strength at that moment was almost non-existent. If an armed ship had appeared anywhere along the coast, it would have encountered practically no resistance. In San Francisco, there was a single cannon; in Monterrey, there were some weapons, but no one who could use them; and the situation was not much better in San Diego and Santa Bárbara. Hence Arrillaga's concern when Vancouver was given such a friendly welcome in San Francisco in 1792 and even permitted to go to the Santa Clara mission. Despite what had been agreed at Nootka, England and Spain continued competing to take control of the region. The Russians were another source of worry, since they might at any time decide to advance southward from their northern settlements, and the comings and goings of American smugglers also had nothing reassuring about them. Ships loaded in Boston with alcoholic beverages, table services, silverware, textiles, and other items exchanged their cargo for sea-otter and beaver pelts and then continued on to China, where the furs were traded for tea and silk.

In 1853 the Corps of Engineers flattened the land of El Cantil Blanc to build the Fort Point and did not conserve the remains of the old walls erected by Arrillaga. www.extranomical.com

Faced with the threat of this growing foreign presence, Arrillaga began to build a fort at San Francisco. This fort, which would be called Castillo de San Joaquín, would be long forgotten now if it had not been built where it was, on what the Spaniards called Punta del Cantil Blanco, or to use a name more familiar today, at one end of the Golden Gate, one of the world's most emblematic locations. It was exactly the same place that the son of another Gipuzkoan, Juan Bautista Anza II, had chosen as the site of the San Francisco presidio fifteen years before, in 1776.

On Arrillaga's orders, Indians brought from the Santa Clara mission began to build the fort in August 1793. Twenty-three yoke of oxen were used to transport logs and other materials, and the construction took a year. By the time it was finished, the weapons that the frigate *Aránzazu* had brought to supply the fort were in place, including six handsome bronze cannons manufactured a hundred years earlier in Peru.

The San Joaquín fort did not last long. The construction left much to be desired, since Arrillaga had no one who knew the trade on whom to rely, and the unstable walls of adobe and brick were soon damaged by earthquakes and shifting soil. Nevertheless, it deserves to be remembered that the entrance to San Francisco Bay was defended for a number of years by the fort built on Arrillaga's orders and the cannons brought by the frigate *Aránzazu*.[5]

The work carried out by the interim governor apparently pleased the authorities, and when the post passed into the hands of Borica, Arrillaga was promoted to the rank of lieutenant colonel. Back in Loreto, over the next five years he tried to bring order to the affairs of the presidios of both Californias. This is the subject of the majority of documents Arrillaga signed during this period, with the notable exception of a manuscript preserved in the Bancroft Library in Berkeley with the title of "Diario que manifiesta los Reconocimientos que a verificado de Orden Superior . . . en las Fronteras a la Gentilidad de la Antiqua California y margenes del Colorado" (Diary setting out the reconnaissances he has verified, on orders from his superiors . . . on the borders with the pagans in Old California and on the banks of the Colorado).

José Joaquín Arrillaga . . . on the Borders with the Pagans in Old California and on the Banks of the Colorado

At the end of the eighteenth century, the territories that stretched from Baja California to the Colorado River and the Gulf of California remained relatively unknown. Made up of the untamed lands where California's Yuma Indians lived, the region was called the frontier. During the century's final years, several expeditions were dedicated to exploring those territories. José Joaquín Arrillaga participated directly in one of them, and as was expected, he set down the details of his journey in a diary.

In 1793, Viceroy Revillagigedo authorized the exploration of the banks of the Colorado River, and Arrillaga, in accordance with his

Reproduced for the Baja California Travels Series, Volume 17, 1969

diligent character, preferred to go in person rather than to leave the enterprise in others' hands. The journey was to have a double objective: investigating the possibility of a land route to Sonora, as the Jesuits Kino and Salvatierra had done a hundred years before, and selecting sites for new Dominican missions. The exploration was carried out in four campaigns, from June 14 to November 21, 1796. In the words of the historian John W. Robinson, who edited Arrillaga's diary, "for the area covered and the detail of observation, these expeditions were without parallel in the early history of Northern Baja California."[6]

The fourth campaign began on October 15. Arrillaga was accompanied by twenty-one soldiers, two corporals, and a sergeant. On the 19th, as soon as the sun rose, they could see the poplars growing along the banks of the Colorado River, the territory where the Yumas had rebelled in 1781. We have already mentioned previously the good relations that the Yuma chief Olleyquotequiebe, whom the Spaniards called Salvador Palma, and his people initially maintained with Juan Bautista Anza, as well as the subsequent rebellion in which the Yumas, feeling themselves humiliated by the Spaniards, murdered all the whites who fell into their hands, including the great explorer Francisco Garcés and the young Navarrese friar Juan Antonio Barreneche. It is no great stretch to suppose that Arrillaga recalled those tragic events as he entered that territory.

On October 20, the group set out at first light to visit a ranchería. The inhabitants took to flight as soon as they saw the soldiers, but Arrillaga indicated to them by gestures that they came in peace, and the Indians dared to approach. There was an exchange of gifts: on the Indians' side, melons and watermelons, and on that of the soldiers, meat, biscuits, and cigars. Through an interpreter, Arrillaga offered the natives his friendship, promising them that if they came to his camp, he would give them more presents.

A few hours later, the Indians were at the camp. There was another exchange of gifts. Arrillaga wanted to know whether the famous chief Salvador Palma was still alive, and he received an affirmative answer. He also asked about the direction he was intending to go that afternoon. Let us allow Arrillaga himself to continue the narration:

> They pointed out two routes to me: a straight one, and another one which went around. Seeing their good will, I resolved to take the first one, and I asked them to guide me. They did it in that manner, two on horseback, with whom I left at two in the afternoon with the troops and the loads. In about two leagues I

spotted several little huts, some people, and their farms of melons, watermelons, and pumpkin. I continued on my way, always between these farms, and a great multitude of people joined me along the way little by little. Many were without weapons, others were with them, and some of them were with sticks . . . It must have been about four o'clock when we came to cross a laguna with some undrinkable water and, noticing that the Indians were amassing themselves, I ordered the sergeant to place himself on the rear guard and, continuing with all due precautions, he should attempt, without offending them, to disperse the Indians. The sergeant did as I ordered him, but they remained in sight, and always following us. The two guides remained here; they had tried to convince me to spend the night, but I did not judge it convenient.

I continued on my way and observed that several gentiles who looked to be of some authority were ahead of me on horseback, going from house to house. With this, I arrived in a laguna which I could not cross. Asking the Indians about the place for crossing, a boy, of whom I learned afterwards to be from the vicinity of Mission San Miguel, offered to show me. We returned to the head of the laguna and, although he showed me the way through, I decided not to take it, because it had much water and it was treacherously muddy. When another gentile started to guide us I realized that he was leading us astray. After having walked a while, the above-mentioned boy came and told me that I could cross the laguna without difficulty. I ordered someone to attempt the crossing and it was accomplished. In this retracing of steps in which it was necessary to go around several times, there gathered a multitude of people, who started to shout and make provoking gestures.

Once across the laguna, without my requesting him, another gentile started to guide us. At the same time, the sergeant notified me from the rear guard that he could no longer contain such a multitude of people, and asking me if they should put on their cueras. I ordered that they should do so at once, that they should unsheath their lances, and that everyone should have his weapons ready. The gentiles calmed down somewhat upon this demonstration. Distrusting my situation of being surrounded by some lagunas and by the Indians, plus the fact that it was already getting late, I called the above-mentioned boy and told him to guide me to a safe place, threatening him that if he should not do it, I would kill him with the lance. I made him walk with the scouts, being forced to do so by the knowledge that the

Indian who placed himself as our guide was leading us astray. The boy, seeing himself threatened, told me through the interpreter that I should hurry up. At this time I was notified by the sergeant that they had given a soldier a blow with a jara,[7] and that they had wounded a horse. I had him follow the train, in order to get out of the place, where there were some reed thickets, advising the sergeant not to make a big issue of it as long as they did not continue to attack him.

We had not gone a quarter of a league when we found another laguna, partly dry, and the boy guide told me that I was already in a safe place. And in fact a plain with some mezquite tree clusters presented itself to us. The Indians stopped on its edge. I entered the plain and ordered a stop, so that the troops could change horses and fix the loads.

Not being able to trust being completely free oruightf lagunas and reed thickets, I sent two soldiers to a nearby sierra, so that they would explore to see if we had a way out and, in case that such did not exist, to fire upon the Indians and use lances, and go out the way we came. In this interval one of the interpreters advised me that the gentiles wanted to kill me, according to what they said, and that one of them was there, wanting to talk to me. In fact, he came and assured me that farther ahead many people were waiting to kill us. The crowd within my sight divided itself in five groups, and each of them approached me from time to time. But as soon as I pointed the troops toward them, they retreated. One of the chieftains, as he would make himself to be, approached, asking me for the boy guide who led us to the place. I replied to him that as long as the soldiers whom I sent to look for the route did not return, I was not giving him up. They made various threats at me, including hurling several blows with their jaras, but I ignored them. Seeing that night was approaching, I went to them and warned them through the interpreter that if they did not leave I would kill them. They minded very little and, seeing that they insisted on staying, I ordered the sergeant and some soldiers to attack and frighten them and, this failing, to strike them with the butts of their lances. The sergeant broke his in this manner and the Indians, with great daring, threw him several blows with their jaras, but he casually eluded all of them.

Around Evening Prayer the two soldiers returned, saying that there was a clear way out. I resolved with this news to get out of the vicinity of the rancherías, leaving the Indians who had provoked me so much. Also, I did not ignore the notice that they were waiting for me farther ahead, and so I changed route in the early evening, in case they were following me. Noticing that they did not follow me, I retraced my steps, heading toward the north, which I had planned, and which was known by the friendly Indian guides who were with me.

I continued my journey in good order, the whole troop together, when at seven-thirty in the evening the Indians attacked me in the front. From a cluster of mezquite trees near the route I ordered fire to be opened up on them. The horses ran away at the sound of the shots, but on good ground. As soon as we left the hillside, the Indians stopped, and the horses were brought back and refitted. They hit the sleeve of one of the interpreters with a jara. I don't know if they wounded any of the animals. We did have the misfortune that one of the corporals went down with his horse and was dragged a considerable stretch. He lost his shotgun and lance, which could not be located.

As the night was dark, I resolved to put myself on good ground and to wait for the moon to come out in order to continue. I found a good site and halted until nine-thirty, in which interval I saw several torches pass. As soon as the moon lighted sufficiently, I went on with great precaution, about ten o'clock. The guide told me that there was a bad spot near, with the sierra and rocky cliffs on one side and a laguna on the other, and that only one at a time could cross. The odds being fairly even, I decided not to turn back. I put seven men with the sergeant in front, the loads and horses with the same number, and a corporal in the rear guard. We all entered the bad spot and, as we carne out, we encountered the ambush, part on the path, part on the hillside, and part opposite the laguna in such a way that at the same time they rained jara blows on us from all sides. I ordered fire to be opened first on those who obstructed the path, and the way was cleared at once. Having come out of the bad spot with my first people, I ordered fire to be opened on the hillside. At the sound of the shots the horses retreated and I ordered the sergeant to go aid the rear guard. I remained with two soldiers and my page, firing on the reed thicket of the laguna. The sergeant gave his orders, he had some soldiers go up the hillsides, and he was able in this manner to let the loads and the horses through.

Once free of this bad spot, I counted all my people, and saw that no one was missing, and that no one was seriously wounded. Although several soldiers and two of my attendants were hit with jaras, it was nothing of consequence. They only wounded one soldier who was with me, his horse, and several others, but I did not know about them until later.

I continued my journey, and sometime after eleven found another laguna which I tried to cross but was not able to. I found myself at one o'clock at night next to the place where a short time before I had fought. I asked the guide, and he assured me that he did not know the laguna, since it was not there when he came by ten years ago with Pedro Fages.[8] I deliberated about the route to take, considering that if I halted until dawn it would be necessary to kill many Indians, with the risk to my own people, not knowing if perhaps I would be forced to come back again.

With these considerations I judged it best to return the same way I came in, and save myself without wagering the fortune of everybody, for the longer I lingered, the more people that would gather. I was forced to stand watch all night because the enemy was near, whose loud yelling we could hear in all directions, particularly in the direction of the route I intended to follow.

I resolved, therefore, to return by the before-mentioned bad spot, which was near, and with all possible silence I arrived there, but there were Indians there already. We surprised them, firing upon them, and they left the route clear for us. But before the rear guard had entered the narrow spot, it was attacked violently by the Indians who had come ahead to wait for us. They succeeded in killing a mule with a blow of a jara, which mule was loaded with a little pinole, some squash, and the tent poles. Frightened by the gun shots fired at them, they were forced to retreat, and all of us were able to pass without further incident.

Although we did not notice anything when going, upon returning through the same pass two bodies were found on the path, and three others in the laguna. Two of these were killed by the vanguard in the last battle, and one of them by the muleteers. Having already left us free (for although they followed us at a distance, they did not attempt another attack), I inspected my troops and other things, and I found nothing new. I continued my way toward a laguna near the route by which I had reached the river. I arrived at daybreak. Fearing that they would attempt to attack me, I decided to move about three leagues away, in order to give the people and the horses some rest. I arrived at seven in the morning at a well. About nine o'clock they notified me that from the heights of the nearby sierra there were about eighty Indians descending. I ordered the sergeant and eight men to advance, and they remained within sight of the gentiles. They no doubt had come to look us over.[9]

After repeating that none of his men was seriously hurt, even though some of them were hit by the Indians' *jaras* or pointed sticks, Arrillaga ends his account with these words:

> I must frankly confess that, although the previous afternoon they [the Indians] gave me ample reason to punish them, I had pity on their wretched state. Because they attacked me three times at night I could have revenged myself with the blood of many of them, and could have destroyed their rancherías and families . . . But I used consideration, reflecting that my purpose was the exploration of the land, and not their destruction.

In the report he wrote for his superiors after the campaign, Arrillaga recommended building a good presidio on the lower Colorado, in order thereby to facilitate communication with Sonora, as well as founding a new mission at the eastern end of the Alamo River plain. The king gave his approval for the second project, and in 1797, the mission of Santa Catalina Virgen y Mártir was founded. The natives were always opposed to this mission. Thefts and attacks were continuous until the Indians set the mission on fire and burned it to the ground in 1840.

José Joaquín Arrillaga's Caution with Regard to the Foreign Threat

While the mission of Santa Catalina Virgen y Mártir was being built in the Alamo River valley, Arrillaga learned that Spain and England had declared war on each other. The likelihood that the English would try to take control of California appeared greater than ever, and the governor took measures to defend the territory. He ordered the formation of militia companies and the distribution of arms to the natives, "for the English," Arrillaga wrote, "have a great dread of the Indians, especially in their war-paint and feathers."[10] In fact, Arrillaga had no choice but to rely on them, since there were no more than fifty soldiers in total in the entire peninsula. On this occasion, in the end, no English soldiers appeared in the California ports, only the usual whalers, smugglers, and the like, but Arrillaga's worries did not disappear as a result.

In 1804, Baja California and Alta California became two separate administrative units: Old California (Antigua California) and New California (Nueva California). The former would have its capital at Loreto and would encompass the entire province of Baja California, including the Dominican missions. Its governor would be Felipe de Goicoechea. The second would begin slightly south of San Diego and would encompass all the territory to the north, with Monterrey as its capital and José Joaquín Arrillaga as its governor. Both governors would answer to the viceroy of Mexico, who also had a Basque surname: José de Iturrigaray.

The friars received the news of Arrillaga's appointment with pleasure. They knew that he was a faithful believer and a pious man. The warmest welcome he was given was the one at the Soledad mission, the residence of Father Ibáñez, a native of Tarragona and a great friend of Arrillaga. Ibáñez, who was a musician, composed some verses of welcome for the new governor, and Arrillaga made his entrance into the mission to the music of voices and instruments conducted by the friar.

In his new post, territorial defense was again Arrillaga's chief concern. California's military forces were constituted in their totality by around four hundred men; the white population was too small to supply more recruits; the Indians were very poor soldiers; and Anglo-American ships were arriving ever more frequently in California's waters, in search of pearls, fish, or furs. With great insolence, they even dared to fish under the Spaniards' noses. They had been seen tranquilly hunting sea otters in San Francisco Bay, making use of the skills of Indians brought from the Aleutian Islands for the purpose.

In view of the evident threat, Arrillaga decided in 1806 to impose stricter laws against smuggling. The coast was to be closely watched, and as soon as the soldiers caught sight of a foreign ship, they were to notify the nearest presidio; in addition, no provisions were to be offered to the foreigners. Arrillaga acted with his habitual diligence and observed the regulations strictly, especially in the case of Anglo-American ships. Nevertheless, in the case of the Russians, he had to make some concessions before the year was out.

Arillaga's "Role" in the Romance between the Russian Nobleman Rezanov and the Daughter of the San Francisco Presidio Commander

As we have explained, the desire to prevent the Russians from moving south was one of the reasons the Spaniards wanted to occupy San Diego and Monterrey in 1769. During the following decade, several expeditions were sent to find out what the Russians were doing in the north: Pérez's expedition in 1774, Heceta's in 1775, Arteaga's in 1779 . . . The ones who found Russians found them very far to the north, in latitudes where Spain had never taken possession. (Spain claimed the territory as far as 56° latitude.) Starting with the voyages of the Dane Vitus Bering (1725–30), Russia had sent a number of expeditions to reconnoiter that coast; Russian fur traders had been established there since 1745; the

Nikolái Petróvich Rezanov

great monopoly known as the Russian-American Company had been set up in 1799 . . . but Spaniards and Russians had scarcely set eyes on one another throughout this entire time. However, events would soon lead the inhabitants of the remote north to make contact with the Spaniards living in California.

A year earlier, in 1805, the Russian chamberlain Nikolai Petrovich Rezanov, imperial inspector of the northeastern settlements and plenipotentiary authority of the Russian-American Company, arrived in Sitka.[11] Rezanov, along with Krusenstern and Lisiansky, had participated in the first Russian voyage around the world two years earlier, on the ships *Nadezhda* and *Neva*. Subsequently, together with the naturalist Langsdorff, he travelled to the Aleutian Islands and from there to Sitka. Rezanov was to examine the situation of the Russian colonies and make proposals for extending them. He seems to have devoted all his skill and all his courage to the task, but in Sitka he met an enemy difficult to conquer: hunger. One ship that was supposed to arrive with provisions sank, another failed to appear, and hunger became a serious problem for the two hundred men on the island. Bread was running out, they were unable to fish, and dried fish and the meat of sea lions and seals were growing scarce. The men ate eagles, crows, manta rays, and whatever else they could get. Scurvy spread among the weakened crew. An icy rain never stopped. The only thing that kept the men in Sitka was the hope of fleeing the place, Rezanov wrote.

In these circumstances, the arrival of the American ship *Juno*, under the orders of Captain Wolfe, was a great relief. Rezanov bought the ship, including its cargo, for eight thousand dollars. The improvement in conditions did not last long, however. By spring, the situation was critical, and lacking any other alternative, Rezanov decided to try to obtain food in Califtornia. He knew that trading with foreigners was prohibited there, but starvation frightened him more than violating the Spanish administration's laws. In addition, if everything went well, he could do a good business in furs, if not with the viceroy's permission, then privately, with the missionaries as intermediaries.

Once the plan had been conceived, it did not take much to put it into practice. The *Juno* was prepared immediately. A cargo that might be able to tempt California's inhabitants was selected, and on March 8, 1806, Rezanov set out to sea, accompanied by the naturalist Langsdorff. Half the crew, weakened by the hunger endured during the preceding months and ill with scurvy, was soon completely useless. On the point of shipwreck, they tried three times to enter the Colombia River, without success. They thought that they would never reach California, but scurvy left them no option but to keep going or die. At a certain point, fortunately, the phase of the moon brought favorable winds, and on April 4, they reached the latitude of San Francisco, although the dense fog prevented them from seeing anything. The *Juno* anchored outside the promontories, and on the following day, with all sails set, it headed directly for the port. Since the situation on the ship was so serious, Rezanov decided to pass in front of the San Joaquín fort without stopping, even at the risk of being fired at by the cannon.

At the fort on that morning of April 5, the soldier on watch saw a ship approaching the entrance to the port. He gave the alarm, the soldiers of the presidio made ready, the five gunners ran to the two operable cannons, and they saw with astonishment that the ship passed in front of the fort without even a salute.

"What ship?" they shouted from land, with the help of a speaking trumpet.

"Russian!" the men on the ship replied.

"Drop anchor!" came the authoritarian order from land.

"Yes, sir; yes, sir," the Russians repeated . . . until they dropped anchor at a prudent distance.

Even out of range of San Joaquín's cannons, the Russians were still apprehensive about the Spaniards' welcome. A few years earlier, when Krusenstern and Lisiansky were trying to become the first Russians to circumnavigate the globe, the Spanish king had sent instructions that they be provided assistance when their journey brought them to California. In the end, the *Nadezhda* and *Neva* did not visit California, but the men on the *Juno* were wondering now whether the king's instructions would also apply to them. In any event, the Spaniards were not to find out about the lamentable state of the Russian colonies.

While the *Juno*'s crew were worrying about these things, twenty armed men approached along the shore on land. They were under the command of Ensign Luis Argüello, since the garrison commander, José Darío Argüello, Luis's father, was absent. A Franciscan was also part of the group: José Antonio Uría y Larrañaga, from Azkoitia, Gipuzkoa. Langsdorff and Lieutenant Davidov went on shore to meet with them. How were they going to communicate? Langsdorff himself gives us the answer:

> As neither Lieutenant Davidov nor myself understood Spanish, the conversation was carried on in Latin, between me and the Franciscan padre, this being the only medium by which either one could make himself intelligible to the other.[12]

Relations got off to a good start. The Spaniards promised the Russians that they would give them provisions to alleviate the immediate crisis, and they invited Rezanov and his officers to dine at the presidio. Uría and his companion from the San Francisco mission were present at the dinner, as were Mrs. Argüello and her children, including the young Concepción. In the following days, Rezanov would pay greater attention to the fifteen-year-old Conchita (a nickname for Concepción), but that first night, there were other topics to discuss. The younger Argüello was uneasy. He wanted to know why the *Juno* had appeared there, and not, as they had been told to expect, the *Nadezhda* and the *Neva*, the ships that were going to sail around the world. News was late in coming to San Francisco, and the Spaniards were unaware that the two ships' voyage was over. In addition, Argüello found it very strange that the Russian ambassador would turn up so informally. Rezanov explained himself as well as he could, without confessing the true reason for his visit. Argüello immediately sent a message to Governor Arrillaga to inform him of the situation.

Rezanov also wrote to the governor, offering to go to Monterrey to meet with him in person. Arrillaga was now a man of a certain age, fifty-six years old, but despite everything, fearless of the more than 120 miles of distance, he replied to Rezanov not to trouble himself, that he would come to San Francisco. The Russian chamberlain saw in this reply evidence of the governor's wariness, suspecting that it was a way of preventing the Russians from seeing the interior of the territory and witnessing how scant Spain's military strength was. He was not wrong.

Until Arrillaga arrived, Rezanov dedicated himself to distributing gifts at the presidio and the mission, proudly exhibiting to soldiers and friars the tempting cargo the *Juno* carried. It was a matter above all of manufactured products that could not be obtained in California: knives, scissors, textiles, carpenter's tools, paper . . . Rezanov said not a word of his plan to carry grain away in exchange, nor, above all, of the dramatic situation the northern settlements were experiencing.

The *Juno*'s crew, who were waiting in San Francisco, began to ask themselves why they had to live on Sitka, that sad, dark island, while the Spaniards were living in the paradise of San Francisco, where the land

and climate were so benign. Some of them asked permission to remain there. It was not granted, and two Russian sailors jumped ship.

Arrillaga arrived in San Francisco on April 18. The following morning, two friars visited Rezanov to make the governor's excuses for him, as Arrillaga was unable to come to greet him, due to his age and weariness. Rezanov and all his officers went to the presidio and were brought to the governor, a grey-haired man of venerable appearance. He appeared to Rezanov to be exhausted after having covered the 120 miles from Monterrey to San Francisco on horseback, the only mode of transportation available in early-nineteenth-century California. The governor spoke French, facilitating communication between the two men. In addition, Rezanov was now capable of stammering a few words in Spanish, thanks to his interaction with San Francisco's inhabitants, and especially with the presidio commander's daughter. In reality, Rezanov's circumlocutions and diplomatic lies were a greater obstacle than language to understanding between the two. The chamberlain aimed to make Arrillaga believe that trade would be beneficial to both parties and that the only reason to load his ship with California's products was to find out whether there was a market for them in the northern settlements. The cautious Arrillaga was not as easy to deceive as the Russians supposed, however. He saw clearly that the visit's real purpose was to exchange the *Juno*'s cargo for grain, and that was something that Arrillaga could not permit.

In effect, all Rezanov's eloquence and all his flattery were useless against Arrillaga's firmness. The governor admitted that trade could be beneficial to California's inhabitants, but he was not prepared to violate the law. At most, he would allow the Russians to buy grain for cash. It was not a good solution, since the *Juno* would be unable to transport more than a small amount of grain if it did not unload its existing cargo first. Rezanov argued that, once the appropriate report had been sent to the viceroy, the friars could use the money they received in exchange for the grain as they wished, including to buy a few little things from the *Juno*. Nevertheless, Arrillaga rejected the proposal. During his nearly sixty years of life, his conduct had been irreproachable, and he had no desire to soil his conscience with such evasions. The friars would surely have accepted the deal without so many scruples, but as far as the governor was concerned, that was his final answer. Or his next-to-final answer, since Rezanov still had one card to play.

In his visits to the Argüello family, Rezanov had gotten to know Conchita, the commander's fifteen-year-old daughter, and little by little, a relationship had developed between the two of them that went beyond mere courtesy. In the romantic versions of this story, it is said that Conchita's beauty had no equal in California and that her black eyes lit a fire of true love in the chamberlain. Other, more prosaic versions affirm that it was a carefully calculated plan by Rezanov, who dazzled the girl, accustomed to the presidio's rough way of life, with his marvelous tales of the court of St. Petersburg. When he saw the possibility of obtaining aid for his compatriots slipping away, he decided to play his last card, asking for the girl's hand in marriage. Conchita accepted, and her parents and the friars gave their approval, on condition that the "heretic" obtain papal license to marry. From then on, the Argüellos welcomed Rezanov as a member of the family, and Conchita's brother and father had no secrets from the foreigner.

In these new circumstances, where was Arrillaga left? The governor was disconcerted to see that Don José confided his household's most private affairs to Rezanov and that he had suddenly become a kind of guest of the chamberlain.

With things in this state, Rezanov made a final attempt to get rid of the *Juno*'s cargo, and this time, Arrillaga did not have sufficient courage to oppose all those who had allied against him: the inhabitants of San Francisco, the friars, and his old friend José Argüello. The discord would have disheartened them all, and he decided to give way, although he did come up with a truly complicated procedure for conducting the trade. The mission's inhabitants were to state in writing that they were really in need of the goods that the *Juno* had brought, and Arrillaga, in response, would buy the ship's entire cargo. He would not buy it from Rezanov himself, however, but from the Russian commissioner, so that the chamberlain's name would not appear in the transaction. With the money obtained, the commissioner would buy the grain and provisions the Russians needed from the friars. Finally, the friars would return the money to where it had started, in Arrillaga's hands, after having acquired what they needed from the Russians' cargo.

That was what happened, according to Rezanov's own account. We do not have Arrillaga's version; perhaps he preferred not to set down so unusual an agreement on paper. Before taking their leave of each other, the two men again spoke of the benefits that a good commercial relationship would entail for their respective countries, but with his habitual caution, Arrillaga reminded Rezanov that he could do nothing without authorization from his superiors.

Having attained his objective, Rezanov had no desire to extend his stay. The grain was immediately brought to the ship, and the *Juno* was soon loaded and ready for the return voyage. On May 19—or May 21, according to other accounts—the *Juno* passed in front of the San Joaquín fort, saying goodbye with a cannonade, and receiving the same salute in response. After a very difficult voyage, with severe storms, the ship arrived at Sitka on June 19. The men learned there that scurvy had ravaged their comrades during their absence, but matters soon improved thanks to the *Juno*'s cargo.

Nevertheless, the romance that was so influential in the course of events did not have a happy ending. After offering his help to the Sitka colony, Rezanov set out for St. Petersburg, in order to inform the court of his recent efforts and also in order to seek authorization from the king of Spain and the pope to marry Conchita. Rezanov was weakened by his labors of the preceding year, however, and travelling through the Siberian snows at the height of winter was too much for him. Stricken by a very high fever, he was taken to a cabin. Apparently recovered, he struggled onward for twelve days until, utterly exhausted, he fell off his horse. The resulting bruises and a relapse of fever kept him in bed for several days in Yakutsk, but he left there too soon as well. He made it as far as Krasnoyarsk, where on March 1, 1807, his wanderings came to an end.

The Russian dignitary died without having demonstrated the sincerity of his plans to marry Conchita, but the girl remained faithful to her lover's memory throughout her life, without deviating in the slightest from the romantic script. She rejected all her suitors, and almost forty years later, when she learned that her fiancé had died some time before, she entered a convent.

The story of the love between the Russian nobleman and the young Conchita has been told hundreds of times. It has inspired literary compositions, such as Bret Harte's poem "Concepción de Arguello," and also a rock opera. The farther we get from the original sources, however, the more the protagonists become cardboard figures. There is no doubt that the real people and events were much more interesting. The personality reflected in Rezanov's writings is not that of a sophisticated Russian diplomat and noble lover, but rather that of a haughty man who used quite vulgar language. With regard to Conchita's beauty, the naturalist Langsdorff, who knew her, speaks of her lively eyes and . . . her beautiful teeth! Apparently, he did not discern other admirable traits in her, and her manners struck him as quite rough. As far as our Arrillaga is concerned, he showed that he was not as naive as Rezanov, with his courtier's arrogance, thought, and when all the rest, including the friars, succumbed to the foreigner's charm, he knew how to uphold his position.

Arrillaga's Last Years

California's white population was growing little by little: 990 in 1790, 1,800 in 1800, 2,130 in 1810. There were forty friars at the beginning of the decade, and 20,355 Indians in 1805.[13] As far as the territory was concerned, inland California was still to a large extent *terra incognita* when Rezanov visited San Francisco in 1806. Exploration of that territory would be Arrillaga's most noteworthy enterprise during the following years. After saying goodbye to Rezanov, he returned to Monterrey and began to issue instructions from his desk. He was too old to go in person this time, as when he set out to explore the banks of the Colorado River in 1796.

On May 9, 1806, he gave the order for the first expedition's departure. It set out from San Diego and was headed by Ensign Maitorena, a Mexican of Basque origin. We do not know exactly what its route was, since the expedition diary has been lost. The second expedition left in July of the same year. Among its members was the Bizkaian Fray José María de Zalvidea, and the diary he wrote has been preserved in the Bancroft Library; we will have more to say about him later. Throughout the decade, thanks to these expeditions promoted by Arrillaga, there were more incursions in all directions, and great advances were made in knowledge of the territory.

It was a tranquil period for the missions, without the accusations and disputes of Borica's time. There were the usual tensions between the friars and the secular authorities, but no major conflicts broke out, perhaps because everyone was thinking about the secularization that was soon to come. In addition, Arrillaga had always maintained good relations with the Franciscans. Of all the governors, he was the only one who received a letter of thanks from the guardian of the Colegio de San Fernando.

Around 1810, due to his advanced age and health problems, Arrillaga asked the king for authorization to retire to his native region, perhaps because he wanted to die among his family, since he never married and had no relatives in California. Nevertheless, the court replied that his service there was absolutely necessary, and in compensation, he was named a cavalry colonel. That same year, Hidalgo's rebellion took place in Mexico, the start of the Mexican War of Independence, but the call for revolution found no echo in California, and Arrillaga died without experiencing the new age. In July 1814, on an inspection tour, he fainted. As fate would have it, Soledad was the closest mission. He was brought there, to his old friend Father Ibáñez, and he died there of an intestinal hemorrhage on July 24. He was sixty-four years old. A few days earlier, on the 15th, he had made his will:

> First, I direct that my lifeless body shall be clothed in the habit which the religious of our Father St. Francis wear, and my tomb shall be in one of the churches where I may die.[14]

Ibáñez buried him there in the Soledad church on July 26. Of all the Basque governors, Arrillaga is the only one who is buried in California.

According to eyewitnesses, Arrillaga's funeral was an impressive one. One of Bancroft's collaborators, Enrique Cerruti, asked an informant, Dorotea Valdez, whether she remembered the governor's funeral. The year was 1874, sixty years after Arrillaga's death, but she had a good memory:

> Q.: Do you remember the funeral of Gov. Arrillaga?
> Answer: I do. His Excellency lies buried in the ex-mission of Soledad, his funeral was a very imposing one, and was witnessed by hundred of good citizens of Spain, the missionaries of four missions, a great many Indians and every soldier belonging then to the Presidio of Monterey. At his funeral José el Cantor and upward of four hundred neophytes kept up a continuous singing of the Miserere. By way of digression I will observe that José el Cantor, though then a young Indian, was an excellent singer, understood music and Latin of the church as well as any priest. After Governor Arrillaga was buried, a monument was raised over his grave, and during many years afterwards on the 2d day of November hundreds of Indians and many white men and women visited his grave for the purpose of placing flowers over it. The mission of Soledad is now in ruins, only a part of the church exists, yet I can point out the place where Arrillaga was buried, for I have often prayed in front of his tomb.[15]

José Joaquín Arrillaga marker at NuestraSeñora de la Soledad mission.

Juan Bautista Alvarado also mentions Arrillaga's funeral in his *Historia de California* (History of California). He says that all the region's white inhabitants and friars were present, as well as hundreds of neophytes and catechumens,

> who accompanied José the Cantor as, wearing the habit of a lay brother, he walked before the catafalque, singing the sad and moving *Miserere mei Deus.* The esteem the neophytes had for Governor Arrillaga was so great that they set up a monument over his grave, by common agreement, and for many years, they came from far away to the mission of La Soledad to put flowers on his grave on the Day of the Dead.[16]

Arrillaga asked in his will that a hundred masses be said for his soul at San Miguel and San Antonio. His servants received amounts that varied between twenty-five and one hundred dollars. He also mentioned his siblings: an older brother, Miguel Ignacio, three married sisters, and one unmarried one, María Josefa. He had promised María Josefa that he would help her, and he named her his heir. She was the youngest sister, the one who appeared in the Aia baptismal records with the name of María Xaviera Josepha. We do not know whether the legacy made it to the Basque Country, and it was not a great deal of money in any case. After thirty-seven years of service, the governor's fortune was less than three thousand dollars.

We also have other contemporaries' opinions of Arrillaga. José María Romero recalled, "I knew Governor Arrillaga. He was a tall man, very white, blond, blue eyes . . . Governor Arrillaga was a very agreeable man and loved by all the people."[17] José Brígido Rodríguez explained that the governor "was Bizkaian" and "crusty in his manner," but kind and generous to the troops.[18] In José de Jesús Vallejo's opinion, "Mr. Arrillaga was a person of the greatest piety, extremely zealous in carrying out his obligations, and so good that the soldiers gave him the name of 'Papa Arrillaga.'"[19]

In view of the information he gathered, Bancroft concluded that from the day of his appointment until that of his death, neither his superiors nor his subordinates nor the friars found anything to reproach in the governor's conduct.[20]

Of all those who knew Arrillaga, George Vancouver was the only one who did not have a good opinion of him. The English captain never forgave him for the cold welcome he gave him when he visited California for the second time in 1793. All the other opinions indicate that Arrillaga was a beloved man. In his last years, not only the soldiers, but the whole world called him "Papa Arrillaga," since there was no baptism or wedding in the region at which the elderly governor did not act as a godfather or sponsor.

We see emerge from these accounts the portrait of an Arrillaga who resembles the prototype of the upright, religious, hard-working, and austere Basque. Nonetheless, a great deal of information is lacking. Neither the official documents that came from his pen nor the testimonials of those who knew him say anything about his private life. No one explains why his trunks were found at his death to be full of silk handkerchiefs and stockings. Only a writer of fiction could fill this gap.

Fr. Andrés Quintana's Murder at the Santa Cruz Mission

On October 12, 1812, Fr. Andrés Quintana was found dead in his room at the Santa Cruz mission. Initially, it was thought that he had died a natural death, since he had been sick. He had gone to Monterrey for treatment, but he had to return before he had recovered, since his companion, the other friar at Santa Cruz—a fellow-countryman of his, Marcelino Marquínez, "a native of Treviño, Vizcaya, Spain," in Bancroft's words[21]—had fallen ill. Nevertheless, murder was also suspected from the beginning, and the governor Pablo Vicente Solá, also Basque, wrote to Father Marquínez telling him to allow the surgeon to examine the corpse. The autopsy[22] concluded that violence had played no role in Quintana's death, and the event was record in the mission register in these words: "In the morning, he was dead in his bed of natural causes." However, this terse explanation, signed by Marquínez, was later supplemented by an asterisk, which takes the reader to the following note:

> The investigative activities were repeated, and it was discovered that the Christian Indians of this mission and of Santa Clara killed him; they called him to this mission's orchard to anoint a pretended sick man, and there they strangled him. *Virilia vulnera quae pudet dicere* [He had wounds to his male members that it is shameful to state].[23]

What happened at Santa Cruz? What led the Indians to kill the friar?

The Santa Cruz mission was not an easy posting. Founded by Fermín Lasuén in 1791, California's twelfth mission was located halfway between Monterrey and San Francisco. Lasuén ordered the construction of some huts, which became the home of the mission's first two friars, Isidro Alonso Salazar and Baldomero López, both of whom had arrived on the frigate *Aránzazu*. Everything had to be built from scratch, and as was customary, the older missions made donations, each according to its capacity: Santa Clara gave sixty-four head of cattle, twenty-two horses, seventy-seven fanegas of wheat, and twenty-six loaves of bread; San Francisco, five yoke of oxen, seventy sheep, and two celemines of barley; San Carlos, seven mules and eight horses. Vestments for religious services also arrived. Despite all the aid, however, Salazar and López soon asked to be transferred to another post, after the Indians rebelled in 1793. Salazar wrote to Lasuén in a state of desperation, "In a short time, there will be no missionaries who want to be here or come from Mexico."[24]

A church and a plaza were built, and a mill as well, but at century's end, the mission's future did not look at all promising. Salazar and López finally succeeded in leaving, and one of the friars who replaced them, Manuel Fernández, wrote in 1798 complaining that at Santa Cruz, everything went badly. Only 30 or 40 neophytes were left to work, 138 having deserted; the fields were flooded and only half cultivated; floods had damaged the church; the livestock were half dead; and the cadaver of a whale that had washed up on the beach was attracting a large number of wolves and bears to the area. In the friars' opinion, nevertheless, the chief reason for the Indians' discontent was the settlement of Branciforte, founded alongside the mission by Governor Borica. The colonists stole, did not leave the Indians in peace, and tried to convince them to leave the mission. To make matters worse, an epidemic that was spreading from mission to mission arrived in Santa Cruz in 1802.

Father Fernández left the same year he came, and his place was filled by Fr. Domingo Carranza, a native of Loza, Araba. Carranza was at the mission until 1808. Between 1806 and 1808, the Gipuzkoans Jose Antonio Uría and Francisco Xavier de la Concepción Uría made brief stays at Santa Cruz, and other friars did as well, but they all left immediately. Compared to the others, Andrés Quintana lasted a long time in his post: from his arrival in 1805 until he was murdered on October 12, 1812.

The only biographical data we have for Andrés Quintana are the few facts set down in his baptismal record. The son of Ramón de Quintana and Josefa Ruiz de Alda, he was born on November 27, 1777, in Antoñana, Araba, and was baptized three days later by Fr. Andrés Ochoa de Alda in the church of San Vicente Mártir in that locality. He entered the Franciscan order at the age of seventeen, and after finishing his studies in 1804, he embarked in Cádiz for Mexico. The passport register tells us that he was of medium height and had a strong constitution, dark hair, blue eyes, and thick eyebrows. After a very brief stay at the Colegio de San Fernando in Mexico City, he volunteered for the California missions. On August 31, he was in Monterrey, and by November, he was at Santa Cruz. In other words, this young man, twenty-eight years old, went almost directly from the convent of Vitoria to the Santa Cruz mission; he took up his post as a missionary in Alta California with the education and training he received as a child in Antoñana and as a young man in the Vitoria convent.

In 1811, with the aim of learning about the situation of the inhabitants of the Alta California missions, the Spanish authorities in Mexico sent a questionnaire to all the missions, to which the friars were supposed to respond. The resulting reports provided information about different peoples and languages that would soon disappear. According to the anthropologist A. L. Kroeber, they are one of the very few sources of information we have about the natives' way of life before their first contact with Europeans. In this scholar's opinion, it was Andrés Quintana who replied to the questionnaire at the Santa Cruz mission, and the Indians he described were the Awaswas towns of Chatu-Mu, and the Ohlone towns like Cheyenne or Yuma.

In his report, Quintana offers curious information that is of great interest for anthropologists. For example, discussing customs related to marriage, he explains that when an Indian man wanted to get married, he went to the home of the woman he wanted to marry and sat

Ohlone dance ceremony at the San José mission, ca. 1806. Robert B. Honeyman, Jr. Collection of Early Californian and Western American Pictorial Material, The Bancroft Library, University of California at Berkeley.

down next to her. Subsequently, without saying a word, he sighed, cast some pieces of shell or small spiral shells threaded on a string at the feet of the woman's father, and left, considering himself now married.

Leaving these curiosities aside, however, Quintana's authoritarian perspective is the most striking aspect of his replies. He had been at Santa Cruz six years by that time, but his mental framework did not permit him to see anything positive in the way of life or customs of those peoples. His mentality was that of an eighteenth-century friar educated in a provincial convent, and he judged everything from this perspective. He found the Indians' dances dreary, and the songs with which they accompanied them disagreeable. In war, their behavior was ruthless.[25]

This was how Andrés Quintana saw the Indians of Santa Cruz, not very differently from the way other friars and all the whites in general saw them. In addition to his disdain, however, Quintana apparently possessed another trait that made him hated among the natives. According to some accounts, he was especially cruel when it came to imposing physical punishments.

Ohlone Indians. By Louis Choris, 1816.

In 1877, Thomas Savage, one of Bancroft's collaborators, had the opportunity to speak with Lorenzo Asisara, who gave him first-hand information about Quintana's murder. Asisara was the son of an eyewitness to the friar's death, and he knew in great detail how and why the Indians of Santa Cruz and Santa Clara took vengeance on Andrés Quintana, because his father had told him.

Asisara's narrative tells the story of one of the most dramatic events in those first years in Alta California. Until then, murders of the missionaries had taken place in the broader context of a general rebellion against the mission as an institution. Andrés Quintana's murder, however, was something else: the result of a perfectly organized plan to get rid of that man and no one else.

Andrés Quintana's Murder, Narrated by Lorenzo Asisara

> The following story which I shall convey was told to me by my dear father in 1818. He was a neophyte of the Mission of Santa Cruz. He was one of the original founders of that mission. He was an Indian from the *ranchería* of Asar on the Jarro coast, up beyond Santa Cruz. He was one of the first neophytes baptized at the founding, being about twenty years of age. He was called Venancio Asar and was the gardener of the Mission of Santa Cruz.
>
> My father was a witness to the happenings that follow. He was one of the conspirators who planned to kill Father Quintana. When the conspirators were planning to kill Father Quintana, *they* gathered in the house of Julián the gardener (the one who made the pretense of being ill).
>
> The man who worked inside the plaza of the mission, named Donato, was punished by Father Quintana with a whip with wire. With each blow it cut his buttocks. Then the same man, Donato, wanted vengeance. He was the one who organized a gathering of fourteen men, among them the cook and the pages serving the Father. The cook was named Antonio, the eldest page was named Lino, the others were named Vicente and Miguel Antonio.
>
> All of them gathered in the house of Julián to plan how they could avoid the cruel punishments of Father Quintana. One man present, Lino, who was more capable and wiser than the others, said, "The first thing we should do today is to see that the Father no longer punishes the people in that manner. We aren't animals. He [Quintana] says in his sermons that God does not command these [punishments], but only examples and doctrine. Tell me now, what shall we do with the Father? We cannot chase him away, nor accuse him before the Judge, because we do not know who commands him to do with us as he does." To this, Andrés, father of Lino the page, answered

"Let's kill the Father without anyone being aware—not the servants or anyone, except us that are here present." (This Lino was a pure-blooded Indian, but as white as a Spaniard and a man of natural abilities.) And Julián the gardener said, "What shall we do in order to kill him?" His wife responded, "You, who are always getting sick—only this way can it be possible—think if it is good this way." Lino approved the plan and asked that all present also approve it. "In that case, we shall do it tomorrow night." That was Saturday. It should be noted that the Father wished all the people to gather in the plaza on the following Sunday in order to test the whip that he had made with pieces of wire, to see if it was to his liking.

All of the conspirators present at the meeting concurred that it should be done as Lino had recommended.

On the evening of Saturday at about six o'clock [October 12] of 1812, they went to tell the Father that the gardener was dying. The Indians were already posted between two trees on both sides so that they could grab the Father when he passed.

The Father arrived at the house of Julián, who pretended to be in agony. The Father helped him, thinking that he was really sick and about to die. When the Father was returning to his house, he passed close to where the Indians were posted. They didn't have the courage to grab him, and they allowed him to pass. The moribund gardener was behind him, but the Father arrived at his house.

Within an hour, the wife of Julián arrived [again] to tell the Father that her husband was dying. With this news the Father returned to the orchard, the woman following behind, crying and lamenting. He saw that the sick man was dying. The Father took the man's hand in order to take his pulse. He felt the pulse and could find nothing amiss. The pulse showed there was nothing wrong with Julián. Not knowing what it could be, the Father returned to pray for him. It was night when the Father left. Julián arose and washed away the sacraments (oil) that the Father had administered, and he followed behind to join the others and see what his companions had done. Upon arriving at the place where they were stationed, Lino lifted his head and looked in all directions to see if they were coming out to grab the Father. The Father passed and they didn't take him. The Father arrived at his house.

Later, when the Father was at his table, dining, the conspirators had already gathered at the house of the allegedly sick man to ascertain why they hadn't seized Father Quintana.

Julián complained that the Father had placed herbs on his ears, and because of them, now he was really going to die. Then the wife of Julián said, "Yes, you all did not carry through with your promised plans; I am going to accuse you all, and I will not go back to the house." They all answered her, "All right, now, go and speak to the Father." The woman again left to fetch Father Quintana, who was at supper. He got up immediately and went, where he found the supposedly sick man. This time he took with him three pages, two who walked ahead lighting his way with lanterns and behind him followed his majordomo Lino. The other two were Vicente and Miguel Antonio. The Father arrived at the gardener's house and found him unconscious. He couldn't speak. The Father prayed the last orations without administering the oils and said to the wife, "Now your husband is prepared to live or die. Don't come to look for me again." Then the Father left with his pages, to return to his house. Julián followed him. Arriving at the place where the two trees were (since the Father was not paying attention to his surroundings, but only the path in front of him), Lino grabbed him from behind, saying these words: "Stop here, Father, you must speak for a moment." When the other two pages who carried the lanterns turned around and saw the other men come out to attack the Father, they fled with their lanterns. The Father said to Lino, "Oh, my son, what are you going to do to me?" Lino answered, "Your assassins will tell you." "What have I done to you children for which you would kill me?" "Because you have made a horsewhip tipped with iron," Andrés answered him.

Then the Father replied, "Oh, children, leave me, so that I can go from here now, at this moment." Andrés asked him why he had made this horsewhip. Quintana said that it was only for transgressors. Then someone shouted, "Well, you are in the hands of those evil ones, make your peace with God." Many of those present (seeing the Father in his affliction) cried and pitied his fate, but could do nothing to help him, because they were themselves compromised. He pleaded much, promising to leave the mission immediately if they would only let him. "Now you won't be going to any part of the earth from here, Father, you are going to heaven." This was the last plea of the Father. Some of them, not having been able to lay hands on the Father, reprimanded the others because they talked too much, demanding that they kill him immediately. They then covered the Father's mouth with his own cape to strangle him. They had his arms tightly secured. After the Father had been strangled, [they did not beat him but] took a testicle so that it would not be obvious that he had been attacked, and in a moment Father expired. Then Lino and the others took him to his house and put him in his bed.

When the two little pages, Vicente and Miguel Antonio, arrived at the house, the former wanted to tell the guard, but the others dissuaded him by saying, "No, the soldiers will also kill your mother, father, all of the others, and you, yourself, and me. Let them, the conspirators, do what they want." The two hid themselves. After the Indians had put the Father in his bed, Lino looked for the two pages, and he found them hidden. They undressed the body of Father Quintana and placed him in the bed as if he were going to sleep. All of the conspirators, including Julián's wife, were present.

Andrés asked Lino for the keys to the storeroom. He handed them over, saying, "What do you want?" And they said silver and beads. Among the group there were three Indians from the Santa Clara Mission. These proposed that they investigate to see how much money there was. Lino opened the box and showed them the accumulated gold and silver. The three Indians from Santa Clara took as much as they could carry to their mission. (I don't know what they have done with that money.) The others took their portions as they saw fit.

Then they asked for the keys to the convent, or *monjerío* [women's dormitory]. Lino gave the keys to the *jayunte*, or barracks of the single men, to one of them in order to free the men and gather them together, below in the orchard, with the unmarried women. They gathered in the orchard so that neither the people in the plaza, nor in the *ranchería*, nor in the guardhouse would hear them. The single men left and without a sound gathered in the orchard at the same place where the Father was assassinated. There was a man there cautioning them not to make any noise, that they were going to have a good time. After a short time the young unmarried women arrived in order to spend the night there. The young people of both sexes got together and had their pleasure.

At midnight Lino, being in the Father's living room with one of the girls from the single women's dormitory, entered the Father's room in order to see if he was really dead. He found him reviving. He was already on the point of arising. Lino went to look for his accomplices to tell them that the Father was coming to. The Indians returned, and they crushed the Father's other testicle. This last act put an end to the life

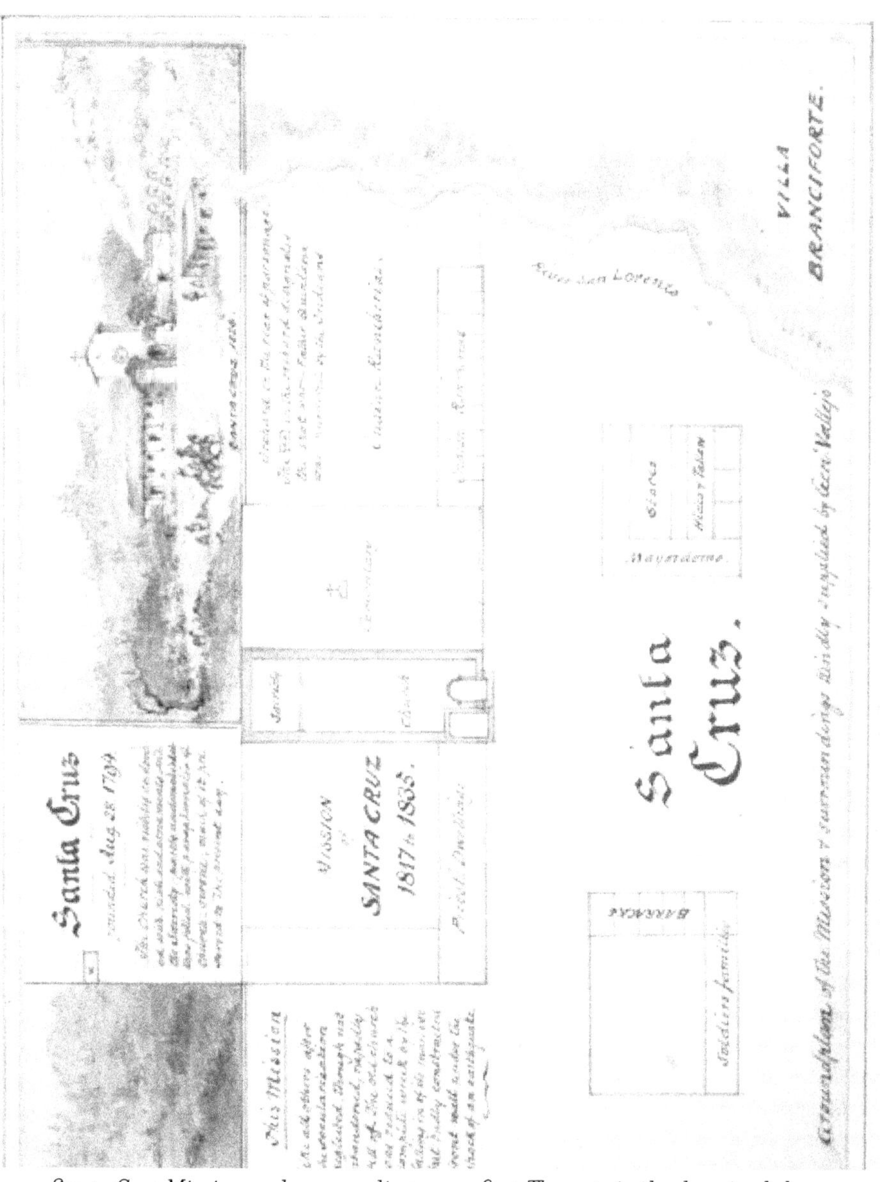

Santa Cruz Mission and surroundings, ca. 1825. The note in the drawing below mentions the murder of Father Quintana. The plan was made by General Vallejo around 1878. UC Berkeley, Bancroft Library. Calisphere http://content.cdlib.org/

of Father Quintana. Donato, the one who had been whipped, walked around the room with the plural results of his operation in hand, saying, "I shall bury these in the outdoor privy."

Donato told Lino that they should close the treasure chest: "Close the trunk with the colored silver (that is the name that the Indians gave to gold), and let's see where we shall bury it." The eight men carried it down to the orchard and buried it secretly, without the others knowing.

At about two o'clock in the morning, the young girls returned to their convent and the single men to their *jayunte*, without making any noise. The assassins gathered once more after everything had occurred, in order to hear the plans of Lino and Donato. Some wanted to flee, and others asked, "What for? No one except us knows." Lino asked them what they wanted to take to their houses—sugar, *panocha*, honey, or any other things—and suggested that they lie down to sleep for a while. Finally everything was ready. Donato proposed to return to where the Father was, to check on him. They found him not only lifeless, but completely cold and stiff. Lino then showed them the new whip that the Father was planning to use for the first time the next day, assuring them that he (Father Quintana) would not use it now. He sent them to their houses to rest, remaining in the house with the keys. He asked them to be very careful. He arranged the room and the Bible in the manner in which the Father was accustomed to doing before retiring, telling them that he was not going to toll the bells in the morning until the majordomo and corporal of the guard came and he had talked to them. All went through the orchard very silently.

This same morning (Sunday), the bells should have been rung at about eight o'clock. At that hour the people from the *Villa de* Branciforte began to arrive in order to attend the Mass. The majordomo, Carlos Castro, saw that the bells were not being rung and went to Lino, who was the first assistant of the Father, to ask why the Father had not ordered him (to toll the bells). Lino was in the outer room feigning innocence and answered the majordomo that he couldn't tell him anything about the Father because he was still inside, sleeping or praying, and that the majordomo should wait until he should speak to him first. The majordomo returned home. Soon the corporal of the guard arrived, and Lino told him the same thing he had told the majordomo. The majordomo returned to join in the conversation. They decided to wait a little while longer. Finally, Lino told them that in their presence he would knock on the door of the room, observing, "If he is angry with me, you will stand up for me." And so he did, calling to the Father. As he didn't hear noise inside, the majordomo and corporal asked Lino to knock again, but he refused. They then left, charging him with calling the Father again, because the hour was growing late. All of the servants were busy at their jobs, as always, in order not to cause any suspicion. The majordomo returned after ten o'clock and asked Lino to call the Father to see what was wrong. Lino, with the keys in his pocket, knocked at the door. Finally the majordomo insisted that Lino enter the room, but Lino refused. At this moment, the corporal, old Nazario Galindo, arrived. Lino (although he had the key to the door in his pocket) said, "Well, I am going to see if I can get the door open," and he pretended to look for a key to open the door. He returned with a ring of keys, but he didn't find one that opened the lock. The majordomo and the corporal left to talk to some men who were there. Later, Lino took the key that opened the door, saying that it was for the kitchen. He opened another door that opened into the plaza (the key opened three doors), and through there he entered. Then he opened the main door from inside, in front of which the others waited. Lino came out screaming and crying and carrying on in an uncontrolled manner, saying that the Father was dead. They asked him if he was certain, and he responded, "As this light that illuminates us. By God, I'm going to toll the bells." The three entered, the corporal, the majordomo, and Lino. He didn't allow anyone else to enter. The corporal and the majordomo and the other people wrote to the other missions and to Monterey to Father Marcelino Marquínez. (This Marquínez was an expert horseman and a good friend.) The poor elderly neophytes, and many other Indians who never suspected that the Father was killed, thought he had died suddenly. They cried bitterly. Lino was roaring inside the Father's house like a bear.

The Fathers from Santa Clara and from other missions came, and they held the Father's funeral, all believing that he had died a natural death, but not before examining the corpse in the entrance room and opening the stomach in order to be certain that the Father had not been poisoned. Officials, sergeants, and many others participated in these acts, but nothing was discovered. Finally, by chance, one of those present noted that the testicles were missing, and they were convinced that this had been the cause of death.[26] Through modesty they did not reveal the fact, and buried the body with everyone convinced that the death had been a natural one.

A number of years after the death, Emiliana, the wife of Lino, and María Tata, the wife of the cook Antonio, became mutually jealous. They were both seamstresses and they were at work. This was around August, at the time of the lentil harvest. Carlos Castro was with his men, working in the cornfields. Shortly before eleven o'clock he returned to his house for the meal. He understood the language of the Indians. Returning from the cornfields, he passed behind one of the plaza walls near where these women were sewing and heard one tell the other that she was secretly eating *panocha*. Castro stopped and heard the second woman reply to the first, "How is it that you have so much money?" The first replied, "You also have it because your husband killed the Father." Then the second accused the husband of the first woman of the same crime. The war of words continued, and Castro was convinced that Father Quintana had been assassinated, and he went to tell Father Ramón Olbes, who was the missionary at Santa Cruz, what he had heard. . . . Then the Father sent for the corporal, Nazario Galindo, to arrest the assassins. They began with the orchard workers and the cook, without telling them why they were under arrest. Antonio was the first prisoner. They put him in jail and asked him who his accomplice was. He said who his accomplice was, and the man was arrested, and they asked each one the name of their respective accomplices. In this way they were all arrested, except Lino, who was looked upon as a valiant man of great strength. He was taken through the deceit of his own *compadre* Carlos Castro, who handed him a knife to trim some black and white mares, in order to make a hackamore for the animal of the Father. Suspiciously, Lino said to Castro, "*Compadre*, why are you deceiving me? I know that you are going to arrest me." There were already two soldiers hidden behind the corral. "Here, take your knife, *compadre*, that which I thought is already done. I am going to pay for it—and if I had wanted to, I could have finished off the soldiers, the majordomos, and any others that might have been around on the same night that I killed the Father."

The result of all this was that the accused were sent to San Francisco, and among them was my father. There they were judged, and those who killed the Father were sentenced to receive a *novenario* (nine days in succession) of fifty lashes for each one, and to serve in public works at San Diego. The rest including my father, were freed because they had served as witnesses, and it was not proven that they had taken part in the assassination.

> All returned, after many years, to their mission.
>
> The Spanish Fathers were very cruel toward the Indians. They abused them very much. They had bad food, bad clothing, and they made them work like slaves. I also was subject to that cruel life. The Fathers did not practice what they preached in the pulpit. The same Father Olbes was once stoned by the Indians for all his cruelties.[27]

How much credibility should we grant to Asisara's narrative? The Franciscan historian Engelhardt's opinion is that abuse of the Indians was merely an excuse, but is Engelhardt's judgment trustworthy? Doesn't he always take the Franciscans' side whenever there is an accusation against them?

In this case, Engelhardt based himself on the opinions of the governor and the father president of the missions in taking Father Quintana's side. According to this historian, Solá, after reading the trial documents, set in motion what he himself called, in a letter sent to the viceroy on June 2, 1816, "the most secret and closest investigations."[28] After examining information from all nineteen missions, the governor came to the conclusion that the friars treated the neophytes "perhaps more lovingly than natural parents treat their children." With regard to Father Quintana himself, Solá maintained that "he was excessive not in punishing his Indians, but rather in the love with which he always looked on them."[29]

In a letter addressed to Vicente de Sarría, the president of the missions, Solá considered Quintana innocent. Sarría agreed with the governor and replied that his description of Father Quintana struck him as very accurate.[30]

Andrés Quintana's name has remained linked *per saecula saeculorum* to the abuse of the Indians. Rightly so? In law, the value of testimony depends on the witness's credibility. In this case, knowing that Lorenzo Asisara was the son of one of the conspirators who plotted Father Quintana's murder, and that theft also played a role, prudence counsels retaining some degree of doubt about his testimony's truthfulness.

Pablo Vicente Solá, Alta California's Last Colonial Governor

The inhabitants of Monterrey organized the most splendid possible welcome for the governor who was arriving to take possession of his post, not because they thought that his personality or his career made him deserving of such honors—Pablo Vicente Solá had just been appointed to the position and was entirely unknown in Monterrey—but because they rejected the Mexican independence movement and were eager to show their attachment to the king of Spain. For this reason, when the ship carrying the province's highest-ranking official appeared in Monterrey Bay on August 30, 1815, the majority of the region's missionaries were there, with the father president, Esteban Tapis, at their head, along with the province's military authorities and many other whites and Indians who did not want to miss the great celebration.

The Monterrey presidio, a quadrangle of adobe buildings, had been decorated the day before with tree branches from which hung tallow lamps with cotton wicks. At nightfall, gathered in that plaza formed by the buildings, Monterrey's inhabitants could take an elegant stroll and exchange a few words with the governor by the light of the strategically placed lamps.

The next morning, the troops waited in formation in the atrium of the church, and when the governor made his entrance, all those present sang the *Te Deum*, accompanied by the Indian musicians the friars had brought from other missions, at the same time that cannon and musket salvos underlined the solemnity of the moment. At the end of the ceremony, in the presidio plaza, Solá made a speech in which he spoke with admiration of California and its inhabitants. It was then time to enjoy the banquet that the ladies of Monterrey had prepared for the governor, the officers, and the missionaries. When Solá entered the room, he was approached by a group of girls, all dressed in white, who came to kiss his hand. At table, the most exquisite dishes from the surrounding area awaited the guests: olives from San Diego, grapes and wine from San Gabriel, sweets made with flour from San Antonio, and many other delicacies.

Once the banquet was over, the governor was invited to attend a bullfight. Solá had attended other bullfights, and he was not surprised when the bull entered the presidio plaza. What came next, however, was unlike anything he had ever seen before. Four cowboys mounted on horseback brought in a grizzly bear, dragging it by ropes tied around its paws. Enraged to the point of frightening even those accustomed to a spectacle of this kind, the wild animal tried to get loose. The governor looked questioningly at the commander, who explained that bears were abundant in the surrounding mountains and often came down to fill their bellies with the valley livestock.

Next, the bear and the bull were chained together at the legs with a strong chain that left them both sufficient space to move, and the ropes were removed. The animals were left facing one another. The

Monterrey Presidio. Drawn by José Cardero, 1791-1792. (Robert B. Honeyman, Jr. Collection of Early Californian and Western American Pictorial Material, The Bancroft Library, University of California at Berkeley).

bull lowered its head and looked about threateningly; the bear, rearing up on its hind legs, appeared to await the start of the fight. For ten long minutes, however, neither animal took a step forward. The spectators began to grow impatient. The cowboys approached and pricked the bull with goads, and the animal, with a bellow of pain, charged its opponent. Then the bear, more agile than would ever be expected from so heavy a body, slashed at the bull's neck, avoiding its horns, and both animals went down. The noise was tremendous, the two exasperated animals rolled about amid a cloud of dust, and the spectators shouted at the top of their lungs, seeing the trails of blood and understanding that the fight would continue until one of the animals died. At a certain point, the bull, exhausted and thirsty, stuck out its tongue, and the bear, changing position, tried to rip it out. It paid for the attempt with its life. The bull was alert, and in a sudden attack, it buried a horn in its enemy's flesh and lifted it up in the air. When the bear fell, severely wounded, the bull, infuriated by its own wounds, pressed its advantage with a new charge that concluded the combat.

At night, a dance was organized, the most elegant ever held in those territories, but the governor retired early. The next morning, he had to go to the mission of San Carlos, where the inhabitants also wanted to offer him a ceremony of welcome.

The following day, missionaries, incense-bearers, and a very large number of Indians came out to meet Solá and his entourage, and all went together in procession to the San Carlos church, where another high mass was celebrated. After that, the whites sat under the arcade, and the Indians, organized in groups, offered a demonstration of their games. Some of them, adorned with feathers and warpaint, simulated various battles, after which the leaders of each group came up to lay their weapons at the governor's feet. When the performance had ended and Solá mounted his horse to return to Monterrey, he declared that he felt very honored by everything he had seen and that he had enjoyed it all, but that there were two things that had especially impressed him: the grizzly bears of Monterrey and the simulated combats of the San Carlos Indians, since he had never seen anything similar.[31]

The new governor was now established in Monterrey, and the friars were obligated to make a courtesy visit to King Ferdinand VII's representative. The missionaries were curious to learn what that man who had arrived from the Basque provinces was like. They had read favorable opinions in a letter sent from the Colegio de San Fernando, but they had also heard that he was an arrogant man who had alienated all his men. The moment had arrived to get to know him in person. After discussing the matter in private, the friars decided that Fr. Vicente Sarría was the best person to pay him a visit, since in addition to being the prefect, he came from the Basque provinces like the governor. Hence, accompanied by two other friars, Sarría set out to visit him. Sarría had a reputation as an educated and sagacious man, and he soon gave new proof of it. When they arrived at the governor's residence, he told his companions that, since the governor was alone in his office, it would be best if he also went in unaccompanied. That way, the two men could speak alone.

> So it was that he entered the salon alone, where he was welcomed with the urbanity his status deserved, and after reciprocal compliments, they had a long and serious conversation, which was followed by another, in a mixture of Spanish and Basque, with the result that both the official and the prelate forgot the gravity with which they began, and when they said goodbye, they took their leave of one another with such good understanding as if they had already been old friends.[32]

At all events, despite the cordiality of their first meeting, their future relationship would not be as good as the one between Lasuén and Borica, undoubtedly because they did not agree politically: Solá was liberal, and Sarría was conservative.

Pablo Vicente Solá, one of twelve children of Nicolás Solá Ursola and Theresa Arrizavalaga, was born in Arrasate, Gipuzkoa in 1761.[33] He was not the only sibling who went to California. Another brother became a Franciscan friar and had lived in California since 1786; he had been suffering from mental illness for thirty years when he died at the Colegio de San Fernando in 1820. Solá came from a family of means and had received a good education. Those who knew him in California described him as a man of medium height, strong, and using a formula of the time, "of a florid complexion." With regard to his character, his contemporaries' opinions differed notably. According to Osio, he was a proud man who lacked Arrillaga's prudence. Alvarado affirmed that he was an agreeable, peaceful, and compassionate person and that his education and manners were better than those of all previous governors. Vallejo praised him, but Romero judged him to be an "ill-humored and despotic man." Boronda said that he was a very strict man, but impartial and just, and a great lover of children.[34] Among the Franciscans, he maintained very good relations in particular with Francisco Xavier de la Concepción Uría, that is, the friar praised by everyone who knew him for his good humor. We have already mentioned that in the friendly letters they exchanged, it seems that Uría was in the habit of interspersing phrases in Euskara. The historians who have studied Solá emphasize his courtesy, but they also mention another, not very heroic quality: in the seven years he held the post of governor of California, he stood out as a man much given to complaining.

Hipólito Bouchard, the Enemy No One Expected

Once the welcome celebrations were over, the first task Solá tackled was an inspection of the territory. For two years, he dedicated himself to travelling the province, stopping at all the presidios and missions. At the time, around 2,400 whites lived in Alta California, and there were around 2,000 Indians at the missions. At the nineteen missions, hard work went on. Beautiful churches had been built at some of them and were under construction at others. The number of cattle and sheep had increased enormously, and the horses had multiplied to such an extent that the decision was made to kill them in order to leave the pastures for more necessary animals. The Indians, for their part, were at peace, except for the occasional flight by some neophytes and the occasional cattle theft.

The presidios, in contrast, struck Solá as neglected, entirely unprepared to confront an invasion or defend themselves against a single warship. There were only forty-two cannons in all of Alta California, and half of them were unusable. North of San Francisco, the Spaniards lacked stable settlements, and Solá came to the conclusion that the greatest threat was located there, on account of the Russians, who were expanding and reinforcing their settlements at Bodega and Fort Ross. He could not imagine that the real risk would ultimately arrive at the hands of the Buenos Aires rebels, led by Hipólito Bouchard.

On November 20, 1818, the lookout at Punta de Pinos in Monterrey saw two frigates and immediately sounded the alarm. Solá gathered all his men—forty in total: twenty-five members of the presidio company, four gunners, and eleven members of the militia—and sent them to the battery. At eleven o'clock at night, one of the frigates dropped anchor. The men at the battery tried to identify it, shouting questions through a speaking trumpet, but as Solá would explain to Viceroy Don Juan Ruiz de Apodaca[35] later, the men on the ship replied in English, and no one could understand them.[36] In effect, the frigate's captain, Peter Corney, was an Englishman, and in the early nineteenth century no one spoke English in what was then California's capital.

In the following days, some artillery fire was exchanged, but the forces on each side were very unequal. The two frigates had sixty-six cannons between them, and in Monterrey there were no more than eight cannons of small caliber. There were also attempts at negotiation. Bouchard sent a note to Solá proposing the latter's surrender. Solá, according to his own account in his letter to the viceroy, received the note with the disdain it deserved, proudly declaring that his men were ready to die for the king. Nevertheless, when Bouchard's forces—four hundred men and four cannons—disembarked on the 24th, Solá stopped flaunting his pride and gave the order to retreat, after making a weak defense. He ordered the soldiers' families and the area's only colonists to take refuge at the Soledad mission, while he and his troops headed for Rancho Real, about thirteen miles from the presidio, with the ammunition they had managed to save and with the contents of the provincial archive.

Bouchard remained in Monterrey for another five days, repairing his ships, and during this time he stole everything he could, killed livestock, and set fire to the presidio, the governor's residence, and all the other residences and gardens. In his letter to the viceroy, Solá complained that he had lost his furniture and other things that were very necessary to him. For Bouchard's part, once he had carried out his plans in Monterrey, he sailed south, continuing to attack Spanish interests along his entire journey to Valparaíso, Chile.

Subsequent historians—certainly Chapman, and Bancroft as well to some extent—have accused Solá of not defending Monterrey and of justifying himself with excuses. At the time, however, Viceroy Ruiz de Apodaca approved the governor's conduct and promoted him to the rank of colonel of the provincial militia in recognition of his services. As far as Bouchard and his men are concerned, some see them as insurgents who wanted to bring to Alta California the revolution against Spain that was spreading in South America; others consider them riff-raff of the same caliber as the pirates and *pichilingues* of the past. In any case, they were the protagonists of the only foreign attack Alta California suffered during the period of Spanish control.

These unexpected events made Alta California's military weakness plain. In response to Solá's anguished plea, the viceroy sent two ships carrying weapons and around two hundred men. Solá soon realized, however, that many of those men served only to create problems. They were *cholos* ("half-breeds"), criminals, and beggars, many of them recruited in the jails, men with no military discipline and with no knowledge of how to handle military weapons. Solá wrote to the viceroy that it was better to send no one if they were going to send rabble like this. Another complaint from the bad-tempered governor, it seemed, but Solá had a point. Neither the civil authorities, nor the friars, nor the population in general were happy about these people's arrival.

Solá, Interested in the Education of California's Inhabitants

We have already mentioned that Borica was very interested in the education of the inhabitants of California's towns and presidios. He founded schools and tried to convince parents of the advantages of educating their children. Schools had also been founded in Arrillaga's time, but not much progress had been made.[37] Solá, in contrast, took up the matter again, and thanks to his efforts, schools were set up in Monterrey and in other towns and presidios as well. In his reports for 1817 and 1818, the governor informed the viceroy that there were schools in each of the four presidios and in two towns, where colonists or soldiers "of good character" taught the children religion, reading, writing, and arithmetic. Solá founded and maintained two schools for boys and one school for girls, to a large extent with his own money. In addition, he had two men, Aspiroz and Santa María, come to found a secondary school, but they did not adjust to the territory and returned to Mexico the same year they arrived.[38] Solá also tried to convince the viceroy of the importance of founding schools for neophyte boys who could become the educators of young people of their own race in the future, as well as the need to educate neophyte girls in order to free them from the influence of their parents and relatives, but his plans did not receive support in Mexico.

In Monterrey, the schoolteacher was Miguel Archuleta, who has a Basque surname, who had learned to read and write from Father Ibáñez (whom we have previously mentioned: José Joaquín Arrillaga's friend who offered him some verses of welcome when he visited the Soledad mission as the newly appointed governor). Archuleta's students included, among others, Mariano Guadalupe Vallejo and Juan Bautista Alvarado, destined to play an important role in California history.[39] In their memoirs, both described a school that was extremely poor in every way: in methods, resources, and subjects of study.

Solá was in the habit of visiting the school, but given his progressive opinions on educational matters, he did not much like what he found:

> He suggested to Archuleta that there were other useful branches of learning besides the doctrina; that besides Ripalda and the caton and the novena de nuestra señora and the lives of saints, martyrs, or virgins, there were other books worth reading.[40]

Solá distributed copies of the *Gazeta de México*, the Spanish Constitution of 1812, and *Don Quijote* among the students, and he permitted the older students to use his library. On other occasions, he invited the students to his office and spoke to them about the importance of education.

In Monterrey, the custom apparently existed of allowing the schoolchildren to run down to the shore when a ship arrived. On one of those occasions, the door flap was left open, even though the teacher had warned them to be careful, and when they returned to class, they found the classroom full of chickens, the inkwells toppled over, and all the work they had been doing ruined. They had earned quite a punishment. The older boys were supposed to hold the guilty parties down by their legs, one by one, but that day the students refused to obey and threw the teacher out of the school. Such a rebellion had never taken place in Monterrey. In the end, thanks to Solá's mediation, the teacher pardoned the students after making them promise to behave, and order was reestablished.

The Spanish Governor Becomes the Mexican Governor

From 1810 onward, the Spanish authorities' attention and the majority of their funds were directed toward halting the Mexican independence movement, but the effort was in vain. In 1821, Col. Agustín de Iturbide, instead of crushing the Acapulco rebels as he was expected to do, suddenly took up the revolutionary banner and declared New Spain's independence. Solá had never had a good opinion of the revolutionaries and had always been loyal to the king. At this point, however, his friends in Mexico informed him that the Spanish cause was lost and that it was better to act prudently. Accepting their advice, he set aside his old loyalties and accepted the new authorities: he was a soldier, always ready to obey his superiors' orders. He swore allegiance to the Mexican government, and the officers under his command did the same. The news spread throughout the province, and Mexican flags were soon flying throughout the territory. California ceased to be Spanish and became a province of Mexico, but Solá remained in his post for several months longer. Later on, he represented California in the new Mexican Congress. After that, he disappears from the documentary record.

Vicente de Sarría: An Educated and Sagacious Bizkaian, Father President of the California Missions

In 2009, a foundation dedicated to the study of Basque language and culture, Labayru Fundazioa, published a collection of the sermons of a Bizkaian Franciscan who served as a missionary in California. Titled *Bizente Sarria (1767–1835): Sermoitegia*,[41] the volume is based on the friar's manuscripts found in the University of California at Berkeley's Bancroft Library. The texts constitute a magnificent sample of the old Bizkaian dialect and offer, in their editor's words, "a beautiful example of different lost expressions." A press release reported that the author had risen to become the highest-ranking Franciscan authority and a man of great prestige in California. Who was this Bizente Sarria or Vicente de Sarría, who attained such fame far from his native land?

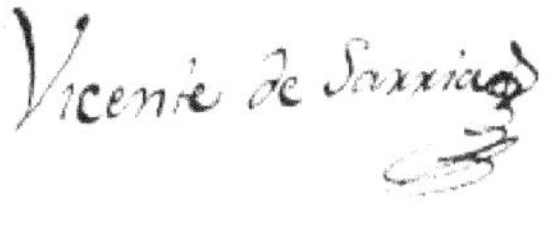

Vicente Francisco de Sarría y Lezama—we will write his name as it was written in his own time—was born in November 1767 in Etxebarri, Bizkaia. His mother, María Antonia, was likewise a native of Etxebarri, and his father, Tomás, came from Larrabetzu. He entered the convent of San Francisco in Bilbao as a novice in 1783, and he professed the following year. From 1794 to 1797, he served as a teacher in this same convent, teaching philosophy to lay students and theology to the friars. He spent the following three years teaching philosophy in Arantzazu, and it is from this period that the sermons preserved in the Bancroft Library in Berkeley date. We will never know what motivated Sarría to include his notebook of sermons in Euskara in the scant baggage he took to the Americas.

In Mexico, Sarría's first place of residence, as was customary, was the Colegio de San Fernando, where he remained until he was sent to California in 1809. He arrived in Monterrey on board the *Princesa* on June 22, 1809, and on September 10, he made his first entry in the register at his first posting, San Carlos in Carmel.

In 1811, the questionnaire or "interrogatory" that the Mexican authorities had prepared in order to learn about the Indians' situation arrived at San Carlos, as at the rest of the missions. At that time, the Catalan Juan Amorós and Vicente de Sarría were the friars in charge of the mission. In the anthropologist A. L. Kroeber's opinion, the report signed by the two friars stands out above the others for the quantity of details provided and the quality of the writing. In addition, it offers one of the most complete accounts we have of the Esselen people, including the only complete sentence we have in the Esselen language, "Egenoch lalucuimxs talogpami ege salegua lottos tahezapami laxlachis," meaning "The men who shoot well with a bow are esteemed and well liked."

Much is said today about the clash of cultures, but any such clash today would seem minor compared to what Sarría and his fellow missionaries experienced in late-eighteenth- and early-nineteenth-century California. The natives' way of life, their habits, their beliefs, their style of dress . . . everything was utterly strange to them, as is clear in these replies signed by the two San Carlos friars:

> At this mission there are seven nations of Indians. They are called Excelen and Egeac, Rumsen, SargentaRuc, Sanconenos, Guachirron and Calendo Rue . . . The languages which there are among these seven nations are two, one called Rumsen, and the other Excelen, entirely different. For instance in Rumsen they say, muxina muguiant jurriquimo igest oyh laguan eje uti maigin. In Excelen, egenoch lalucuimxs talogpami ege salegua lottos tahezapami laxlachis. Both of these examples mean: "The men who shoot well with a bow are esteemed and well liked."
>
> The kind of idolatry which has been found among these natives is that they sometimes smoke, blowing the smoke to the sun, the moon, and to certain people who they believe live in the sky; and with this they say: "Here goes this smoke in order that you will give me good weather tomorrow." Thus also of the seeds which they gather and of which they make pinole or flour. Of these they throw a handful to the sun, the moon, or the sky,

> saying: "I send you this so that another year you will give me greater abundance." Thus they recognize in the sun and the moon influences bearing upon their necessities, and recognize also that in the sky there is another people which sends them what they wish, and for this reason they offer them flour, seeds, and tobacco smoke.
>
> They have often been asked if they have heard tell anything of the place of their origin. To this all answer that they do not know. And this ignorance is not strange, for these natives hold it for the greatest affront that one should speak of their dead parents and relatives; to such a degree, that a boy whose parents should die while he is quite small, would have no one who would tell him how his deceased father, grandfather, and other kindred were called. If they quarrel among one another, they say in order to be more vituperative: "Your father is dead (a ti se te murio tu padre)" and then they become more angry. On account of these practices they have no way of retaining a recollection of their ancestors, the more so since when anyone dies, they burn all his clothing and property, and if he has animals, like chickens, dogs, or a horse, they kill them, and pull up his plants. If they are asked the reason, they say that it is in order that they may no longer remember the dead.[42]The final report that compiled the information from all the missions was completed in 1815. The replies were organized by topic: race, origin, language, love between spouses and between parents and children, attitudes toward foreigners, disposition to read and write, prominent virtues, superstitions, idolatry, medicine, calendar, food, drink, adoration of the sun and moon, burials, character, commerce and money, government, music, clothing . . . As Bancroft argues, it is a document of great significance, since it gathers the testimony of talented men who had the first direct and continuous contact with peoples who, at the time Bancroft was writing, were on the point of disappearing.[43]

Some of those talented men charged with producing this important testimony have already been mentioned: José de Miguel and José María de Zalvidea at San Gabriel, Andrés Quintana at Santa Cruz, Martín de Landaeta and José Antonio Urresti at San Fernando, José Antonio Calzada and Francisco Xavier Uría at Santa Inés . . . Regrettably, the Indians did not set down in writing the customs and superstitions of those friars in their long grey habits. It would have been interesting to know what vision they had of the friars.

Vicente de Sarría Takes on the Administration of the California Missions

Only three years after his arrival in California, Sarría was named prefect commissioner of the missions for six years.[44] In his new post, he wrote a pastoral letter that discussed matters related to the Indians and the missions. He mentioned the need to learn the native languages—"the only means to achieve the purposes of our mission is the study of the Indians' language"[45]—and recommended that the friars prepare catechisms in each mission's language. Along the same lines, he noted that the elderly who could not go to the church had to be instructed in their own homes and in their own language: "This is a burden," he confessed, "but we absolutely cannot throw it from us. The duty of pastors is not to look after the strong only, but after the weak and feeble."

In 1813, immediately after taking possession of his office, Sarría carried out the first canonical visitation of the whole territory. With the Napoleonic invasion, the Spanish administration had little attention to spare for those remote colonies, and as a consequence of the Mexican revolt, not one ship had arrived from San Blas with provisions in 1811 and 1812. In view of the grave situation, Arrillaga, who was then governor, wrote to Sarría requesting aid for the four Alta California presidios: Monterrey, San Francisco, Santa Bárbara, and San Diego. The prefect replied that the missions would provide what help they could. The majority donated flour and cloth, but Sarría's own mission, San Carlos, was unable to donate either one, since it did not even have enough for its neophytes. Sarría always knew how to remain firm in relation to the authorities when the pressure exerted on the missions seemed excessive to him.

Around the same time, specifically in 1814, Sarría was a protagonist in a historic event: on September 29, he baptized the Scotsman John Gilroy, the first foreigner to settle permanently in California, with the name of Juan Antonio María.

Also in this period, faced with the accusation that the Indians' high rate of mortality might be related to neglect by the missionaries, Sarría ordered an investigation. The conclusion was not a new one: it was the "French disease" that was to blame. According to Sarría, immoral relationships with the presidio soldiers were weakening the native race. At some missions, the friar wrote, officiating at someone's wedding was equivalent to sending him or her to the grave.

Sarría wanted to see the soldiers far away from the friars. The troops sent from Mexico lacked discipline and religion, in his view, and were a bad influence on the neophytes, pushing them to abandon the mission and return to the mountains. In a letter written to Governor Solá, his fellow-countryman, Sarría said that soldiers might be necessary when the friars went to explore the interior, but not in order to preach the gospel. He was convinced that the Indians would welcome the fathers with open arms if they went alone.

Sarría again visited all the missions in 1816. When he returned to San Carlos, he wrote his second pastoral letter to the friars, reminding them of their vow of poverty and urging them to engage in study and reading. On December 14, 1817, he founded California's twentieth mission, to which he gave the name of San Rafael Arcángel. In 1818 and 1825, he again visited all the missions, on the latter occasion not as prefect commissioner, but as father president of the California missions.

Sarría held the post of father president of the California missions between 1823 and 1825. Consequently, he was in office when the revolt of the Chumash Indians of the Santa Barbara Channel, in which he played a decisive role, took place in 1824.

Vicente de Sarría's Mediation in the Chumash Revolt

The Chumash population had declined dramatically in the preceding hundred years, and in the first decades of the nineteenth century, a movement arose in favor of maintaining autochthonous traditions among the few thousand Chumash who remained. Tensions were evident, and rumors of rebellion were not lacking. The reason for the discontent, in Governor Argüello's opinion, was the Indians' desire to free themselves from white domination and return to their pagan freedom. From the friars' perspective, however, the motive was different: the lack of compensation for their labor. Despite working hard to supply the presidios, they had not received anything for their efforts since 1810.

Probably for both reasons, the discontent grew, and in 1824, the Chumash decided to rebel. They chose February 22 as the date for a simultaneous uprising at three missions, Santa Inés, La Purísima, and Santa Bárbara. However, the day before, an Indian from La Purísima arrived at Santa Inés and asked permission from the garrison corporal to visit a relative who was imprisoned there. The corporal denied the request, and the man protested, "Does the king perhaps forbid relatives to speak with prisoners?" The corporal replied, "There's no king but the captain,"[46] and had him punished for his insolence, arousing such indignation among the Chumash of Santa Inés that they decided to begin the revolt right there and then.

It was the most organized revolt that had ever occurred in California. Santa Inés was almost entirely burned down. At La Purísima, after a fierce battle, the natives forced the garrison to surrender. They allowed the soldiers, their families, and the mission's resident friar to retreat to Santa Inés and tried to maintain their position. The Mexican army needed almost a month to recover the mission. At Santa Bárbara, the Chumash disarmed the soldiers stationed at the mission and sent them to the presidio. For their part, the presidio soldiers attacked the mission, but were unable to expel the Indians. Shortly thereafter, the majority of the rebels abandoned Santa Bárbara and withdrew to the interior, camping at Buena Vista Lake in what is now the San Joaquín Valley, sixty miles from Santa Bárbara. An expedition was sent to bring them back, but without result. The decision was then made to send a new expedition.

Vicente de Sarría agreed to accompany this second expedition, together with Father Ripoll, after making Gov. Luis Argüello promise that the Indians would receive a full pardon. Antonio María Osio, probably basing himself on what he heard from Governor Argüello, his brother-in-law, summarized Sarría's participation in the expedition in these words: "only his persuasion had the necessary power to take away the Indians' fear."[47]

Several months later, in a letter to the bishop of Sonora, Sarría explained the reasons for the rebellion and how he succeeded in getting those who had fled to the mountains to return to the mission.

Vicente Sarría Offers Details about the Chumash Rebellion in a Letter to the Bishop of Sonora

> With regard to the uprising at Missions Santa Inés, Purísima and Santa Bárbara, I previously stated the Indians from Santa Bárbara had fled to the valley of tules and the mission had been abandoned. An expedition of soldiers and armed civilians set out to bring them back, but nothing was achieved. In fact, as I indicated, the neophytes then regrouped on a small island in a large lagoon which was surrounded by dense tules along its shore. The path to the lagoon was defended by a muddy and marshy area. People on horseback could not pass through without experiencing extreme difficulty and danger. It was decided that a second expedition should be sent out. While it was preparing to depart, the Reverend Father from Mission

Sta. Bárbara wrote me a long and detailed account of the uprising of the neophytes, what had possibly contributed to it, and how the Indians were being oppressed at that time.[48] I was very moved by his account in favor of the Indians and I appeared before the Governor of the Province and presented it to him. I negotiated with this *Jefe* and requested that he grant the Indians a general pardon, if they returned to the mission. I easily achieved my goal, because when the *Señor Gobernador* heard this account, he felt the same way about it that I did. He and I agreed that I should accompany the expedition which would be commanded by *Don* Pablo de la Portilla, captain of the auxiliary company from Mazatlán, which has been in this province since 1819.

I wanted to go to assure the neophyte fugitives that they would be pardoned, to eliminate their fears that they would be pursued by the soldiers, to dispel any doubts about punishment, and, above all, to convince them to return to their mission. Everything worked out. We left Sta. Bárbara on June 4 and headed toward the interior. After a five day journey we arrived at the valley of the tules. After a day's rest, Captain de la Portilla, Reverend Fr. Antonio Ripoll, the administrator of Mission Sta. Bárbara, and I, went to speak with the fugitives. The three of us were unarmed, and we kept ourselves at a fair distance from the soldiers so that the Indians would not be afraid to speak with us. They displayed considerable distrust and fear as they came out to receive us. They did not want to lay down their weapons, which consisted mainly of bows and arrows and a few firearms which they had taken from the mission. We did not make an issue of that. They proceeded fully to reveal their complaints. We heard them out respectfully and offered them safe conduct. They met with us a number of times at the same spot. Finally, in peace, mutual joy, and satisfaction, they were convinced to take advantage of the general pardon and return to the mission. On June 13, a mass of thanksgiving was celebrated in a very beautiful wooded area at the place where we had met with the Indians. This year the date coincided with the Feast of the Holy Trinity. The same Indians who had fled displayed their musical talent as they sang under the direction of their choir master, Jayme, who had been one of the first to have taken part in the uprising. We remained there for three more days so that many families who had scattered through the nearby areas could be reunited. On June 16 we left for Mission Sta. Bárbara, accompanied by many neophytes, male and female, of all ages, who previously had been fugitives. Since we walked very slowly so they could follow us, the trip took seven days. Others then followed in large

> groups. Very few are still missing, and so the mission is back to the way it was before. The fugitives from Sta. Inés and La Purísima returned to their respective missions in the same manner and now there are very few still missing.
>
> This is how the uprising, which began at Mission Sta. Inés and continued at La Purísima and Sta. Bárbara, ended. Only at Mission Sta. Inés did the Indians express their hostility by shooting arrows at the priest.[49] This did not happen at La Purísima or at Sta. Bárbara, where they treated the priest with great kindness. Before they fled after their skirmish with the soldiers, they handed the father the keys to the church and sacristy. Promising to take good care of him and provide him with clothing, they invited him to go with them. They told him that they were very sad that the Indians who had the misfortune to perish in the skirmish had not received the last rites.[50]

Here the narrative of events ends. Sarría goes on to explain to the bishop of Sonora the reasons that drove the Indians to rebel, saying that they were overwhelmed by the excessive taxes, donations, and loans that were demanded from them in order to feed and provide clothing for the soldiers. Faced with this exploitation, the Indians no longer had any way to ensure that the laws and decrees that protected them were observed, nor did they have lawyers who could help them to defend themselves. According to the *Recopilación de Leyes de los Reynos de las Indias* (Recompilation of laws of the kingdoms of the Indies), their lawyers were to be heard with great attention, but Sarría charged that those who were appointed judges were in reality people interested in the neophytes' destruction.

Sarría then takes up another issue that was in the forefront of attention at the time: the distribution of mission lands. As has been said, the missions had been founded for a term of ten years, after which the lands were to be returned to their original owners, the Indians. However, the government had begun to distribute the farms among the "people of reason." On this point, Sarría's opposition was total, and in his letter to the bishop, he declared himself ready to publicly defend the Indians and their land rights.

Last Years: From the Bustle of Politics to the Quiet of the Soledad Mission

News traveled slowly and was late in arriving in California. For this reason, although Mexican independence was proclaimed in September

1821, the news of Agustín de Iturbide's assumption of power was not known in Monterrey until the end of the year. In April of the following year, Governor Solá called together the highest-ranking authorities of the presidios and missions to learn their opinions of the new regime. Sarría attended as the representative of the mission president, and like all the others, he agreed to swear allegiance. He also participated in the election of California's representatives in Mexico, as well as in the meeting held to discuss the territory's self-government. Nonetheless, Sarría found the continual tensions with the civil authorities ever more difficult to bear, and when the republican government that succeeded Agustín de Iturbide promulgated a new constitution in 1824, he refused to swear allegiance to it, not because he disapproved of independence, but because he felt that such oaths had become a mere game.[71] He likewise refused to celebrate a high mass or sing a *Te Deum* in honor of the new constitution, as Governor Argüello had requested. In consequence, Mexican President Guadalupe Victoria ordered him to be arrested and deported to Mexico. Trying to avoid the punishment, Sarría offered to go to the Sandwich Islands to set up a mission there. In the end, the deportation order was not carried out, undoubtedly because the authorities feared that if Sarría was expelled from California, the friars who shared his opinion—that is, almost all of them—would leave as well. He was not granted authorization to go to the Sandwich Islands, and he continued in his post as prefect until 1830.

Due to the instability in Mexico, the Colegio de San Fernando was unable to send new missionaries to fill the positions that became vacant. In 1828, when Francisco Xavier Uría left the Soledad mission for San Buenaventura, Sarría found himself forced to leave San Carlos to fill the place that had been left vacant at Soledad.

The mission of Nuestra Señora de la Soledad was the thirteenth in the chain of Alta California missions. It was founded by Fermín Lasuén in 1791, at a location that the natives called Chuttusgelis, and as we have already mentioned, it was the burial place of José Joaquín Arrillaga, the Gipuzkoan governor born in Aia. The region was one of Alta California's poorest, due to its arid soil and harsh climate. Adobe walls crumbled in the dry heat of summer and the damp cold of winter. Surely for this reason, the area was thinly populated, and from the beginning, it was very difficult to obtain workers for the mission. Six years were needed to construct an adobe building to replace the shelter of branches that Lasuén had consecrated.

It was also difficult from the beginning to find friars who could adapt to the place. It was immediately evident that the first two whom

Lasuén assigned to build the mission, Father Gili and Father Rubí, were utterly unsuited for the task. Lasuén wrote to the guardian of San Fernando that both felt "complete and total repugnance . . . for this kind of life and for this country." Lasuén asked himself what could be done with "minds filled with an unqualified abhorrence for everything that is to be done here."[52]

Soledad mission. By A. B. Dodge. http://www.missionscalifornia.com

During the mission's brief life, almost thirty friars passed through Soledad. One after another, as soon as they could, they requested a transfer to a less harsh location, offering rheumatism or some other illness as an excuse. There were two exceptions to this continual churning. The first was the Aragonese Florencio Ibáñez, Arrillaga's friend, who spent fourteen years at Soledad and was buried alongside the governor. Ibáñez had to deal with two epidemics, the first of which struck when he had been in his post no more than a year. Despite the care the friar provided, all the Indians fled in fear, and the mission was left empty, as recorded in the mission register in the entry for February 5, 1802. In 1806, another epidemic ravaged the mission, and on that occasion as well, Ibáñez and his companion had to fight the sickness with very few resources.

The second exception—the second friar who remained at Soledad for an extended period—was the Bizkaian Vicente de Sarría. For seven years, Sarría concerned himself with keeping the mission running and with attending to the material and spiritual needs of its inhabitants.

Sarría had another very unusual occupation during this period: the composition of a treatise on Caesarean sections. Around a hundred

Soledad mission ruins. http://www.missionscalifornia.com

years later, Sherburne F. Cook translated the text and published it in *California and Western Medicine*. According to Cook, there were neither doctors nor midwives in California in the mission period who could remove the fetus from a woman who had died before or during labor. This was the topic of Sarría's work, which Cook evaluates as follows:

> Although himself by no means versed in medicine, he read what literature he had available, utilized a wide personal experience, and wrote out a treatise on the cesarean operation for the benefit and guidance of his followers. This treatise, which occupies itself as much with theologic as with strictly medical matters, represents the serious attempt of an intelligent man to contribute to the existing knowledge of his place and tine. As such it may be regarded as the first original contribution ever offered by a resident of California in the field of medicine.[53]

We see once again that necessity drove the friars to educate themselves in all fields: construction, agriculture, livestock raising, medicine . . . or all of them at once.

Alfred Robinson visited the Soledad mission in 1829 and had the opportunity to get to know Sarría, or "Seria," as he called him. In his *Life in California*, he wrote:

> It was near sundown when we arrived and dismounted at the door of La Soledad. The gloomiest, bleakest, and most abject-looking spot in all California!

Indians transport Sarría's corpse from Soledad to San Antonio de Padua. By Alexander Harmer.

This mission was founded in 1791; and, although it presents a very unpromising aspect to the traveller from the gloominess of its exterior, its interior exhibits a striking contrast. A pious old man controls its concerns, and pours out to his guests with free hospitality the abundance thereof. His charities, his goodness, and meekness of character are proverbial; and to have known the old Pádre Seria was a happiness indeed.[54]

By that time, the process of secularization, to which Sarría was openly opposed, was unstoppable and truly discouraging for the friars. Elderly and ill, Sarría spent his last years at Soledad without any other friar to accompany him, and that was how he died, without receiving the last rites, on May 24, 1835. He was sixty-eight years old when his worn-out body was found beside the altar in the church. The previous day, he had felt ill and sent a messenger in search of Father Mercado, but the latter did not arrive in time. Mercado ascribed the death to "scant nutrition." Angustias de la Guerra told the story that once she and Sarría dined together at Soledad. It was a fast day, and the friar ate only a borage leaf dusted in flour and fried, accompanied by a little water.[55] Bancroft does not share Mercado's opinion, however. He says that Sarría died suddenly, perhaps when he was at the altar celebrating mass.

In Bancroft's view,

> He was a scholarly, dignified, and amiable man; not prone to controversy, yet strong in argument, clear and earnest in the expression of his opinions, devoted to his faith and his Order, strict in observing and enforcing Franciscan rules and conscientious in the performance of every duty; yet liberal in his views on ordinary matters, clear-headed in business affairs, and well liked by all who came in contact with him. As prefect no California friar could have done better, since in the misfortune of his Order he never lost either temper or courage.[56]

He also mentions Sarría's writings:

> He wrote several little works, among which was also a curious volume of manuscript sermons in his native Basque

The last Indians who remained at Soledad carried the friar's body on a litter to San Antonio de Padua, about twenty-five miles away, where he was buried in the mission church, on the epistle side of the sanctuary.[57]

Vicente Sarría's death was also the death of Soledad. As soon as they saw that no one was coming to replace him, the Indians abandoned the mission, and the adobe walls soon began to crumble.

José María de Zalvidea and Other Witnesses of the End of the Missions

Early in the morning of June 11, 1804, two Franciscan friars arrived at the Hospicio de Indias (Indies Hospice) in Puerto de Santa María. Both were Bizkaian, and they wanted to sail for the Americas as soon as possible. One was a mature man, around forty years old. In his scant baggage, he carried a folder containing the sermons in Euskara written during his time in Arantzazu. As the reader will have guessed, he was Vicente de Sarría, whom we have discussed in the previous section. His companion, a young man of twenty-four, was José María de Zalvidea, born in Bilbao on March 2, 1780: tall, thin, with an olive complexion and a face pocked with smallpox scars, blue eyes, and a deep cleft in his chin, according to the ship's passenger list. After waiting eighteen long days, the two men embarked on the frigate *Constante* on June 29, accompanied by the countryman Francisco Sarasola. They disembarked without problems at the port of Veracruz and continued their

Fr José María de Zalvidea

journey by land, arriving at the Colegio de San Fernando in Mexico City on September 10.[58]

At San Fernando, despite Zalvidea's youth, his superiors judged him to be capable and mature and decided to send him to the missions without further preparation. Consequently, before a year had passed, on August 31, 1805, Zalvidea set foot in California at the port of San Francisco. As his first posting, so that he could adapt and acquire experience, he was assigned to the San Fernando mission. He spent a year there, in the course of which he was able to visit the nearby missions, where he immediately gave evidence of the capacities his superiors had seen in him. At Santa Bárbara, in order to ensure a supply of water for the mission's gardens, fruit trees, and residences, and with the help of the native Chumash Indians, he built a large cistern, a stone-and-mortar construction 120 square feet in size and 7 feet deep.[59] It was located on a height, and the water descended to the mission by way of an aqueduct. This cistern, built in 1806, is still admired by the tourists who visit the mission buildings.

In the same year, 1806, José María de Zalvidea participated in a reconnaissance expedition in the California interior. It was not the first expedition to enter what is now the Central Valley. In 1772, Cmdr. Pedro Fages had been there looking for two deserters, and a few years later, in 1776, Fr. Francisco Garcés had explored the territory, when he was travelling with Juan Bautista Anza in search of a route between Sonora and Monterrey. Zalvidea's expedition was organized on Governor Arrillaga's orders, and the friar was charged with a double mission: he was to inspect the territory to see whether he could find an appropriate site for setting up another mission, and he was to record a description of the territory explored in a diary. We know this expedition today as "Zalvidea's expedition," since we know about it thanks to the notes taken by the friar from Bilbao.

Diary of an Inland Expedition

Zalvidea's "Diario de una expedición tierra adentro" (Diary of an inland expedition), as well as offering concrete information about the Central Valley—geographical location of the rancherias, number of inhabitants in each one, detailed information about the vegetation and water resources—it offers details about Indian peoples who would never be named again in any other document. In other words, Zalvidea's manuscript speaks about groups that had already disappeared by the time ethnographers began to take an interest in California's native peoples.

The expedition left Santa Bárbara on July 19, 1806. The group's route was first from Santa Inés northward, and then eastward toward the valley floor. They gave the name of Buenavista to a ranchería at the edge of Tulare Lake. The majority of the territory through which they passed was arid, alkaline, and poorly suited for setting up a mission, but the area around what is now Visalia appeared to Zalvidea to be an appropriate location for this purpose. Continuing north, they reached what is now the southern border of Fresno County, after which, turning south, they left the valley behind, crossing Tejon or Tehachapi Pass. They then followed the eastern foothills of the San Gabriel Mountains until, turning west, they crossed the mountains that separated them from San Gabriel on August 14.

Throughout the journey, the Indians showed themselves to be friendly and desirous of hosting the missionaries. At no time did Zalvidea forget his missionary zeal, and upon arriving in a new ranchería, he sought to baptize as many elderly people as possible. "Very early in the morning we set out toward the north," he began his entry for July 22, continuing:

> At the beginning of our journey we had to climb a mountain by a very bad path. Soon we came out upon some plains and at two leagues we reached the village of Talihuilimit where I baptized 3 old women, the first of sixty years, one of whose legs was paralyzed. To her I gave the name Maria Magdalena. This woman has a son at Santa Ynez. The second might have been sixty-five years old, and had been bitten in the hip by a bear. To her I gave the name Maria Marta. She has a Christian son at La Purisima. The third whom I baptized might have been over one hundred years old and I called her Maria Francisca.[60]

Day after day, Zalvidea noted down in his diary information about the lands through which the expedition passed, as well as the number of baptisms administered. In the entry for July 24, we read:

> In the little ranch mentioned I baptized five old women and one old man, their names being respectively Maria Lucia, Lucia Maria, Maria Dominga, Dominga Maria, Fernandina, and Fernando.
>
> On the 27th, however, a moment of great pathos breaks the monotony of the narrative:
>
> After one league we came upon an old woman, in a little hut, who was at her last breath, destitute of all human assistance. After having labored very hard to revive her, so that I

might make her a Christian, I finally attained my desire and named her Maria Gertrudis: two hours after baptism she surrendered her soul to its Creator.

Zalvidea had just arrived in the region, and he could not understand the woman. In his diary, there is mention of an interpreter. In any case, the scene is full of significance. We see on the one hand the European friar who believes that he is in possession of the truth, trying to save the woman's soul, and on the other a poor, dying woman asking herself what this man dressed entirely in grey might be[61]—a spirit? Someone come from the world of the dead to take revenge?—and entirely unable to understand his words and gestures.

The expedition's members ran into difficulties only once, and the cause on that occasion was not the Indians' mistrust, but the usual conflicts between neighboring groups. The incident occurred on July 26.

At dark we arrived at a village on the extremity of the lake called Sisupistu. We were accompanied by several Indians from Buenavista. As soon as the Indians of the village at the end of the lake saw the others coming they fled from their village to a tule swamp near by. At the same time their warriors caused an uproar by firing a spear at the chief of the Buenavista Indians. The cause of the excitement was the arrival of the Buenavista Indians, who were enemies of the others; of all this we were in ignorance. As soon as I discovered the reason for the riot I managed to talk to the chief of the village of Sisupistu and convince him that we came to be his friends and we did not know that the Indians of Buenavista were his enemies. I called together the two hostile chiefs and made them become friends and soon everything quieted down. We slept within sight of the village and the Buenavista Indians remained all night in our camp. In order that there might be no conflict among the natives I collected the bows and arrows carried by the Buenavista Indians. The night passed quietly and on the next day I returned the weapons.

Zalvidea was twenty-six years old when the expedition took place. It was not a useless journey. The friar selected the location for a new mission in the area around where Visalia is today, baptized a good number of elderly Indians, and left us the diary we have quoted. Some authors who have discussed this expedition also credit Zalvidea with another achievement, affirming that he was the one who gave Tejon Pass its name after finding a dead badger (in Spanish, *tejón*) there. We have no desire to take away any of Zalvidea's merits, but after reading his diary with care, we are able to declare that no badger appears in it.

San Gabriel

Zalvidea's next posting was the mission of San Gabriel Arcángel, a few miles from today's city of Los Angeles. Zalvidea arrived at San Gabriel on December 19, 1806, and during the twenty years he exercised his ministry there, the mission became the largest and most prosperous of its time: it was there that wine was made on a large scale for the first time, that California's first orange trees were planted, along with many other fruit trees, and that the best wheat harvests ever known in the missions were achieved. The orchards and fields extended for hundreds of acres, and in order to protect them all from the horses and wild animals that wandered the region, the friar planted an impressive cactus hedge, parts of which still survive. In addition, Zalvidea's efforts were not limited to San Gabriel and its neophytes. He planted fruit trees in every hollow and ravine so that when the Indians passed by, they would have something to eat. Since he was sensitive to less practical matters as well, he also planted a beautiful garden in front of the mission, the highlight of which was a sundial surrounded by rosebushes.

The French explorer and naturalist Duflot de Mofras recalls for us what San Gabriel became thanks to Zalvidea's efforts:

> Near the mission, there are beautiful clusters of palm trees, three large contiguous vineyards enclosing nearly two hundred thousand vines, four superb orchards and vegetable gardens, an immense olive grove, and another one containing four hundred orange trees. The vineyards, groves, and gardens were surrounded by impenetrable hedges or palisades of prickly pears or Barbary figs.

Mofras also mentions Zalvidea's importance as a precursor of California viticulture:

> It is to Reverend Father Zalvidea, of whom we have already spoken, that San Gabriel owes the introduction of viticulture. He made a first attempt with a planting of seventy thousand vines, which earned him the nickname in the region of "Father of the seventy thousand vine stocks" (*el Padre de las setenta mil cepas*).

This prosperity was not limited to the agricultural sphere. As far as livestock was concerned, according to Mofras, there were twenty

THE OLD MILL ~ *El Molino Viejo*

A fascinating link to the past this architectural landmark is a notable California cultural center.

"The Old Mill." For historian R. Newcomb, the building retains the architectural taste of the monks: austerity, solidity, and beauty. Jean Bruce Ward; Gary Kurutz, 1974: 156

The Old Cave of Zalvidea, converted into The Old Mill (San Marino, California), is now a museum and cultural center.

thousand horses and more than forty thousand sheep at San Gabriel in 1834. Around three thousand Indians took care of all this, and in order to provide shelter for the large number of neophytes, forty-seven Indian residences were built all around the perimeter of the plaza, alongside the friars' residence, as well as weaving workshops, carpentry workshops, warehouses, granaries, tanneries . . . Construction then began on the church, which still stands.

More than for building the church, however, Zalvidea is remembered for the mill that he built a few miles from the mission around 1816. It was the first watermill in the region and meant enormous progress for the local inhabitants, especially the women, who were thereby freed from the heavy labor of grinding grain on stone *metates*. What is now the Old Mill Museum is located in San Marino and it is considered the most beautiful example of civilian architecture of its time. In 1971, it was one of the first ten sites in Los Angeles County included on the National Register of Historic Places, and it has also been named a

Women grinding grain with a metate. *By A. B. Dodge. http://www.missionscalifornia.com/*

California Historical Landmark.

Vicente de Sarría—the other Bizkaian who crossed the ocean together with Zalvidea—witnessed all this progress at San Gabriel, and he dedicated words of praise to his companion, emphasizing that, in his opinion, he was one of the province's best missionaries.[62]

José Zalvidea or Salvideo, San Manuel Reservation, 1933. Gabrielino Indian origin. It was not strange that the neophytes took the name of the mission sheriff. Zalvidea was informant for the linguists and ethnologists, among others, J. P. Harrington, C. Hart Merriam, A. L. Kroeber. C. Hart Merriam Collection of Native American Photographs, ca. 1890-1938. http://www. oac.cdlib. org/

In 1812, when he had been at San Gabriel for six years, Zalvidea replied to the questionnaire that the Spanish authorities sent to the missions with the aim of gathering information about the Indians.[63] According to those who knew him, he had a gift for languages and was in the habit of preaching in the Indians' language, but we do not know which language that was, since one of the responses to the questionnaire mentions that four languages were spoken at the mission: "The first is called Kokomcar; the second Guiquitamcar; the third Corbonamga; the last Simbamga."[64]

The report includes much interesting information about San Gabriel's inhabitants. Question twenty-one, for example, which aims to collect information about funerary rites, receives the following answer:

> No other ceremonial has been observed than for the mourners to cut their hair; throw beads into the air; make a disordered clamor at night for the first three days of mourning; and place some seeds on the dead body; and if he had some particular trade, they place the instrument or tool characteristic of that exercise on him. Some observe what is almost a natural fast for three or four days, but both these and those who do not fast try not to remember the deceased any longer. Among the pagans,

> when a famous captain dies, they summon the nearest bordering villages, even if they are distant, and hold a great festival, which is nothing but dancing and eating. Afterward, they either bury the body, or burn it and bury the ashes. The dance and the banquet continue for a period of three days, after which the deceased falls into eternal oblivion.

At the time the questionnaire was circulated, the Indians' mortality rate continued to be high at San Gabriel. Like the other friars, Zalvidea thought that venereal disease was the cause:

> Many of those who are born show at a glance the sole inheritance that their parents give them, on account of which three-quarters of those who are born die in their first or second year of life, and of the quarter who survive, the majority do not reach the age of twenty-five.

Around 1810, out of San Gabriel's 1,200 inhabitants, some 300 or 400 were infected with syphilis, and in order to keep the epidemic from spreading, Zalvidea ordered a hospital to be built some distance from the mission. It was a hospital only in name, of course, and the two ministers at San Gabriel, Zalvidea himself and his fellow-countryman José de Miguel, had to care for the sick who crowded it without any help from medicine. It was the legacy of Juan Bautista Anza's 1774 expedition, and a plague spread by the "riff-raff" whom the Mexican authorities sent to guard the missions and populate California. "Here we have the real cause," the historian Engelhardt insists, "of the extraordinary mortality and of the final extinction of the Indians in Central and Southern California."[65]

At the end of his report, Zalvidea requested doctors and medicine, and he concluded by announcing the future that awaited them if they did not receive help: "Alta California will be left bare of Indian inhabitants."

San Juan Capistrano

In 1826, José María de Echandía, California's Mexican governor, promulgated a plan for the emancipation of the mission Indians, according to which the friars were to release those neophytes who were capable of looking after themselves. From this time forward, they would become Mexican citizens. The neophytes at all the missions were informed that a new authority had arrived in the region—Echandía himself—who wanted to be their friend and was ready to fight for their rights. The message got through to the Indians, and at San Juan Capistrano in particular, it received an immediate response: rebellious neophytes refused to work for the friars.

In order to implement his plan, Echandía promulgated an edict that asked the friars for a detailed inventory of each mission. It was at this time that Jose María de Zalvidea arrived at San Juan Capistrano. With the help of his fellow friar José Barona, he drew up the inventory, but added some reflections that no one had requested. Zalvidea was convinced that Echandía's plan hid a desire to confiscate the missions' assets in order to distribute them among the landowners of Spanish origin.

As a consequence of these additional reflections, the document signed by Zalvidea and Barona became a clear assertion of the Indians' rights, one of the most uncompromising of its time. "[I]t would never do harm but prove rather advantageous to consider, that all these lands did belong and do belong to the Indians," the Franciscans insisted. "On these lands they were born, and on them were born likewise all their fathers and all their forefathers."[66] In an attempt to demonstrate that the only just path consisted in returning the lands to their original owners, the friars enumerated the Indians' rights as they were set out in the *Recopilación Indiana*, the Spanish compilation of laws applying to the Indies. Their effort came too late, however. The era of the California Franciscan missions was drawing to a close.

At San Juan Capistrano, many Indians abandoned the friars, and the mission's deterioration quickly became evident, as did, it seems, the deterioration of Zalvidea's health. According to accounts by his contemporaries, the friar's "eccentricities" increased. When they spoke to him, he always answered, "Let's go, yes, sir," without meeting their eyes. At meals, he served himself whatever was put in front of him on a single plate, whether it was solid or liquid, sweet or bitter, and ate it all mixed together. He liked devotional books, and when he read them while strolling around the mission, he often stopped and began to gesture, shouting, "Away with you, Satan," as if he was fighting with the devil or trying to drive away evil thoughts. He flagellated himself frequently and wore belts with spikes that tore into his flesh. Bancroft affirms despite all this that where practical matters were concerned, he continued to have a clear mind and liberal ideas,[67] but it is possible that his mental health had been undermined, like his physical health. In an 1831 letter to the father president, he confessed that he had been suffering from asthma for some time:

> I have consulted with the doctors as to what kind of life I should lead. Along with other instructions, they have told me that the northern climate is harmful for me. They have also told me that I need to wear shoes and that my tunic has to be of linen at the level of my lungs. With the permission of the previous prelate, I have done accordingly. Now, I again ask Your Reverence for the necessary permission to wear the said shoes and linen.[68]

In a postscript, he added that his companion at San Juan Capistrano, Fray José Barona, was unable to get out of bed due to a nervous debility. In 1832, after Barona's death, Zalvidea remained at the mission alone.

End of an Era and End of Zalvidea

Zalvidea showed himself reluctant to intervene in the political debates of the time. When California became part of Mexico, he was prepared to swear allegiance to the republic, so long as it did not violate his conscience. Later on, when the law secularizing the missions was approved, his youthful energy was gone, and feeling sick himself and worn out by having to care for so many other sick, he informed Governor Echandía that there was nothing he desired so much as to be freed from the mission's temporal administration, a responsibility that he had come to hate.[69]

Zalvidea's feelings were shared by the other friars, and two of them—the Bizkaian Tomás Esténaga at San Gabriel and the Navarrese Francisco González de Ibarra at San Fernando—did what no one had dared to do before. In June 1835, without asking permission, they abandoned the mission, took ship, and fled to Sonora. It was an act that went against all the rules and could even be understood as apostasy, but the father president took their side and excused them.

Before a year had passed, both friars had returned to their post. When the French explorer Duflot de Mofras passed through San Gabriel in 1842, Esténaga was still there. With his sleeves rolled up, he was teaching the Indians to make bricks when Mofras arrived. "The Indians owe a remnant of well-being today only to the protection of the youngest and most active of the Spanish Franciscans, Reverend Fr. Tomás Esténaga, Bizkaian,"[70] the explorer wrote in his *Exploration du territoire de l'Orégon, des Californies et de la Mer Vermeille* (Exploration of the territory of Oregon, the Californias, and the Gulf of California).

As he passed through San Buenaventura, Santa Cruz, San Juan Bautista, San Miguel, Carmel, San Rafael . . . , Duflot de Mofras found that all the missions were abandoned or in ruins. Mofras recalled what San Gabriel was in its days of greatest prosperity, in Zalvidea's time:

> Zalvidea sent a ship loaded with oil, hemp, and linen to San Blas every year; he often sent another to Lima with a cargo of soap or tallow. The number of hides produced by the mission was between thirty and thirty-five thousand a year.

He goes on to describe what it had become:

> Everything has been looted by the civilian administrators: a few steps from the mission, the land has been given out, and some Americans and English have already built houses there.
>
> Zalvidea, Esténaga, Ibarra, and a few others, the last representatives of the group of missionaries, once so powerful, were destined to witness the missions' slow decadence. With the secularization law, the establishments passed into the hands of administrators appointed by the government, while the *californios*[71] took over the lands, divided into farms. In a letter to Gov. J. B. Alvarado, Zalvidea expressed his profound disagreement with what was happening:
>
> The Indian community came and informed me that efforts had been made to deprive them of Trabuco, Mission Vieja, and Yuiguilli. If their land is taken from them, how will they (the Indians) maintain their few thousand cattle which in time might be reduced? I am acquainted with their solid reasons as also with their rights, favored by the laws of nature and by the wise laws of the Indies which I refrain from quoting because your wisdom is not ignorant of them. But, in order not to hear the clamors of the poor without power to help them, I again ask Your Honor for my passport. The permit of my Prelate I already have in writing. In justice Your Honor can not refuse the passport, since I have been serving in the territory these thirty-six years. Excuse the molestations, and command your servant, etc.[72]

It was not the first time that Zalvidea requested permission to leave, since he wanted to end his days surrounded by his fellow Franciscans. In those thirty-six years, he had more than completed his obligatory term of service. There was no one to replace him, however, since the Mexican government had prohibited individuals of Mexican origin from working in the missions, and in the end, he had to remain at San Juan Capistrano, where obtaining even the most necessary items cost enormous effort.

The merchant José Antonio Aguirre[73] visited San Juan Capistrano on more than one occasion on his voyages along the Alta California coasts in the ship *La Joven Guipuzcoana* around 1840, and he found Zalvidea badly in need of money. On one of those visits, Aguirre advanced the friar goods worth four hundred dollars, accepting liquor and cowbells in exchange.

On his 1842 visit, Duflot de Mofras found the San Juan Capistrano mission practically in ruins, despite Zalvidea's efforts to maintain it.[74]In a letter written that same year, the friar confessed that he had spent the last four years confined to his bed. By that time, San Gabriel's gardens and orange groves, its vineyards, its abundant wheat harvests and great herds of cattle, and its large groups of neophytes were distant memories for Zalvidea. At San Juan Capistrano in 1842, the situation was very different. "I am here without chocolate," Zalvidea lamented. "This Mission has no wheat, no wine, nor brandy. The circumstances of my debility require strengthening nourishment."[75]

The same year, Zalvidea moved to the mission of San Luis Rey, hoping to find there the care he needed, but that mission too was in ruins. When Mofras visited it in 1841, he found its elderly friar, the Navarrese Francisco González de Ibarra—the one who some years previously had taken ship, together with Esténaga, and deserted his post—"à l'état plus deplorable [in the most deplorable state]." Zalvidea died there in 1846, as preparations were underway to take him to San Juan Capistrano in a wagon.

According to Bancroft, Zalvidea never had an enemy or said a bad word about anyone. Nevertheless, there was someone who spoke badly of him. In 1852, the Scotsman Hugo Reid, who lived near San Gabriel, accused Zalvidea harshly in an article published in the *Los Angeles Star* newspaper:

> He was not only severe, but he was, in his chastizements, most cruel. So as not to make a revolting picture, I shall bury acts of barbarity known to me through good authority, by merely saying that he must assuredly have considered whipping as meat and drink to them, for they had it morning, noon and night.[76]

The Scotsman's words have been often quoted in works that denounce the Indians' treatment in the missions, but it is just to keep in mind that, alongside this single negative opinion, favorable opinions of Zalvidea are numerous. To cite Bancroft once again, in his view, Zalvidea was doubtless in those days a model missionary, and then and later was regarded by the common people as a saint.[77]

Bancroft based his opinion on the accounts of contemporaries who had direct contact with Zalvidea. One of them, Agustin Janssens, recalled that the priest often experienced episodes of religious exaltation and sometimes writhed as if he wanted to expel the devil from within him, but that he was otherwise mentally healthy. “He carried on conversations perfectly and one could take advice from him about any matter, as he gave the impression that whatever was said to him would be well considered. The goodness of his heart had no limit.”[78]

The Englishman Michael C. White—“Miguel Blanco” to California’s inhabitants—maintained a close relationship with Zalvidea. He describes him as a tall, lean, and vigorous man, very hardworking and intelligent, and “in the full sense of the word a saint. He planted fruit trees in the ravines and in many places distant from the missions, for the benefit of the bronco Indians.”[79]

Caption reads “Eulalia Perez, 139 years of age.”

Doña Eulalia Pérez also knew the friar personally. The reminiscences that Doña Eulalia dictated to Thomas Savage, Bancroft’s collaborator, are preserved in the Bancroft Library. The document is dated 1877 and has this curious title: “Una vieja y sus recuerdos: Dictados por Doña Eulalia Pérez que vive en la mision de San Gabriel a la edad avanzada de 139 años” (An old lady and her memories: Dictated by Doña Eulalia Pérez, who lives at the San Gabriel mission, at the advanced age of 139 years). She says in her account that both José María de Zalvidea and his companion, Father Sánchez, treated the Indians very well, and that the neophytes and all the other natives loved them very much. She also comments that Zalvidea taught the Indians to pray in their language and that he always had great respect for them.[80]

Doña Felipa Osuna continued defending the friar thirty years after his death, taking the view that the eccentricities of his last years were due to the many years of effort and sacrifice that preceded them. She was a witness of Zalvidea's last hours. When some of his friends heard that he was gravely ill, they went to San Luis with the aim of taking him to San Juan Capistrano in a wagon. However . . . "When he found out that they were coming for him, he said, 'Come on now, come on now. Yes, lord, they are coming for me, but I cannot go because I am dying like a good soldier. I hear confessions and baptize here. What will this place be like without a Father?'"[81] Against his will, and although Felipa Osuna herself was opposed to moving him, his friends decided to take him to San Juan Capistrano the next day. That evening, Father Oliva took the precaution of administering extreme unction, after which Zalvidea made everyone leave the room. The next morning, he was found dead.

That is what really happened. Father Zalvidea was so revered by everyone. Before he was buried, everybody cut off a little piece of his habit or his cord. He was practically left without any habit at all.

In a letter written a few years earlier, Zalvidea confessed that, after working at San Gabriel for twenty years, he had left the salary and the mass stipends he had collected there for the community, departing for the San Juan Capistrano mission without a real.[82] He made his final journey equally poor, and almost naked as well.

Epilogue

Jose María de Zalvidea died in 1846, the same year that the United States declared war on Mexico. In 1847, Tomás Eleuterio Esténaga drew his last breath at San Fernando. As he was dying, he rose from his bed, and going over to the small altar that had been set up in his room, he exclaimed in a firm voice, "I have served at San Gabriel and Los Angeles for fifteen years. Should I, during that time, have scandalized or offended anyone, forgive me for the love of God."[479]

In this way, the last two members of the group of Basque missionaries died on the eve of 1848, a decisive year in California history. On February 2 of that year, the Treaty of Guadalupe Hidalgo was signed, ending the war between Mexico and the United States. The treaty required Mexico to give up more than half her territory, including all of today's states of California, Utah, Nevada, New Mexico, and Texas and parts of Arizona, Colorado, Kansas, Wyoming, and Oklahoma. The international border was set at the Río Grande. Almost at the same time, an event occurred that would have enormous repercussions for the new American territory. On January 24, James W. Marshall found some gold nuggets at a place called Sutter's Mill in Coloma, near Sacramento. It was not a major discovery, but it turned out to be far more decisive for increasing California's population than anything else that had happened up to that time. During the following seven years, California became the destination of thousands of people from around the world who, infected by "gold fever," were aiming to get rich quick.

As is well known, among those thousands of people, there were, again, many Basques. While the first to arrive were emigrants from the southern Basque Country, Hegoalde, who had settled in Latin America, they were soon joined by others who came directly from Europe, from the northern Basque Country, Iparralde. These Forty-Niners tried their luck panning for gold, but they quickly opted for more reliable economic pursuits, turning first to cattle raising, then to the care of sheep. Scattered throughout the western United States, many of them made their homes in the most barren parts of Nevada, Oregon, and Idaho. They belonged to a people that had not set down its history in writing, and they were unaware that many of their compatriots had been there earlier, exploring unknown lands and seas, seeking silver or pearls, trying to save the indigenous inhabitants' souls, or dedicating themselves to more ordinary occupations. They did not know that they were merely one link in a long chain. How could they have known it, if the achievements of those first Basques in California never made it back to their native land? Today, happily, we have the opportunity to fill in this gap, thanks to the documents that have been preserved in the archives of Spain, Mexico, and California.

Endnotes

Chapter 1. First Maritime Explorations, 1533–1767

1. Díaz del Castillo, *Historia verdadera,* 1904, 2: 413–14 (1st ed. 1632).
2. Archivo General de Indias (AGI), *Catálogo de Pasajeros a Indias,* PASAJEROS, L.1, E.3487.
3. "Hernán Cortés: Información sobre la muerte de Diego Becerra," AGI, PATRONATO, 180, R.52.
4. Cutter 1961, 233–44.
5. Rodríguez de Montalvo 1510, fol. CVIII verso. English translation from en.wikipedia.org/wiki/Origin_of_the_name_California.
6. "Cartas del Virrey Luis de Velasco 1550-1564," AGI, México 19, N 23 a.
7. "Carta de fray de Andrés de Urdaneta al rey don Felipe II, 18 de mayo de 1560," cited in Prieto, *El Océano Pacífico,* 1984, 182–83.
8. Now Jalisco, Mexico.
9. www.euskomedia.org/aunamendi.
10. www.sge.org/sge07/base.asp?Id=25&pag=11.
11. Fernández de Navarrete 1851, 70–74.
12. Griffin and Aguirre, "Letter of Fray Andres de Aguirre," 1891, 8.
13. According to Donald C. Cutter, Mathes reads this "Rufano," while the Sutro documents have "bufano," but the sense would require "bufalo."
14. Andrés Aguirre's complete letter is found in Spanish and English in Griffin and Aguirre 1891, 7–13. English translation from *The California Coast: A Bilingual Edition of Documents from the Sutro Collection,* translated and edited in 1891 by George Butler Griffin, re-edited with an emended translation, annotation, and preface by Donald C. Cutter (Norman: University of Oklahoma Press), 10–17.

15. Fray Martín de Rada, "Relación sobre el estrecho de Terranova," AGI, INDIFERENTE, 1528, N.13.
16. "Relacion del viage y navegacion que hizo el Capitan Pedro de Unamuno," in Mathes, *Californiana I,* 1965, 8–37.
17. Wagner, "The Voyage of Pedro de Unamuno to California in 1587," 1923, 140–60.
18.The complete narrative in Mathes, *Californiana I,* 1965, 8–37.
19. English translation from H. R. Wagner and Pedro de Unamuno, *The Voyage of Pedro de Unamuno to California in 1587* (San Francisco, Calif.: California Historical Society Quarterly), 147–48.
20. Ibid., 149.
21. Ibid., 149.
22. Ibid., 150.
23. These rituals were customary in Spanish ceremonies of possession: they struck the trees with their swords, tossed sand and rocks, pulled up grass, carried water from the sea to the land, and made a cross with tree branches in order to legitimate their ownership of the territory.
24. The name given to a group of Indian huts.
25. English translation from H. R. Wagner and Pedro de Unamuno, *The Voyage of Pedro de Unamuno to California in 1587* (San Francisco, Calif.: California Historical Society Quarterly), 147–48., 152–53.
26. Ibid., 155.
27. Ibid., 155.
28. Ibid., 157.
29. Preston, "Serpent in Eden," 1996, 2–37.
30. "Declaracion que hizo en la ciudad de Guadalaxara del Nuevo Reyno de Galicia en 24 de Enero de 1588 Antonio de Sierra," ," in Mathes 1965, 1: 67.
31. "Declaracion que hizo Tomás de Alzola maestre de la Nao nombrada Santa Ana que robaron los Yngleses," ibid., 73.
32. Ibid., 73.
33. Ibid., 73.
34. Ibid., 74.
35. "Declaracion que hizo . . . Antonio de Sierra," ibid., 70.
36. Alzola's testimony is reported in the third person.
37. "Declaracion que hizo Tomás de Alzola," ibid., 75.
38. "Declaracion que hizo . . . Antonio de Sierra," ibid., 70
39. "Declaracion que hizo Tomás de Alzola," ibid., 75–76.
40. "Declaracion que hizo . . . Antonio de Sierra," ibid., 71
41. Héctor Santos, www.bibingka.com/sst/santana/santana.htm.
42. Pourade, *The Explorers,* 1962, 62.
43. www.sandiegohistory.org/books/pourade/explorers/explorerschapter5.htm.

44. Sebastián Vizcaíno's letter was stolen by an English ship and published in the late sixteenth century, in Richard Haklut's *The English Voyages*.
45. Vizcaíno is referring to the *Santa Ana*, which Thomas Cavendish had looted and burned.
46. "A letter from Mexico, of Sebastián Biscaino to his father Antonio Biscaino," Herbert Eugene Bolton collection, BANC MSSC-B840, Box 13, Bancroft Library, University of California, Berkeley.
47. "Relacion de Sebastián Vizcaíno: 8 de diciembre 1596," in Mathes 1965, 1: 264. English translation from Sebastián Vizcaíno, "Vizcaino's Narrative," *Hispanic American Historical Review* 10, no. 2 (May 1930): 204–18, at 205.
48. These first accounts of the indigenous people of California are entirely mediated by the new arrivals' perspective. It has to be taken into account, in addition, that their contact with the indigenous people was usually very brief.
49. "Relacion de Sebastián Vizcaíno: 8 de diciembre 1596," in Mathes 1965, 1: 264. English translation from Sebastián Vizcaíno, "Vizcaino's Narrative," *Hispanic American Historical Review* 10, no. 2 (May 1930): 204–18, 205–6.
50. "Relacion hecha por Sebastián Vizcaíno: 16 de Abril 1598," in Mathes 1965, 1: 317–18. English translation from *The California Coast*, 67–68.
51. Vizcaíno here passes over in silence the true reason for the attack, that the soldier assaulted the woman in order to take the pearls she had around her neck. Vizcaíno was reprimanded by the viceroy, by order of the Council of the Indies, for not having punished the soldier involved.
52. Mathes 1965, 1: 319–20.
53. Now Bahía San Carlos.
54. "Relacion de Sebastián Vizcaíno: 8 de Diciembre 1596," in Mathes 1965, 1: 275. English translation from Vizcaíno 1930, 215.
55. "Carta de Sebastián Vizcaíno al Rey: 27 de febrero de 1597," in Mathes 1965, 1: 285.
56. Vizcaíno's diary is signed by the expedition's senior notary, Diego de Santiago. While Vizcaíno is sometimes referred to in the third person, the majority of the text is narrated in the first-person plural, undoubtedly as in the original ship's log, and it is believed to be a copy of Vizcaíno's diary.

Fray Antonio de la Ascensión laments in his summary that they had turned back before reaching the Strait of Anián, the legendary Northwest Passage. In addition, Fray Antonio's narrative reinforced the mistaken idea that California was an island.

57. "Relaciones y demarcaciones del descubrimiento que hizo Sebastián Vizcaíno en los puertos y ensenadas de la mar del Sur en donde va

puesto con precisión todo ello," ibid., 568–613.

58. "In more than eight hundred leagues that I went, it was all inhabited with countless Indians, who said that there were large towns inland, inviting me to go with them" ("Carta escrita al Rey por Sebastián Vizcaíno: 23 de Mayo 1603," in Mathes 1965, 1: 456–57).
59. Relations between natives and colonizers began with exchanges of this kind. The colonizers most frequently offered clothing and foodstuffs, and the Indians, for their part, customarily offered animal skins and food.
60. Now Bahía de San Quintín.
61. Now Bahía Colnett.
62. They were probably referring to the members of Juan de Oñate's expedition, who had just arrived in New Mexico.
63. 'Dance' in Nahuatl.
64. Now Cedros Island.
65. "Carta escrita al Rey por Sebastián Vizcaíno: 23 de Mayo 1603," ibid., 455–58.
66. "Memorial de Nicolás de Cardona: 1618," in Mathes 1970, 2: 66.
67. Ibid., 66.
68. A type of flea.
69. Ibid., 66–67.
70. "Información que se hico acerca de averse gastado en la fábrica de los viajes," ibid., 18–38.
71. The indigenous inhabitants gave this name to pirates of different nationalities, both Dutch and English. According to one theory, the word comes from "speak in English," that is, the order that the pirates kept repeating to the locals.
72. Andrés Pérez de Ribas, *Historia de los triumphos de nuestra santa fe,* cited in Mosk 1934, 54–55.
73. Speilbergen 1906, 110.
74. Venegas 1757, 1: 204.
75. Mosk, op. cit., 60.
76. Niehuis 1939, 12–14, 25, found at www.scribd.com/193901-Desert-Magazine-1939-January/d/2095007.
77. Mathes 1969, 213.
78. The port of Palos de la Frontera, in Spain.
79. Bolton 1960, 91.
80. "Auto de Don Ysidro de Atondo y Antillon de 1 de abril de 1683," in Mathes 1974, 2: 509.
81. Ibid., 508–9.
82. "Testimonio de Don Ysidro de Atondo y Antillon a 5 de abril de 1683," ibid., 287.
83. Fruit of the plant *Cercidium microphylum.*

84. "Información de Don Ysidro de Atondo y Antillon: 16 de noviembre de 1684," ibid., 527–28.
85. Hittell 1898, 157.
86. A type of corn-based stew.
87. Ibid., 158.
88. Mathes 1974, 1: 300.
89. "Respuesta del sr. fiscal," ibid., 373.
90. Bolton 1936, 207.
91. Mathes 1974, 2: 490–91.
92. "Testimonio de don Isidro de Atondo y Antillon del veinticinco de octubre de 1684," ibid., 502–3.
93. Venegas 1757, 2: 232–33, cited in Hittell, op. cit., 160.
94. Chapman 1921, 169.
95. Hittell 1898, 161.

Chapter 2. The Jesuit Missions of Baja California, 1697–1767

1. Hittell, op. cit., 188.
2. "Salvatierra: Carta al P. Ugarte firmada en Loreto a 3 de julio de 1698," in Venegas, op. cit., 44–45.
3. Ibid., 46.
4. The Fondo Piadoso de California was created in Mexico in 1697 with the objective of receiving donations for the Jesuit missionaries working to spread the Catholic faith in California.
5. Ibid., 112.
6. The story derives from the writings of members of the Society of Jesus (Venegas, Clavijero . . .), explaining its evident hagiographic tone.
7. Ibid., 112.
8. "Carta del padre Sebastián de Sistiaga al padre visitador José de Echeverria: San Ignacio, 27 de octubre 1730," cited in Del Río 2003, 100.
9. Venegas, op. cit., 112.
10. Ibid.,114.
11. Clavijero 1852, 50–51.
12. Ibid., 51.
13. Clavijero says that it was Ugarte who planted the first vineyards in Baja California, after having seen abundant wild grapes in the peninsula. As mentioned above, vines sent by Diego Marquina were planted in Atondo's time. In any event, Ugarte's were the first that prospered.
14. Cited in Venegas, op. cit., 119.
15. Ibid., 121.
16. "Carta del padre Sebastián de Sistiaga al provincial Cristóbal de Escobar y Llamas: San Ignacio, 19 septiembre 1743," cited in Del Río, op. cit., 90.

17. Bancroft 1884 (Works XV), 1: 297.
18. Juan Bautista Muguzabal (Portugalete, 1675 – California, 1761) was employed for almost forty years in the warehouses of the missions and of the Loreto presidio. He was in charge of paying the soldiers and sailors and directed the comings and goings of the ships. He also served as sacristan of Loreto and as a catechist.
19. Venegas, op. cit., 183–84.
20. The best portrait of Fr. Kino is the one drawn by H. E. Bolton in his book *Rim of Christendom*.
21. Venegas, op. cit., 183–84, 316.
22. Ibid., 318.
23. Ibid., 327
24. Bancroft 1884 (Works XV), 1: 451. English text from www.archive.org/stream/cihm_14166#page/n517/mode/2up/search/Ugarte.
25. Sebastián Sistiaga was born in Teposcolula, New Spain, in 1684. He was teaching literature at the Colegio de San Andrés in Mexico City when he decided to go to the missions. He spent almost thirty years in California.
26. Juan Bautista Luyando was born in Mexico City in 1700. He worked as a missionary for only six years, due to health problems. He subsequently returned to central Mexico and held senior positions in various Jesuit schools.
27. Clavijero, op.cit., 75.
28. Venegas, op. cit., 394.
29. In a letter written in 1730, visitor-general José de Echeverría (Donostia-San Sebastián, 1688) affirmed that more progress had been made in California in the last thirty-four years than in the two hundred that had preceded them since the beginning of the conquest of New Spain ("Carta del padre visitador Jose de Echeverria al marqués de Villapuente, 10 de febrero, 1730," cited in Crosby 1974, 48).
30. Ibid., 397.
31. Del Barco 1988, 265.
32. Burrus 1984, 115–17.
33. Dunne 1968, 432.
34. Jackson 1981.
35. Dunne, op.cit., 417–18.

Chapter 3. First Land Explorations, 1598–1781

1. Fray Marcos de Niza returned telling marvelous tales of the cities of Cíbola, saying that he had found a city even larger than Tenochtitlán (Mexico City), where the people used gold and silver dishes and decorated their houses with turquoises, enormous pearls, emeralds, and

other similar jewels. When Francisco Vázquez de Coronado's expedition arrived there after a year's travel, with Fray Marcos as their guide, they had a huge surprise: "And when they saw the first town that was Cíbola, the curses that some hurled at Fray Marcos were so many that God grant they not fall on him" (words of the chronicler Pedro de Castañeda de Nájera, quoted in León-Portilla 2001, 63).

2. Oñate chose many other Basques for his expedition. We give their names and origins as they appear in the lists of the time: Asensio de Arechuleta ("native of Ybar"), Sebastián de Gaceta ("born in the city of 'Villalobo,' Bizkaia, servant of the *maese de campo*, with armor for himself and for his horse"), Pedro Giménez from Vitoria, Domingo de Lezama from Bilbao, Cristóbal de Lizaga, Leon de Ysasti, Juan Lopez de Yllareta ("Of the city of San Sebastián, in the province of Gipuzkoa, the son of Juan Pérez de Yllareta, with a coat of mail and a harquebus and with a servant provided with armor for himself and for his horse"), Jorge de Zumaya, the brothers Miguel, Juan, and Francisco Olagüe ("Francisco de Olagüe, born in Panuco, with a scar over his right eye, beardless, medium height, seventeen years old"), Hernando de la Rea ("Born in the city of 'Lorio' in Bizkaia, who brought armor for himself and for his horse"), Martín Ruiz de Aguirre ("sergeant, born in the city of 'Leinestro,' Bizkaia"), Juan de Velasco y Zúñiga, Martín de Sorchaga, Juanes de Isasti, Marcos de Zamudio . . . (George P. Hammond and Agapito Rey, *Don Juan de Onate, Colonizer of New Mexico 1595–1682*, garyfelix.tripod.com/~GaryFelix/index5E.htm).
3. Simmons 1999, 24.
4. Oñate's first headquarters was at San Juan, but it was soon transferred to San Gabriel. Starting in 1610, the capital was Santa Fe.
5. Craddock and Polt, *Oñate's Report to the Viceroy, March 2, 1599*, Research Center for Romance Studies, International and Area Studies (Berkeley: Research Center for Romance Studies, 2009), 2; escholarship.org/uc/item/8s90h6b6.
6. *Bacas de Cíbola* or Zívola, a name given to the American bison.
7. There were other men with Basque surnames in the group: Joan de Olagüe and Diego de Ayarde, born in Mexico, and Domingo de Lezama, "born in the city of 'Vilbao,' tall of body, with a red beard and a wound on his nose, twenty-seven years old" (Hammond and Rey, op. cit.).
8. "Vaquero," Spanish for "cowboy," refers to the fact that they lived by hunting the bison or "cows of Cíbola."
9. Craddock and Polt, *Zaldívar and the Cattle of Cíbola: Vicente de Zaldívar's Report of His Expedition to the Buffalo Plains*, Research Center for Romance Studies, International and Area Studies (Berkeley: Research Center for Romance Studies, 2008); escholarship.org/uc/item/6hz1x4s4.

10. They would soon begin to use horses, however. It was Christopher Columbus who brought the first horses to the Indies, on his second voyage in 1493; a few years later, in 1519, Hernán Cortés introduced them to the mainland. They rapidly became a fundamental element of indigenous culture, and escaped horses spread throughout western North America.
11. The Spaniards were called "castillos" in New Mexico, a corruption of "castellanos," Spanish for "Castilians," the term they used for themselves.
12. Underground or partly underground room used by the Pueblo Indians for ceremonies and gatherings, for men only.
13. Mohoqui or Moqui, a Hopi town.
14. Name given to the Pacific in the era of the first explorations.
15. "Son of Juanes de Arechuleta, born in the town of 'Ybar,' medium height, black beard, a small scar on his forehead, twenty-six years old." He married Anna Pérez Bustillo, and they established one of the first families to colonize New Mexico (Hammond and Rey, op. cit.).
16. Craddock and Polt, *The Trial of the Indians of Acoma 1598–1599*, Research Center for Romance Studies, International and Area Studies (Berkeley: Research Center for Romance Studies, 2008), 56; escholarship.org/uc/item/14v3j7sj.
17. Craddock, *Acoma: Teoría y práctica de la guerra justa*, Research Center for Romance Studies, International and Area Studies (Berkeley: Research Center for Romance Studies, 2008), 11; escholarship.org/uc/item/6cp5j0fs.
18. Kessell 2002, 84.
19. Craddock and Polt, *The Trial of the Indians of Acoma 1598–1599*, Research Center for Romance Studies, International and Area Studies (Berkeley: Research Center for Romance Studies, 2008), 210; escholarship.org/uc/item/14v3j7.
20. Zaldívar returned to the Americas with an Indian named Miguel and three brothers from the Valdegovía Valley, (Araba) as aides or servants (AGI, PASAJEROS, L.8, E.2370).
21. The natives interpreted Christian teaching and symbols in their own way. When Capt. Juan de Ullíbarri, a Basque went to El Cuartelejo to free a group of Picuris Indians who had apparently been kidnapped by the Apaches, he saw that the latter were wearing crosses, Christian religious medals, and rosaries. Ullíbarri asked them why they were wearing all those things if they did not know their meaning, and they answered that "for many years they had traded and had commerce with the Spaniards and that they knew they [the Spaniards] wore crosses and rosaries and images of the saints," and "that when they fight . . . the Pawnees and the Jumano and become tired they remember the Great

Captain of the Spaniards who is in the heavens and then their weariness leaves them and they feel refreshed" (Thomas 1935, 72).

22. Colorado River.
23. Amacava: the Mohave people. Bahacecha: cannot be identified with any tribe today. The term "nation" is used in the sense it had in the texts of the time, meaning "human group defined or related by birth," from Latin *nascere* 'to be born'.
24. Gila River.
25. Caso et al., *La "Relación" del padre Francisco Escobar de la expedición al Mar del Sur de Juan de Oñate (1604–1605)*, Research Center for Romance Studies, International and Area Studies (Berkeley: Research Center for Romance Studies, 2008); escholarship.org/uc/item/1t41z1jz. English translation from Herbert Eugene Bolton, "Father Escobar's Relation of the Oñate Expedition to California," www.archive.org/details/fatherescobarsreooboltrich.
26. Omaetxebarria 2001, 181.
27. "Autos Drawn Up as a Result of the Rebellion of the Christian Indians," Santa Fe, August 9, 1680, in Hackett 1942, 8: 3.
28. "To the Governor and Captain General," La Salineta, October 3, 1680, in Twitchell 1914, 2: 46.
29. "Letter of the Governor and Captain-General, Don Antonio de Otermin, from New Mexico," April 8, 1680, www.pbs.org/weta/thewest/resources/archives/one/pueblo.htm.
30. Mission location without a priest.
31. Omaetxebarria, op. cit., 184.
32. *The Handbook of Texas Online*, www.tshaonline.org/handbook.
33. Bancroft 1884, 1: 284.
34. "Auto de don Antonio Otermin, 25 de agosto de 1680," in Twitchell, op. cit., 16–17.
35. "Auto de don Antonio Otermin, 6 de septiembre de 1680," ibid., 20.
36. Hackett, op. cit., 245–49.
37. "March of the Army from El Paso to La Isleta," November 5–December 8, 1681, in Hackett, op. cit., 9: 205.
38. "To the Governor and Captain General," in Twitchell, op. cit., 44.
39. Chapman 1921, 195.
40. For more information on the Basque origin of the name of Arizona, see the website of Tumacácori National Historical Park (www.nps.gov/tuma/historyculture/arizona-planchas-de-plata.htm) and Douglass, "On the Naming of Arizona," *Names* 27, no. 4 (December 1979).
41. The northern part of what was then called Pimería Alta corresponds to today's state of Arizona, and the southern part to Sonora in Mexico. Its borders were the Gila River to the north, the San Pedro to the east, the Altar to the south, and the Gulf of California and the Colorado to the

west.

42. "Informe de Juan Bautista de Anza al arzobispo virrey Juan Antonio Vizarrón: Pimería Alta, 25 de junio de 1737," AGI, Sevilla, Guadalajara, leg. 88, f. 442v.

43. Agustín de Vildósola was born on August 28, 1700, in Arenaza (Bizkaia). In 1741, he founded the presidio of San Pedro de la Conquista del Pitic, and he was governor of Sonora and Sinaloa between 1741 and 1750.

44. "Representación del padre Luis Pindi a Matías Goñi sobre los graves daños que los indios padecen con los vecinos de su feligresía," Aconchi, October 20, 1709, in Mirafuentes Galván 1993, 1: 157–71; www.simposio.uson.mx/memorias/PDF%20AHD/memo%20XVI-1/8%20Agustin%20Ascuhul.pdf.

45. Among the Basques who fought the Apaches, another Gipuzkoan should be mentioned, José Urrutia. The son of Juan Urrutia Excurra and Juana Ibizi Zelaia, he emigrated to the Americas along with his brother Toribio. In 1691, not yet fifteen years old, he took part in Terán de los Ríos's expedition to Texas. In winter 1693, while the expedition was in flight from the Texas Indians, Urrutia suffered an accident and had to stay with friendly Indians, the Kahonatinos, Tohos, and Xarames. He learned their languages and lived according to their customs for seven years, and the natives came to respect him to such an extent that he was named a "great captain," assembling all the Indian nations that were enemies of the Apaches under his command, "sometimes ten thousand or twelve thousand Indians, and other times more," according to his later account (Bolton 1912, 79). Years later, in 1733, he was named captain of the presidio of San Antonio de Béxar due to his long experience with the Indians, in which post he sought to forge an alliance with his old friends with the aim of conducting a campaign that could defeat the Apaches.

46. Borrero Silva 2007, americanistas.es/biblo/textos.

47. A famous religious site in the Basque Country.

48. Arricivita 1792, 339.

49. Garate 2003, 115.

50. Some months before, on passing the promontory known as El Morro, in New Mexico, Elizacoechea had left an inscription engraved in the stone, as Juan de Oñate had done previously: "On the 28th day of September in the year 1737, the most illustrious lord Dr. Don Martín Elizacoechea, bishop of Durango, arrived here, and on the 29th he went on to Zuni." His secretary also wanted to leave a record of his passage: "On the 29th day of September in the year 1737, the graduate [*bachiller*] Don Juan Ignacio de Arrasain arrived here."

51. When George Bush, the former president of the United States,

speaking with Spanish Prime Minister José María Aznar, called him, "My friend Ansar," was he perhaps confusing Aznar's name with Anza's? In effect, his pronunciation was similar to the American pronunciation of "Anza," with the stress on the first syllable and without the final *r*.

52. Gabriel Antonio Vildósola (Elexabeitia, Bizkaia, 1722–78) was named captain of the Fronteras presidio in 1754 for his services during the Pima rebellion. He held that post until 1776, when due to his poor health, he was permitted to return to his native region together with his wife Josefa Gregoria Anza and his two daughters. Both spouses died in the Basque Country, he in 1778 and she in 1800.
53. San Ignacio de Cuquiárachi, September 9, 1754, AGI, Guadalajara 419, 3m–10, 13–14. *Mission 2000 Database*, www.nps.gov/applications/tuma/Detail.cfm?Personal_ID=1219. English translation from www.nps.gov/tuma/historyculture/gabriel-antonio-de-vildosola.htm.
54. The mission of San Pedro y San Pablo de Tubutama was founded by Father Kino at the end of the seventeenth century and was the first fortified settlement established in Pimería Alta. An image of the Virgin of Aránzazu can still be seen in the local church, evidence of the influence Basques had there.
55. *Mission 2000 Database*, home.nps.gov/applications/tuma/Results.cfm.
56. "Diario de Bernardo Urrea," AGI, Guadalajara 419, 3M–20. *Mission 2000 Database*, www.nps.gov/applications/tuma/Detail.cfm?Personal_ID=471.
57. Jose Díaz del Carpio, a native of Gamarra Mayor, a locality near Vitoria-Gasteiz, Araba, had just been named captain of the presidio of Terrenate when the Pima rebellion took place.
58. *Gente de razón*, a name the Spaniards gave to themselves in their New World colonies.
59. Salmón 1988, 70.
60. McCarty 1976, 72–79; www.southwest.library.arizona.edu/desertdoc/welcome.html.
61. Actually in the province of Gipuzkoa.
62. Bringas y Encinas 1819, 35.
63. *Engelhardt* 1899, 40.
64. From Nahuatl *pinolli*, cornmeal.
65. A type of porridge prepared by boiling cornmeal in water.
66. Arricivita 1792, 406–9.
67. *Noticia de la expedición militar contra los rebeldes Seris y Pimas del Cerro Prieto, Sonora, 1767–1771, ed. Mirafuentes and Máynez 1999.*
68. Elizondo became a member of the Real Sociedad Bascongada de Amigos del País (Royal Basque Society of Friends of the Country) in 1773.

69. As his surname indicates, Bucareli y Ursúa was of Basque origin on his mother's side. He was the grandson of Pedro de Ursúa y Arizmendi and a sponsoring member of the Real Sociedad Bascongada de Amigos del País. Of the society's 1,181 members in 1793, 496 lived in the New World, 378 scattered among various Spanish provinces, and only 211 in the Basque Country. The institution "found a clear positive response among émigré Basques. This in itself constitutes eloquent testimony to the persistence of ethnic loyalties in the Basque diaspora" (Douglass and Bilbao 1986, 146).
70. Archivo General de la Nación, México, fol. 263, vol. 47, Provincias Internas. McCarty, op. cit., 4–7; www.library.arizona.edu/exhibits/desertdoc/index.html.
71. "Diario de Anza: Expedición exploratoria, 1774," www.anza.uoregon.edu.
72. The Quechan or Kwtsaan Indians, known as Yumas in English, live on the Fort Yuma Indian Reservation, spanning the Arizona-California border along the lower course of the Colorado River. The relations they maintained with Juan Bautista Anza and his group in the winter of 1774 were their first significant contact with individuals of European origin.
73. "Diario de Garcés de 1774," anza.uoregon.edu.
74. Bolton 1921, 270.
75. Juan José de Echeveste y Arrieta was a native of Donostia and, like Viceroy Bucareli y Ursúa, a member of the Real Sociedad Bascongada de Amigos del País. He was a capable administrator of the tobacco monopoly and an active member of New Spain's Basque community, serving from 1774 to 1775 as director of the Aránzazu confraternity and the Colegio de las Vizcaínas, a school and residence for orphan girls and widows, preferably of Basque origin.
76. Street 2004, 16.
77. Engelhardt 1927, 82.
78. "Diario de Anza: Expedición colonizadora, 1775–1776," anza.uoregon.edu.
79. Pedro Antonio Arriquibar (Zeanuri, Bizkaia, 1745 – Tucson, 1820) arrived in Mexico in 1770 together with forty-four other Franciscan friars. In 1775, he was transferred to Tumacácori, and he spent the next forty-five years in Pimería. Starting in 1796, having obtained dispensation from his vow of poverty, he served as chaplain of the Tucson presidio. His will is one of the oldest documents of this kind that has survived to our days. In it, the friar expresses his desire to be buried in the church, at the altar steps, with a solemn requiem mass, and that his body be carried in procession through the plaza, with the honors due him as chaplain, so that upon seeing it, people would pray for his soul. He goes on to name as his legal heir Teodoro Ramírez, his godson,

to whom he leaves everything he has accumulated during his years as chaplain, except for two hundred pesos reserved for the redemption of captives and for Jerusalem. The inventory of his goods has been published by Stoner and Dobyns (1959, 71–79). As a missionary, Arriquibar had the reputation of a fairly negligent friar, but as chaplain, he became one of the wealthiest residents of the Tucson presidio.

80. The Moraga family's website mentions their ancestors' Basque origin ("they came from the high Basque country in northern Spain," parentseyes.arizona.edu/moraga/moraga.html).

81. One of the members of the expedition was Domingo Albizu, who appears in some documents as Domingo Alviso. In the Mission 2000 database, in the field for "Race or Tribe," he is considered "Vizcaíno" ("Bizkaian"). He was thirty-nine years old and was a soldier at the San Miguel de Horcasitas presidio when he was recruited to take part in the expedition to San Francisco, along with his four children, aged between three and ten. He died on March 11, 1777, shortly after arriving in San Francisco. The town of Alviso in California owes its name to his son Ignacio.

Juan Antonio Amézquita was another pioneer who formed part of Anza's group, accompanied by his wife and his five children (www.sfgenealogy.com/spanish/anzaexp.htm).

82. Chapman 1916, 461–66. For the full list, see www.archive.org/stream/foundingspanishoochapgoog#page/n514/mode/2up.

83. "Diario extendido de Font," October 22, 1775, anza.uoregon.edu.

84. "Diario extendido de Font," March 11, 1776.

85. Fr. Pedro Font called it the Sierra Nevada, the "snow-covered mountain range," on his map, giving it the name by which it continues to be known.

86. "Carta de Fray Luis Jayme a Fray Rafael Verger, Padre Guardián del colegio de San Fernando, 17 de octubre de 1772," in Beebe and Senkewicz 2001, 155–61.

87. Domaikia, Araba, 1715 – Santa Clara, Kalifornia, 1785

88. Chapman 1921, 313.

89. Ibid., 274.

90. From Nahuatl *mizquitl*, a New World tree in the Mimosaceae family.

91. The letter was translated into English from the original in two folios, folder 40, box 202, Civezza Collection, Biblioteca Antonianum, Rome, Italy, and published in Kieran McCarty, *Desert Documentary* (Arizona Historical Society, 1976), 35–39.

92. Arricivita 1792, 550.

93. Ibid., 552.

94. Ibid., 553.

95. Chapman 1921, 341.

Chapter 4. Exploration of the Pacific Northwest from San Blas to Alaska, 1775–1794

1. Many of the officers, engineers, and outfitters who worked at the San Blas de Nayarit naval base were Basques. According to Douglass and Bilbao, they made up the most important and most numerous ethnic group in San Blas. The region's first administrator was Juan de Urrengoechea y Arrinda. Pedro de Yzaguirre, chief outfitter between 1767 and 1777, was the one who supervised the construction of the schooner *Sonora* and the frigates *Santiago* and *San José*. Francisco Segurola subsequently occupied the same post. Later on, between 1790 and 1792, the position was held by Manuel de Basterrechea, who built four ships: the *Valdés*, *Activo*, *Sutil*, and *Mexicana* (Douglass and Bilbao 1986, 232–36).
2. Sierra, Baker, and Wagner 1930, 204.
3. Heceta himself wrote his name in different ways: Heceta, Heçeta, Ezeta, Eceta . . . We have chosen Heceta here because it is the spelling that has endured in various place names: Heceta Island in Alaska and Heceta Head and the Heceta Head Lighthouse on the Oregon coast.
4. Blanca Carlier 1996, 135–40.
5. Cutter 1961, 115. For Bodega y Quadra's genealogy see www.euskalnet.net/laviana/gen_bascas/bodega.htm.
6. The name "Golden Gate" first appeared on John C. Fremont's 1848 map of Oregon and California.
7. Santa María, "Diario de lo acaecido en el nuevo descubrimiento del Puerto de San Francisco," ed. John Galvin, 1971.
8. familysearch.org.
9. "Copia del Diario de navegación que hizo el teniente de fragata Don Juan Manuel de Ayala en el paquebot 'San Carlos', alias 'el Toisón de Oro', desde el Puerto de San Blas al presidio de Monterrey y descubierta del puerto de San Francisco en 1775," AGI, ESTADO, 38A, N.4. pares.mcu.es/ParesBusquedas/servlets/Control_servlet?accion=2&txt_id_fondo=1928215.
10. "Carta del virrey Bucareli a Julián de Arriaga, 1775," AGI, Estado, leg. 20. Fuster 1998, 212.
11. "Copia del Diario de navegación que hizo el Teniente de navío Don Bruno de Hezeta en la fragata Santiago," AGI, ESTADO, 38A, N.11.
12. Rodríguez-Sala 2006.
13. "Fray Benito de la Sierra's account of the Hezeta expedition to the Northwest coast in 1775," in Sierra, Baker, and Wagner 1930, 221.
14. "Diario de Antonio Maurelle en goleta *La Sonora*," AGI, ESTADO, 38A, N.5.
15. Now Point Grenville.

16. Hezeta, op. cit.
17. Cutter 1961, 114.
18. "Carta de Bruno de Hezeta al rey, Madrid, 15 de diciembre de 1789," AGI, Guadalajara 500.
19. www.historylink.org.
20. Hezeta, op. cit.
21. "Diario de Francisco Antonio Maurelle [sic] en goleta 'La Sonora'," AGI, ESTADO, 38A, N.5.
22. They were probably Sitkas from the Tlingit nation.
23. Alfred Hitchcock's famous film *The Birds* takes place in Bodega.
24. Bodega y Quadra to the king, Havana, 1784, AAB. Archer 1991, 6.
25. "Llegada a San Blas de la fragata *Santiago* y la goleta *La Sonora*," AGI, ESTADO, 20, N.22.
26. Tovell 2008.
27. Now Prince of Wales Bay in Alaska.
28. Goicoetxea Marcaida 1992. www.euskomedia.org/PDFAnlt/congresos/11/11523527.pdf.
29. Both diaries can be read in full in the Archivo General de Indias database.
30. Ignacio de Arteaga, "Diario navegación de la fragata 'Nuestra Señora del Rosario'," AGI, ESTADO, 38A, N.13, 141.
31. Juan Bautista de Aguirre, "Diario de navegación de 'Nuestra Señora de los Remedios'," AGI, ESTADO, 38B, N.18.
32. Ibid., 119–23.
33. Ibid., 101.
34. "An Account of the Voyage Made by the Frigates 'Princesa' and 'Favorita' in the Year 1799 from San Blas to Northern Alaska," *Catholic Historical Review* 4, no. 2 (1918): 222–29. www.jstor.org/stable/25011566.
35. A kind of seaweed that grows in shallow ocean waters.
36. Ignacio de Arteaga, op. cit., 230.
37. Ibid., 250–51.
38. Ibid., 250.
39. Now Elizabeth Island.
40. Now Mount Iliamna.
41. Ignacio de Arteaga, op. cit., 298–99.
42. Arteaga to Gálvez, August 5, 1779, AGI, México I. Tovell, op. cit., 102.
43. Alessandro Malaspina (1754–1810) was a nobleman of Italian origin. He circumnavigated the world in the king of Spain's service between 1786 and 1788. Subsequently, between 1789 and 1794, he led a scientific expedition in the Pacific Ocean, drawing maps from Cape Horn to the Gulf of Alaska.
44. The *Nuestra Señora de Aránzazu*, built in Cavite (Philippines), was

initially a 205-ton packet boat. It began to be used in San Blas in 1781, and it was overhauled in 1788, when seven feet were added to its prow and it was equipped as a frigate. Between 1748 and 1792 it made more than thirty voyages to supply the California missions and presidios.

45. There is a genus of plants named Echeveria, belonging to the Crassulaceae family and containing more than 393 species. Originating in the region between Mexico and northwestern South America, it was named in honor of the botanical artist Atanasio Echeverría.

46. Engstrand 2005, 4–21.

47. A gift-giving ceremony among the natives of the Pacific Northwest.

48. Gabriel de Aristazabal, of Basque origin but born in Madrid in 1743, was a famous commander in his day. On Captain Vancouver's maps, the Basque surname takes on an English flavor: "Aristizable."

49. Tovell, op. cit., 223.

50. Lavastida to Eliza, March 11, 1795, AGN, Marina 73, f. 53–54. Tovell, op. cit., 225.

51. Bernabeu 1990, 25.

52. Revillagigedo to Mourelle, in Tovell, op. cit., 230.

53. Juan Francisco de la Bodega y Quadra, "Viaje a la Costa Noroeste," in Bernabeu 1990, 166.

54. Ibid.

55. Vancouver 1798, 1: 385.

56. See Atanasio Echeverría's drawing on p. 223.

57. Vancouver, op. cit., 397.

58. Vancouver 1798, 2: 9–10.

59. Ibid., 34.

60. Felipe Antonio de Goicoechea (Basque Mexican) was born in Cosalá, in the state of Sinaloa (Mexico), in 1747. He was the commander of the Santa Bárbara presidio for eighteen years. On one occasion, he described himself as exiled in those "infinite lands" of Alta California, a sentiment undoubtedly shared by many of the soldiers and friars who served there. In 1805, he was named governor of Baja California, a post he held until his death in Loreto in 1814. In Bancroft's opinion, he was one of the most competent presidio commanders of his time (Lamadrid 1963, 386).

61. Vancouver 1798, 2: 452.

62. Ibid., 455.

63. Ibid., 459.

64. Ibid., 464.

65. Bodega to the king of Spain, May 25, 1793, in Tovell, op. cit., 323.

66. Fuster, op. cit., 476.

67. By 1825, the officers of the Hudson Bay Company were calling it Vancouver's Island, and by the end of the century, it had lost the

possessive marker.

Chapter 5. Franciscan Missions in Alta California

1. Bolton 1917.
2. After getting to know the Yumas of Colorado, Father Font, who accompanied Anza on his colonizing expedition of 1775–76, asked himself a question that is a good reflection of the friars' biases: "I might inquire what sin was committed by these Indians and their ancestors that they should grow up in those remote lands of the north with such infelicity and unhappiness, in such nakedness and misery, and above all with such blind ignorance of everything that they do not even know the transitory conveniences of the earth in order to obtain them; nor much less, as it appeared to me from what I was able to learn from them, do they have any knowledge of the existence of God, but live like beasts, without making use of reason or discourse, and being distinguished from beasts only by possessing the bodily or human form, but not by their deeds" (Bolton 1931, 110–11).
3. "Carta de Lasuén a Fray José Gasol, Santa Clara, 21-07-1802," in Lasuén 1965, 2: 284.
4. "Carta de Lasuén al virrey, 25-4-1797," ibid., 17.
5. Diego de Borica, a governor of California and a native of Vitoria, summarized the causes of the fall in California's indigenous population in these words: "the French disease with which they are infected, the active life to which they are obligated in the missions, and the little sustenance they are given due to the scarcity of seed, along with the slovenliness in which they live crowded together, are the reason that these unhappy people are coming to an end" (Monterrey, July 13, 1795; Martínez Salazar 1992, 213).
6. Bolton 1917, 61.
7. Geiger 1969, x.
8. Solaguren 2007, 2: 363.
9. "Carta de Lasuén a Fray Miguel Lull, San Buenaventura, 28-2-1798," in Lasuén 1965, 2: 71.
10. Landaeta 1949, 26.
11. Ibid., 49.
12. Ibid., 44.
13. Bancroft 1885 (Works XIX), 115–16.
14. Geiger 1969, 258–59.
15. Langsdorff 1927, 44–45.
16. Ibid., 121.
17. Solaguren 2007, 2: 226–28.
18. Bancroft 1886 (Works XX), 659.

19. Beebe and Senkewicz 2006, 207.
20. Robinson 1891, 61.
21. Geiger 1969, xi.
22. Hittell, op. cit., 444.
23. Street, op. cit., 30.
24. Engelhardt 1922, 39.
25. Omaechevarria 1959, 331.
26. "Carta de Pablo de Mugártegui a su hermano Pedro Valentín, Monterrey, julio de 1775," in Omaechevarria 1959, 149–55.
27. A dry measure, roughly an eighth of a bushel.
28. The historian Finbar Kenneally, who translated and published all Lasuén's writings, summarizes the importance Arantzazu has had for Basques in these words: "What the shrine of Guadalupe is to the devout Mexican, and what Beaupré is to the Catholics of Quebec, Aránzazu is to the Basques of Spain. It is their sacred city, the home of a religious shrine that, century after century, has symbolized their faith, their culture, and their uniqueness among the people of Spain" (Lasuén 1965, 1: xvi).
29. Lamadrid 1963, 1: 39.
30. Ibid., 47.
31. Lasuén 1965, 1: 16.
32. Ibid., 15.
33. Lamadrid 1963, 1: 90–91.
34. Lasuén 1965, 1: 22.
35. Lasuén 1965, 1: 78.
36. Chapman 1921, 367.
37. "Carta de Lasuén a Fray Francisco Pangua, San Gabriel, 23-04-1774," in Lasuén 1965, 1: 38.
38. "*Similitudo est causa amoris*" ("Like attracts like.") "Carta de Lasuén a Fray Francisco Pangua, San Gabriel, 1774-04-23," ibid., 40–41.
39. Ibid., 39.
40. A herbaceous plant that grows in marshy soil or along the shores of lakes and ponds; the name comes from Nahuatl.
41. Lasuén 1965, 1: 40.
42. "Carta de Lasuén a la junta del Colegio de San Fernando, San Gabriel, 1774-5-2," ibid., 42.
43. Ibid., 42–43.
44. Ibid., 38.
45. "Carta de Lasuén al Padre guardián del Colegio de San Fernando, fray Francisco Pangua, 29-07-1774," ibid., 43.
46. "Carta de Lasuén al gobernador Borica, Santa Barbara, 03-12-1779," ibid., 2: 61.
47. "Carta de Lasuén a Fray Francisco Pangua, San Diego, 13-09-1776,"

ibid., 1: 67.
48. “Carta de Lasuén a Fray Francisco Pangua, presidio de Monterrey, 17-08-1775,” ibid., 57.
49. From Nahuatl *metlatl*, a stone for grinding grain.
50. “Carta de Lasuén a Fray Juan Prestamero, San Diego, 28-01-1776,” ibid., 60.
51. Ibid., 46.
52. Ibid., 46.
53. The excommunication, an extremely severe punishment in those days, was quickly resolved, but Rivera would die a few years later without any spiritual assistance, in the 1781 rebellion of the Colorado River Yumas.
54. Geiger 1969, 139.
55. “Carta de Lasuén a Fray Francisco Pangua, misión San Diego, 6-12-1780,” in Lasuén 1965, 1: 77–78.
56. www.sandiegohistory.org/journal/71fall/br-letter.htm.
57. “Carta de Lasuén a José de Jesús Vélez, O.F.M., San Diego, 03-10-1782,” in Lasuén 1965, 1: 87.
58. Bancroft 1885 (Works XIX), 9 and 490.
59. “Carta de Lasuén al Padre Guardián de San Fernando Fr. Francisco Pangua, 8-6-1782,” in Lamadrid 1963, 1: 275–77.
60. Lasuén 1965, 1: 83.
61. Engelhardt 1930, 2: 424.
62. Bancroft 1885 (Works XIX), 8–9.
63. Lasuén 1965, 1: 300.
64. Diego de Borica was baptized on November 12, 1742, in the church of San Vicente in Vitoria. His father was Cosme de Borica, and his mother was María Bentura de Retegui. His paternal grandparents were Prudencio de Borica, from Abando, and María Antonia de Othero, from Bilbao; his maternal grandparents were Miguel Antonio de Retegui, from Oiartzun, and Ursola de Arzac, from Vitoria (www.snae.org).
65. Jose María Romero, “Memorias: San Juan Capistrano, California,” ms., 1877, Bancroft Library, Berkeley, California. content.cdlib.org/ark:/13030/hb6z09p30p/?order=21&brand=calisphere.
66. Bancroft 1884 (Works XVIII), 727.
67. I. B. Richman, *California under Spain and Mexico*, 169. Martínez Salazar 1992, 98.
68. Hittell, op. cit., 561.
69. If we accept the testimony of the chronicler Fray Juan de Torquemada, Santa Bárbara owes its name to the seaman Sebastián Vizcaíno. When he was sailing among the islands in the channel in 1602, Vizcaíno suffered a terrible storm that lasted from the afternoon of December 3 until nightfall the following day. The 4th was Saint Barbara’s feast day, and following the custom of the times, Vizcaíno named the location for

the saint of the day (Juan de Torquemada 1964, 714).
70. A dry measure, in the neighborhood of one and a half bushels.
71. Geiger 1969, 140.
72. "Carta de Lasuén a Borica, 15-06-1795," in Lasuén 1965, 1: 339.
73. Ibid., 339.
74. Ibid., 340.
75. Ibid., 340.
76. "Carta de Lasuén a Borica, San Buenaventura, 14-04-1798," ibid., 2: 77.
77. "Carta de Borica a Lasuén, 22-09-1796," in Lamadrid 1963, 2: 200.
78. Ibid., 564.
79. Ibid., 200.
80. Ibid., 203–4.
81. "Carta de Lasuén a Fray Antonio Nogueyra, San Carlos, 02-11-1796," ibid., 404.
82. Bancroft 1884 (Works XVIII), 1: 726.
83. Hittell, op. cit., 590.
84. Bancroft 1884 (Works XVIII), 1: 589.
85. Lasuén 1965, 2: 202.
86. Ibid., 203.
87. Ibid., 204.
88. Ibid., 202.
89. Ibid., 199.
90. Lamadrid 1963, 2: 338.
91. "Carta de Lasuén a Don Pedro Fages, San Carlos, 21-08-1787," in Lasuén 1965, 1: 151.
92. Solaguren 2007, 2: 626.
93. "Carta de José Joaquín de Arrillaga a Fray Martín de Landaeta, Loreto, 23-03-1801," in Landaeta 1949, 31–32.
94. Lasuén 1965, 1: vii.
95. Ibid., xxxiii.
96. Chapman 1921, 378.
97. Later, Malaspina would write these words about Lasuén: "his activity for our natural-history collections was such, his information and reflections on the prosperity of these missions were so prolix and detailed, and finally, his hospitality was so caring, natural, and religiously abundant at whatever hour we visited him at the mission, whether the officers or the members of the other subaltern classes, that they could be but poorly described by any other pen than one of perpetual acknowledgment and appreciation" (Malaspina 1990, 194).
98. Ibid., 380–81.
99. Ibid., 141.
100. "Carta de Lasuén a Fray Tomás Pangua, San Juan Capistrano,

27-12-1793," in Lasuén 1965, 1: 298.
101. Ibid., 298.
102. Chapman 1921, 381–82.
103. Bancroft 1885 (Works XIX), 8.

Chapter 6. Other Protagonists of Alta California History

1. A measurement of weight, approximately a hundred pounds.
2. Archivo Municipal de Hernani, C. S. III-4, 194–96. Garmendia Larrañaga and Peña Santiago 2007, 10; www.euskomedia.org/PDFAnlt/jgl/07001110.pdf.
3. mendezmende.org.
4. Between 1776 and 1804, the two Californias were governed as a single province. The governor resided in Monterrey, in Alta California, and the vice governor in Loreto, in Baja California. The vice governor in Loreto was under the authority of the governor in Monterrey, but due to distance and the problems of communication, he had *de facto* executive power.
5. Gordon Chappell, "Historic California Posts: Castillo de San Joaquin," California State Military Museum, www.militarymuseum.org/CastilloSanJoaquin.html.
6. Arrillaga, ed. John Robinson, 1969, 15.
7. A stick with one end sharpened and hardened in the fire, used as a projectile weapon.
8. Gov. Pedro Fages had explored the Colorado's lower reaches in 1785.
9. "Diario de los reconocimientos verificados por el Capitán de Loreto de orden superior en la Frontera: 1796," Bancroft Library, University of California at Berkeley, BANC MSS M-M-1831.
10. Bancroft 1884 (Works XV), 735.
11. We follow Bancroft's narrative here. Bancroft 1885 (Works XIX), vol. 2, chap. 4.
12. Langsdorff 1927, 38.
13. Bancroft 1885 (Works XIX), 2: 158–60.
14. Engelhardt 1930, 3: 8.
15. Dorotea Valdez, "Reminiscences, Monterrey, Calif.," ms., 1874, Calisphere, University of California, content.cdlib.org/search?-facet=type-tab&relation=calisphere.universityofcalifornia.edu&-style=cui&keyword=arrillaga&x=31&y=5, frame 0530–0531. English translation from cdn.calisphere.org/data/13030/1j/hb3s20071j/files/hb3s20071j-FID26.jp.
16. Juan Bautista Alvarado, "Historia de California, 1876," vol. 1, 1769–1824, Calisphere, content.cdlib.org/ark:/13030/hb1z09n-8qz/?order=49&brand=calisphere, frame 46–47.

17. Jose María Romero, "Memorias, San Juan Capistrano, Calif.," ms., 1877, Calisphere, content.cdlib.org/ark:/13030/hb6z09p-30p/?order=21&brand=calisphere, frame 0102, lin. 17.
18. Jose Brigido Rodríguez, "Recuerdos historicos sobre California," ms., 1877, Calisphere, content.cdlib.org/ark:/13030/hb7j49p3b-j/?query=Rodríguez%20Jose%20Brigido&brand=calisphere, frame 0081–0082.
19. Jose de Jesus Vallejo, "Reminiscencias historicas de California, San Jose, Calif.," ms., June 22, 1875, Calisphere: content.cdlib.org/ark:/13030/hb1489n8zb/?query=Vallejo%20Jose%20de%20Jesus&brand=calisphere, frame 0070.
20. Bancroft 1885 (Works XIX), 206.
21. Engelhardt 1897, 371.
22. The examination of Andrés Quintana's body is considered the first autopsy performed in California.
23. missions.huntington.org/DeathData.aspx?ID=46048.
24. Omaetxebarria 2001, 290.
25. Putnam and Kroeber 1908–10, vol. 8, no. 1, 1–27; www.archive.org/stream/universityofcal08univuoft#page/n7/mode/2up.
26. Fray Narciso Durán gave news of the murder to Fray Norberto de Santiago in a letter written on October 2, 1814: "Those of the house murdered him in so barbarous a manner that I doubt if such cruelty has ever been resorted to in the most barbarous nations for they tortured him *in pudendis* and suffocated him at the same time with the cloths he used in administering extreme unction" (Geiger 1969, 205).
27. Mora-Torres 2005, 78–95.
28. Engelhardt 1930, 3: 13.
29. Ibid., 14–15.
30. Ibid., 16.
31. The account is based on Juan Bautista Alvarado's testimony; Hittell 1898, 633–40.
32. Antonio María Osio, "Historia de la California, 1815–1848," ms., Calisphere, content.cdlib.org/ark:/13030/hb8b-69p3q7/?order=6&brand=calisphere, frame 0124.
33. mendezmende.org.
34. Bancroft 1885 (Works XIX), 2: 471–72.
35. Juan José Ruiz de Apodaca y Eliza (Cádiz, 1754 – Madrid, 1835), viceroy of New Spain between 1816 and 1820. His father was an Araban from Ondategi, and his mother was born in Cádiz but of Basque origin.
36. "Carta de Pablo Vicente Sola a Don Juan Ruiz de Apodaca, Monterrey, 12-12-1818," in Beebe and Senkewicz 2001, 298–304.
37. Jose María Romero, "Memorias, San Juan Capistrano, Calif.," ms., December 1877, Calisphere, content.cdlib.org/ark:/13030/

hb6z09p30p/?order=21&brand=calisphere, frame 0103.

38. Bancroft 1885 (Works XIX), 2: 426.
39. Mariano Guadalupe Vallejo (1807–90) was a *californio* politician, military man, and estate owner. Juan Bautista Alvarado (1809–82) served as governor of Alta California between 1836 and 1837 and again between 1838 and 1842.
40. Bancroft 1885 (Works XIX), 2: 428–29.
41. Sarria, Etxebarria, and Apraiz 2009; www.euskalkultura.com.
42. Putnam and Kroeber, 1908–19.
43. Ibid.
44. He occupied the post again from 1823 to 1830.
45. San Carlos, July 2, 1813, in Engelhardt 1930, 3: 4–5.
46. Beebe and Senkewicz 1996, 275–76.
47. Antonio María Osio, op. cit., frame [illegible].
48. The text's author was Fray Antonio Ripoll of Santa Bárbara. Ripoll considered the soldiers responsible for the revolt, and the friars accused them of not having taken into consideration the pleas they made to them in favor of the Indians.
49. The friar at Santa Inés was Francisco Xavier de la Concepción Uría, a native of Aizarna (Gipuzkoa). Born in 1770, he would have been fifty-four years old when the Chumash revolt occurred. Antonio María Osio, in his memoir *Historia de la California* (History of California), narrates Uría's curious behavior at Santa Inés: "It has been said that Sunday was the appointed day to raise the warcry, but they started earlier at the Santa Inés mission, around two o'clock in the afternoon on Saturday, at which time Fr. Fray Francisco Javier Uría was taking his siesta, despite knowing his neophytes' intentions. If he had been asleep, they would have murdered him, but a little Indian page who loved him a great deal ran to remind him, in order to warn him that they were going to kill him now and that he should get up quickly. Upon hearing that interesting news, the Father jumped out of bed to go and look out the window, from which he saw a multitude of Indians heading toward the door of his house, already painted and armed with darts. This reverend father was an excellent religious, and so that people would not believe in his goodness, he had made it a habit to say obscene words. He was a Bizkaian and had an entirely Bizkaian soul, a shotgun like the ones that are forged in Eibar, and in that moment of crisis, he made his resolution. He spoke to a Camillian lay brother who was with him by chance and quickly armed him with a rifle, and in order to set a good example for his companion to imitate, he put a bullet into the first rebel who set foot on the threshold of the door. When those who were following him saw the effects of the Bizkaian weapon , they stopped briefly, and the Father did not waste this short time to be ready

with a second shot, which he put to good use on one of those who were best painted, who threw a dart at him and who fell dead in the same moment that he was struck by the bullet. The lay brother already had three darts in him and was spitting up blood when the Father, with a keen eye that saw everything, came quickly to help him. He pulled out of his chest two darts that were causing him great suffering and then wrapped several pieces of soft leather around his neck, which saved his life, considering the many darts that hit him there, while his accurate aim became deadly and his arms, quick to load and fire, moved more swiftly than they usually did when he was receiving alms, so that the Indians fell back. He went out into the corridor, where he observed that one of them, also armed with a rifle, was loading it behind a pillar. He took shelter behind another, and the two were laying in wait for each other, but finally the Indian was less cautious and stuck his left elbow out from behind the pillar, and he received right in that spot a bullet that shattered the bone as far as the shoulder" (Antonio María Osio, "Historia de la California, 1815–48," ms. 61–64, Calisphere, content.cdlib.org/ark:/13030/hb8b69p3q7/?order=6&brand=calisphere, frame 0181–0184).

50. Beebe and Senkewicz 1996, 277–83.
51. "Carta de Fray Vicente Francisco Sarria a Fray Narciso Duran, 23-04-1825," Archivo de Santa Barbara. Engelhardt 1930, 3: 218.
52. "Carta de Fray Fermín Lasuén al padre guardián Fray Tomás de Pangua, 28-05-1794," Archivo de Santa Barbara. Lasuén 1965, 1: 305.
53. Sarría, *Descripción de la operación cesárea*, trans. Sherburne F. Cook, 1937, 1: 107–9; 2: 187–89; and 3: 248–50.
54. Robinson 1846, 90.
55. Beebe and Senkewicz 2006, 226.
56. Engelhardt 1897, 385.
57. Libro de Entierros de San Antonio, in Bancroft 1886 (Works XX), 3: 689–90.
58. Solaguren 2007, 2: 834–37.
59. Bancroft 1886 (Works XIX), 2: 120.
60. "Zalvidea's Diary," Bancroft Library, Berkeley, BANC MSS C-B oversize box 20. English translation from www.gutenberg.org/files/36387/36387-h/36387-h.htm.
61. The Franciscan habit in the period of the Alta California missions was grey.
62. Geiger 1969, 267.
63. In the historian Maynard Geiger's opinion, Zalvidea was the author of the San Gabriel report. It was written by Fray Luis Gil y Taboada, in his view, but Gil had recently arrived at San Gabriel and acted as Zalvidea's assistant and secretary.

64. Geiger and Zalvidea 1955, 77–84.
65. Engelhardt 1927, 91.
66. Engelhardt 1922, 86–94.
67. Bancroft 1886 (Works XXII), *History of California*, 5: 622–23.
68. “Carta de Jose María de Zalvidea al Padre Principal Narciso Durán, San Juan Capistrano, 6-7-1831,” in Engelhardt 1922, 105.
69. “Carta de Jose María de Zalvidea al gobernador Echeandia, San Juan Capistrano, 3-12-1932,” in Engelhardt 1922, 109–10.
70. Duflot de Mofras 1844, 352–53.
71. Spanish-speaking, Catholic descendants of the early Spanish colonists in California.
72. “Carta de Jose María de Zalvidea al gobernador J. B. Alvarado, San Juan Capistrano, 21-1-1841,” in Engelhardt 1922, 130–31.
73. José Antonio Aguirre, born in Donostia-San Sebastián around 1798, left for the New World at the age of fifteen. After becoming a rich merchant in Guaymas (Mexico), he dedicated himself to trading in Alta California. He owned several ships, including one named *La Joven Guipuzcoana* (“The young woman from Gipuzkoa”), and visited California often. He maintained residences in San Diego and Santa Bárbara, and his house in Santa Bárbara was said in 1842 to be the most beautiful residence in the city. He married a daughter of wealthy landowner José Antonio Estudillo, and when she died, he married her sister as his second wife. He built a warehouse on the beach at San Diego, where he did his business. He exported hides and tallow from San Diego and imported luxury goods for the *californios*: silks, satins, and embroidered shawls. During the 1830s, he partnered with Miguel Pedrorena, who later became his brother-in-law. Aguirre quickly became the most prosperous merchant in Alta California. His house in San Diego, known as the Casa de Aguirre, is still standing in Old Town San Diego State Historic Park. The church that Aguirre had built has also been reconstructed after having been torn down and is known as the Old Adobe Chapel. It preserves many original elements, including Aguirre’s own tomb. The French naturalist Duflot de Mofras said of Aguirre that he was the richest man in the region and that almost everyone in the area had some economic relationship with him (Duflot de Mofras 1844, 370). Bancroft also mentions him in his *History of California*: “On account of his great size he was sometimes nicknamed Aguirron; of fine presence, affable in manner, and well liked by all” (Bancroft 1886 [Works XIX], 2: 688).
74. In Mofras’s words, “San Juan Capistrano est un des établissements les plus ruinés, malgré la résistance qu’opposa à sa dévastation son missionnaire le R. P. espagnol Fr. José María de Zalvidea, Biscayen [San Juan Capistrano is one of the most ruined establishments, despite the

resistance opposed to its devastation by its missionary, the Spanish Reverend Fr. Fray José María de Zalvidea, a Bizkaian]" (Duflot de Mofras 1844, 347).

75. "Carta de Jose María de Zalvidea al Padre Principal Narciso Durán, San Juan Capistrano, 13-6-1842," in Engelhardt 1922, 152–53.

76. Heizer; memory.loc.gov/cgi-bin/query/r?ammem/calbk:@field%28DOCID+@lit%28calbk007div21%29%29.

77. Bancroft 1886 (Works XXII), *History of California*, 5: 621–23.

78. Ellison and Price 1953, 109.

79. Michael C. White and Thomas Savage; lcweb2.loc.gov/cgi-bin/query/r?ammem/calbk:@field%28DOCID+@lit%28calbk080div30%29%29.

80. Hijar, Pérez, and Escobar 1988, 76, 82.

81. "Felipa Osuna: 'The Oldest Resident of Old Town in 1878,'" in Beebe and Senkewicz; www.sandiegohistory.org/journal/v55-4/v55-4osuna.pdf.

82. "Carta de Zalvidea al gobernador Echeandia, 1831," in Engelhardt 1922: 109–10.

Epilogue

1. Engelhardt 1927, 302.

Bibliography

Alzugaray Aguirre, Juan José. *Vascos universales del siglo XVI*. Madrid: Ediciones Encuentro, 1988.

Archer, Christon I. "Los viajes de Juan Francisco de la Bodega y Quadra, 1775 y 1779." Paper presented at Coloquio Internacional sobre Bodega y Quadra, Lima, 1994.

Arricivita, Juan Domingo. *Crónica seráfica y apostólica del colegio de Propaganda Fide de la Santa Cruz de Querétaro en la Nueva España*. Mexico City, 1792.

Arrillaga, José Joaquín. *Diary of His Surveys of the Frontier, 1796*. Edited by John Robinson. Los Angeles: Dawson's Book Shop, 1969.

Arteaga y Bazán, Ignacio, and Caamaño Moraleja, Jacinto. *Colección de diarios y relaciones para la historia de los viajes y descubrimientos, 7*. Madrid: CSIC-Departamento de Publicaciones, 1975.

Bancroft, Hubert Howe. *History of the North Mexican States and Texas*. Vol. I, 1531-1800, San Francisco, 1884. (Works XV).

——. *History of Arizona and New Mexico: 1530-1888*. San Francisco, 1889. (Works XVII).

——. *History of California*. Vol. I, 1542-1800. San Francisco, 1884. (Works XVIII).

——. *History of California*. Vol. II, 1801-1824. San Francisco, 1885. (Works XIX).

——. *History of California*. Vol. III, 1825-1840. San Francisco, 1886. (Works XX).

——. *History of the Northwest Coast*. Vol. I, 1543-1800. San Francisco, 1884. (Works XXVII).

Barry, J. Neilson. "Who Discovered the Columbia River" *in Oregon Historical Quarterly*, vol. 39, no. 2 (1938), 152-161. www.jstor.org/stable/20611111

Bass, Steve, and Ansolabehere, George. *Basques in Kern County: 1870 to 1940*. Kern County Basque Club, 2010.

Beebe, Rose Marie, and Senkewicz, Robert M. "The End of the 1824 Chumash Revolt in Alta California: Father Vicente Sarría's Account" *in The Americas*, vol. 53, no. 2 (1996), 273-283. www.jstor.org/stable/1007619

——. *Tensions among the Missionaries in the 1790s*. California Mission Studies Association, Santa Clara University, 1996.

——. *Lands of Promise and Despair: Chronicles of Early California: 1535-1846*. Berkeley, California: Santa Clara University, Heyday Books, 2001.

——. *Testimonios: Early California through the Eyes of Women: 1815-1848*. Berkeley, California: Heyday Books, 2006.

Bernabeu Albert, Salvador. *Juan Francisco de la Bodega y Quadra: El Descubrimiento del Fin del Mundo (1775-1792)*. Madrid: Alianza Editorial, 1990.

Blanca Carlier, José María. "Osuna y sus marinos" *in* Apuntes 2: Apuntes y documentos para una historia de Osuna, vol. 1 (1996), 135-140.

Bolton, Herbert Eugene. "The Jumano Indians in Texas, 1650-1771" *in* The Quarterly of the Texas State Historial Association, vol. XV, no. 1 (1912), 67-84. www.archive.org/details/jumanoindiansintooboltrich

——. Anza´s California Expeditions.

——. *Spanish Exploration in the Southwest: 1542-1706*. New York: C. Scribner´s Sons, 1916.

——. "The Mission as a Frontier Institution in the Spanish-American Colonies" *in* The American Historical Review, vol. XXIII, no. 1 (1917), 42-61.

——. "Father Escobar´s Relation of the Oñate Expedition to California" *in* The Catholic Historical Review, vol. V (1919), 19-41.

——. "The Iturbide Revolution in the Californias" *in The Hispanic American Historical Review*, vol. 2, no. 2 (1919), 188-242. www.jstor.org/stable/2505905

——. *The Spanish Borderlands: A Chronicle of Old Florida and the Southwest*. New Haven: Yale University Press, 1921.

——. *Rim of Christendom: A Biography of Eusebio Francisco Kino*. New York : Russell & Russell, 1960.

Borrero Silva, Mª del Valle. "El proceso colonizador en Sonora: La población civil y presidial en un ambiente de frontera" *in* Orbis incognitus, Asociación Española e Americanistas, 2007.

Bringas y Encinas, Diego Miguel. *Sermon que en las solemnes honras celebradas en obsequio de los VV. PP. Predicadores apostólicos Fr. Francisco Tomás Hermenegildo Garcés, Fr. Juan Marcelo Díaz, Fr. José Matías Moreno, Fr. Juan Antonio Barreneche: Misioneros del Colegio de propaganda fide de la Santa Cruz de Queretaro...* D. F. Villalpandoren inprenta, 1819.

Burriel, Andrés Marcos. *Noticia de la California y de su conquista temporal y espiritual*. Madrid, 1757.

Burrus, Ernest J., ed. *Baja California Travels Series,* 47. Los Angeles: Dawson´s Book Shop, 1984.

Caso, Nicole; Crouse, Marina; McMichael, Heather; and Polt, John H. R. *La "Relación" del padre Francisco Escobar de la expedición al Mar del Sur de Juan de Oñate (1604-1605).* University of California, Berkeley, Research Center for Romance Studies, 2008. escholarship.org/uc/item/1t41z1jz

Cervera Jiménez, José Antonio. "Andrés de Urdaneta (1508-1568) y la presencia española en el Pacífico durante el Siglo XVI" *in* Revista de la Sociedad Española de Historia de las Ciencias y de las Técnicas, vol. 24, no. 49, 59-88.

Chapman, Charles E. *The Founding of Spanish California, the Northwestward Expansion of New Spain, 1687-1783.* New York: Macmillan Co., 1916.

——. *A History of California: The Spanish Period.* New York: Macmillan Co., 1921.

Clavijero, Francisco Javier. *Historia de la Antigua o Baja California.* Mexico City, 1852.

Cook, Sherburne F. "Sarria's Treatise on the Cesarean Section, 1830" *in* California and Western Medicine 37 (1937).

Craddock, Jerry R.*Acoma: teoría y práctica de la guerra justa.* UC Berkeley, Research Center for Romance Studies, 2008. escholarship.org/uc/item/6cp5j0fs pagina 11

Craddock, Jerry R., and Polt, John H. R. *The Trial of the Indians of Acoma 1598-1599.* UC Berkeley, Research Center for Romance Studies, 2008. escholarship.org/uc/item/14v3j7sj

——. *Zaldívar and the Cattle of Cíbola.* UC Berkeley, Research Center for Romance Studies, 2008. escholarship.org/uc/item/6hz1x4s4

——. *Oñate's Report to the Viceroy March 2, 1599.* UC Berkeley, Research Center for Romance Studies, 2009. escholarship.org/uc/item/8s90h6b6

Crosby, Harry. *The King's Highway in Baja California.* Salt Lake City, Utah: Copley Books, 1974.

Cutter, Donald C. "California, Training Ground for Spanish Naval Heroes" *in California Historical Society Quarterly, vol.* 40, no. 2 (1961), 109-122. www.jstor.org/stable/25155386

——. "Sources of the Name California" *in* Arizona and the West: Journal of the Southwest, vol. 3, no. 3, 1961. www.jstor.org/stable/40167930

Del Barco, Miguel. *Historia natural y crónica de la Antigua California.* Edited by Miguel León-Portilla. 2d ed. Mexico City: Universidad Nacional Autónoma de México, 1988.

Del Río, Ignacio. *El régimen jesuítico de la Antigua California.* Mexico City: Universidad Nacional Autónoma de México, 2003.

Díaz del Castillo, Bernal. *Historia verdadera de la conquista de la Nueva España. Mexico City: Oficina tipográfica de la Secretaría de Fomento, 1904. (First edition, 1632).*

Díez de Salazar Fernández, L. M. *Ferrerías Guipuzcoanas: Aspectos socio-económicos, laborales y fiscales (siglos XIV-XVI).* Donostia-San Sebastián: Fundación Social Kutxa, 1997.

Dobyns, Henry F. *Spanish Colonial Tucson: A Demographic History.* Tucson, Arizona: University of Arizona Press, 1976.

Douglass, William A. "On the Naming of Arizona" *in* Names, vol. 27, no. 4 (1979).

Douglass, William A., and Bilbao, Jon. *Amerikanuak": Los Vascos en el Nuevo Mundo. Servicio Editorial Universidad del País Vasco, 1986.*

Duflot de Mofras, Eugène. *Exploration du territoire de l' Orégon, des Californies et de la Mer Vermeille, éxécutée pendant les années 1840, 1841 et 1842.* Vol. 1. Paris, 1844.

Dunne, Peter M. *Black Robes in Lower California. Berkeley, 1968. (First edition, 1952).*

Elizondo, Domingo. *Noticia de la expedición militar contra los rebeldes Seris y Pimas del Cerro Prieto, Sonora, 1767-1771. Edited by José Luis Mirafuentes and Pilar Máynez. Mexico City: Universidad Nacional Autónoma de México, 1999.*

Ellison, William H., and Price, Francis, eds. *The Life and Adventures in California of Don Agustin Janssens.* San Marino, 1953.

Engelhardt, Zephyrin. *The Franciscans in California.* Harbor Springs, Michigan: Holy Childhood Indian School, 1897.

——. *The Franciscans in Arizona.* Harbor Springs, Michigan: Holy Childhood Indian School, 1899.

——. *San Juan Capistrano Mission.* Los Angeles, California, 1922.

———. *San Fernando Rey: The Mission of the Valley.* Chicago, Illinois: Franciscan Herald Press, 1927.

———. *San Gabriel Mission and the Beginnings of Los Angeles.* San Gabriel, California: Mission San Gabriel, 1927.

———. *Missions and Missionaries of California.* Santa Barbara, California: Mission Santa Barbara, 1930.

Engstrand, Iris H. W. "Seekers of the "Northern Mystery: European Exploration of California and the Pacific" *in California History, vol.* 76, no. 2/3, Contested Eden: California before the Gold Rush (1997), 78-110. www.jstor.org/stable/25161663

———. "Perception and Perfection: Picturing the Spanish and Mexican Coastal West" *in The Western Historical Quarterly, vol.* 36, no. 1 (2005), 4-21. www.jstor.org/stable/25443099

Erlandson, Jon M., and Bartoy, Kevin. "Cabrillo, the Chumash, and Old World Diseases" *in Journal of California and Great Basin Anthropology,* vol. 17, no. 2 (1995), 153-173. escholarship.org/uc/item/3k52f936

Espinosa, J. Manuel. The Pueblo Indian Revolt of 1696 and the Franciscan Missions in New Mexico: Letters of the Missionaries and Related Documents. Norman and London: University of Oklahoma Press, 1991.

Etulain, Richard W., and Echeverria, Jeronima, eds. Portraits of Basques in the New World. Reno & Las Vegas: University of Nevada Press, 1999.

Fernándes de Navarrete, Martín. *Biblioteca Marítima Española, vol. 1.* Madrid: Imprenta de la viuda de Calero, 1851.

Font, Pedro. *The Anza Expedition of 1775-1776.* Edited by Frederick J. Teggart. Publications of the Academy of Pacific Coast History, vol. 3, no. 1. Berkeley, California: University of California, 1913.

Garate, Donald T. *Juan Bautista de Anza: Basque Explorer in the New World, 1693-1740.* Reno: University of Nevada Press, 2003.

Garmendia Larrañaga, Juan, and Peña Santiago, Luis Pedro. *El mar de los vascos, II: del Golfo de Vizcaya al Mediterráneo: Leyendas, tradiciones y vida.* Juan Garmendia Larrañaga bilduma 7. Donostia: Eusko Ikaskuntza, 2007.

Geiger, Maynard. *Franciscan Missionaries in Hispanic California, 1769-1848.* San Marino, California: Huntington Library, 1969.

Geiger, Maynard, and Zalvidea, José María de. "Reply of Mission San Gabriel to the Questionnaire of the Spanish Government in 1812 Concerning the Native Culture of the California Mission Indians" *in The Americas,* vol. 12, no. 1 (1955), 77-84. www.jstor.org/stable/979580

Goicoechea Marcaida, Angel. *Aportacion vasca al desarrollo de la cartografía de América durante el siglo XVIII.* Donostia: Eusko Ikaskuntza, 1992.

Griffin, George Butler. *The California Coast: A Bilingual Edition of Documents from the Sutro Collection.* Norman: University of Oklahoma Press, 1969.

Griffin, George Butler, and Aguirre, Andres de. "Letter of Fray Andres de Aguirre to the Archbishop of Mexico, Giving an Account of Some Rich islands Inhabited by Civilized People, Discovered by a Portuguese Trader, and Situate in Latitude 35° to 40° North -Written in 1584-5" *in* Historical Society of Southern California, vol. 2, no. 1, 7-13. Documents from the Sutro Collection (1891). www.jstor.org/stable/41215025

Hackett, Charles Wilson. *Revolt of the Pueblo Indians of New Mexico and Otermín's Attempted Reconquest 1680-1682.* Albuquerque: University of New Mexico Press, 1942.

Hezeta, Bruno de. *For Honor and Country: The Diary of Bruno de Hezeta. Translated and edited by* Herbert K. Beals. Oregon Historical Society Press, 1985.

Hijar, Carlos; Pérez, Eulalia; and Escobar, Agustín. *Three Memoirs of Mexican California.* Berkeley, California: Friends of the Bancroft Library, 1988.

Hittell, Theodore Henry. *History of California.* Vol. 1. San Francisco: N.J. Stone & Company, 1898.

Izengabea. "An Account of the Voyage Made by the Frigates 'Princesa' and 'Favorita' in the Year 1799 from San Blas to Northern Alaska" *in The Catholic Historical Review*, vol. 4, no. 2 (1918), 222-229. www.jstor.org/stable/25011566

Jackson, Robert H. "The 1781-1782 Smallpox Epidemic in Baja California" *in Journal of California and Great Basin Anthropology*, 3(1), 1981. escholarship.org/uc/item/82c3d9x0

Kessel, John L. *Spain in the Southwest: A Narrative History of Colonial New Mexico, Arizona, Texas and California.* University of Oklahoma Press, 2002.

Kino, Eusebio Francisco. *First from the Gulf to the Pacific: The Diary of the Kino-Atondo Peninsular Expedition: December 14, 1684-January 13, 1685.* Translated and edited by W. Michael Mathes. Los Angeles: Dawson's Book Shop, 1969.

Lamadrid Jiménez, Lázaro. *El alavés Fray Fermín Francisco de Lasuén, O.F.M. (1736-1803): Fundador de Misiones en California.* Vol. 2. Diputación Foral de Álava, 1963.

Landaeta, Martín. *Noticias acerca del puerto de San Francisco.* Mexico City: Antigua Librería Robredo, de José Porrúa e hijos, 1949.

Langsdorff, Georg Heinrich. *Langsdorff's Narrative of the Rezanov Voyage to Nueva California in 1806.* San Francisco, California: Private press of Thomas C. Russell, 1927.

Lasuén, Fermín Francisco de. *Writings of Fermín Francisco de Lasuén.* Translated and edited by Finbar Kenneally. Washington D. C.: Academy of American Franciscan History, 1965.

León Portilla, Miguel. *Cartografía y crónicas de la antigua California.* Universidad Nacional Autónoma de México. (First edition, 1989; second edition, 2001).

Lightfoot, Kent G., and Simmons, William S. "Culture Contact in Protohistoric California: Social Contexts of Native and European Encounters" *in* Journal of California and Great Basin Anthropology, vol. 20, no. 2 (1998), 138-170. escholarship.ucop.edu/uc/item/0935d5zx#page-1

Malaspina, Alejandro. *En busca del paso del Pacífico.* Edited by Andrés Galera Gómez. Crónicas de América. Madrid: Historia 16, 1990.

Martínez Salazar, Ángel. *Diego de Borica y Retegui (1742-1800): Gobernador de California.* Arabako Foru Aldundia, 1992.

Mathes, Michael W., ed. *Californiana I: Documentos para la historia de la demarcación comercial de California 1583-1632.* Vol. 2. Madrid: Ediciones José Porrua Turanzas, 1965.

——. "A Biographical Note on Isidro de Atondo y Antillón, Admiral of the Californias" *in California Historical Society Quarterly*, vol. 48, no. 3 (1969), 211-218. www.jstor.org/stable/25154366

——. *First from the Gulf to the Pacific: The Diary of the Kino-Atondo Peninsular Expedition, December 14, 1684-January 13, 1685.* Los Angeles: Dawson's Book Shop, 1969.

——, ed. *Californiana II: Documentos para la historia de la explotación comercial de California, 1611-1679.* Vol. 2. Madrid: Ediciones José Porrua Turanzas, 1970.

——. "Sebastian Vizcaino and San Diego Bay" *in* The Journal of San Diego History, vol. 18, no. 2 (1972). www.sandiegohistory.org/journal/72spring/vizcaino.htm

——. *Californiana III: Documentos para la historia de la transformación colonizadora de California 1679-1686.* Vol. 3. Madrid: Ediciones José Porrua Turanzas, 1974.

Maximin Piette, C. J. G. "The Diarios of early California" *in* The Americas, vol. II, no. 4 (1946), 409-422. www.jstor.org/stable/977712

McCarty, Kieran. *Desert Documentary: The Spanish Years, 1767-1821.* Tucson, Arizona: Arizona Historical Society, 1976.

Mirafuentes Galván, José Luis. "Agustin Ascuhul, el profeta de Moctezuma: Milenarismo y aculturación en Sonora (Guaymas, 1737)." Memoria del XVI Simposio de Historia y Antropología, vol. 1, 157-171. Universidad de Sonora, Departamento de Historia y Antropología, 1993.

Mora-Torres, Gregorio, ed. *Californio Voices: The Oral Memoirs of José María Amador and Lorenzo Asisara.* Denton, Texas: University of North Texas Press, 2005.

Moriarty, James R. "The Discovery and Earliest Explorations of the Gulf of California" *in* The Journal of San Diego History, vol. 11, no. 1 (1965). www.sandiegohistory.org

Mosk, Sanford A. "The Cardona Company and the Pearl Fisheries of Lower California" *in* Pacific Historical Review, vol. 3, no. 1 (1934), 50-61. www.jstor.org/stable/3633457

Myers, Paul A. *North to California: The Spanish Voyages of Discovery, 1533-1603.* Coral Springs, Florida: Llumina Press, 2004.

Niehuis, Charles C. "Lost Ship of the Desert" *in* Desert Magazine (1939), 12-14, 25. El Centro, California: Desert Publishing Company.

Omaechevarria, Ignacio. *Fr. Pablo José de Mugártegui.* Bilbao: Desclée de Brouwer, 1959.

Omaetxebarria, Ignazio. *Franciscanos misioneros vascos: Biografías y semblanzas.* Oñati: Arantzazu E. F., Arantzazuko Santutegia, 2001.

Osio, Antonio María. *The History of Alta California: A Memoir of Mexican California.* Madison, Wisconsin: University of Wisconsin Press, 1996.

Pourade, Richard F. *The Explorers, 1492-1774.* Union-Tribune Publishing Company, Copley Press, 1962.

Preston, William. "Serpent in Eden: Dispersal of Foreign Diseases Into Pre-Mission California" *in Journal of California and Great Basin Anthropology, vol.* 18, no. 1 (1996), 2-37. www.jstor.org/stable/27825595

Prieto, Carlos. *El Océano Pacífico: Navegantes españoles del siglo XVI.* Madrid: Alianza Editorial, 1984.

Putnam, Frederic Ward, and Kroeber, A. L., eds. *University of California Publications in American Archeology and Ethnology.* Vol. 8. Berkeley: University Press, 1908-1910.

Robinson, Alfred. *Life in California during a Residence of Several Years in That Country.* San Francisco: William Doxey, 1891.

Rodríguez-Sala, María Luisa. *De San Blas hasta la Alta California: los viajes y diarios de Juan Joseph Pérez Hernández.* Mexico City: Universidad Nacional Autónoma de México, 2006.

Salmón, Roberto Mario. "A Marginal Man: Luis of Saric and the Pima Revolt of 1751" *in The Americas*, vol. 45, no. 1 (1988), 61-77. www.jstor.org/stable/1007327

Santa María, Vicente. *The First Spanish Entry into San Francisco Bay, 1775*. Edited by John Galvin. San Francisco, California: John Howell Books, 1971.

Santos, Héctor. "The Sacking of the Galleon Santa Ana" in *Sulat sa Tansô* at www.bibingka.com/sst/santana/santana.htm. US. 1997ko apirilaren 5a.

Sarria, Bizente. *Bizente Sarria (1767-1835): Sermoitegia*. Edited by Nagore Etxebarria and Ainara Apraiz. Bilbao: Labayru Ikastegia, 2009.

Shea, John. *Catholic Missions: Among the Indian Tribes of U.S.* Carlisle, Massachussets: Applewood Books, 2010. (First edition, 1855).

Sierra, Benito de; Baker, A. J.; and Wagner, H. R. "Fray Benito de la Sierra's Account of the Heceta Expedition to the Northwest Coast in 1775" *in California Historical Society Quarterly, vol.* 9, no. 3 (1930), 201-242. www.jstor.org/stable/25178081

Simmons, Marc. *In* Etulain, Richard, and Echeverria, Jeronima, eds., *Portraits of Basques in the New World.* Reno, Nevada: University of Nevada Press, 1999.

Smith, Frances R. "The Mission of Nuestra Señora de la Soledad" *in California Historical Society Quarterly*, vol. 23, no. 1 (1944), 1-18. www.jstor.org/stable/25155824

Solaguren, Celestino OFM. *Los Franciscanos vasco-cántabros en el siglo XIX: Vicisitudes y nomenclador bio-bibliográfico.* Vol. II. Oñati: Arantzazu, 2007.

Speilbergen, Joris van. *The East and West Indian Mirror: Being an Account of Joris van Speilbergen's Voyage Round the World (1614-1617), and the Australian Navigations of Jacob Le Maire.* London: Hakluyt Society, 1906.

Stoner, Victor R., and Dobyns, Henry F. "Fray Pedro Antonio de Arriquibar, Chaplain of the Royal Fort at Tucson" *in Arizona and the West*: Journal of the Southwest, vol. 1, no. 1 (1959), 71-79. www.jstor.org/stable/40166914

Street, Richard Steven. *Beasts of the Field: A Narrative History of California Farmworkers, 1769-1913*. Stanford, California: Stanford University Press, 2004.

Thomas, Alfred Barnaby. *After Coronado: Spanish Exploration Northeast of New Mexico, 1696-1727.* University of Oklahoma Press, 1935.

Thurman, Michael E. "The Establishment of the Department of San Blas and Its Initial Naval Fleet: 1767-1770" *in The Hispanic American*

Historical Review, vol. 43, no. 1 (1963), 65-77. www.jstor.org/stable/2510436

——. *The Naval Department of San Blas, New Spain's Bastion for Alta California and Nootka, 1767 to 1798.* Glendale, California, 1967.

Torquemada, Juan de. *Monarquía Indiana.* Edited by Miguel León-Portilla. Biblioteca Estudiantil Universitaria. Mexico City: Universidad Nacional Autónoma de México, 1964.

Tovell, Freeman. *At the Far Reaches of Empire: The Life of Juan Francisco de la Bodega y Quadra*. Vancouver and Toronto: UBC Press, 2008.

Tuthill, Franklin. *The History of California.* California: H. H. Bancroft & Company, 1866.

Twitchell, Ralph Emerson. *The Spanish Archives of New Mexico.* Vol. 2. Cedar Rapids, Iowa: Torch Press, 1914.

Vancouver, George. *A Voyage of Discovery to the North Pacific Ocean.* Vol. 3. London, 1798.

Venegas, Miguel. *Noticia de la California, y de su conquista temporal, y espiritual hasta el tiempo presente.* Madrid: Viuda de M. Fernández, 1757. www.archive.org

Vizcaino, Sebastián. "Vizcaino's Narrative" *in* The Hispanic American Historical Review, vol. 10, no. 2 (1930), 204-218.

Wagner, Henry R. "The Discovery of California: A Paper Read before the Society, May 7" *in California Historical Society Quarterly*, vol. 1, no. 1 (1922), 36-56. www.jstor.org/stable/25613567

——. Unamuno, Pedro de. "The Voyage of Pedro de Unamuno to California in 1587" *in California Historical Society Quarterly, vol.* 2, no. 2 (1923), 140-160. www.jstor.org/stable/25177703

——. "The Last Spanish Exploration of the Northwest Coast and the Attempt to Colonize Bodega Bay" *in California Historical Society Quarterly*, vol. 10, no. 4 (1931), 313-345. www.jstor.org/stable/25160479

Ward, Jean Bruce, and Kurutz, Gary. "Some New Thoughts on an Old Mill" *in California Historical Quarterly,* vol. 53, no. 2 (Summer 1974), 139-164. www.jstor.org/stable/25157502

Winnemucca, Sarah. *Life among the Piutes: Their Wrongs and Claims.* University of Nevada Press, 1994. (1st edition, 1883)

Zalvidea, José María de. "Preguntas y Respuestas: Mission San Gabriel in 1814" *in* Quarterly of the Historical Society of Southern California, vol. 53, no. 3 (1971), 235-50. (Translated and edited by Maynard Geiger, OFM.)

Zubiri, Nancy. *A Travel Guide to Basque America: Families, Feasts, and Festivals.* Reno, Nevada: University of Nevada Press, 2006.

Online Sources

anza.uoregon.edu (Anzaren web-a)
escholarship.org (University of California)
familysearch.org
home.nps.gov/applications/tuma/search.cfm (Mission 2000: Searchable Spanish Mission Records)
missions.huntington.org
pares.mcu.es (Portal de Archivos Españoles)
southwest.library.arizona.edu (The University of Arizona)
www.americanistas.es (Asociación Española de Americanistas)
www.archive.org
www.calisphere.universityofcalifornia.edu
www.euskomedia.org
www.historylink.org (The Free Online Encyclopedia of Washington State History)
www.jstor.org
www.nps.gov/history (National Park Service, U. S. Department of the Interior)
www.sandiegohistory.org (San Diego History Center)
www.snae.org (Euskadiko Artxiboen Sistema Nazionala)
www.tshaonline.org (Texas State Historical Association)

www.ingramcontent.com/pod-product-compliance
Lightning Source LLC
LaVergne TN
LVHW010050110826
845155LV00028B/279
* 9 7 8 1 9 4 9 8 0 5 0 7 9 *